FASHIONING SPACES

Mode and Modernity in Late-Nineteenth-Century Paris

Fashioning Spaces

Mode *and Modernity in Late-Nineteenth-Century Paris*

HEIDI BREVIK-ZENDER

UNIVERSITY OF TORONTO PRESS
Toronto Buffalo London

ISBN 978-1-4426-4803-6

Printed on acid-free, 100% post-consumer recycled paper with vegetable-based inks.

Library and Archives Canada Cataloguing in Publication

Brevik-Zender, Heidi, 1973–, author
Fashioning spaces: mode and modernity in late nineteenth-century Paris/
Heidi Brevik-Zender.

Includes bibliographical references and index.
ISBN 978-1-4426-4803-6 (bound)

1. French literature – 19th century – History and criticism.   2. Paris (France) –
Social life and customs – 19th century.   3. Modernism (Literature) – France.
4. Fashion in literature.   5. Public spaces in literature.   I. Title.

PQ298.B74 2015   840.9'357   C2014-905013-5

University of Toronto Press acknowledges the financial assistance to its
publishing program of the Canada Council for the Arts and the Ontario Arts
Council, an agency of the Government of Ontario.

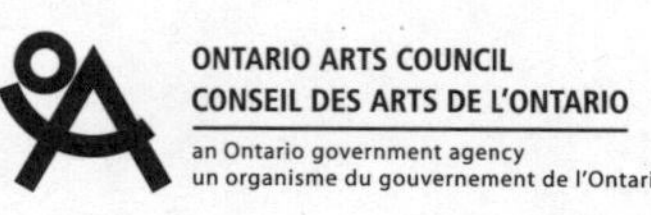

University of Toronto Press acknowledges the financial support of
the Government of Canada through the Canada Book Fund for its
publishing activities.

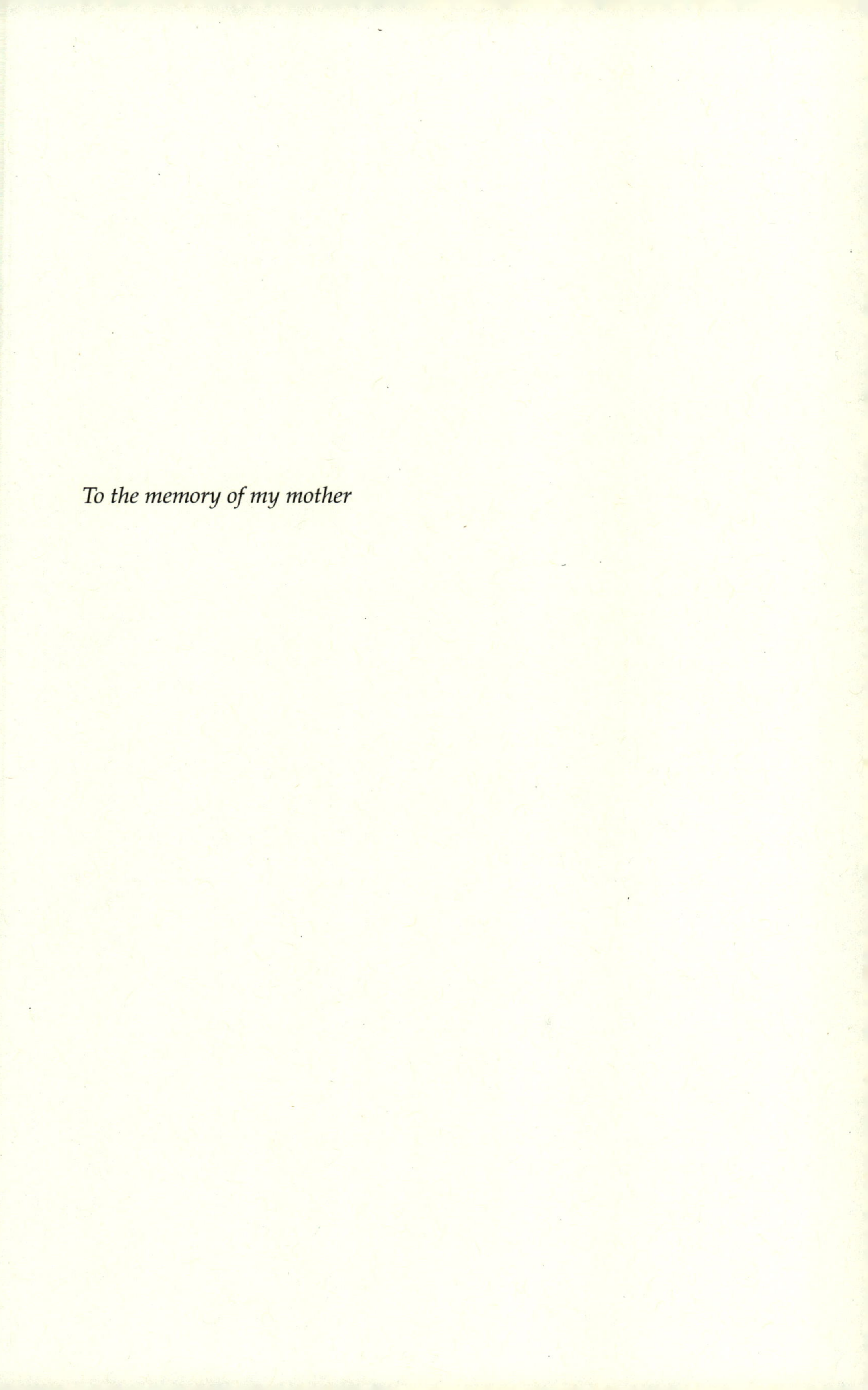

To the memory of my mother

Contents

Illustrations

Acknowledgments

Funding for this project was generously provided by the Department of Comparative Literature and Foreign Languages, the College of Humanities, Arts, and Social Sciences, the Academic Senate, and the Office of Research at the University of California, Riverside. A fellowship from the Borchard Foundation for International Education afforded me time and an idyllic locale in which to complete the manuscript.

I am profoundly grateful to those who have supported me and this project over the years. To Gretchen Shultz, Edward Ahearn, Mary Gluck, and Pierre Saint-Amand, my mentors at Brown University who first inspired me to explore the intersections of Parisian modernity, gender, and fashion and who shaped my thinking through thoughtful critique, intellectual rigour, enthusiasm, and encouragement. To subsequent guides who offered important critical insights, a shared passion for my research, steady warm counsel, and sometimes all three: Catherine Nesci, Michelle Bloom, Eric Haskell, and Margherita Long. To those who provided not just friendship but inspiration through their own fascinating books on fashion: John Potvin, Susan Hiner, and Andrea Denny-Brown. To the three anonymous readers of the manuscript whose comments improved it immeasurably. To Siobhan McMenemy, my editor, who navigated me expertly through the process with professionalism and kindness. To dear friends who have impacted, always for the better, my experience of writing this book: Claudia Esposito, Rudabeh Pakravan, and Karim Daanoune.

I thank my family – the Zenders, the Omis, and the Breviks – for their encouragement when I encountered challenges and for their joy when research and writing were progressing well. I thank my father George for his abiding care and support, as well as his incomparable instincts and insights on printing and book culture, my brother Mark, and my sister Erika.

Finally I thank John, for reading countless drafts of these materials by which he has become, doubtless, more knowledgeable about nineteenth-century French literature and culture than most abstract mathematicians, for the spirited discussions from which this book has benefited, and, most of all, for showing me love and support every step of the way.

FASHIONING SPACES

Mode and Modernity in Late-Nineteenth-Century Paris

Introduction

Poised to lift her bow, statuesque and elegant in a white and yellow dress, a violinist waits patiently for the room to fall quiet. Posh society, recognizable by its formal gowns and crisp black and white suits, suggests the scene is highly fashionable, a standing-room-only event not to be missed. For French painter James (né Jacques-Joseph) Tissot (1836–1902), the salon is a site of sartorial excess. Lace skirts spill across the floor, flounced chiffon abounds, coloured ribbons trail down necks and backs, all highlighted through Tissot's fastidious attention to details of clothing. Concert attendees, as though displaced in some way by the room's surfeit of smart attire, crowd the doorway and flow over into the corridor. It is not the musician but fashion that reigns in this high-society setting, a soirée where sartorial finery is de rigueur and the importance of showing off one's own stylish outfit is eclipsed only by the need to see the latest fashions being worn by others (see figure 0.1).

Easily overlooked against the garment-laden scene in the foreground is a staircase, which rises up the top left section of the canvas. Although separated from the main hall, the stairwell remains connected to the fashion dynamics playing out in the larger salon. The figures on the stairs are clad in similar garments to the concertgoers in the painting's primary space, forming cohesion through clothing. Although located in the background, they are still implicated in the visual networks at play, as suggested by the elderly woman seated on the right who seems to train her glasses on the violinist but is positioned in such a way that she might also be focusing her gaze on the partygoers situated on the ascending steps. The contrast between this woman's proper comportment – seated quietly on a chair – and the brazen informality of the guests chatting and perched casually on the steps, points to a tension

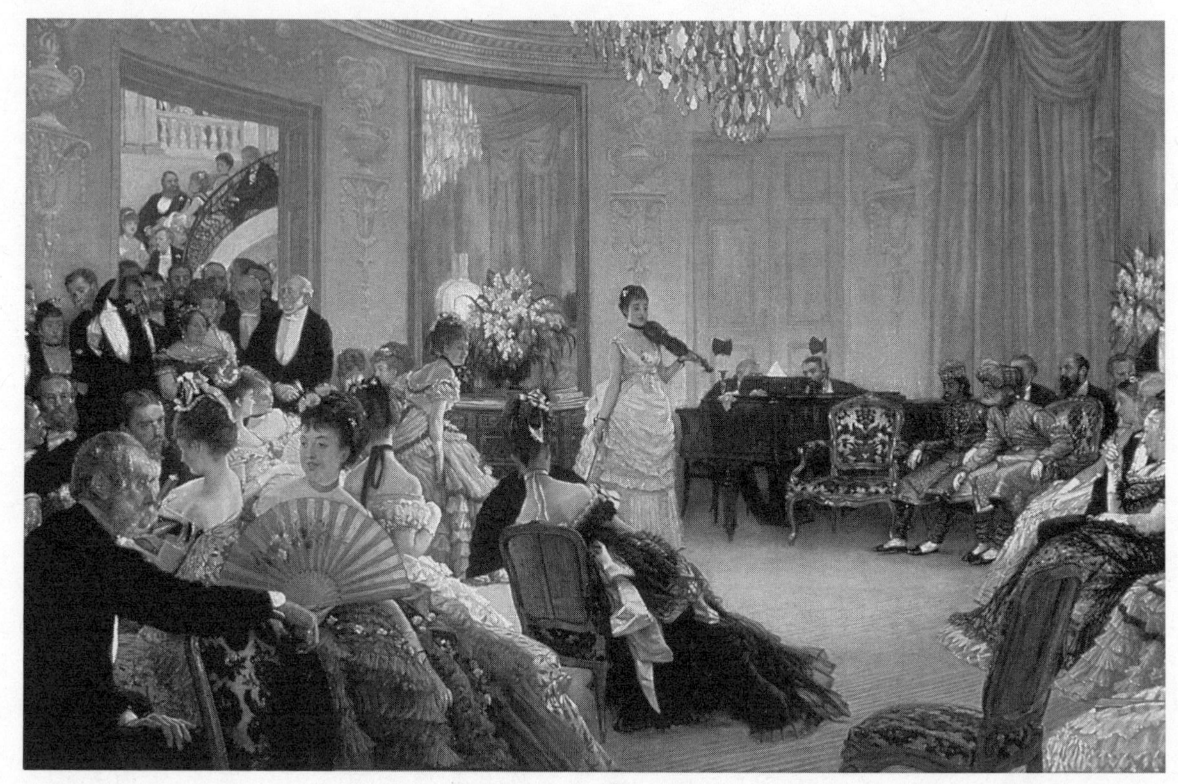

0.1 James Tissot, *Hush!* (*The Concert*), c. 1875. Oil on canvas. Manchester Art Gallery. Reproduced by permission of the Bridgeman Art Library.

inherent to the staircase, which has been appropriated for an unintended use, one that is likely unsanctioned by those more in tune with social respectability, who sit in the concert salon. The staircase is dislocated from the scene but still located within its visual, sartorial, and cultural discourse: it is what I will be calling in this book a *dislocation* of modernity.[1]

The garment-centred rendition of high society in Tissot's painting *Hush!* provides a fitting introduction to this study of fashion, space, and modernity in early Third Republic Paris. Tissot's staircase "dislocation," filled with elegantly dressed spectators who are separate from yet imbedded discursively in the primary space of the canvas, illustrates my argument that authors, as well as painters and journalists of this period, were preoccupied by the intersections of space and fashion in the modern metropole. *Fashioning Spaces* will argue that Paris-based writers situated charged depictions of garments not exclusively in what are widely understood as the settings of fashionable modernity but, with even greater frequency, in dislocations, where exteriority, intimacy, transgression, and subversion converge. That the last decades of the nineteenth century were subject to this "spatial turn" in representations of Paris is not surprising, given that this period, from roughly 1870 to 1900, followed the implementation of the dramatic urban renewal project that we now refer to as "Haussmannization" for the city planner, Baron Haussmann, who spearheaded the razing and rebuilding of the capital's streets, parks, and neighbourhoods. The body of aesthetic representation that I examine here engages with the changing complexities of what it meant to inhabit a new metropolitan landscape rising out of Second Empire urban expansionism. To put it succinctly, I seek to understand through their own spatial and sartorial fixations how authors, in concert with many artists of the period, were responding to Haussmannization and its aftermath.

Locations and Dislocations of Modernity

Space has been a subtext of much interdisciplinary work by scholars investigating Parisian modernity, although an understanding of which locales constituted the spaces of the modern has undergone some noticeable shifts. A first wave of powerful studies that were interested in issues of class centred on the public urban locations that we now think of synonymously with Haussmannization. In his influential *The Painting of Modern Life* (1985), art historian T.J. Clark found inspiration in the

Impressionists and Manet, examining their treatments of working-class bars, forest picnics, café-concerts, the balcony, the theatre, and the opera.[2] The department store emerged as another key locale in works such as Rachel Bowlby's *Just Looking* (1985) and Michael B. Miller's *The Bon Marché* (1981).[3] Christopher Prendergast's *Paris and the Nineteenth Century* (1995) took its cues from the *flâneur*, organizing itself around the venues encountered by the iconic wanderer: cafés, panoramic vistas, sewers, catacombs, markets, barricades, parks, canals.[4] The boulevard took pride of place: works such as Joachim Schlor's *Nights in the Big City* (1991) turned our focus to the street as the symbolic nexus of modern experience.[5] The enormous impact of Walter Benjamin's *Arcades Project* (1999) and works examining it such as Susan Buck-Morss's *The Dialectics of Seeing* (1989) brought intense interest to the philosopher's iconic *passages*, the covered commercial pathways of nineteenth-century Paris in which modernity's contributions to the twentieth century were seen to be summarized.[6] Building on these perspectives and addressing, in particular, a rising interest in visual mass culture, Vanessa Schwartz's *Spectacular Realities* (1998) called attention to arenas of mass spectacle: panoramas, the wax museum, and perhaps most compelling, the public morgue.[7] Simultaneously, urban space was productively complicated by interventions that turned the focus from the public arena to the domestic sphere, such as Sharon Marcus's *Apartment Stories* (1999), which analysed what she termed "the interiorization of Paris"[8] while concentrating on the home apartment and its implications in discourses surrounding bourgeois private life.

Fashioning Spaces seeks both to contribute to and to innovate spatial inquiry through the concept of dislocations and its interplay with sartorial fashion. It understands dislocations of the modern as alternate, heretofore overlooked areas of the city, in which fashion is deployed by authors for a variety of purposes, among them the following: to transgress gendered norms; to critique social and political turmoil; to memorialize the past; and to look defiantly, trepidatiously, and even hopefully towards the future. Given that the category of dislocations is itself infinite, I have chosen to focus on settings that involve important elements related to clothing that recur persistently in literary works of the period. These locales include the apartment staircase, the servant stairwell, the hallway antechamber, the theatre foyer, the dressing room, the dressmakers' studio, the high-fashion couturier atelier, and the garment-manufacturing workshop. In addition to representations of these literal spaces, the notion of space in metaphorical terms will also be explored: a Maghrebi capital city as a symbolic antechamber to North African colonies, a staircase as cipher for Commune barricades, a waiting room as an expression of authorial anticipation.[9] I term all of these areas *dis*-locations because they are spaces of *dis*ruption in which challenges to traditional relationships of power – primarily those of class and gender – provocatively occur. Yet, not unlike Tissot's staircase, they remain *located* within the discursiveness of modernity, for although they appear to fade inconsequentially into the background of the metropolis, the very presence of stylish sartorial elements in them marks them as crucial sites of the modern.

Fashion and Modernity

One innovation of this book, then, is that it engages with questions related to modern city space by focusing on fashion. In recent decades, the topic of fashion as a metaphor for modernity in nineteenth-century France has received sustained and rigorous academic attention that has convincingly discredited the stereotype that fashion is tantamount to frivolity and has asserted the value of fashion as a critical concept. I build on now classic studies such as Philippe Perrot's *Les Dessus et les dessous de la bourgeoisie* (1981) [*Fashioning the Bourgeoisie*, 1994], Elizabeth Wilson's *Adorned in Dreams* (1985), Gilles Lipovetsky's *L'Empire de l'éphémère* (1987) [*The Empire of Fashion*, 1994], and Valerie Steele's *Paris Fashion* (1988), along with more recent works such as Ulrich Lehmann's *Tigersprung* (2000) and Susan Hiner's *Accessories to Modernity* (2010), which have done much to examine the nexus of fashion and modernity against the literary, historical, cultural, and philosophical contexts of the period.[10] As these works all demonstrate, fashion played a primary role in aesthetic constructions of Parisian modernity in the late nineteenth century. Lehmann's philosophical intervention charts the development of the *mode-modernité* correlation to the late 1850s when Charles Baudelaire's iconic fashion-inflected essay on modernity, *Le Peintre de la vie moderne* [*The Painter of Modern Life*], first appeared, tracing the trope as it developed in Stéphane Mallarmé's fashion magazine *La Dernière Mode* (1874) and eventually evolved into Benjamin's treatment of Parisian modernity in *The Arcades Project*, written primarily in the 1930s. Hiner uncovers the link between fashion and modernity earlier, in the literature of the 1840s and 1850s by Honoré de Balzac and Gustave

Flaubert, which she adeptly connects to later echoes in Marcel Proust's version of the fin-de-siècle, *À la Recherche du temps perdu*, drafted in the 1910s and 1920s.

My study on literature from 1870 to 1900 is concerned with a more concentrated period of time, roughly that of a single generation.[11] In historical and political terms, these were the years following the fall of Napoléon III, an event that marked the last time France would be ruled by an emperor and that ushered in a new republican regime. In the Parisian world of letters, this was the period when Haussmannization was chronicled by its inheritors, a group of authors who did not necessarily remember the urban landscape before the Second Empire or even the intense phase of demolition, the erection of buildings, and the paving of Haussmann's boulevard axes in the 1850s and 1860s. To be sure, construction and destruction were still a part of their lived experience, as neighbourhoods continued to expand, more suburbs of Paris were incorporated, and public transportation and routes of circulation carried on growing.[12] But the nostalgia of Baudelaire, as expressed in poems such as "Le Cygne" ["The Swan"] (1861), where the poet's well-known exclamation, "Paris changes!" ["Paris change!"][13] communicated a melancholic sense of loss about a city seeming to crumble to dust before him, would be replaced by a set of different concerns held by a rising generation of writers. These authors – Emile Zola, Guy de Maupassant, Rachilde, Alphonse Daudet, Georges Feydeau, and Joris-Karl Huysmans among them – perceived their own matrix of relationships between fashion and space in the years following the death of Baudelaire in 1867, years before Proust had yet to begin penning *À la Recherche* and Benjamin was still a child.

The novels, short stories, plays, and essays of these writers are my primary sources. Paintings by contemporaries including Edgar Degas, Félicien Rops, and Gustave Caillebotte, as well as newspaper reports and period garments housed today in fashion museums and archives, provide visual, historical, and material context for my close textual readings. *Fashioning Spaces* asks what this corpus can tell us about the ways in which those living through the period used fashion not only to conceive *of* modernity, but also to imagine *where* they saw modernity manifested. It argues for taking into account the places in which authors and artists imagined garments to be displayed, worn, bought, tried on, and fabricated, because the texts themselves repeatedly suggest inherent associations between dress and location. This perspective represents a fundamentally new way of thinking about sites of French modernity because it highlights contingencies, both perceived and created, between garments and space during this vibrant period of aesthetic production. This book, thus, (1) refines our understanding of the sites important to literary representations of Parisian modernity, (2) reveals sustained connections between metaphorically charged items of clothing and urban locations of fashion, and (3) posits a novel way of considering the early Third Republic by exposing a specific set of anxieties, questions, and hopes of writers using fashion to react to the political, social, and cultural contexts of the late nineteenth century.

Fashioning Space

Why is fashion a useful critical lens through which to study conceptions of space during this period? One can begin to answer this question by recognizing that during this era a number of links were forged between fashion and urban spatiality, both discursively and in more material terms. For an example of the former, we can look to Charles Blanc, the director of Paris's École des Beaux-Arts, who wrote an entire book-length study entitled *L'Art dans la parure et dans le vêtement* [*Art in Adornment and Clothing*] (1875) devoted to examining similarities among decorative elements in art, architecture, and dress.[14] Organizing his volume into three subjects, namely "the adornment of people" ["la parure des personnes"], "ornaments of houses" ["ornements de la maison"], and "the decoration of cities and monuments" ["la décoration des villes et des monuments"], Blanc posited that these categories should be understood as naturally intertwining.[15] His perception of such direct correlations between garments and city architecture, outlined in a book destined for readers associated with the high-art sphere of the École des Beaux-Arts, was echoed, too, in more popular mass-circulating texts such as the fashion magazine *Le Journal des Modes*. In an issue that was published the following year, for instance, one of the periodical's reporters instructed female readers that the day's style was to merge into the urban environment "dressed in unnoticeable colours like the stone of the walls and the dust on the pavement."[16] Privileging sartorial practicality over flamboyancy, for sombre fabric hues were advocated as a way of minimizing the appearance of dirt from city streets, the report bears witness to an understanding that clothes and the urban landscape in which they would be worn were inherently related. These writings from the art world and the popular fashion press project a rather neutral attitude towards an association between city spaces and fashionable garments. Other voices were more pessimistic. A detractor of Haussmannization, for instance, took up the metaphor of clothing to criticize the Baron's buildings and the society they accommodated, disparaging Paris's new look as "crinoline architecture."[17] The term "crinoline" referred to the stiff underskirts and steel cages created to buttress the enormous bell-shaped dresses in vogue from the 1850s to the 1870s. As T.J. Clark reads it, the word "crinoline" is here used pejoratively to communicate the author's censure of the superficiality of both fashion and the new edifices of the metropolis.[18] Still darker undertones pervade another representation of the crinoline depicted in a caricature published in the satirical newspaper *Le Charivari* in 1858 (see figure 0.2). In this illustration by Charles Vernier denouncing the capital's controversial proposal to incorporate the suburbs into the city proper, Paris is allegorized as a stylish woman who advances menacingly on the helpless outlying neighbourhoods, threatening to imprison them under her fashionable hoop undercage.

Commentators who expressed urban spatiality through sartorial metaphors may have been inspired by the fact that buildings and garments of the late century had a number of construction materials and design aesthetics in common. The steel in crinoline cages that supported the skirts of stylish women, for instance, was alloyed from the same metal used in the exposed wrought-iron skeletal structures that became one major emblem of Second Empire construction.[19] As Julie Wosk remarks in her study of the crinoline, "In a century that introduced steel-cage frameworks to reduce the need for heavy masonry in architectural design, manufacturers began promoting steel-cage construction to lighten the load in women's dress."[20] By the 1870s, the crinoline cage had fallen out of vogue, but the highly architectural approach to women's undergarments endured in, for instance, the structural bustles that protruded at 90 degree angles to extend the shape of women's posteriors during the 1880s. Not only were crinoline cages, bustles, and buildings signifying modernity produced using similar methods, but they could have comparable forms and operational concerns as well. As Leila Whittemore concludes in her analysis of the period's new shopping emporiums, "the crinoline, like the department store, combined outward monumentality and inward lightness. Both reflect the curious blend of functionality and fantasy that characterized the new architecture of consumption."[21] Fashion and architecture also overlapped in terms of decorative themes, as seen in the number of similar motifs that were present in both garments and buildings of the period. Jean Sagne

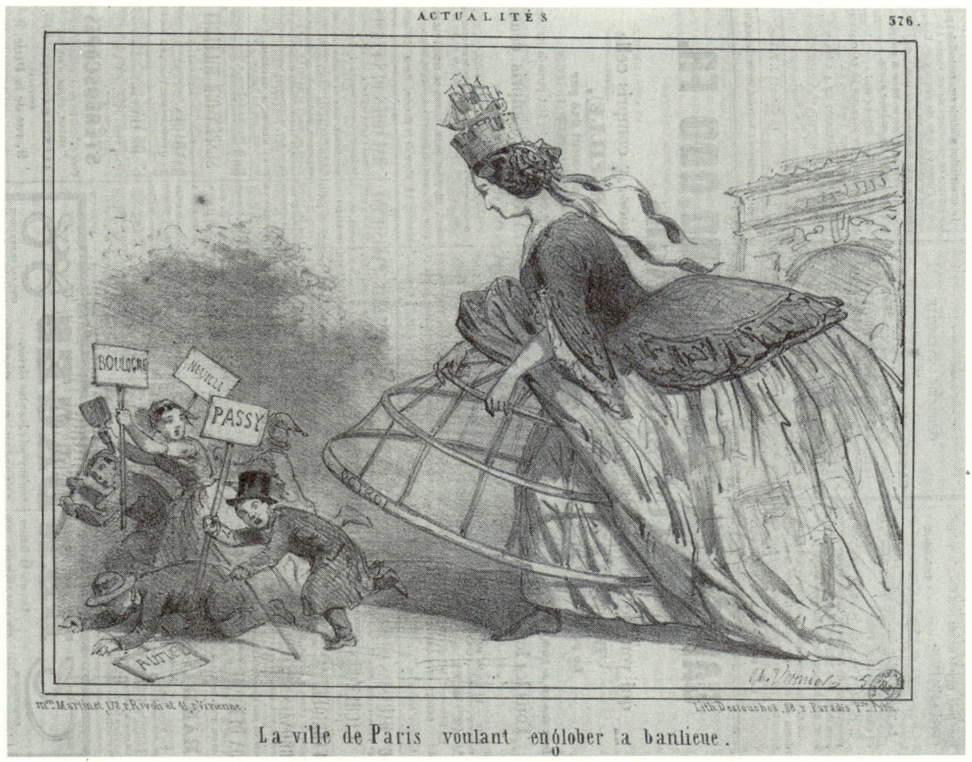

0.2 Charles Vernier, *Paris voulant englober la banlieue: Le Charivari*, 6 November 1858. Reproduced by permission of the Bibliothèque nationale de France.

observes, for instance, that "fashion, like architecture of the time, was founded on eclecticism, impregnated with allusions to the Orient and historical references" ["La mode, comme l'architecture du temps, se fondait sur l'éclectisme, imprégnée d'allusions à l'Orient, de rappels historiques"].[22] Remarking that Parisian couturiers well understood that "dressmaking is, after all, a form of engineering; it is three-dimensional construction work,"[23] fashion historian Diana de Marly points to another reason that architectural aesthetics of the period may have found themselves perpetuated in dress.

As fashion and city architecture developed somewhat in tandem in the physical urban landscape, an analogous overlap emerged in the literature of modernity. Anne Green, examining the intersections of fashion and text during the 1850s and 1860s observes, "Throughout this period the imagery of dress seeps into the language, so that the boundaries between the rituals of reading, writing and dressing come to blur and merge."[24] Also tracing this trend back to the Second Empire, Prendergast foregrounds Baudelaire's use of the metaphor of dress in "Dawn" [Le Crépuscule du matin] and "To a Red-haired Beggar" [À une mendiante rousse], two poems from "Tableaux Parisiens." As Prendergast observes, in the former poem morning breaking over the city is pictured as "dawn shivering in a pink and green dress" ["L'aurore grelottante en robe rose et verte"] and in the latter an urban beggar is "clothed" in lavish garments and accessories only to be stripped naked of them in the final stanza.[25] Baudelaire's treatment of fashion in these two urban poems, Prendergast contends, implies the poet's attitude that "the very act of translating the city into the terms of poetic metaphor, especially the pastoral metaphor of Dawn, ha[d] itself grown threadbare."[26] For Baudelaire, fashion thus articulates not the pastoral romanticism of an earlier era but a new poetics of the rising city. A related set of concerns would emerge several decades later in Zola's *Le Roman expérimental* (1880) [*The Experimental Novel*], the novelist's essay on the aims of naturalism and his methods of producing this distinctive brand of narrative. Insisting that modern realist fiction was best served by underscoring links among spatial environment, structures, and clothing, Zola famously declared, "Man cannot be separated from his milieu … he is shaped by his clothing, by his house, by his city" ["L'homme ne peut être séparé de son milieu … il est complété par son vêtement, par sa maison, par sa ville"].[27] Taking up Baudelaire's juxtaposition of urban space, fashion, and the writer's own reflections on literature, Zola recalibrated these converging concepts not for the sake of Second Empire poetics but rather for the new narrative form of Third Republic naturalism. For the critic reading both of these writers today, garments are not simply metaphors but clues to understanding the methods behind the creation of literary forms and approaches to reading them.

Dislocating the Public/Private Divide

One leitmotif that appears throughout work on Parisian urban space is the notion that representations of city locales tend to trouble a public/

private dichotomy. This line of thinking is present, for example, in *The Arcades Project* insofar as the fragments comprising the opus foreground Benjamin's interests in public passageways but also consider modernity in relation to interiority, as expressed in organizing themes such as Convolute I, which is entitled "The Interior, the Trace."[28] Ultimately, Benjamin problematizes the binary of internal and external, examining "the Parisians' technique of *inhabiting* their streets"[29] from which he concludes that "Parisians make the street an interior"[30] and develops his own seductive formulation of "the intoxicated interpenetration of street and residence."[31] Contemporary scholarship across a number of disciplines has followed suit. Marcus's investigation of the apartment building exposes "houses that were not enclosed cells, sealed off from urban streets, markets, and labor but fluid spaces perceived to be happily or dangerously communicating with more overtly public terrain."[32] Likewise, in Schlor's proposal to examine the nocturnal city street in terms of "'external,' material urbanization" as opposed to "'internal' urbanization,"[33] the author's inserted quotation marks rightly suggest a more complex overlap of these two not-so-oppositional categories. In an inspired reading of such spatial troubling in Zola's *La Curée*, David Van Zanten argues that representations of the boulevard in the novel indicate that "it is less that the discipline of the interior had been extended into the street than that the street became fantasized as formerly only the interior could be."[34] Ruth Iskin points out that Degas's paintings of milliners (a subject I discuss at length in chapter 6) depict women shopping for hats in areas that evoke both "the public spaces of consumption" and "an atmosphere of a private space."[35] In another recent study of French images of late-century femininity, Kathryn Brown analyses "the act of reading as a moment of private reflection in public" in paintings depicting women perusing texts.[36]

It is likely not a coincidence that some of these investigations that centre on depictions of female experience are by historians and critics of art, for many (including me) have been inspired by Griselda Pollock's influential concept of the "interstitial" spaces in Impressionist paintings of and by women.[37] For Pollock, writing in the 1980s when vibrant new analyses of gender across various fields of representation were being pioneered by way of feminist critique, the designations of public and private were useful to demonstrating broader class and gender dynamics that had arisen in the nineteenth century from contesting or upholding the notions of interiority and exteriority. It is not that I disagree with any of the astute analyses above, all of which complicate spatial constructions of public and private in fascinating and valuable ways.[38] But I perceive a consequence arising from this method of problematizing the spatial dichotomy, which is that the dichotomy is thus highlighted in the critical apparatus. That is, to suggest that a space complicates a public/private separation risks according pride of place to a binary opposition between public and private. Although this can be illuminating, as we have seen above, what I am calling for is a critical paradigm that addresses a new and broader spectrum of prevailing meanings expressed in late-century literary representations of Parisian space.[39]

   Hollis Clayson's recent work on "thresholds" in paintings of Impressionist interiors is a move in this direction.[40] Her study, citing Victoria Rosner's modernist model, focuses on nineteenth-century balconies, drawing rooms, cabarets, and omnibuses and understands them as "diverse composite, transitional, intermediate, and hybrid locales."[41] Clayson's regard is deliberately trained on interior spaces (although she treats the notion of "indoors" in productively figurative ways) and images. In the literary works that I discuss, some spaces have qualities of a threshold, such as the antechambers treated in part 2. However, in-betweenness, hybridity, and transitoriness are not always attributes of space that authors choose to underscore. Somewhat different, then, is my notion of dislocations, which seeks to offer a more comprehensive description of the spatial concerns arising in literature. A particular hallmark of dislocations, for example, is that they are relational to the "locations" of Haussmann modernity, specifically those associated with fashionable display such as boulevards, theatres, and department stores. I am interested in the ways in which authors rework such spaces, "dislocating" them and turning them into sectors frequently characterized by literal or figurative disorder that responds to a destabilization of traditional social norms. The grand staircase at Garnier's opera house in Paris, for instance, was a glamorous, high-profile site where elegant women and men débuted their latest sartorial finery. The direct product of Haussmannization – Garnier's design was the winning entry in a national competition, and its construction was funded by Second Empire coffers – the building's glitzy opulence made it, in many eyes, the very architectural symbol of Napoléon III's self-glorifying and wasteful administration. In her dislocated versions of Garnier's staircase, I argue in chapter 1, Rachilde recasts the space into flights of steps where, through fashion, fixed notions of gender identity are questioned, contested, and transgressed. Her writing thus illustrates what John Potvin maintains, that "fashion's impact on [everyday] spaces and places does not only make them 'fashionable,' but exposes and complicates social relationships within them."[42]

Dislocations can also comprise a system linking elements together, one that we might consider in terms of a network or *réseau*, a term that appears frequently in period references to Haussmannization. Henri Lefebvre, who wrote extensively about late-nineteenth-century Paris and urban spatiality alike, evokes this idea of space as a network when he describes the staircase as a part of a larger connection that "links particular houses and dwellings back to their distribution in urban space."[43] As I demonstrate in chapter 5, citing a related notion in Michel Foucault's essay on heterotopias,[44] the dislocation of the fashion atelier in *La Curée* expresses Zola's uneasy reaction to the connective spatial organization of Haussmannization because the network upon which the new city was based seems directly to enable, for the novelist, the dangerous spread of declining social morals. Spatial connectivity appears similarly troubling to Maupassant, whose *Bel-Ami* anti-hero Georges Duroy learns to access and master urban geography – to "conquer his place" ["conquérir sa place"],[45] as Maupassant puts it – in his cruel rise to power. In an episode featuring what might be deemed the nineteenth-century version of "networking," Duroy visits Madeleine Forestier, the woman journalist who will facilitate his social and spatial ascent, and finds her in her book-lined office (*cabinet de travail*). The study, normally a masculine space,[46] is here feminized[47] and sartorialized by the books bound in a ray of hues which are repeated in the colourful garments worn by the female characters in the novel. It is also a conduit to Duroy's infiltration into the social network essential to his conquest of the metropolis. Madeleine's role as a conduit to Paris's networks is expressed through fashion, as her garment falls open at the arm and her "wide-open sleeve"[48] ["manche largement ouverte"[49]] hints at the penetration – both sexual and social – that she will later afford him. In Maupassant's depiction of this dislocated space, the *cabinet de travail* is bureau, boudoir, and boulevard in one, a microcosm of the network of spaces through which men pass en route to the top.

This example from *Bel-Ami* highlights another feature of literary portraits of early Third Republic city spaces, namely, their polyvalence. In the sites of pleasurable phantasmagoria for which Paris had by then become well known – locations of entertainment and leisure that had been one of the priorities of the amusement-seeking regime of Napoléon III

– this multiplicity of overlapping meanings seems often an inherent trait. Italian writer Edmondo de Amicis's account of visiting Paris in 1878 illustrates how the destabilization of fixed meanings had come to characterize the city's glittering locales for awestruck eyewitnesses: "Here the street becomes a square, the sidewalk a street, the shop a museum, the café a theater, beauty, elegance, splendor, dazzling magnificence, and life a fever."[50] At the same time that spectacular diversions such as those described by Amicis became emblematic of the capital's topography, however, Haussmannization sought to regulate, order, and arrange the landscape as a form of imperial control. It was in reaction to these paradoxical spatial contexts – one promoting "fever-inducing" entertainments and the other controlled organization – that writers of the period created their own complex textual versions of the metropole.

Their renditions pictured the city not for how it conformed to Haussmannization's "functionalist rationalism" ["rationalisme fonctionnaliste"],[51] as Jean-Pierre Leduc-Adine, with some neutrality, has called it, but more often in terms of confusion and uncertainty, particularly as a place of profound class instabilities that were expressed through fashion. As I point out in chapter 3, for instance, it is an overcoat in Zola's *Au Bonheur des Dames* that provides the catalyst for a momentary levelling between social unequals, the salesgirl Denise and her wealthy client, Mme Desforges. The sartorial object marks an erosion of class hierarchies that poses a threat to those of high status and enables those born to inferiority to imagine an upended social dynamic. This motif is a recurring one in texts of the period that feature fashion prominently, a fact that highlighting writers' awareness of the complex links between clothing and class. As Hiner explains, "nineteenth-century literary discourse is acutely aware of both the paradox and the slippage of fashion's role from a normalizing system upholding social hierarchies to an equalizing system in which those hierarchies are increasingly less visible."[52] Noting the urgency with which fashion was called on by those in power who used it in attempts to retain their social distinction, Hiner notes, "In Second Empire France, as more attention was falling on public spaces with the explosion of boulevards, cafés, department stores, and public gardens … there was even greater potential for class mixing and thus a more acute urgency for displaying one's distinction."[53] That Hiner's apt discussion of how fashion enables social distinction includes references to boulevards, cafés, department stores, and gardens, suggests the importance of space to this process.

Class tension is, therefore, one recurring topic in this study but, as *Fashioning Spaces* illustrates, early Third Republic writers' concerns about modernity were far from homogeneous. In fact, in the texts analysed here, garments do the work of pointing to unease across a wide range of modernity's concerns. We will see that fashion functions as a cipher for contemporary reactions to political turmoil and traumas of the previous empire that haunted Parisian spaces of daily life and marked the capital's future. Garments are drawn on to recognize the limits that urban sites continued to impose on gender and identity expression. Dress posits the problematic implications of France's overseas expansion, linking the city to the colonies abroad and demonstrating that the notion of "modern space" involved locales beyond the French capital. If Haussmannization was an attempt to imbed particular cultural memories within the cityscape – the glorification of Napoléon III and the Baron himself, for instance – dislocations in literary works communicate a cultural memory of things that empire builders might have wished society to forget, such as the catastrophe of the Commune or the insidious violence of overseas colonization.

At the same time, as a generative, creative endeavour, literature expresses a desire to engage with the changing urban environment, to reclaim, perhaps, some measure of control over it by representing, reformulating, and translating it through writing. It introduces new possibilities for the performance of identity in the metropole and privileges the role of the reader, who becomes the indispensable observer upon which fashion depends, for fashion is never "made" without a public envisioned to acknowledge it. Some literary works use dislocations to rebel against a society hostile to non-normative desires and lifestyles; when Jacques Silvert, the feminized male protagonist of Rachilde's novel *Monsieur Vénus* (1884) declares that he will love his masculinized female companion Raoule, in his words, "*wherever* I please: *here, elsewhere*, in a *drawing room*, in a *garret*" (emphasis added)[54] ["*où* il me plaira: *ici, ailleurs*, dans un *salon*, dans une *mansarde*" (emphasis added)[55]], his defiance of constricting sexual norms is registered in spatial terms. Texts demonstrate fashion's connection to urban accessibility through movement, influenced, perhaps, by the subtext of motion sewn into garment designs emblematic of the Third Republic. The extreme bustle of the 1880s, for instance, fetishized a woman's posterior as an erogenous object but also called attention to her accentuated movement in a city to which she was gaining ever more access. Ornaments such as the tassel, which hangs down the back of this stylish 1885 day dress, would have swung conspicuously from side to side and pointed to the modern woman's physical mobility with each step she took (see figures 0.3 and 0.4). In her analysis of the handbag, Hiner labels the purse a "portable *foyer*,"[56] fittingly calling to mind that fashion objects can be thought of as dislocations in and of themselves. Hiner goes on to observe the important gendered implications in recognizing the accessory as a space, nothing that in some fiction, "the sac … is portable and ventures away from home and family to accompany women in their move toward greater visible agency in the public sphere."[57] As I discuss in chapters 2 and 6, if fashion is often rightly denounced for the constraints it places on women, the female writer Rachilde could also envision its liberating potential in terms of urban movement.

A Word on Theorizing Space

Readers familiar with scholarship on fashion and nineteenth-century modernity may find it curious that the writings of Baudelaire, Mallarmé, and Benjamin are not highlighted more overtly in this book. This is a deliberate choice informed by the fact that others have already done much to examine the quintessential paradigms that we associate with these thinkers, in particular, the dialectical nature of the ephemeral and the eternal in modernity that Baudelaire so influentially posited and that is (rightly) cited in most critical work on the nexus of fashion and modernity.[58] Instead, then, I look to theorists of space who are often associated with the twentieth-century urban conditions during which they were writing but whose works are grounded, implicitly or sometimes quite explicitly, in the nineteenth century. Thus, readers will find my discussions illuminated by Michel Foucault's thoughts on heterotopias, Henri Lefebvre's writings on the Commune and spatial rhythm, Jurgen Habermas's theories on the development of the bourgeois urban environment, Yi-Fu Tuan's analyses on spaces and places, and Michel de Certeau's notions of tactics and strategies in the practices of everyday life.[59]

These critical thinkers represent approaches to spatiality that are widely heterogeneous, deploying, in some instances, the same terms as one another but inscribing them with disparate, even contradictory meanings. Certeau, for example, understands an urban "place" to refer to "a field of programmed and regulated operations,"[60] an arena constructed by forces of power seeking to control it. When agents undermine these regularizing forces through their own set of tactical negotiations, they create a new spatial configuration that Certeau calls "space" or a "practiced place"[61] informed by the agent's presence in and navigation through it. In contrast, Tuan sees "space" as an arena of possibility, as "a symbol for openness and freedom,"[62] while a "place" corresponds to a "built environment"[63] that provides a sense of stability, belonging, and security. Certeau and Tuan thus define the terms "space" and "place" in radically different ways, but I find each one separately useful, the former for my analysis of subversive urban navigation in Rachilde's novels and the latter for my discussion of how the possibility of the city as refuge seems lost in Feydeau's absurdist version of modernity in *Tailleur pour dames*. Foucault's concept of heterotopias helps to illustrate the virtual, surface qualities that Maupassant inscribes into dislocations in the novel *Bel-Ami*, while Lefebvre and Habermas, who apply historically contextualized, Marxist viewpoints to the Commune uprising and the emergence of the bourgeoisie respectively, are deployed to illuminate how these social occurrences were spatially understood by their literary chroniclers, most notably, Zola. It is not, then, that *Fashioning Spaces* privileges a singular theoretical model, but rather that it recognizes that the works of a variety of twentieth-century critics who have meditated deeply on space can be brought fruitfully to bear on how Haussmannized Paris was perceived and represented in the 1800s. In bringing what is typically thought of as "modernist" and "postmodernist" cultural theory (beyond Benjamin) into deeper conversation with the nineteenth century, I hope to invigorate scholarship of late 1800s aesthetics, particularly in the area of fashion, with a new critical vocabulary.

This said, if the names Baudelaire, Mallarmé, and Benjamin are not routinely emphasized in this book they have, nonetheless, deeply influenced it, acting as the underlying trifecta of philosophers who examined the modern in terms of the sartorial and always with an eye towards metropolitan space. Thus, veiled but present in my analyses of fashion's intersections with gender is Mallarmé's periodical *La Dernière Mode*, whose feminine pseudonyms have long intrigued scholars studying fashion in relation to the author's poetics of high symbolism. Likewise, Benjamin's declaration in *The Arcades Project* that "fashion has the scent of the modern,"[64] which posits dress as a measure of modernity and associates it with the nineteenth-century urban sphere, has

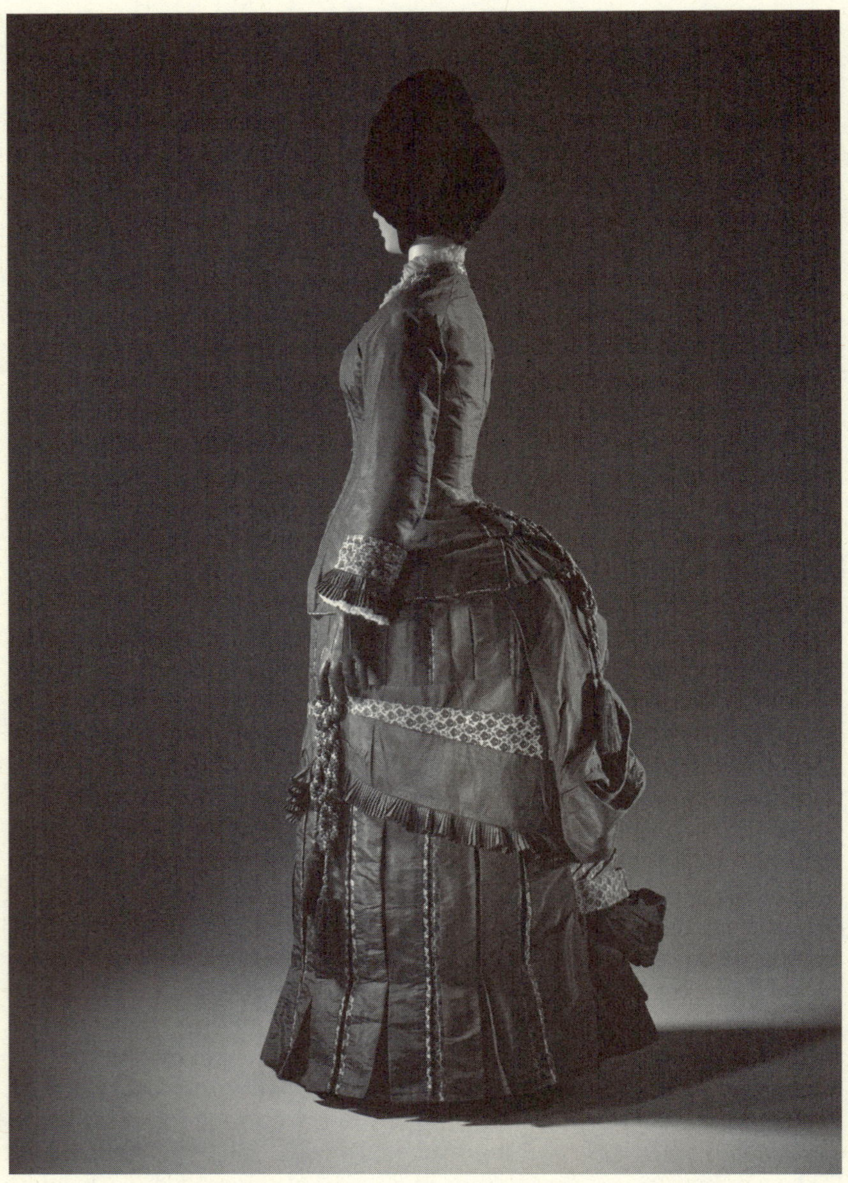

0.3 *Woman's Dress*, France, c. 1885. Los Angeles County Museum of Art. Image copyright © The Metropolitan Museum of Art. Image source: Art Resource, NY.

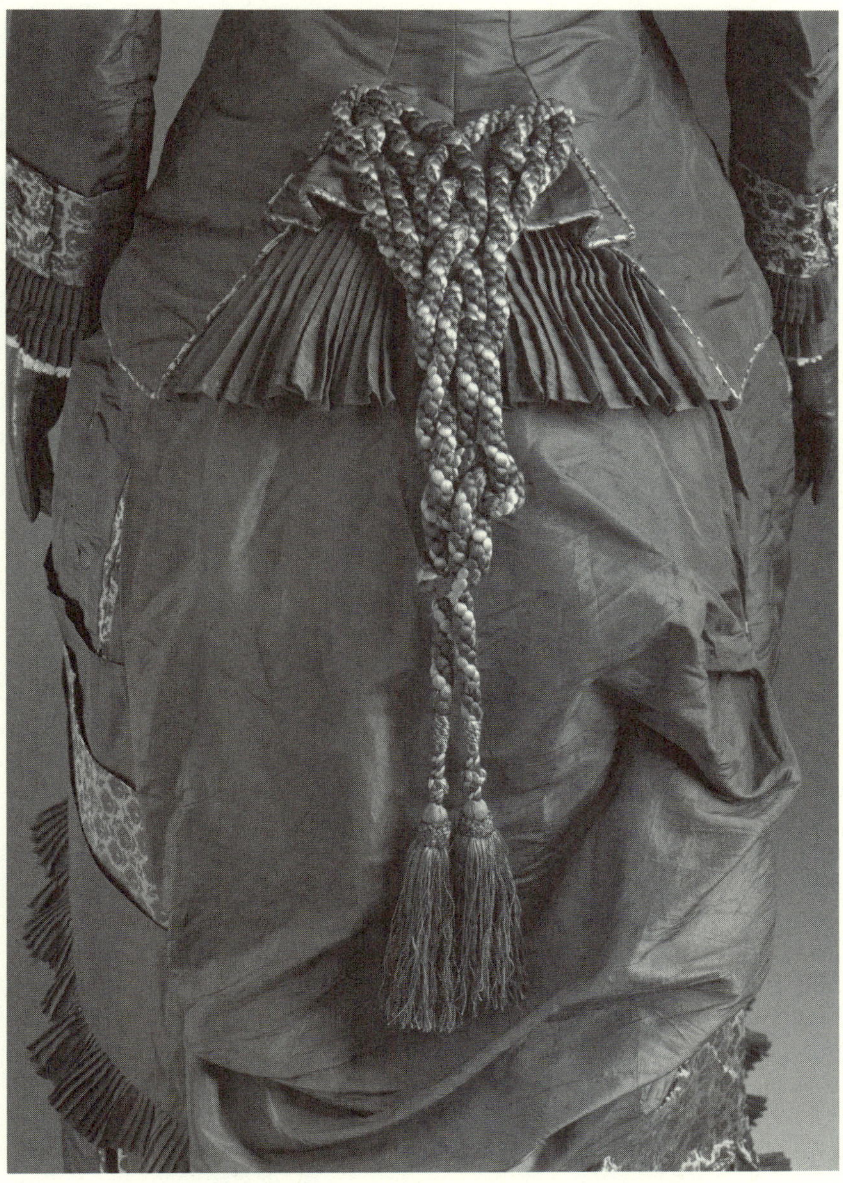

0.4 *Woman's Dress*, close-up, France, c. 1885. Los Angeles County Museum of Art. Image copyright © The Metropolitan Museum of Art. Image source: Art Resource, NY.

never been far from my thoughts. Finally, as evidenced by his appearance throughout these pages, it would be impossible (and impoverishing) to ever exclude Baudelaire.

Method and Organization

Fashioning Spaces offers an innovative look at some well-studied texts such as Zola's *Rougon-Macquart* novels, as well as explorations into works by well-known names such as Feydeau and Huysmans that are less familiar but equally compelling for the role they play in representing modernity. The lenses of fashion and urban spatial theory are thus combined to re-examine the priorities and aesthetic choices of canonical writers of the late nineteenth century from a reinvigorating point of view and to break new ground, too, through readings of understudied texts and authors. Furthermore, unlike many studies of fashion that focus solely on women, this book explores masculine garments (such as those in Caillebotte's paintings of stylish city dwellers in top hats and dark suits as well as protagonist Georges Duroy's transformative eveningwear in Maupassant's *Bel-Ami*) to demonstrate how fashion was conceived broadly across gender lines. This comparative study of men's and women's dress allows for a more comprehensive understanding of the work of fashion in aesthetic depictions of the period.

The book comprises six chapters, which are grouped into three sections having two chapters each: part 1 examines staircases; part 2 studies antechambers; and part 3 analyses fashion ateliers. This arrangement permits us to treat three categories of dislocations in depth while still exploring a wide breadth of concerns about writers' experiences of the modern city. Chapter 1, "Fashioning the Commune Barricade," begins with a discussion of Paris's grand urban staircases as key locations for sartorial display in the Third Republic city. It draws on newspaper reports, lithographs, and advertisements of the debut of Charles Garnier's opera house in 1875 as well as Félicien Rops's painting *L'Attrapade* of the staircase outside a high-profile restaurant. The chapter traces how elements of these monumental urban staircases are transformed in Zola's novel *Au Bonheur des Dames* from areas of fashionable spectacle to dislocated spaces of modernity. I focus on stairs in Zola's titular department store, from the customer staircases located inside the store to the employee stairwells integrated behind the scenes within its machinelike structure. Reading these sites as locations haunted

by the spectre of the bloody Paris Commune of 1871, I link Zola's staircases to the stepped barricades erected during this catastrophic civil conflict, one that might have plagued the author's memory during his
drafting of the novel and influenced his vision of the future city.

Chapter 2, "Ups and Downs, Surface and Spectacle," starts with close
readings of stairwells in the novels *Monsieur Vénus* and *La Jongleuse*
by Rachilde, examining the staircase as a space of gender subversion
in the former and a location illuminating the ambivalent status of the
female performer in the latter. Through the notion of spectacle,
Rachilde's writings connect to works by Maupassant and Daudet, all
three of whom express dwindling confidence about their place in the
modern city. In this section, I incorporate a discussion of Caillebotte's
paintings of Paris from the 1880s, which emphasize the verticality of
city buildings and echo in pictorial form the metaphors of ascent and
decent in Maupassant's and Daudet's texts. My analysis of Duroy's
famous climb up the Forestiers' staircase in *Bel-Ami* makes use of
Foucault's essay on heterotopias, which illuminates Maupassant's
criticism of the surface quality of urban dislocations. The chapter's
study of *Sapho*, Daudet's relatively understudied novella, centres on
the multisensorial qualities of clothing that Daudet draws out in a
working-class staircase at the beginning of the text. I suggest that the
physical pain and tactile nature of garments conveyed in this pivotal
scene imply Daudet's larger distrust of the phantasmagoria that modern space had become.

Part 2 turns to a second dislocation, that of the antechamber. This
section includes analyses of a number of types of antechambers, including entry halls in upper-class homes, theatre foyers, backstage loges,
and drawing rooms. Chapter 3, "Waiting for Change," begins with an
analysis of Degas's painting *L'Absinthe*, which, I argue, exemplifies the
same waiting and changing dialectic that informs literary representations of late-century antechambers. The chapter explores a frequently
overlooked episode in Zola's *Au Bonheur des Dames*, which takes place
in two separate antechambers in the apartment of wealthy Mme
Desforges. Zola's treatment of a jacket fitting gone awry is understood
to represent his broader endorsement of high capitalism and his prediction of its future success in France's developing liberal democracy. We
then analyse *Nana* by situating it in the context of the author's aesthetic
development. In particular, this text about a highly fashionable courtesan is read as a reflection of the author's state of mind as he waited,

apprehensively, for the public's response to the brand of literary naturalism that he sought, famously, in these years to promote. The chapter discusses male fashion through the dandified fop La Faloise, who is made to wait in a backstage theatre loge for Nana, a character figuring in the text as the very personification of an emerging vulgarized form of high fashion.

Chapter 4, "Maupassant, Transformation, and the Unexotic Exotic," is a reading of the antechamber in Maupassant's short story "La Parure" and novel *Bel-Ami*. It begins with the *robe à transformation*, a garment including multiple tops that could be worn interchangeably with the same skirt. I use the robe à transformation to contextualize "La Parure," a tale in which the main character is victimized by her slavish adherence to fashions that she hopes will "transform" her. The story concludes, unpredictably for Maupassant, with an optimistic ending about the possibility of modern human compassion in the urban landscape. The second part of the chapter examines what I interpret as Maupassant's critique of France's colonization of North Africa by arguing that, through the metaphor of the antechamber, Maupassant provocatively links France's imperialist activities in the Maghreb back to the metropolis of Paris. This section focuses on the orientalized garments of Duroy's mistress Clotilde and their connections to various forms of exoticized waiting rooms in the text.

Part 3 is concerned with fashion ateliers, dislocations in which garments are "made" in various senses of the word. Chapter 5, "Places and Spaces of Haute Couture," examines the haute couture workshop, the space par excellence wherein fashion was designed or created. The chapter begins with *Le Muscle du grand couturier*, Félicien Rops's watercolour of a tailor's fitting room, which is linked to Feydeau's play *Tailleur pour dames*, a rollicking comedy taking place in a dressmaker's atelier. Reading beyond the work's surface comedy I argue that the vaudevillian farce masks the playwright's darker anxieties about destiny and chance in the modern cityscape. *Tailleur pour dames* is thereby understood as a precursor to later twentieth-century movements including Surrealism and Existentialism, which sought to understand the meaning of human existence in ways that Feydeau's play anticipates. This discussion incorporates Yi-Fu Tuan's theories about the difference between "spaces" and "places," which inform my analysis of the fashion atelier as symbolic of a loss of security in modernity. The subsequent discussion of Zola's novel *La Curée* centres on Worms, a fictional analogue for the actual high-fashion designer Charles Frederick Worth. The analysis here posits that Zola's treatment of space is a critique not of Haussmannian regularization but, rather, of a dangerous network that the Baron's city planning might have unintentionally engendered.

The final chapter, "A Woman's Work(space)," focuses on the figure of the woman garment maker and her relationship to her space of work. The chapter begins with Degas's paintings *Chez la Modiste* and *Les Modistes*, which resonate with the depiction of women's work in the fashion atelier in Joris-Karl Huysmans's novel *En Ménage* and related piece "Robes et Manteaux." To a degree, the portraits of the female fashion worker by Degas and Huysmans illustrate her labour in a positive light. However, I argue that such depictions are created in service not of the *ouvrière* herself but rather of the male "high" artist. The study concludes with an analysis of the fashion atelier in a series of Rachilde's late-century novels. These works address misogynist prejudices about women fashion workers and show how Rachilde's feminist challenge to such prevailing gender ideologies was advanced spatially, in terms of women's increased access to the modern metropolis.

Fashioning Spaces demonstrates that writers of the early Third Republic frequently used clothing to make and describe textual spaces of the city. Dislocations – staircases, antechambers, and fashion ateliers – were related to newly emerging arenas of the Haussmannized city but in authors' works the latter spaces are shown to be more compelling, imaginable, penetrable, and potentially subversive than the empire-memorializing, mass-spectator, consumerist locales that had been created by urban planners to symbolize Parisian modernity. These texts collectively point to the space that fiction itself inhabits in urban life, one both discursive and material. Mallarmé illustrated this best, describing his fashion magazine *La Dernière Mode* as a work of poetry that would allow an elegant woman to "dress her soul as well [as her body]"[65] ["se parer aussi l'âme"[66]] while simultaneously envisioning the periodical as a physical object, situated in her dressing room, "half-opened like a scent-bottle, on the silks of sofa cushions embroidered with dreams"[67] ["entr'ouvert, comme un flacon, sur les soieries, ornées de chimères, des coussins"[68]]. Published in bound volumes, serial newspapers, periodicals, and play scripts – concrete items that occupied space and circulated through it even as they represented it – literary works of this period joined paintings, lithographs, photographs, and worn garments in impacting and animating the lived urban environment. The literature of fashion represented a way to make sense of new spatial paradigms, offering writers a presence in everyday discourse and allowing them to insert themselves into modernity's dynamics. If the dislocations they imagined existed on a metaphorical plane, they were deeply implicated in the historical, social, and political contexts that they alternately challenged and upheld. In this way, authors contributed to the formation of urban behaviours; they turned to writing to negotiate their own experiences of urbanization and their words were part of an analogous process for their readers. What I will demonstrate in the pages that follow are the ways in which a subject as seemingly frivolous as fashion actually provided a tremendously powerful metaphor through which to index and negotiate modernity in late-nineteenth-century Paris.

PART ONE

The Staircase

1 Fashioning the Commune Barricade: Zola's *Au Bonheur des Dames*

It was 5 January 1875, the highly anticipated date of the most fashionable event of the season in Paris. After fifteen years of construction and numerous delays, Charles Garnier's gilded rococo opera house, a belated homage to the opulent aesthetic of the recently deposed Second Empire of Napoléon III, was finally to be celebrated that night with a gala opening. Four days later the city remained abuzz, with public interest in the Opéra's debut remaining so high that the editors of *Le Monde Illustré* elected to devote an entire special issue to coverage of the spectacular event. According to reporter Albert de Lasalle, among the most notable features of the new concert hall was its *grand escalier*, the primary interior staircase by which opera-goers accessed the main concert hall. Lasalle called it "the majestic staircase of honour" ["le majestueux escalier d'honneur"][1] and marvelled at its "dazzling marble and onyx décor" ["éblouissant décor de marbre et d'onyx"].[2] Next to appear were images of this impressive structure: on 16 January the periodical featured a prominent lithograph engraving that centred on the marble staircase, Garnier descending it flanked by crowds of finely dressed onlookers.[3] With the passing months, it became increasingly evident that such glowing appreciation of the staircase was widely shared. In fact, the elegant stairs captivated visitors to such a degree that, for many, they appeared to be the highlight of the entire building. In *Le nouvel Opéra* (1875), a volume commemorating the structure's début, the Opéra's archivist Charles Nuitter paid homage to the newness of the staircase's design, its clever layout, and the rich brilliance of the materials that Garnier had insisted upon integrating into its construction.[4] Proclaiming it to be "one of the most remarkable design concepts of the new Opéra" ["l'une des conceptions les plus remarquables du nouvel Opéra"],[5] Nuitter later amended this, declaring that the staircase was actually more than remarkable as it was, in fact, "a monument inside a monument" ["un monument dans un monument"].[6] Garnier himself, somewhat bewildered that the grand escalier appeared to have eclipsed the rest of his elaborate design, noted in 1878 that, for many, "the Opéra is the staircase, just as the Invalides is the dome" ["l'Opéra, c'est l'escalier, comme les Invalides, c'est le dôme"].[7] Like the gilded hemispherical roof that memorialized France's history of empire building and military triumph, the grand escalier had become a synecdoche, a representative not just of the edifice as a whole, but of Parisian modernity itself.

To be sure, as Nuitter noted, the triumph of Garnier's staircase was attributable, in part, to physical construction: its breathtaking monumentality, the lavishness of its design, the marbled grandeur of its stairs and balconies, and the majesty of its vaulted ceilings and arcades. Yet, its success derived also from the way in which the space appealed to the nineteenth-century public's enjoyment of both viewing and being part of the spectacle of urban life, a spectacle in which fashion played a key role. An 1875 lithograph by Emile Thérond illustrates how Garnier deliberately structured the space so that patrons would arrive in direct view of spectators already situated in the surrounding balconies (see figure 1.1). In this way, attendees could observe the arrival of crowds of stylish Parisians to the opera house and enjoy watching, or indeed, being watched, as a form of pre-show entertainment before the curtain went up on the official musical performance. Théophile Gautier, writing in 1863, over a decade before the building was completed, had already anticipated that the balconies placed strategically over the grand escalier would become a place where "curious people will be able to lean on their elbows as in a painting by Paul Veronese, spectators and spectacle at the same time" ["les curieux pourront s'accouder comme dans une toile de Paul Véronèse, spectateurs et spectacle en même temps"].[8] The importance of the staircase as a space of spectacle in and of itself was reinforced by the fact that, according to Le Monde Illustré's reporter Lasalle, the lights in the lobby and grand staircase glowed brighter than the beams trained on the actual stage: "The foyer and the majestic staircase of honour are … the only rooms of the monument that are lit to the required degree. The hall leaves a little, and the stage a lot, to be desired on this account" ["Le foyer et le majestueux escalier d'honneur sont … les seules pièces du monument qui soient éclairées au point requis. La salle laisse un peu, et la scène beaucoup à désirer sous ce rapport"].[9] Lasalle's report

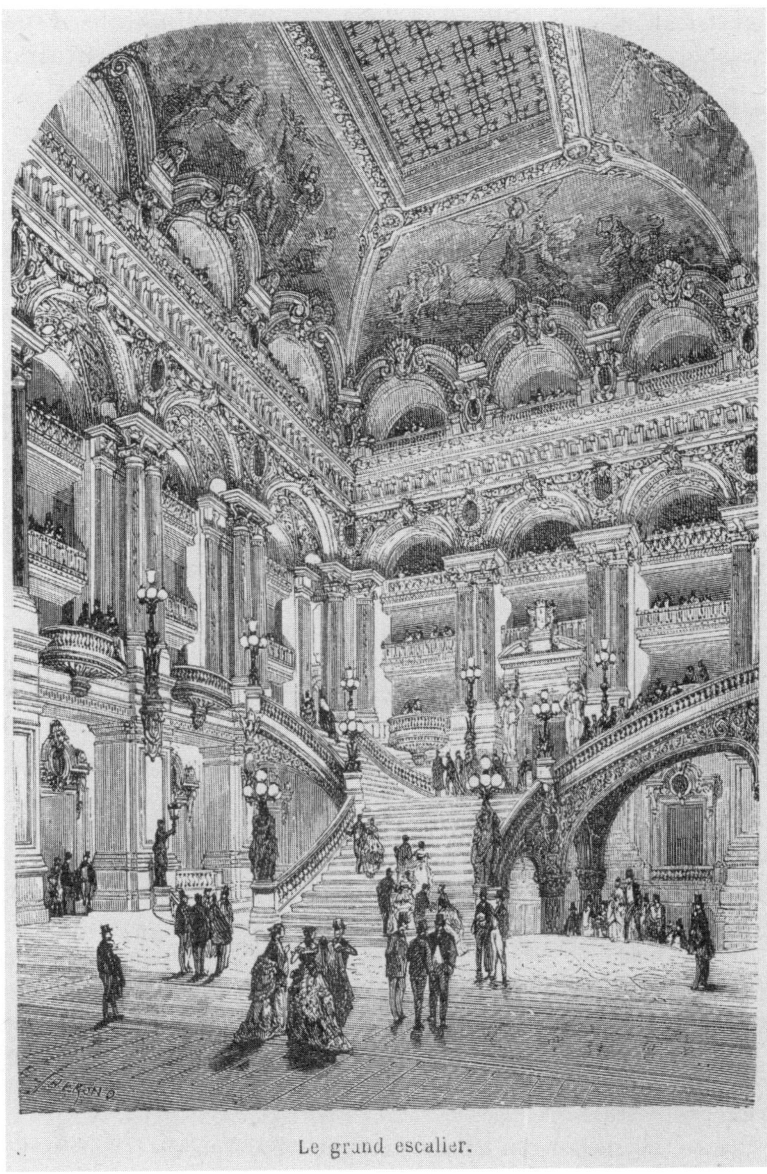

1.1 Emile Thérond, *Le grand escalier*, 1875, in *Le nouvel Opéra* by Charles Nuitter, 87. Reproduced by permission of the Getty Research Institute, Los Angeles (2582-814).

suggests that, even in structures erected ostensibly to promote costumed entertainment, it was not the stage but rather the public's own sartorial display that was privileged in the new architecture of modernity.

Indeed, like the grand escalier, other public locations built in the nineteenth century were created with the exhibition and consumption of clothing in mind. Locales such as the racecourse, the park, and the boulevard had for decades drawn Parisians wishing to exhibit their garments, as well as couturiers hoping to stimulate sales of their creations. Yet, the Opéra staircase, symbol not only of a past empire but also of a nascent republic, equally represented the dawn of an era in which space, fashion, and notions of modernity would mutually inform one another in increasingly complex ways. This is illustrated by an advertisement for a new fabric called "Le Nouvel-Opéra," which appeared in the same issue of *Le Monde Illustré* dedicated to the building's début. The text, demonstrating the network connecting garment fabrics and the commercial fashion industry to the modern spirit evoked by spaces of the city connected to high style, is worth citing in its entirety:

Allow us to announce the arrival of a new material of silk brocade, imitating antique fabrics, having an inimitable suppleness and shine, with which one makes ravishing outfits by combining it with velvet, satin, or faille. One would have to attach to this notice a swatch of this fabric, which is the latest fashion of the day, because it is almost impossible to give an accurate idea of its supreme elegance by way of a brief summary. Let us content ourselves with adding that the NOUVEL-OPÉRA, as this remarkable creation of modern industry is named, is already very much in vogue, and this is evident since it has been chosen by all women desiring to achieve or preserve the reputation of elegance that is attached to certain figures of note. The NOUVEL-OPÉRA will also be appreciated, as it deserves to be, by reasonable and thrifty women who will quickly recognize how solid this double-faced fabric is, woven in such a way as to be supple, shiny, and hard-wearing. These precious qualities also render it appropriate for interior furnishings: fabric wall coverings, drapes and door curtains, padded seats, etc. The NOUVEL-OPÉRA can be found at the shop of M. Lehoussel, maison de l'Union des Indes, 1, rue Auber.

[Signalons l'apparition d'un nouveau tissu de soie broché imitant les anciennes étoffes, d'une souplesse et d'un brillant inimitables, avec lequel on fait de ravissantes toilettes en l'associant au velours, au satin ou à la faille. Il faudrait pouvoir joindre à cette note un échantillon de cette étoffe, qui est la nouveauté du jour, car il est presque impossible de donner une juste idée de sa suprême élégance par des indications aussi sommaires. Contentons-nous d'ajouter que le NOUVEL-OPÉRA, ainsi se nomme cette remarquable création de l'industrie moderne, jouit déjà d'une vogue très-grande, et cela s'explique, car il est adopté par toutes les femmes jalouses de conquérir ou de conserver cette réputation d'élégance qui s'attache à certaines personnalités féminines. Le NOUVEL-OPÉRA sera aussi apprécié, comme il mérite de l'être, par les femmes raisonnables et économes qui reconnaitront bien vite combien est solide cette étoffe à double face, tissée de façon à être à la fois souple, brillante et inusable. Ces qualités précieuses la rendent aussi très-propre aux combinaisons d'ameublement: tentures de murs, rideaux et portières, sièges capitonnés, etc. Le NOUVEL-OPÉRA se trouve chez M. Lehoussel, maison de l'Union des Indes, 1, rue Auber.][10]

The advertisement, appearing a mere four days after opening night, suggests that associations between Garnier's structure and notions of modernness and fashionability had already been established. The name of the silk is perhaps the most obvious sign of its producers' desire to capitalize on the stylishness that the long-awaited building seemed immediately to evoke. But the advertisement also accentuates two other important characteristics linking "le Nouvel-Opéra" to its architectural namesake. The first is the silk's up-to-the-minute quality, emphasized in descriptions of the cloth as "new" and "the latest fashion of the day." The second is the fabric's opulent elegance, conveyed in descriptive terms including "ravishing" and "brilliant," which linked it to other sumptuous and pricey fabrics such as velvet and satin.

The advertisement is a striking testament to the complex interconnectivity of the diverse populations supporting and supported by fashionable consumption in the capital city, including fabric manufacturers, distributors, and the mass-circulating press itself.[11] Even more remarkable are allusions to urban spaces located beyond the Opéra's walls. The suggestion, for instance, that consumers could recreate the lavish stylishness of Garnier's space by using the silk for furniture, wall coverings, and curtains created a sense of a network between the monumental locations of the city and readers' living quarters. More provocatively, the very name of the fabric implied that, in donning a garment made from the silk, one could metaphorically "wear" the opera house itself, an abstract mapping of urban space onto the body by way of clothing.

This symbolic link between physical building and stylishly clothed bodies relates in interesting ways to Garnier's design process, which he outlined in 1878 in a multivolume tome, the title of which echoed that of the silk: *Le Nouvel Opéra de Paris*. In it, Garnier specifies that, while designing the grand escalier in particular, he had drawn on his memories of the costume balls once held at Paris's former opera house, a structure that had burned down several years prior and which his own monument had replaced.[12] He describes thinking about the fabrics, accessories, and jewelry worn by "the colourful crowd who would animate the grand staircase" ["cette foule colorée, qui devait animer le grand escalier"],[13] enthusing over the accessories and opulent fabrics, "gold, brocade, damask, velvet" ["l'or, le brocart, le damas, le velours"] that, in his words, "spring from Veronese's palette and now shine and sparkle under the vaulted staircase!" ["jaillissent de la palette de Véronèse, et qui, maintenant, éclatent et scintillent sous les voûtes de l'escalier!"].[14] Garnier's writings demonstrate that the spatial organization of the staircase and its sumptuous décor were, at their inception, informed by the interactions that the architect had foreseen occurring among space, garments, and the bodies that would breathe life into both.[15]

Staircase Scoldings: Rops's *L'Attrapade*

Garnier was not alone in his attention to the nexus of stairways and the sartorial. Belgian painter Félicien Rops (1833–1898) memorably rendered a convergence between staircase and fashion in his watercolour *L'Attrapade*, a title often translated as "The Scolding" because of the word's informal connotations linking to the notion of insult,[16] but the literal root of which is the verb *attraper* meaning "to catch" (see figure 1.2). In the painting, two well-dressed women confront one another on a red carpet–lined staircase, the brunette on the left depicted in mid-descent and looking over her shoulder at her rival clad in blue, who in turn, gestures angrily at her departing adversary. Rops's 1877 satire of Parisian high life simultaneously draws attention to haute couture fashion and a staircase, the charged site of the watercolour's dramatic "scolding." As the attention to garments in *L'Attrapade* suggests, clothing was an important theme to Rops, an aesthetic choice likely stemming from his direct involvement in the late-century fashion industry. When *L'Attrapade* debuted, Rops was working as an illustrator for re-editions of texts by authors who had written prominently about fashion, writers including Baudelaire, Théophile Gautier, and

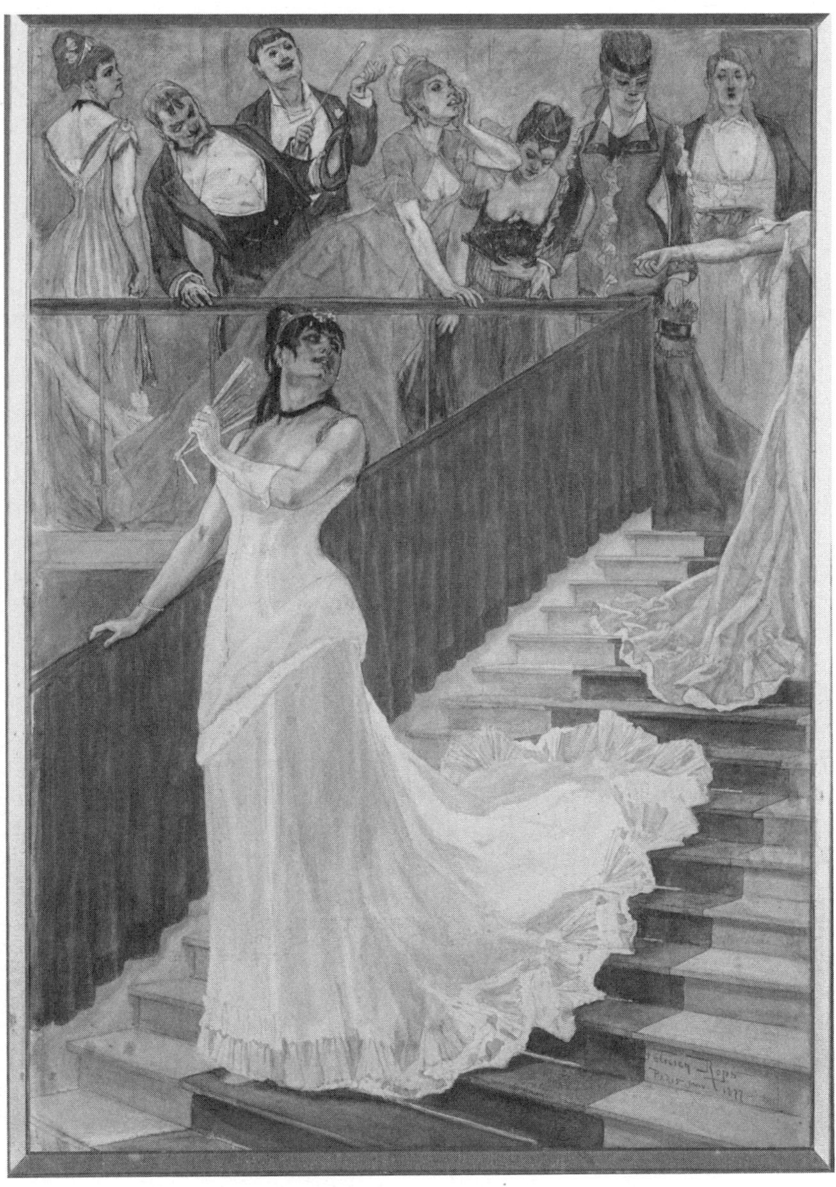

1.2 Félicien Rops, *L'Attrapade* (*The Row*), 1877. Pencil and watercolour on paper. Namur, Le Musée Félicien Rops. Reproduced by permission of the Bridgeman Art Library.

Barbey d'Aurevilly. The artist had moved to Paris from Brussels to seek his fortune as a painter, but also, significantly, to continue his romantic liaison with two French *couturières*, the sisters Aurélie and Léontine Duluc.[17] The 1880s and 1890s saw the rise of their joint fashion house, first called "Maison Duluc, Rops et confections" and then renamed "Aux mannequins," which Rops supported by illustrating fashion plates and occasionally designing women's wear.[18] Due to Rops's decades-long participation in the fashion industry, it is not surprising that garments would become a focal point in the many works of Decadent and Symbolist art that he was also producing at a prolific rate during this period.

In *L'Attrapade*, Rops highlights the radiant pastel evening dresses worn by the pair of women at the centre of the composition both in celebration of fashionable high society and as a critique of its superficial privileging of luxury and scandal. Spotlighting in painstaking detail the tailoring of the two women's gowns, from the ruffled and pleated trimming of their trains to their fitted bodices, Rops also deliberately calls attention to space by way of a large staircase that dominates the bottom third of the composition and creates movement through the strong diagonal line it cuts descending from right to left. Sartorial cues – ball gowns and formal menswear – establish the location as an arena of heightened public spectacularity, a space of Parisian modernity par excellence. The spectators in the background, who react with comic shock (and delight) to the altercation between the two luxuriously clad adversaries, aid in dramatizing how the staircase served as an extension of the theatre stage and could even surpass it as a space of both diversion and the display of opulent garments.

The year he completed *L'Attrapade*, Rops referred to the painting as "the most important thing I have done" ["ce que j'ai fait de plus important"].[19] It is likely that this striking declaration was referring less to the subject matter of the composition and more to an innovation in painting method that Rops had been toiling for months to achieve. This was an approach by which the painter enhanced his preliminary watercolour with pastels in order to augment the work's radiance without sacrificing the delicateness of its colours.[20] The many versions of *L'Attrapade* from this period that Rops produced suggest that this new procedure was an aesthetic preoccupation. Even so, the painting's subject matter and its location seem also of importance, as demonstrated by the specificity with which Rops described them to friends. In a letter to the artist Maurice Bonvoisin, for instance, the painter explained the scene as "a great devil of a prostitute descending the stairs" ["une grande diablesse de fille descendant l'escalier"],[21] clarifying, too, that the location was the Café Anglais, a high-profile restaurant well known for attracting the same stylish clientele as Garnier's Opéra. This deliberate decision to set his image in a prominent space of modern glamour and to highlight the brilliance of fabrics catching light and minute details on garments indicates that fashion, and one of the city's most recognizable staircase locales, dually contributed to Rops's achievement of a new painting technique, one that he had laboured to perfect and that art historian Michel Draguet terms a "milestone" ["un jalon"][22] in the artist's career. Moerover, by providing a necessary signifier for Rops's staircase, fashion communicated the artist's tongue-in-cheek criticisms of the upper-class society lampooned in his painting while simultaneously demonstrating his admiration for the beauty of luxury garments. In this last way Rops was not unlike Garnier, whose architectural vision for the grand escalier was also influenced by an appreciation for haute couture. Garments and their relationship to urban space thus played key roles in helping both men realize new forms of aesthetic expression.

What is more, as we will investigate later in this chapter, Rops's scene of confrontation resonates (however unintentionally) with a far more serious type of altercation also related to Parisian urban space: the devastating Commune of 1871. For the painting's staircase is, in effect, a space of advancement and retreat staged between two adversaries that, if read in more sober terms, has connotations relating to war. Warfare is evoked also by the title *L'Attrapade*, literally "The Catch," which calls to mind the tactical manoeuvres of capturing an evader. These militarized metaphors will be discussed in a later examination of staircases in Zola's *Au Bonheur des Dames*, which will analyse the novel's underlying commentary on military and militia advancements, retreats, and entrapments that took place during the bloody 1871 civil clash.[23]

The Staircase in Fashion

Let us return first, though, to spectacle and garment. The importance that Garnier and Rops both ascribed to the staircase may have been informed by the fact that women's fashions in this period were transforming in a way that was not subtle but conspicuous, a way that would encode the new style, clearly different from what had come before it, as "modern." Architect and artist, like stylish women of the day, doubtless intuited that few locations were better than a grand escalier to display one's attractive modernness, especially as the most striking elements of the major clothing style change of the 1870s would have been enhanced when ascending and descending stairs. The change to which I am referring is that the enormous bell-shaped crinoline, which had been the height of fashion for nearly two decades, had begun to give way to a silhouette that flattened in the front of a woman's body while concentrating its volume behind it.[24] As a result, from the front, the female figure appeared more slender overall than in previous years (see figure 1.2 for Rops's rendition of this slimmer skirt shape), and indeed in the late 1870s, looks became so column-like as to approximate more a man's trim build than the ultra-femininized hourglass – the tiny waist engulfed in full petticoats – that had previously reigned. Although skirt fronts were certainly embellished in the years that Garnier and Rops debuted their respective works, arguably the most elaborate ornamental and structural attention was to be found on the backs of gowns, where, in some cases, stairs seemed even a discernible motif reproduced in the outfits themselves.

There was, for instance, a skirt style that grew out of an earlier vogue for evenly spaced, multilayered flounces, such as those seen on many of the young women in Tissot's painting *Hush!* (figure 0.1). When the tiered layers were extended on the back of the body, as seen in the 1870s fashion plate from *La Mode Illustrée* (see figure 1.3), they resembled staircases of fabric, which mimicked the structural design of the grand escalier on which they were paraded. In figure 1.4, the petticoat, which features a close-fitting front and an offset stack of regularly spaced semi-circle metal hoops moving down from the wearer's lower back, demonstrates how undergarments of the period foundationally enhanced the steplike quality of such skirt designs. To be sure, many style innovations are made with the goal of attracting attention; in this case, location was an especially crucial factor in the visual impact of modern looks, since wearers would have created a seductive eye-catching sway as their hips, radically expanded with poufs of fabric over many-layered underskirts, shifted to and fro on alternate steps.

Tellingly, the practice of concentrating a focal point of women's wear on the back of the skirt through fit or decorative detail remained a general trend until the end of the century. By the mid-1880s the dome shape in undergarments had been replaced by the *tournure* or bustle, a cage of metal or whale baleen that extended a woman's derrière behind her, sometimes thrusting back as far as several feet and at a rigid right angle from her lower back (see figure 0.3). Instead of an entire flight of steps, one could imagine that the bustle approximated the form of one giant stair, an oversized "step" that exaggerated the female backside into an extreme erogenous zone. Even after the bustle collapsed in later years, and semi-rigid undercontraptions succumbed to a skirt that hung naturally from the waist, an emphasis on the back of the body persisted. Cuts remained long, and, throughout the 1890s, skirts typically included a short train that fanned out, draped, and flowed sensuously over stepped urban terrain, simultaneously highlighting garments and their movement in space. Walter Benjamin's reference to a dreamed image of "stairs like the train of a dress"[25] expresses this correspondence between the structure of stairways and the fabrics trailing behind stylish late-century women as they climbed and descended them. We should note that extended skirt backs were not, in fact, original to the early Third Republic as, indeed, all of the looks described above had antecedents from earlier epochs; nor, naturally, were staircases a new phenomenon. The point to glean is that the very noticeable transformation – or modernization – in silhouettes, particularly from the 1860s to the 1870s, coincided with the heightened emphasis on the display of clothing as a trademark of the architecture of modernity.

The staircase as a design motif in this period also appeared on fashion accessories,[26] in particular, on fans, which were often ornamented with painted scenes of the exteriors of mansions, castles, or other lavish buildings featuring large staircases.[27] In *La Dernière Mode*, Mallarmé imagines fans decorated with "scenes of grand entrance flights-of-steps to noble houses or ancestral parks – or asphalt and gravel" (translation modified)[28] ["Scènes de perrons d'hôtels ou des parcs héréditaires et de l'asphalte et de la grève"[29]]. The staircase (*perron*) is a signifier of traditional aristocratic luxury that the poet reinforces by evoking private mansions of the wealthy (*hôtels*) and inherited land (*parcs héréditaires*). Yet, as fashion must mix the new with the old, Mallarmé juxtaposes these traditional sites of fashionability with "the contemporary *monde*"[30] ["le monde contemporain"[31]] that asphalt, the smooth paving material of Haussmannized boulevards, would have represented to a Third Republic readership.

The presence of the staircase in garments, considered alongside testimonials stressing the newness of the Opéra's grand escalier, its spectacularity, and the role of fashion and clothed bodies to its design invite us to think of the grand public staircase as a quintessential space of Parisian modernity, one that entertained affluent Parisians as well as the petite bourgeoisie hoping to "climb" economically and socially to

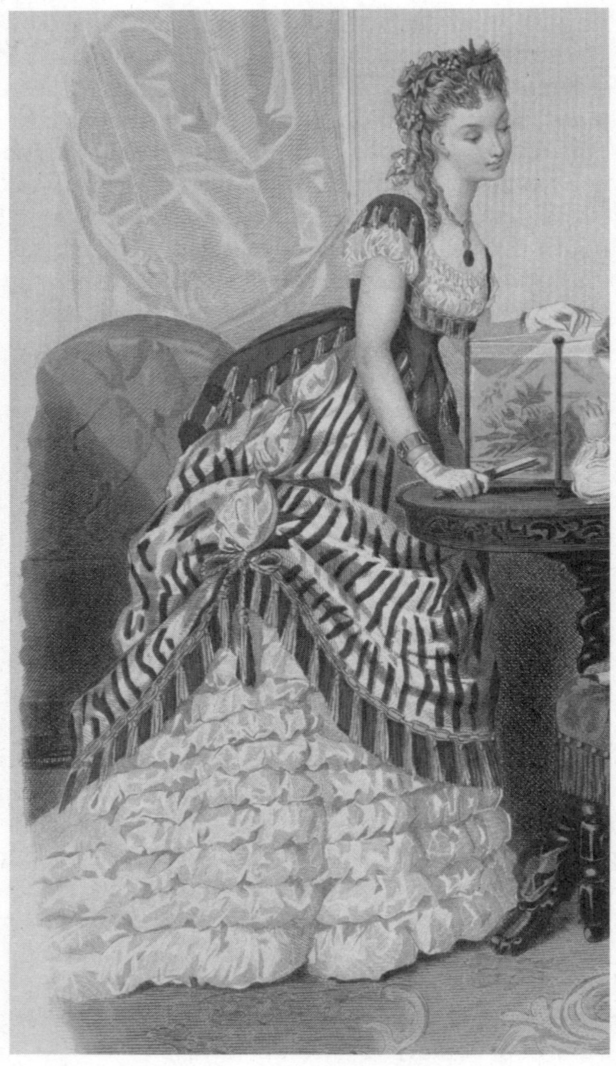

1.3 Detail from *Women and a Child Looking at an Aquarium*, from *La Mode Illustrée*, c. 1870. Coloured engraving. Reproduced by permission of the Bridgeman Art Library.

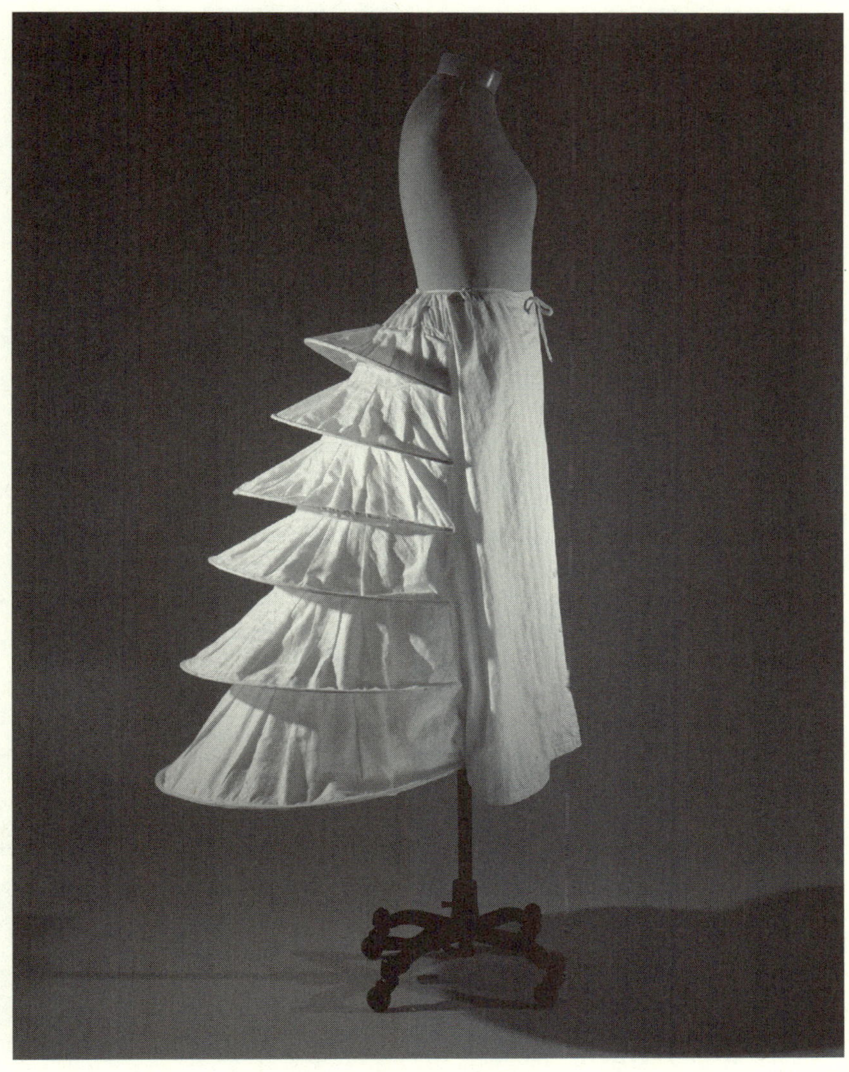

1.4 *British Bustle*, c. 1871. The Metropolitan Museum of Art, Purchase: The New York Historical Society (by exchange) and Louise Moore Van Vleck Gift, 1985 (1985.27.4).

their ranks. In contrast, as we will see, the experience of modernity as depicted in literary texts was not limited to such monumental or diverting urban locales. Rather, the staircases of Garnier and Rops can be understood as large-scale, Empire-sanctioned analogues to the less grandiose, far more politically problematized staircases that occur with surprising regularity in works of fiction of the last three decades of the nineteenth century.

In the literature studied here, staircases transform from such arenas of fashionable elegance into dislocations where garments and space function together to point to subversions of gender and class and to engender political critique. In Zola's works, for instance, the staircase expresses the violent social instabilities heralding the fall of the Second Empire and serves as a metaphor for the Commune barricades built in its wake. Architecturally, staircases are transitional passageways, spaces through which one moves in between two destinations. In her fiction, Rachilde calls upon this threshold quality of the staircase to explore possible freedoms that urban experience could provide women and also to condemn the city as a space in which women had to constantly perform in order to navigate it. As we will see in chapter 2, staircases enable Maupassant and Daudet to criticize the surface spectacularity of modern space even while indulging in lavish descriptions of it. For all four authors, the staircase is intimately linked to the garments worn in and around it. Literature of the period thus echoes, often with less monumentality but with just as much complexity, the relationships between clothing and space performed in the majestic arena of Garnier's grand escalier. Staircases demonstrate how writers used the interplays between garments and their surroundings as a means to examine what the modern city had become and to evaluate their present and future roles in it.

The (Stair)case of the *Rougon-Macquart*

That Emile Zola's *Rougon-Macquart* series includes a number of problematic staircases is not in itself surprising, given the novelist's devotion to documenting urban spatiality in Second Empire France. More noteworthy, perhaps, is the fact that prominent staircases in Zola's novels tend often to be sites where fashion is also highlighted. Hannah Thompson has persuasively shown in *Naturalism Redressed*[32] that garments function importantly throughout the twenty volumes of Zola's masterwork. The focus here will be the moments in which dislocated staircases are underscored in conjunction with highly charged occurrences of fashion. These passages are concentrated in *La Curée* (1871), *Nana* (1880), *Pot-Bouille* (1882), and *Au Bonheur des Dames* (1883), the works that Thompson terms Zola's "novels of luxury"[33] and that can equally be called his "novels of fashion" for their emphasis on the places and players associated with Parisian high style.

I begin with Zola because his staircases highlight a number of concerns about modernity to be discussed throughout this book. If some of these are specific to Zola, such as the author's delayed anxiety about the civil conflict of the Commune of 1871, others – ambivalence over women's transforming roles in society, for example – are shared more broadly. Critiques of bourgeois society levied by numerous writers are another hallmark of the dislocations that I will be examining, such as those illuminated by Zola in *Pot-Bouille*. Rendered in vividly spatial terms, the main stairwell in this novel's primary setting – an apartment building in one of Paris's newly constructed middle-class neighbourhoods – is the location in which Berthe, caught *in flagrante delicto*, flees her cuckolded husband clad only in her filmy undergarments. Because it is shared by all of the inhabitants in the building, the staircase is where Berthe's affair is transformed from a personal infidelity into a spectacle that all of her neighbours can judge. Here Zola's staircase passage seems to anticipate Jurgen Habermas's declaration that the bourgeoisie, the dominant class of the nineteenth century, had become a population "passionately concerned with itself."[34] For Habermas, this self-interestedness manifested in the middle class's growing fascination with the domestic drama, one that *Pot-Bouille* both exemplifies and represents through this key scene on the apartment staircase. Offering a narrative version of Habermas's later theory, Zola uses the stairwell to critique the hypocrisy of the building's residents, who look down upon the young woman disapprovingly while engaging in their own condemnable extramarital activities behind closed doors.

Through its attention to space and dress, the *Pot-Bouille* staircase illuminates another subject of concern during the Third Republic to which I will return throughout: representations of women as disruptions to the place and moral structure of home life. Through the convergence of clothing and location in *Pot-Bouille*, Zola codes disturbances to nineteenth-century domestic respectability as feminine. The inappropriateness of Berthe's transparent garment on the stairwell – a disconnect between fashion and space – bears witness to the adultery she has committed, while her male partner Octave Mouret, who is similarly undressed, is spared from this humiliating sartorial and sexualized exposure by his apartment flat, a space that conceals him and acts as his refuge. Yet Berthe's *chemise* is not merely the fashion object through which her infidelity is laid bare; it also has spatial implications for, as Marcus observes, Zola refers in other passages of *Pot-Bouille* to the dirty underwear or "dubious undergarments [*dessous douteux*]" of women, playing on the fact that "*dessous* can refer to both architectural foundations and women's undergarments."[35] The episode exemplifies the novelist's tendency not simply to portray women as harbingers of the moral downfall of modern society – those whose soiled undergarments signal their unclean selves – but to do so at the junction of fashion and built urban structures.

Another staircase, this one in Zola's novel *La Curée*, highlights the related nineteenth-century trope of women as inherently sexually transgressive. This is a staircase serving as a conduit between the shady Sidonie Rougon's "cramped and mysterious"[36] ["étroite et mystérieuse"[37]] lace shop and the bedroom located above it. The boutique, where "odds and ends of point lace and Valenciennes"[38] ["bouts de guipure et de la valencienne"[39]] hang in its windows, is connected to fashion through this display of lace, an expensive trimming commonly used in haute couture garments and accessories of the period and one that, Thompson illustrates, often symbolizes women's illicit sexuality in the *Rougon-Macquart*.[40] In reality, the shop is nothing more than a front to facilitate the exchanges of money for sex that occur in the upstairs bedroom and that Sidonie arranges as a paid intermediary. Her staircase anticipates Zola's later suggestion in *Pot-Bouille* that it is women who play the roles of transgressors and mediators in society's sexual and moral decline.

As Therese Dolan has shown, it is especially through the figure of the prostitute that connections between fashion and social decline concretize in the late century;[41] the staircase emerges in literature as a site exposing this link. In *Nana*, his courtesan novel, Zola rewrites the hidden stairwell of *La Curée* into the "great staircase"[42] ["vaste escalier"[43]] of the Muffat mansion, an edifice that, through its grandeur, calls to mind Garnier's Opéra. Style communicates the infidelity of countess Sabine as she returns from a night of debauchery and encounters her husband, the Count Muffat, on the central stairway of their austere mansion. The detail that the countess's hairstyle has come undone (she is *mal repeignée*[44] or "poorly recombed") draws parallels with Nana, the courtesan whose golden tresses are frequently unravelled after sexual activity.[45] The tousled hairstyle that associates the countess with the prostitute allows Zola to propagate the misogynist viewpoint that moral and sexual disorder were shared by all women, regardless of their social class. The staircase encounter between the countess and her husband takes it a step further, suggesting a transference from women to men of immoral comportment and symbolizing architecturally the communication of depravities transmitted from courtesan and countess to count. For it is on the stairs that, Muffat's "mud-stained clothes"[46] ["vêtements boueux"[47]] signal that he has been corrupted through his unclean liaison with Nana, whose popularity as Paris's most fashionable courtesan increases her own chances of being sullied by disease. The count's dirty eveningwear bears witness to his tainted religious beliefs, once pure but now soiled by the vice of desire for this contagious woman. Degradation of fashion in the appearances of both characters as they pass one another on the steps mirrors their spiritual and moral decay, while the intertext of Sidonie's illicit stairs from *La Curée* implies that it is corruption itself that lies beneath the surface dazzle of the Muffats' monumental staircase.

The point to emphasize here is that social critiques of modernity are frequently communicated in terms of urban space. We read that Sidonie's hidden stairwell is "a staircase hidden in the wall"[48] ["un escalier caché dans le mur"[49]]; that is, it is constructed, literally, inside a key foundational element of the building. This attention to the stairs' placement in the wall suggests that, for Zola, the structures of the newly constructed metropolis were marked within their very frameworks by the depravity ingrained into the disreputable stairwell in Sidonie's boutique. As discussed in detail in chapter 5, especially in *La Curée*, Zola's biting denunciation of the dishonest real estate speculation that facilitated the reconfiguration of Paris under Haussmannization is spatially conceived. The sordid staircase, where lace and urban construction collide, is the dislocation expressing Zola's critique.

Department Stor(i)es: *Au Bonheur des Dames*

The analysis above suggests no shortage of examples of fashion moments in staircases in the *Rougon-Macquart*. Yet, for the reader familiar with Zola's history of the Second Empire, the convergence of fashion, modernity, and stairways is most likely to call to mind the central staircase in Octave Mouret's department store, Au Bonheur des Dames, particularly given Zola's well-known proclamation that his eponymous novel documenting the rise of the mass-production fashion industry was to be his "poem of modern activity" ["poème de l'activité moderne"].[50] This staircase, located at the hub of the department store and in a novel situated at the very midpoint of Zola's twenty-volume cycle, provides the central fashion site for my discussion of the Zolian staircase.

As has been well studied, Zola took much inspiration for his fictional department store setting from his early 1880s visits to Aristide Boucicaut's real-life establishment, Le Bon Marché.[51] In particular, as his preparatory notes from 1882 demonstrate, the novel's central staircase was modelled after the massive wrought-iron flight of steps in Boucicaut's building. The Bon Marché *escalier*, not unlike the staircase at Garnier's Opéra or at the Café Anglais, also caught the imagination of graphic artists whose works reflect a variety of attitudes about the meanings of these spaces. In his 1875 lithograph of the then-recently constructed staircase at the Bon Marché, Frédéric Lix foregrounded the voluminous skirts and the crush of female shoppers (over)populating the stairs of the department store (see figure 1.5). Lix's image gives a picture of fashionable – and feminine – excess more in line with Zola's hystericizing portrait of female consumerism than with Emile Thérond's more austere, sparse, and male-heavy representation of the Opéra's grand escalier (see figure 1.1). Despite their differences, however, both images feature symmetrical, multifloored flights of steps that are echoed in the stepped tiers of the skirt styles of the 1870s. The prints also showcase smaller balconies and shadowy heads peering over railings at stylish shoppers or opera-goers below, a configuration of spectator and performance that is echoed in Rops's rendition of the scene at the Café Anglais wherein the viewers in the background are as important to the composition as the two protagonists in the foreground. These shared elements suggest similarities between the visual extravaganza that Boucicaut's department store staircase offered patrons and what was also débuting across town at Garnier's Opéra and the Café Anglais.

In *Au Bonheur des Dames*, the central staircase is a key narrative location. Zola repeatedly situates Mouret at its apogee and writes from the dominating point of view of his protagonist's surveilling gaze to document the buzzing activity of the department store below him: "He had gone back to his favorite position at the top of the mezzanine stairs by the banister"[52] ["Il était revenu à son poste favori, en haut de l'escalier de l'entresol, contre la rampe"[53]]; "He paused at the top of the central stairway and looked out for a long time down the central nave"[54] ["Il s'arrêta en haut de l'escalier central, il regarda longtemps l'immense

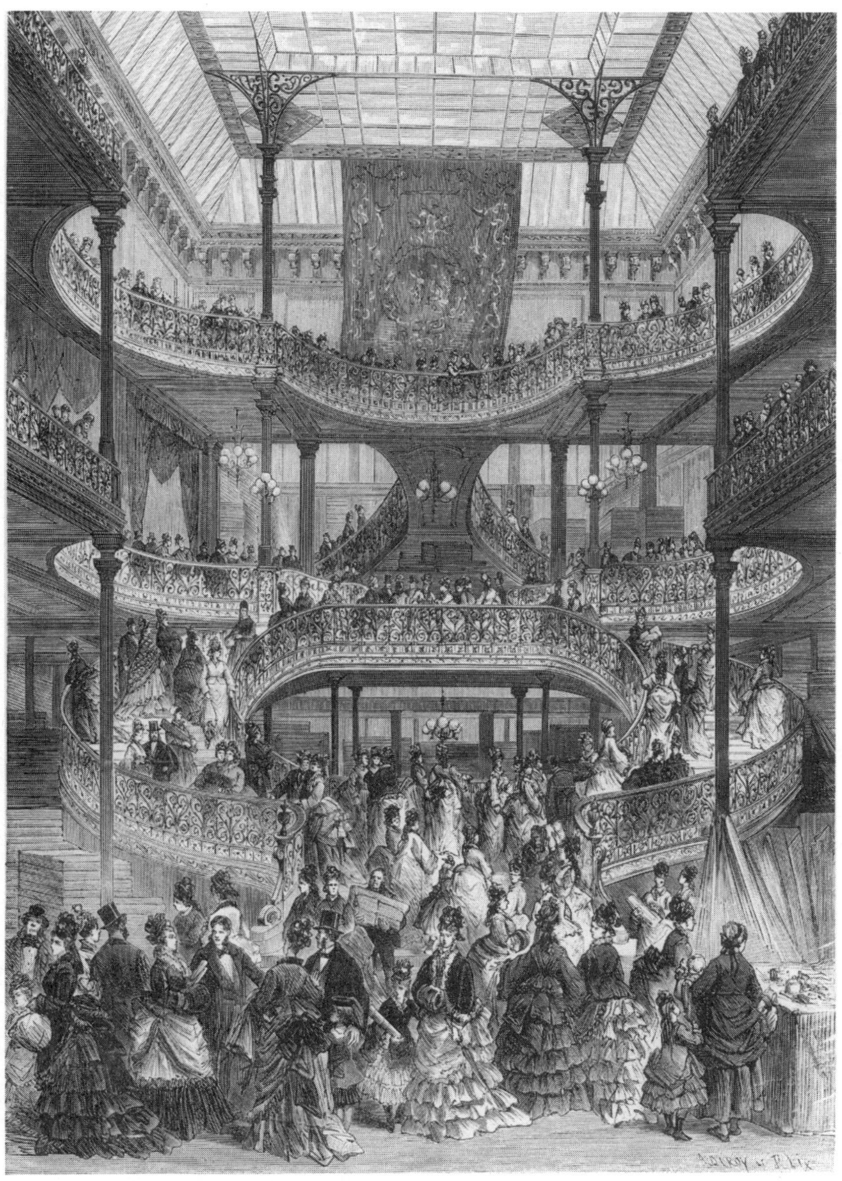

1.5 Frédéric Théodore Lix, *New Staircase in "Au Bon Marché,"* from *Le Monde Illustré*, c. 1875. Engraving, black and white photo. Reproduced by permission of the Bridgeman Art Library.

nef"[55]]; "Suddenly, he appeared at the top of the main staircase leading down to the ground floor and from here he still dominated the whole shop"[56] ["Brusquement, il reparut en haut du grand escalier qui descendait au rez-de-chaussée; et, de là, il domina encore la maison entière"[57]]. A favourite vantage point for Mouret during the three major sales that punctuate the novel's action (in chapters 4, 9, and 14), the view from the top of the staircase is consistent with the narrative stance taken up by the naturalist writer himself, whose notoriously overwhelming descriptions and hyperbolic metaphors, among other techniques, can be understood to exert a similar form of dominance over narrative and reader alike.[58]

Stairways also recur throughout the text as locations of important fashion moments that are tied to the novel's sentimental storyline. It is in an employee stairwell, for example, that Mouret's troubled attraction to Denise is awakened. This "undefinable feeling of surprise and fear, mingled with tenderness"[59] ["sentiment indéfinissable de surprise et de crainte, mêleé de tendresse"[60]] is incited by the unsettling juxtaposition of self-discipline and abandon that her clothing expresses to him. That is, Mouret is intrigued by the contrast between Denise's sartorial restraint – "her little black dress and her plain hat with only a single blue ribbon around it"[61] ["sa petite robe noire, son chapeau garni d'un seul ruban bleu"[62]] – and by what he suddenly views as her sensual untamability. For, despite her modest comportment and appearance, Mouret senses a "little savage"[63] ["sauvageonne"[64]], noting with uneasy interest that Denise's simple bonnet fails to contain "her fine, startled hair over her forehead"[65] ["ses beaux cheveux épeurés sur son front"[66]]. Fashion and the troubling staircase join together to catalyse an important relationship: one of the few romantic love stories of the *Rougon-Macquart* that Zola allows to survive. Later it is the main department store staircase that takes centre stage as the site in which Mouret's affections for Denise are exposed to a bitterly jealous Mme Desforges, an encounter that is described by Zola through the metaphor of a fashion battle. This battle, discussed in chapter 3, will be restaged later between the two female rivals in the semi-democratizing space of the antechamber. In what follows we will focus on how Zola's treatment of fashion and staircase suggests we might understand the encounter not simply as a plot point in the novel's romantic triangle but, more hauntingly, as a cloaked reference to the violent Commune of 1871, an event that was marking its tenth anniversary the year that Zola began writing *Au Bonheur*.

Modelling the Commune

Recent scholarship has called provocative attention to the subtext of the Commune in Zola's work.[67] Citing the repeated metaphors of violence and war in *Nana* and *Au Bonheur*, two of Zola's novels written nearly a decade after the Commune and set just before its eruption, Leslie Ann Minot suggests that this civil clash culminating in the "bloody week" (*semaine sanglante*) of May 1871 is a "spectre" that "lurks just below the surface"[68] of both works. For Peter Starr, Zola evokes the confusion of the Commune through the commercial, as opposed to the violent, revolutions that Mouret effects in the department store throughout the novel.[69] Vaheed Ramazani reads *Au Bonheur* as a male appropriation of female space through the masculine-associated tropes of production and war noting, tellingly,"the 'warring' bodies in *Au Bonheur des Dames* are predominantly those of women."[70] Ramazani's comment in particular gestures towards the gendered subtext of Zola's references to the Commune. As all three scholars note, the fact that many of the symbolic battles in Mouret's department store are waged by women cannot help but evoke the *pétroleuses*, infamous women arsonists who were erroneously blamed for setting fire to numerous Parisian structures in the final throes of the fighting and who became notorious figures of the 1871 conflict.[71] In his novel, Zola both reinforces stereotypes of the pétroleuses and offers them a counterpoint. Ghosts of the legendary women appear in his portrait of sexually deviant, hysterical, criminal female shoppers at Mouret's department store, while their antidote is provided in the protagonist Denise, who balances traditional traits of feminine purity and virginity with what Zola represents positively as a progressive capitalist spirit.[72] Depictions of the pétroleuses written or drawn by contemporaries often showed them grasping the bottles of petroleum that they allegedly used to incinerate targeted locales in Paris.[73] In *Au Bonheur*, Zola replaces these containers of flammable liquid with fashion objects that are clutched by women shoppers, from Mme Marty's purse overflowing with handkerchiefs, ties, garment trimmings, and other accessories, to the handfuls of lace caught up in Mme de Boves's thieving grasp.

On the occasion of the Bonheur's summer sale, this regendered "women's war" is dramatically staged on the grand staircase and complicated through the metaphor of fashion. As Denise and Mme Desforges struggle to climb the central staircase against a descending tide of shoppers, troops of headless mannequins appear to flank the edges of the steps like a double row of soldiers:

> On every step, a tailor's dummy was solidly attached, motionlessly exhibiting an article of clothing: suits, jackets, dressing-gowns ... And they looked like two ranks of soldiers for some triumphal parade, each with a little wooden peg like the handle of a dagger sticking out of the red flannelette, which seemed to bleed from a freshly cut neck.[74]

> [A chaque marche, un mannequin, solidement fixé, plantait un vêtement immobile, costumes, paletots, robes de chambre; et l'on eût dit une double haie de soldats pour quelque défilé triomphal, avec le petit manche de bois pareil au manche d'un poignard, enfoncé dans le molleton rouge, qui saignait à la section fraîche du cou.[75]]

The notion of combat is underscored by oppositions that Zola creates between female camps: Denise and Mme Desforges must fight to climb the stairway against the women descending it, and tensions mount between the two adversaries as they engage in a growing competition for Mouret. Through references to soldiers, daggers, and bloody wounds, Zola makes plain that the mannequins symbolize figures of violent conflict.[76] What is not clear, though, is for which side these "soldiers" are fighting. On the one hand, their double-row configuration (*haie*) evokes the orderly formation of an organized army, represented during the Commune by the military forces sent from Versailles to quash the socialist revolution of the Communards. On the other hand, Zola's mannequins eschew a standardizing uniform and stand erect dressed in a mismatch of outfits, including suits, coats, and housedresses. This sartorial disparity would more readily evoke not the Versaillais forces but rather the Communards, who hailed from different sectors of the bourgeois, working, and artistic classes and whose social diversity was reflected in the assorted range of garments that they wore. Moreover, dressed unambiguously as women, the dagger-impaled mannequins call to mind far less the all-male forces of the Versailles army and more the female pétroleuses, who were the only women on either side of the conflict associated with armed combat.

Although the Communards did not have an official uniform per se, dress was an important marker of their identity, especially clothing made of red fabric. Red signified revolution, and the Communards wore this symbolic shade conspicuously in the form of scarlet sashes, scarves, ribbons, and cockades.[77] Both men and women, then, wore red markers of their political allegiance, this hue differentiating them from the coats of the uniforms worn by the military, which were generally blue.[78] However, the colour red was gendered feminine, too, through its association with the pétroleuses. The most famous example is school-teacher-turned-Communard, Louise Michel, who was nicknamed "the red virgin" (*la vierge rouge*), "red" for her lifelong commitment to revolutionary activities and "virgin" for the fact that she never married.[79] The women brought to trial after the Commune who were accused of being pétroleuses were identified, in part, by the articles of clothing that witnesses said they had been wearing during the conflict, in particular, by the red scarves or sashes that three of the five had allegedly donned.[80] On Zola's staircase, the mannequins, like the Communards, are unified sartorially by a shared textile – red flannel at the base of their headless necks – that recalls, both in hue and in its placement at the neckline, the alleged pétroleuses' conspicuous choice of coloured accessory.

What is worth noting about Zola's staircase passage are not the metaphors of war or violence themselves, which are prevalent throughout the entire novel.[81] Nor is the juxtaposition of fashion with the notion of battle remarkable in itself, for this thematic recurs in other places in the text. Rather, it is the ambivalence about who is fighting whom, the questionable outcome of this sartorially described conflict and the location in which it occurs that stand out as notable, because they suggest the author's fundamentally troubled stance with respect to the urban spaces of modernity that had been profoundly marked not just by Haussmanization but by the Commune as well.

Zola's ambivalence about the Commune is apparent in the journalistic reports that the young novelist wrote as the dramatic events of March through June 1871 unfolded. As Raymond Trousson has convincingly shown, during the days in which the fighting took place Zola was highly critical of the Communards, whom he characterized as "crazy" (*fous*) vandals and drunkards.[82] He disapproved especially of female combatants, whom he qualified either as "brutes" when they took up the arms of fallen male Communards, or as an even more threatening class of women, "others whose type of insanity is more serious" ["d'autres dont le genre de folie est plus grave"].[83] These were the "rational thinkers" ["raisonneuses"] who did not themselves fight, but who posed an even greater danger than those who did, since they used reason to incite others to battle, "pushing Paris toward slaughter" ["poussant Paris au massacre"].[84]

At the same time, although Zola deplored the actions of both male and female Communards, he was equally repulsed by the brutal, seemingly indiscriminate mass killing of accused insurgents. On 25 May 1871, he lamented the gruesome mounds of dead Communards that the Versaillais army had piled, callously and unceremoniously, under the city's bridges in the aftermath of the semaine sanglante. Reporting on this traumatic sight, Zola wrote:

> I just want to tell you about the heaps of cadavers that they piled under the bridges. No, I will never forget the awful heart pangs that I felt facing this mass of bloody human flesh, thrown haphazardly onto the towpath. Heads and limbs were mixed together into horrible discontinuities.

> [Je veux seulement vous parler des tas de cadavres qu'on a empilés sous les ponts. Non, jamais je n'oublierai l'affreux serrement de coeur que j'ai éprouvé en face de cet amas de chair humaine sanglant, jeté au hazard sur le chemin de halage. Les têtes et les membres sont mêlés dans d'horribles dislocations.[85]]

To return to the novel, the term in the staircase passage cited above around which Zola's ambivalence revolves, to my mind, is the word "triumphal" (*triomphal*), which he uses to describe the parade of mannequins and whose meaning is tinged with a bitter irony made more acute by the ambiguous identity of his "marching soldiers." If the marching mannequins on Octave Mouret's staircase were to symbolize the Versaillais army, whose massacre of an estimated 20,000 to 40,000 people he denounced,[86] Zola surely would have been using the term "triumphal" ironically, finding nothing victorious in the slaughter of innocent Parisians erroneously thought to have participated in the insurrection, or of the tragically misled, as Zola believed to be the case of many Communards.[87] If, on the other hand, the feminized mannequins were stand-ins for the red-scarfed pétroleuses, any mention of "triumph" would seem doubly ironic, for the figures appear to bleed from fresh gashes at their necks, headless allegories not of "triumph" but of a mortally wounded, failed revolution. As Zola's violent imagery indicates, the battle to which the troops of mannequins march is one without triumph for either side, a war with no winner as was the agonizing civil clash that had pitted the citizens of France against one another.

In 1880, total amnesty was granted to thousands of exiled Communards who were finally accorded the right to return to France.[88] This final repatriation of those exiled for nearly a decade provoked renewed public interest in the events of 1871 and, likely, latent distress about them.[89] Perhaps, as Ramazani proposes, the horrors of the Commune were still so fresh the following year when Zola began drafting *Au Bonheur* that he could only treat them obliquely, needing still another decade before he could face the incident explicitly in 1892's *La Débâcle*.[90] Whatever the reasons for the indirect nature of his references to the Commune in *Au Bonheur*, the feminocentricity of the department store's central staircase and Zola's ambivalence with respect to the warring tensions on it are an indication that not only had ideas about the fundamental gender of war changed in the aftermath of the highly publicized case of the pétroleuses, but so had conceptions about the space itself – Haussmann's city – in which the civil conflict had occurred.

That is, if we are to understand Zola's fashionable staircase as a reflection of his attitudes about the spaces of the post-Commune metropolis more generally, what emerges is a picture of urbanism that is, on the one hand, navigable and functioning and thus in line with the ideology of a productive capitalist society that was a premise of Haussmannization. On the other hand, some of these stairways are also marked by illegibility, disorder, and internal tensions. These qualities, we have seen, are present on the department store's grand public staircase, but they are equally apparent in the maze of smaller stairwells located both within the *grand magasin*'s public shopping areas and in the sections of the building restricted to store personnel. Zola's references, especially to the former, evoke the chaotic confusion of the Commune and coincide, in one key instance that we will examine below, with sartorial elements that are deeply politically loaded.

Driven by the naturalist's urge to document the layout of the department store as comprehensively as possible, Zola gives the behind-the-scenes locations of the Bonheur – the underground refectory, attic dormitories, distribution centres, and executive offices – equal billing with the sections of the structure open to consumers. The stairways in the former space are conduits in the steam-billowing, roaring, crushing "machine," a favourite of Zola's metaphors to depict the powerful mechanization involved in the distribution of fashion merchandise that is purchased and sold in the building. The employee stairways that are scatteed throughout both narrative and building are epitomized by the set of steps that lead from the basement to the street level of the rue de la Michodière, where goods are "disgorged" ["dégorgeait"][91] for delivery to customers' homes. From this staircase, packages emerge "constantly"[92] ["sans relâche"[93]], their steady, unremitting progress signifying the relentless yet smooth "mechanical operation"[94] ["fonctionnement méchanique"[95]] of the overall fashion system of which the department store is a central location.

In contrast, the web of stairways inside the shopping area is characterized by confusion, a marketing brainchild of Mouret, who creates a multifloored labyrinth in which his female customers get lost, stumble across new products and, as a result, make purchases of textiles, garments, accessories, or furnishings that they would not have otherwise made.[96] Women seem constantly confounded around these stairways: early in the novel, a befuddled Denise repeatedly turns away from the very staircase that will lead her to and from her job interview with Mme Aurélie; during the novel's first sale Mme Desforges's access to the central staircase is blocked by a swelling river of shoppers;[97] while shopping at one of the Bonheur's storewide sales, Mme Bourdelais, frazzled from herding her family of small children, searches in vain for a staircase to ascend to the next floor;[98] on the occasion of the white sale, in the final chapter, Mme Marty loses what little restraint she has, her desire to buy what she cannot afford ignited by a collection of Japanese decorative objects strategically displayed at the top of the grand escalier.[99]

"Revolutionary Urbanism" inside the Machine

If the behind-the-scenes staircases are typically immune from such instances of (feminized) disorder, the overall state of upheaval characteristic of the shopping area does, at one point, invade the inner workings of the "machine." In this passage, Denise and her brother Jean, seeking privacy, descend an employee stairwell leading to the department store's vast basement. Here, they are discovered by the predatory Inspector Jouve, whose romantic overtures Denise has just spurned. Filled with fear, brother and sister flee to the stairs on the rue de la Michodière from which packages are "disgorged" to delivery omnibuses. Jean escapes up the staircase, but not before Jouve catches sight of his untidy locks of hair and loose white blouse. These sartorial clues are enough to confirm that Jean is not an elegantly tailored, impeccably groomed employee of the Bonheur and to suggest that Denise has engaged in an activity that is against store policy – an amorous liaison on the Bonheur's property – for which she is then (unjustly) terminated.

This brief episode can be understood to function primarily to advance the novel's plot by ensuring Denise's temporary departure from the store. However, to my mind, the relative chaos and terror inscribed into this passage, one of few scenes of heightened physical action in the text, also echoes, albeit in less traumatic form, what Zola may have remembered as a witness to the Commune. Jean's billowing white shirt, the attire of an apprentice in the ivory trade, links him to the artisan Communards, men from the skilled working class who were at times referred to as "blouses," named for the garment that they typically wore.[100] Moreover, the young man's impassioned invectives preceding the siblings' flight, when he cries out that he wants to hurt himself ("How I hate myself! I could slap my face!"[101] ["que je suis donc furieux contre moi! Je me flanquerais des gifles!"][102]) gesture towards the brutality that the nation inflicted internally upon itself in the Commune hostilities. As his eyewitness accounts of the events of 1871 attest, Zola believed that some Communards, subject to their own naiveté, were incited by revolutionary rhetoric to fight for a cause they did not fully comprehend. Like them, Zola might have been suggesting, Jean overdramatizes minor inconveniences until he believes he is a victim of major suffering, not even realizing that "he was not himself sure of the precise truth" "[lui-même ne savait plus l'exacte vérité"].[103] To contribute to the hostile tone of the episode, Jean's vehement outbursts come on the heels of Jouve's rough attempt to force a kiss from Denise that the frantic young woman deflects with a violent push, in the process soiling the retired army captain's white tie and military decoration with blood-red wine. When Jouve later catches Denise (and nearly Jean) at the bottom of the delivery staircase, he has replaced his wine-spattered tie with a new white cravate, expunging the evidence of his crime and her forceful shove with an accessory, the large knot of which, Zola emphasizes, "shone like snow"[104] ["luisait comme une neige"[105]].

Zola's irony at the colour of Jouve's replacement tie seems obvious on one level: the inspector is in no way innocent of attacking Denise, as the white purity of freshly fallen snow deceptively implies. If we understand this scene as having a larger relation to the Commune, however, the delivery staircase, typically associated with efficiency and functionality but here a site of confused, chaotic flight, provides an analogous space for a confluence of symbolic fashion, military presence, self-inflicted violence, and problematic attempts at absolution, all elements of the Commune and its aftermath. I do not wish to overstate an allusion to the Commune in this episode; rather, the larger point I wish to stress is that the working staircase, like the grand escalier passage discussed earlier, points to Zola's general anxieties about the meanings that modern urban space would take on in the Third Republic, a period ushered in with bloody urban warfare.

Evoking the streets of a city once intended as a monument to the Second Empire and then, following the Commune, monumentally destroyed, Guy Debord and others from the avant-garde group Internationale Situationniste would later proclaim the Commune a form of "revolutionary urbanism" that "attacked on the spot the petrified signs of the dominant organization of life."[106] In *Au Bonheur*, Zola resituates the location and terms of the battle from public war zone to centre of fashion, setting the Commune's "revolutionary urbanism" not in the boulevards, but "on the spot" of the new urban zone of Third Republic modernity that the department store, nexus of fashion and commodity culture, exemplified for him. In this way, the novelist problematizes the department store, connecting it to changes occurring in the larger urban landscape and pointing out how Parisian spaces had become semiologically obscured by, for instance, rising tensions between the rapid construction of Haussmannization and the subsequent destruction of some of the most iconic historic spaces of the city during the conflict of 1871, such as the Hôtel de Ville.

Thus, glittering locations like Garnier's grand escalier that had been constructed to signify the capital's dramatic Second Empire modernization and to serve as backdrops for fashion and entertainment, for Zola, seem equally imbued with and inseparable from the memory of the bloodshed that had brought in the new Republic. Through Denise's compulsive preoccupation with the painting of Mme Hédouin, one is constantly reminded that the Bonheur is erected over the corpse of Mouret's first wife, the original proprietor of the enterprise. To the reader who follows Mouret's story from his arrival in Paris in *Pot-Bouille* to his rise to power in *Au Bonheur*,[107] the gory demise of Mme Hédouin that occurs in the unnarrated interval between the two novels seems abrupt, morbid, and incongruous, not unlike the Commune's quick escalation and rapid, violent denouement. Echoing Denise, stunned by losing her salesgirl post at the department store because "the catastrophe had been so sudden"[108] ["la catastrophe venait d'être si brusque"[109]], the novel suggests the author's lingering incomprehension following the abruptness of these events. The department store staircase, like the building around it, is a monument to modern fashionable spectacle, yet it equally memorializes a still unfathomable incident from which it originates and which it cannot avoid referencing.

Fashioning Barricades

We have seen that the Commune resonates in Zola's Bonheur staircases in terms of material dress: the mannequins' garments recall the sartorial expressions of revolutionary sentiment that were worn by the Communards and especially associated with the figure of the pétroleuse; Jean's artisan's smock and Jouve's military decorations provide the primary "uniforms" of the two warring sides. But there is a second resonance between the Commune and the convergence of the modern space of fashion that the staircase represents, since the structure, shape, and functions of Zola's department store war zone can also be understood as an echo of the Commune barricades. Barricades, those improvised blockades erected by the insurrectionists across the barely completed boulevards of Haussmann's city, were highlighted in texts by Victor Hugo, Karl Marx, and Frederich Engels[110] and reproduced pictorially in many illustrated newspapers of the day. Through these and other accounts of the conflict, barricades came to be the urban constructions most iconically associated with the Commune.

Fashion provides a connection between Zola's text and the radical upheaval of the urban landscape that took place in 1871 when Paris's boulevards were strewn, almost overnight, with these symbols of rebellion. In his novel, Zola employs the very word "barricade" to describe the aftermath of the department store's first sale, clearly emphasizing the imagery of post-battle rubble: "It was hard to make one's way along the ground-floor galleries, so obstructed were they by the scattering of chairs; in gloves, one had to climb across a *barricade* of boxes piled around Mignot" (emphasis added)[111] ["On longeait avec peine les galeries du rez-de-chaussée, obstruées par la débandade des chaises; il fallait enjamber, à la ganterie, une *barricade* de cartons, entassés autour de Mignot" (emphasis added)[112]]. Although there are obvious differences between impromptu revolutionary blockades and ornate department store escaliers, during the Commune some uses and behaviours associated with the fashionable staircase were equally manifested in street warfare. For instance, the primary functions of barricades, as Mark

Traugott outlines in his history of these structures, included protecting the Communards, impeding the circulation of the Versaillais military, and disrupting the army's communication efforts.[113] These goals were intended to help position the Communards in sites of power, both symbolic and spatial. Thus, as images such as this period photograph suggest, many barricades served as makeshift staircases, some built so far above street level that climbing them required ascending stacks of stone "stairs" fashioned out of *pavés* seized from streets and the debris of destroyed edifices. Both barricades and grand staircases used height to their advantage, configuring space in such a way that those who had ascended them could look down advantageously upon their respective onlookers (see figure 1.6).[114]

Beyond contributing to the tactical goals of the insurgents, barricades also supplied a space on which to "perform" revolution in ways that were not entirely different from those adopted by stylish Parisians, who would later use staircases to stage their own modern fashionability. Scholars, some perhaps inadvertently, call to mind such a comparison. Traugott, for instance, refers to the construction of barricades as a "spectacle"[115] because crowds would inevitably assemble to witness or participate in the communal "show" that barricade building occasioned. Jeannene Przyblyski similarly evokes theatricality in her description of the "posturing" of Communards in photographic images of the barricades, wherein revolutionary action is visually constructed as a type of "street theater"[116] and the barricades as "a stage."[117] In *La Proclamation de la Commune*, a text that both celebrated the event's revolutionary spirit and mourned its disappearance, Henri Lefebvre relied on theatrical metaphors, referring to the Commune as a "festival" ["fête"], one that turned first into a "spectacle" ["spectacle"] and finally a "drama" ["drame"] ending in "tragedy" ["tragédie"].[118] As Janet Beizer notes, nineteenth-century writer Maxime Du Camp likewise called upon a vocabulary of stage and performance in his four-volume invective against the Commune, *Les Convulsions de Paris*. Beizer observes that Du Camp's text is rife with terms associated with the theatre, including *spectacle*, *mascarade*, and *acteur*, among many others. For her, this invocation of theatricality serves Du Camp's ultimate goal to weaken the political significance of the event and mark it as a mere performance, the curtain of which had fallen.[119]

It is beyond the scope of this project to examine to what extent theatricality served to enhance or diminish the overall potency of the Communards' objectives. What is important here is that these allusions

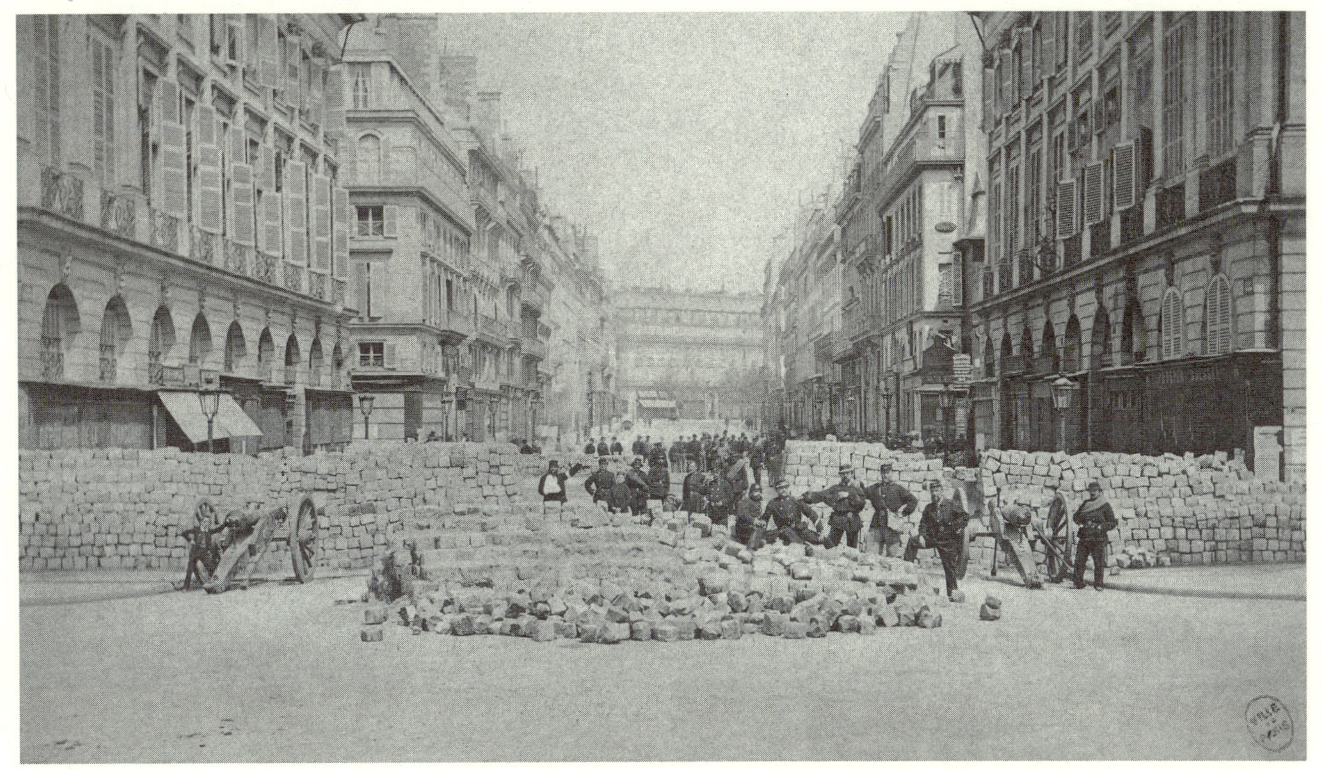

1.6 Anonymous, *Commune de Paris: Barricade rue de la Paix depuis la place Vendôme, vers la place de l'Opéra*, 1871. © The Image Works.

to the stage, acting, and theatre from period authors and contemporary scholars alike call attention to the spectacularity of the barricades, one that would be re-enacted in distorted form in the years that followed, physically on Garnier's grand escalier and novelistically on Zola's department store staircases. Although the revolutionary thrust of the barricades was replaced by the public's desire for fashionable entertainment on the post-Commune staircase, the stairs in Zola's work nevertheless evoke, disquietingly, both the subversion of authority enacted by the Communards and its brutal suppression. Zola's Bonheur staircases thus do more than simply call to mind the civil insurgency of 1871: they also stand as a literary testament to the long-term psychological effects of the Commune, a discursive "commemoration" of trauma, as the title of Peter Starr's book, *Commemorating Trauma: The Paris Commune and Its Cultural Aftermath*, calls to mind. The department store staircase emblematized a larger point: that this infamous moment in Paris's history was inextricably tied to what Zola depicts in *Au Bonheur* and other early 1880s novels as the subsequent domination, not by a new empire but by a culture of consumption that, for him, had exploded forth in the opening decade of the Third Republic.

If Zola's reaction to the events of 1871 in *Au Bonheur* was somewhat delayed, in its more immediate aftermath a link emerged between fashion and the urban spaces most affected by the civil conflict. During the months directly following the fall of the Commune, it was not the ephemeral barricades that characterized the city's landscape; these were quickly cleared by a conservative Third Republic government keen on expunging any suggestion of militia activities.[120] Rather, many first-hand reports from this period focused on the ruins of Parisian monuments, including the Tuileries Palace and the famously toppled column at the Place Vendôme. Among the most devastated sites was the Hôtel de Ville, which had been largely destroyed in a fire allegedly set by the pétroleuses in the final days of the semaine sanglante. The blaze had left most of the stone exterior of the building intact, though, so following the Commune the decision was made to conserve the façade and to raze and rebuild the internal spaces in a contemporary style. As a result, the structure became a curious temporal hybrid, one consisting of the old Renaissance-inspired exterior and a new Third Republic interior.

Before the scorched internal space was demolished in order to accommodate its replacement, however, broken remnants caught the nostalgic imagination of eyewitness Georges Bell, for whom the charred remains of the building's central staircase provided a poignant synecdoche for the larger city. In *Paris in Ashes* [*Paris Incendié*] (1871),[121] his account of the destruction of the city's major monuments, Bell describes entering the rubble of the Hôtel de Ville and seeing the remains of the building's staircase: "A ramp that has resisted all forms of stress, indicates the U-shaped stone staircase opened either left or right into all of the edifice's galleries … [the sight] fills with profound sadness the heart of the Parisian … you hesitate to speak, even to communicate your impressions and thoughts to your companions."[122] Bell's description of the mostly destroyed yet still partially erect staircase expresses a contradiction, for it calls attention to the lasting stability of a ramp that has "resisted all forms of stress" but inflects this description of strength and solidity with indecision about direction, "either left or right," that the two flights of the structure symbolize. The writer's acknowledgment that much of Paris had in fact survived the Commune, encapsulated architecturally in the vestige staircase of the Hôtel de Ville, is simultaneously complicated by "hesitation" and sorrow that the path to rebuilding the city *psychologically* remains unclear.

Tellingly, in training his attention upon the site of the burned municipal edifice, Bell renders it a noteworthy sight to behold, thereby highlighting the attraction-like nature of the Hôtel de Ville's partially destroyed staircase and textually enacting a voguish form of tourism that took hold in Paris in the months following May 1871. For it was during this period that, as Daryl Lee puts it, visiting the ruins of the capital became "a current fashion" for "the massive influx of tourists into Post-Commune Paris."[123] The stylish set had long been taking the "Grand Tour" to exoticized locations such as Rome, Pompeii, Egypt, and Greece to marvel at the haunting elegance of former empires. As readers of period women's periodicals are well aware, this type of tourism and fashion were interrelated, since travel often necessitated new garments and accoutrements that were suitable for voyaging to and navigating through foreign locales. To serve the sartorial needs of tourists, fashion magazines regularly included designs for travelling clothes, accessories, and even hairstyles that would be most appropriate for exploring the typically rougher terrain of locations outside of the city while maintaining one's stylishness (see figure 1.7). The difference in this case is that post-Commune tourism was taking place not abroad but in Paris itself as, suddenly, the capital found itself in the unusual position of being on the receiving end of sightseers interested not in Haussmann's modernity but rather in the city's post-traumatic ruin.

Consistent with other ladies' periodicals that addressed the needs of fashion-conscious tourists, Mallarmé's *La Dernière Mode* included a

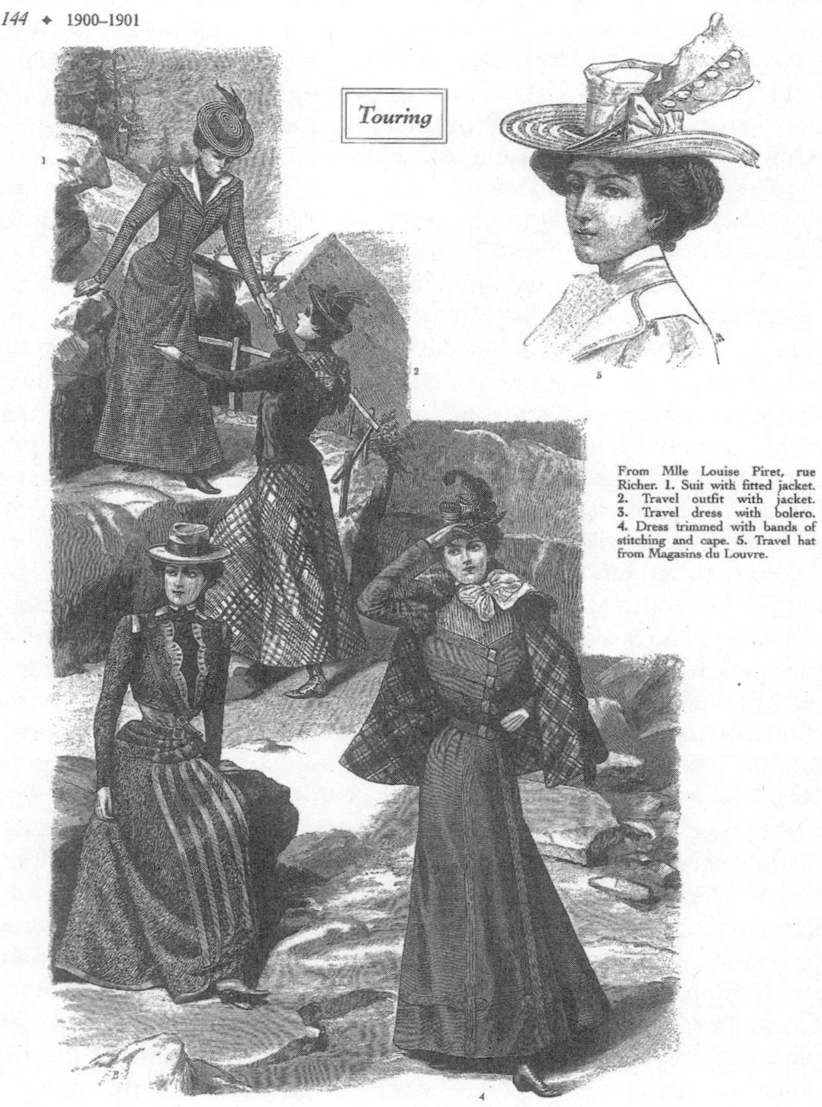

1.7 Anonymous, *Touring*, from *La Mode Illustrée*, 1900–1901, in *Victorian and Edwardian Fashions from 'La Mode Illustrée'* edited by JoAnne Olian, 144. Reproduced by permission of Dover Publications.

column on travel in every instalment, although the poet seemed, at times, unable to retain the objective composure typical of a fashion reporter. In the 20 September issue, for instance, Mallarmé's cynicism erupts as he comments on this invasion of visitors to France's capital. Correctly noting that the remnants of the Hôtel de Ville and the Tuileries Palace are "photographed and minutely described in foreign guide books"[124] ["photographiés et décrits soigneusement dans tous les guides d'outre-mer"[125]], he criticizes the outsiders inundating the city who are motivated primarily by voyeurism and the desire to be fashionable sightseers, tourists who "admire" what he labels with irony "Parisian splendor": "foreigners and provincials profit from this opening of her gates to come, in flocks, to admire the vestiges of Parisian splendor"[126] ["l'etranger et la province profitent de cette ouverture de portes pour venir, par troupes, admirer quelques vestiges de la splendeur parisienne"[127]]. Mallarmé's dismayed description of the ruined city, a place to which he had dreamed of returning in the 1860s when he was residing discontentedly in the provinces, is more dismal elegy than lighthearted fashion report. His list of the destroyed monuments, "facades, with their statuettes still, after three years, blackened by fire ... the Hôtel de Ville, in its devastation knocked to the ground, and the Tuileries empty" (tanslation modified)[128] ["ces frontons gardant, depuis trois ans, leurs statuettes noircies par le feu ... L'Hôtel de Ville jeté à terre, les Tuileries vides"[129]], emphasizes the black, flattened, and hollow qualities of ravaged buildings. This portrait of urban devastation is juxtaposed with a sarcastic critique of crowds of young people, recognizable as fashion mavens because they are dressed in the season's sartorial trend, "young persons in white-veiled Tyrolean hats"[130] ["des jeunes personnes au voile blanc tombant d'un chapeau du Tyrol"[131]], who visit the "ruins"[132] ["ruines"[133]] as though they are nothing more than the latest must-see sites from antiquity.[134] When Mallarmé decries the "lamentable spectacle"[135] ["spectacle lamentable"[136]] that is Paris when the city is deserted during the summer months by its native population and speaks of the "coquetry of a metropolis audaciously new, rich and splendid"[137] ["coquetterie d'une métropole audacieusement neuve, riche at splendide"[138]], his critique may have been levied equally at the vain "coquetry" of those who had built the now-damaged Second Empire city as well as at style-obsessed visitors to Paris who had been treating the remains of the capital as a domestic version of the Grand Tour.

The post-Commune tourists imagined by Mallarmé were not, however, alone in their aestheticization of the devastated capital. Even as they lamented the ruined city, writers of the period reframed the destruction of Paris in terms of its troubling beauty, doing so using metaphors of sartorial adornment. Describing the skeletal remains of the Hôtel de Ville, for example, Edmond de Goncourt enthused, "The ruin is splendid, magnificent. In their rose, ash-green, and white-hot-iron coloration, in the brilliant agatization of stone cooked by petrol"[139] ["La ruine est magnifique, splendide. La ruine aux tons couleur de rose, couleur cendre verte, couleur de fer rougi à blanc, la ruine brillante de l'agatisation, qu'a prise la pierre cuite par le pétrole"[140]]. Goncourt's description of the "brilliant" colours resulting from the intense heating of stone deploys the metaphor of jewels of various hues, the building transformed by way of incineration into masses of pink, green, and white gems. That Goncourt envisions the charred ruins re-emerging as precious stones might have equally occurred for Mallarmé, whose inaugural fashion report in *La Dernière Mode* is devoted to the subject of "Jewelry" (*Bijoux*). In the wake of the Commune, when the Hôtel de Ville ruins were still fresh in readers' minds, Mallarmé cites jewelry made with myriad coloured stones – sapphires, rubies, emeralds, and diamonds – naming the very same hues as Goncourt in his description of the day's most fashionable ornaments.[141]

Théophile Gautier provided another eyewitness account of the burned buildings, this one focusing on fabric. "At one of the windows," he noted, "strangely enough, an awning of blue silk still hung intact without having burned in this incandescent hearth capable of calcining the limestone and melting the metals."[142] Lee notes, "This is the Gautier interested in fashion, a central figure of 'modernity' by his interest in *la mode* as a key index to understanding the new times."[143] Here Lee invokes Gautier's essay *La Mode* (1858), a treatise linking fashion to art, the subject of which might explain why the poet's eye would train in particular on the silk fabric hanging from the charred windowpane. Through his attention to colour, evident also in his art criticism of the period, Gautier may have known that the blue of the silk awning related it to fashion by way of a development in dyeing technology that had radically impacted the clothing industry from the 1860s onward. This was the rise in aniline dyes, chemicals that could tint fabrics more vibrantly and permanently than natural agents, such as indigo, which had previously been used. Following this groundbreaking innovation, bright synthetic blue had become a sought-after colour for garments, as not only writers but artists as well discerned.[144] Renoir, for instance, famously featured the hue in his 1874 painting *La Parisienne*, spotlighting the electric blue of his model's walking dress to emphasize the modern stylishness of the typical Parisian woman.[145] In *Au Bonheur*, Mouret debuts a new blue and silver fabric from Lyon that he names *Paris-Bonheur*, proclaiming it a silk for which shoppers will clamour and that will "revolutionize"[146] ["révolutionne"[147]] the commerce of fashion. It seems no coincidence that the textile, which, in Mouret's words, will be "an item … that is the sensation of its time" ["un article … qui fasse époque"], is the very modern hue of blue.[148] If we return to Gautier's description and read it through the lens of sartorial ornament, the awning fabric hanging at the window might evoke a fashionable blue silk scarf embellishing its wearer's neck, or a stylish azure bonnet shielding her face from the elements. By such associations with fashion, ruined monuments for Goncourt, Mallarmé, and Gautier took on modern qualities but also aesthetic ones that, in some ways, neutralized the enormity of the disaster. Lee offers that, in writers' accounts, "the violent cause of destruction, it seems, transforms the banal urbanism of Haussmann into something sublime."[149] For these authors, a group largely responsible for the nineteenth-century ideology of "art for art's sake" (*l'art pour l'art*), aesthetic sublimation of destruction was, perhaps, the only way of comprehending it.[150]

In contrast, for others such as famed designer Charles Frederick Worth, links forged between the Commune and the fashion industry were directly related to commerce. When Worth reopened his famous Parisian fashion house soon after the Commune, his collections reportedly featured garments made of fabrics that deliberately referred to recent violent events. In the words of an early twentieth-century writer, these included "wonderful creations in silks and satins of a rich orange colour called *Bismarck enragé*, and of a lovely deep grey known as *Cendres de Paris*."[151] "Cendres de Paris, or "Paris's ashes," would have instantly ignited memories of the burned remains of city structures, while "Bismarck enragé," literally "Rabid Bismarck," was an animalistic reference to Otto von Bismarck, the chancellor of Prussia who had commanded the Germanic states to victory in the Franco-Prussian War (1870–71). The fact that Worth likely believed that associations with the Commune would increase sales of his garments suggests that he recognized not only the commodity value of the postwar ruins but their evident beauty as well, which he then linked to his haute couture works of art.

The blazing buildings of the Commune also make their appearance in *Au Bonheur* as a metaphor for the final throes of destruction that take place in the last hour of the second storewide sale. Zola's description of the edifice's central nave calls up a dramatic inferno that seems to engulf the entire building:

In this fiery red glow, thick clouds of dust, stirred since morning by the tramping of the crowd, rose like a golden mist. A sheet of fire spread through the great central gallery, outlining the staircases, the hanging bridges and all the lacework of floating iron against a backdrop of flame. The mosaics and faience of the friezes glistened, the greens and reds of the paintwork glowed in the reflection from the copious amounts of gold. It was like a living heap of embers in which the displays, the palaces of gloves and kerchiefs, the garlands of ribbons and lace, the tall stacks of woollens and calico and the mottled beds blossoming with light silks and scarves, now seemed to be burning away (translation modified).[152]

[Dans cette clarté d'un rouge d'incendie, montaient, pareilles à une vapeur d'or, les poussières épaissies, soulevées depuis le matin par le piétinement de la foule. Une nappe enfilait la grande galerie centrale, découpait sur un fond de flames les escaliers, les ponts volants, toute cette guipure de fer suspendue. Les mosaïques et les faiences des frises miroitaient, les verts et les rouges des peintures s'allumaient aux feux des ors prodigués. C'était comme une braise vive, où brûlaient maintenant les étalages, les palais de gants et de cravates, les girandoles de rubans et de dentelles, les hautes piles de lainage et de calicot, les parterres diaprés que fleurissaient les soies légères et les foulards.[153]]

As the fire rages, the sight seems, on the one hand, tragically beautiful, not unlike the descriptions by Goncourt and others of the Commune blazes that marked the end of the conflict in such spectacular terms. Yet, in Zola's version, the embers do more than destroy the staircases and ironwork of the building, since they set fire as well to the sartorial materials – gloves, ties, ribbons, fabrics, and silks – that remain on the shelves. These "burning" fashions contribute to the splendour of the scene, but also introduce a disquieting truth: when the building goes up in flames, the fashions for which it was built are similarly destroyed. Understanding the novel according to Zola's instructions, as an analogy for "modern activity," the combusting clothing items can be read as symbolic of Parisians, those engaged in modernity's activities and for whom the city's monumental new infrastructure had been constructed, like a department store built to accommodate objects of dress. Steven Wilson notes Denise's impression in first seeing the store that "les étoffes vivaient" or "the fabrics had come alive"[154] and observes that lace in the Bonheur has "animate qualities."[155] Wilson's reading supports the interpretation that the fashion items in the store might symbolize people. The passage thereby calls up a number of troubling questions that may have been in the author's thoughts while penning a novel that systematically overlapped visions of the Commune with visions of modernity. If, for example, the ostensible purpose of grand public structures such as the Hôtel de Ville was to administer, serve, and symbolize the city's population, what would be the fate of Third Republic society following the Commune's destruction? Would the city and its inhabitants, the perpetrators and the site of "modern activity," rise, phoenix-like, from the ashes of smouldering ruins, or did the forces of modernity simply burn everything before them to oblivion, like the accessories and fabrics glowing in the embers of the Bonheur's devastating sale? The ambivalence that characterizes Zola's conflicting depictions of Paris throughout much of the *Rougon-Macquart* suggests that, for him, such fundamental questions about the future of urban modernity may have ultimately remained unresolved.

Conclusion

Walter Benjamin famously described historical development as "one single catastrophe which keeps piling wreckage upon wreckage."[156] In Zola's attempt to write "the history" of the Second Empire by way of the *Rougon-Macquart*,[157] the Bonheur staircase can be understood as a discursive representation of Benjamin's metaphor of wreckage. Built on the spot of its material antecedents – neighbourhoods razed to rubble by Haussmannization, Commune barricades, ruins of monuments – all of these comprising mounds of detritus, the department store *escaliers* are the Third Republic iterations of Benjamin's piles of debris. In the Bonheur department store, a modern monument to capitalist phantasmagoria, broken rock is replaced with mounds of textiles and items of fashionable dress. As the headless mannequin soldiers suggest, however, the opulent luxury of the department store is constructed on the "catastrophe" that preceded it, conveying Zola's apprehension about the ultimate effects of this ominous past on the city yet to come.

The meanings that Zola ascribed to certain urban spaces, as exemplified by the charged dislocation of the staircase, seem deeply informed by prior human occupants and activities. For Michael Mayerfeld Bell, the phantom-like presence of former inhabitants and actions is one of the very defining features of modern locales, "a ubiquitous aspect of the phenomenology of place"[158] that leads him to understand the urban landscape as "haunted" by its past. He writes, "We moderns, despite our mechanistic and rationalistic ethos, live in landscapes filled with ghosts. The scenes we pass through each day are inhabited, possessed, by spirits we cannot see but whose presence we nevertheless experience."[159] Zola's construction of the Communard-haunted staircases in *Au Bonheur* is consistent with Bell's notion of spectres in modernity, those whose ghostly presence remains in contemporaneous representations of the metropolis and informs predictions for its future.

2 Ups and Downs, Surface and Spectacle: Rachilde, Maupassant, and Daudet

As any reader of her novels quickly surmises, the intersection of fashion and gender expression was a preoccupation for the decadent writer Rachilde (1860–1953). The cross-dressing protagonists of her well-studied *Monsieur Vénus* (1884) are perhaps the most famous of her subversively dressed characters, but such figures are equally present across the many works that Rachilde penned in the last two decades of the century. An author who began her career in Paris writing for the fashion press, Rachilde frequently played with the transformative qualities of clothing, often drawing on it to problematize categories of gender rather than reinforcing them like most male writers of her generation. In particular, she drew on transvestism, featuring women who donned men's clothing in an attempt to subvert stereotypes of femininity that had for so long considered women only as pure virgins or as dangerous seductresses. Tellingly, Rachilde's use of fashion to disrupt fixed gender norms conveys a sense of urgency that is absent from the texts of her male counterparts. Outrageous unveilings of cross-dressers and dramatic moments of gender confusion in her texts are echoed in the transgendered titles of some of her novels, such as *La Marquise de Sade* (1887), *Madame Adonis* (1888), and *L'Animale* (1893), all of which deliberately feminize grammatically masculine terms. Scholars have understood this impetus as Rachilde's reaction to her status as a female artist who faced the prejudices of a society that judged women's works as inferior to those of men. Surely aware of what was at stake for her as a woman author in a man's profession, Rachilde called upon metaphors of clothing in literature to challenge the gender politics of her day.

Rachilde's use of dress to trouble gender was not limited to fiction alone. As a young woman, she proclaimed herself a "man of letters" (*homme de lettres*) on her business cards, wore masculine-coded clothing in public, and was also rumoured to have cropped her hair like a man, an unsubstantiated legend that the author herself seemed to enjoy perpetuating.[1] Rachilde was not, of course, the first woman writer to adopt a pseudonym and masculine attire in order to gain recognition from a patriarchal society and readership.[2] Nonetheless, her bold inversions of gender roles and fashions – aggressive challenges to basic tenets of acceptable bourgeois decorum – helped to establish her as one of the few women writers of the 1880s and 1890s to gain acceptance within an artistic circle composed almost entirely of men. As Melanie Hawthorne and Diana Holmes have argued, Rachilde cultivated her scandalous reputation as a strategy to promote herself as a writer, a difficult task for a woman in a male-dominated literary circle.[3] "In some ways," Hawthorne notes, "Rachilde was always dressing up, playing a role, using elements of costume to create a public persona."[4] Fashion was thus a key component to Rachilde's successful attempts to complicate perceptions about her own gender identity and, in so doing, to draw attention to herself as an exceptional woman of letters.

Hawthorne's terms – "playing," "role," and "costume" – aptly underscore the theatricality of Rachilde's self-presentation and also go beyond referencing the author's manipulation of her own appearance by evoking her significant impact to the realm of theatre. Rachilde's work as a writer and producer of plays, especially considerable during the last decade of the nineteenth century, remains understudied relative to her novels. This despite the fact that she wrote over twenty works for the stage, actively supported young playwrights such as upstart Alfred Jarry, and used her influence to promote experimental productions at the Théâtre de l'Art and the Théâtre de l'Œuvre, sites of important literary production in 1890s Paris.[5] As we will see, Rachilde's relationship to theatre is relevant to this discussion because it foregrounds her treatment of fashion as costume and her attention to the interface of spaces and the garments worn in them.

Staircases emerge in key passages of Rachilde's late-nineteenth-century writing, from her works of theatre to her prose. A staircase figures as a critical stage set in the dramatic dénouement of her suspenseful one-act play *Le Rôdeur* (*The Prowler*), for example, and the structure recurs in moments of exaggerated sartorial drama in the novels *Monsieur de la Nouveauté*, *Monsieur Vénus*, and *La Jongleuse*. However, the staircases that Rachilde evokes are not monumental like Garnier's Opéra, nor are they like Zola's teeming department store *escalier*, both overcrowded settings for public spectacle. Rather, in the two episodes examined here, the first from *Monsieur Vénus*, which takes place in a clandestine service stairwell, and the second from *La Jongleuse*, set on a deserted flight of steps, Rachilde stages dramatic fashion moments in spaces of intimacy where an audience is limited to a single male spectator. Dislocations, we recall, serve at times as microcosms for the larger city; as such the visual objectification of the fashioned female body on these staircases can be read to mimic women's problematic experience in the urban environment and suggest a desire to subvert penetration of the masculine gaze.

"She Went On": Staircase Wit in *Monsieur Vénus*

Of Rachilde's numerous publications, *Monsieur Vénus*, a sexually provocative regendering of the myth of Pygmalion, has received the lion's share of critical attention. This is partly due to the fact that the novel launched its young author into the limelight, its scandal and renown helping to establish her as one of few women circulating in the literary intelligentsia of the fin de siècle. The tale of Raoule de Vénérande, a decadent aristocrat who takes up the role of masculine dominator over ephebic working-class painter Jacques Silvert, has been productively examined by scholars focusing on gender in relation to biography, decadence, hysteria, and modernity.[6] The focus in this present chapter on Raoule's masculinized attire on the staircase seeks to open up new ways of thinking about Rachilde's perceptions about modern space, fashion, and the gendered limits and freedoms that both could impart.

That the staircase will be an important locale in *Monsieur Vénus* is implied as early as the novel's opening phrases, which introduce Raoule to the reader just as she has ascended to the Silverts' garret apartment on the "seventh floor"[7] ["septième étage"[8]]. By specifying that the slum flat is located on the top storey of the building, a space typically inhabited by servants and the city's most destitute tenants, Rachilde foregrounds the notion that Raoule's "climb" up the staircase is actually a "descent" in social terms, for as a result of this upward rise the aristocratic protagonist will, ironically, end up marrying a man far below her station. The novel's starting location sets up the critical staircase scene that interests us here, which takes place midway through the novel as Raoule begins adopting menswear in earnest, a sartorial reinforcement of her position of authority over a poor and increasingly feminized Jacques. To prepare for nocturnal visits to her lover's boudoir, she takes to cross-dressing as a man, donning "a man's suit"[9] ["un complet d'homme"[10]] and her equestrian headgear, a "top hat"[11] ["chapeau haute forme" (*sic*)[12]] modelled after the iconic man's accessory, which she tips forward in order to hide her face. Although she scoffs at Jacques's fears that she will be arrested if caught wearing men's clothes in public, Raoule seems aware that such worries are justifiable, knowing as she surely would have that it was illegal in Paris in 1884 for women to dress as men.[13] To hide her transvestism from potentially untrustworthy servants, her deeply religious and disapproving aunt, and indeed, the law, Raoule thus turns to back passageways of her mansion in order to slip out undetected.

It is in the service staircase one night that she encounters her admirer, Raittolbe, who is attempting to penetrate into Raoule's bedroom by way of the back staircase in order to seduce her. In mid-descent, Raoule hesitates, for she risks sanctions if caught in full male attire. Her fears are allayed, though, when her suit and top hat, visual signs of masculinity, are persuasive enough to trick Raittolbe, who addresses her as a man until she laughingly reveals herself to him. Performing masculinity skilfully enough to pass as a gentleman, Raoule subverts her assigned gender with fashion. Rachilde makes use of this episode to underscore Raoule's creativity, pointing out that for a cross-dressed woman to navigate the modern city to her advantage requires "efforts of ingenuity"[14] ["efforts d'imagination"[15]]. The term "ingenuity" ("imagination" in the original French) links Raoule's cross-dressing skills to her creativity, a quality that, since at least the early nineteenth century, had been associated with masculine artistic genius. Through the example of Raoule, Rachilde implies the difficulties that she herself faced as a woman attempting to "pass" in a male-dominated artist's world, and also draws attention to her own writerly creativity (and, perhaps, genius).

Yet, although Raoule's expert cross-dressing affords her mobility and autonomy that most men and fewer women enjoyed in the late nineteenth century, she can only achieve this measure of freedom in spaces of seclusion: specifically, in the isolation of Jacques's boudoir or in her personal carriage en route to visit him. Raoule's predicament echoes that depicted in this 1878 Alfred Grévin illustration of a cigar-smoking woman in male attire who saucily declares, "It's fun to be a man" ["C'est amusant d'êt' homme"], her inverted legs a reinforcement of the upendeding she is effecting on gender codes through dress (see figure 2.1). Like Grévin's model, then, Raoule takes pleasure in donning

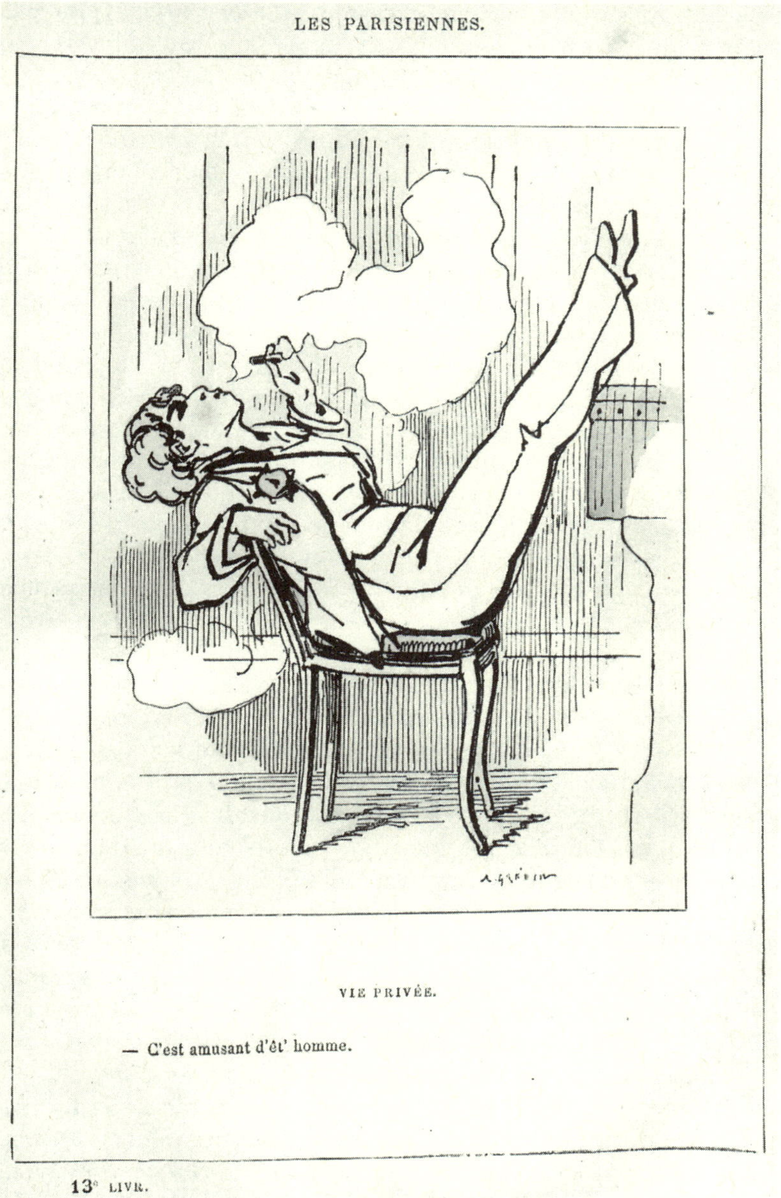

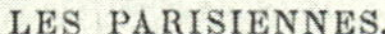

2.1 Alfred Grévin, *Vie Privée – C'est amusant d'êt' homme*, in *Les Parisiennes*, by Alfred Grévin and Adrien Huart (Paris: Librairie illustrée, 1878), 97.

men's suits, but as the caption "Private Life" ["Vie Privée"] indicates, she can only do so when hidden from view of the authorities. Though the subject of Grevin's illustration suggests, on the one hand, an increased awareness that more women than ever had begun adopting men's garments,[16] its caption acknowledges, too, that when women engaged in what was deemed to be cross-dressing they could not do so freely throughout the city.

Not one to be fully restricted by social conventions, Raoule rebels against the notion that she must conceal her performance of masculinity. The service staircase, although hidden, is a passageway to Paris, a conduit to the Haussmannian avenues that will then carry her from her mansion on the Champs-Elysées to Jacques on the boulevard Montparnasse. At first it is a site of constraint in which Raoule is trapped by an ascending Raittolbe. However, the staircase is then transformed by Raoule's determination to forge ahead into a space that will facilitate her goal of a sexual encounter with Jacques. This suggestion, that the staircase is first a space of hesitation and then one of subversive possibility, is inscribed into the very grammar of the passage: "As she started down, she met a man who was lighting his cigar. To turn back was to lose her opportunity, to go out was to risk giving herself away … She went on, passing close to the man, who touched the brim of his hat, not before looking at her very attentively"[17] ["Raoule descendant rencontra un homme allumant son cigare. Rétrograder c'était perdre l'occasion, et sortir était risquer de se trahir … Elle continua, passa près de l'homme, qui toucha le bord de son chapeau, non sans l'examiner attentivement"[18]]. The conspicuous ellipses that Rachilde here inserts register Raoule's hesitation at the choice she makes between quashing her own desires ("lose her opportunity") and punishable exposure ("giving herself away"). The staircase, itself an in-between space, provides an apt setting for Raoule, like the narrative, to pause between these two outcomes. As the text resumes, however, the staircase allows her movement and access, which the text mirrors with the phrase, "she went on."

The prominent role that Rachilde assigns to Raoule's dress on the service staircase in some ways calls to mind Garnier's *grand escalier*: in both spaces garments are self-consciously exhibited in order for wearers to advance meanings about their own identities. Moreover, just as spectators on the Opéra staircase were on hand to critique fashions and, by extension, their wearers, Raittolbe is there to see Raoule and subsequently disapprove of her "masquerade"[19] ["mascarade"[20]] as an act of "depraved women who spoil the best things"[21] [les depravées qui gâtent les meilleures choses[22]]. Both instances point to the necessity of a viewer in order for fashion to be ascribed with meaning, a process that can produce tensions when the wearer's objectives and the viewer's interpretations are in conflict. In *Monsieur Vénus*, for example, Raittolbe's condemnation of Raoule's masculine attire as "depraved" clashes with Raoule's aim to be taken for a man in order to access the mobility that menswear can supply. Thus, unlike in the case of the department store or the Opéra, where stylishness was of chief concern, space and fashion in Rachilde's novel are brought together primarily to challenge patriarchal expectations of how women should dress and behave. Rather than seeking approval from her audience, Raoule takes advantage of her dominant position at the top of the stairs, forcing her spectator to yield, however reluctantly, to her will. As though reversing Diderot's aptly named concept of "staircase wit" (*l'esprit d'escalier*), Raoule's insouciant laugh is a signal that she has succeeded in maintaining her mental acuity, overturning in her favour the implicit power inequities symbolized by the top (authoritative) and bottom (weakened) positions of the stairwell.[23] In an observation that seems to illustrate Rachilde's point of view, John Potvin states, "Fashion is one of those ways we understand our place in the world, and yet it offers us alternatives."[24] Here Rachilde deploys fashion to distort the dynamics of the grand staircase, altering it from a space prescribing a set decorum for women to a dislocation that subverts these very social protocols.

Staircase Theatre: *La Jongleuse*

By 1900, the year she published her novel *La Jongleuse* (a title meaning "the female juggler"), Rachilde had enjoyed several decades not only as a successful novelist but also as a co-publisher of a literary journal, a playwright, and a high-profile patron of modernist theatre. Her increased participation in the experimental theatre scene in the last decade of the century is reflected in the clear influence that the dramatic arts had on *La Jongleuse*, both in content and in form. The novel is, as Hawthorne points out, "permeated with the vocabulary of the theater."[25] Indeed, to my mind *La Jongleuse* is a novelistic adaptation of one of Rachilde's plays, an 1891 symbolist work entitled *Madame La Mort*. Although the play concludes with a different ending, the novel nonetheless reiterates the structure and primary themes of the earlier dramatic work. The metaphors of theatre and performances will prove important for the following discussion of the role of fashion and the staircase in *La Jongleuse*, for they help to illuminate Rachilde's ambivalence towards women's experience of the modern urban landscape. On the one hand, *La Jongleuse* stands as a critique of a society in which women are made constantly to perform. At the same time it depicts theatrical strategies of dress and negotiations of stagelike spaces that open up possibilities of expression for its female protagonist. Like *Monsieur Vénus*, it is a commentary, made by way of the dislocated staircase, on the troubled access to the city afforded to women who did not seek to conform to the gendered norms expected of them during this period.

Madame La Mort, the play in three acts that Rachilde seems to have recast a decade later as the novel *La Jongleuse*, centres on Paul Dartigny, a wealthy and splenetic young decadent who obsessively yearns for death. The first and third acts take place in Paul's private smoking room, while the second act occurs in a hazy garden, which, according to Rachilde's program notes, is meant to symbolize the mind of the protagonist who is dying after having inhaled the fumes of a poisoned cigar.[26] In Act II, the figures of Life (*La Vie*) and Death (*La Mort*), portrayed as two allegorical women, compete over Paul's soul. La Vie, played by the same actress as Paul's first-act lover Lucie, wears a pink evening gown with a fashionable *décolleté*, while La Mort is completely covered by a shadowy, grey dress and veil. Life/Lucie offers Paul a future of earthly pleasures wherein the young man might fill the respectable bourgeois roles of husband and father, but Paul is seduced instead by the void promised by mysterious Death. La Mort eventually defeats La Vie, and Paul expires as the title character wraps him in the folds of her immense, grey veil.

Like *Madame La Mort*, *La Jongleuse* is a love triangle involving struggles for power and affection among its three protagonists: the wealthy older widow Eliante Donalger, her childlike and athletic niece Missie, and the young medical student Léon Reille, who shuns Missie's clumsy advances, entranced instead by her mysterious and elegant aunt. Meeting one night at a dinner party, Eliante invites Léon to her home, a mansion in which the affluent woman's private chambers have been transformed into a space of fin-de-siècle orientalist fantasy reflecting her hybrid origins as a *créole*, a white woman born in a French colony abroad. Eliante's otherness informs the eclectic array of outfits that she dons in subsequent encounters with Léon, outfits that include a juggler's sleek leotard, a statuesque ivory dressing gown, a widow's visiting outfit, and a risqué flamenco dress. The novel's vivid conclusion is highly theatrical: Eliante lures Léon to her bed with the promise of giving herself to him physically at long last. When day breaks, however, Léon finds to his horror that, through Eliante's orchestration, he has spent the night with Missie. Just as Léon makes this startling discovery, Eliante, juggling her knives next to the bed, allows one of the heavy blades to fall upon and penetrate her at the neck, committing suicide in an expression of "supernatural joy"[27] ["une joie surnaturelle"[28]]. The reader experiences the heroine's gruesome demise through the young man's shocked perspective rather than through a third-person narrator.[29] The theatrical quality of the novel is thus underscored as the reader becomes, like Léon, a live audience to Eliante's spectacular suicide/performance.

Through overlapping thematics, then, *La Jongleuse* revisits elements of *Madame La Mort*, but another similarity exists in the carefully choreographed structure that they share. By alternating between odd-numbered chapters that are driven by plot and even-numbered epistolary chapters that represent the characters' subconscious dreams and memories, *La Jongleuse* approximates the play, in which the physical settings of Acts I and III serve as bookends to the abstract "cerebral" setting of the Act II garden scene inserted between them.[30] Rachilde's structural referencing throughout her novel to the play has two effects: (1) it imbeds the narrative in a tradition of performance whereby space is constructed as stage set and garments as costumes, and (2) it alludes to an inherent theatricality present in the locations and dress of the urban Parisian world in which the story is set.

As scholars have noted, Eliante experiences life as a series of performances, "juggling" the multiple facets – or characters – of her identity throughout.[31] Léon repeatedly refers to her as an "actress" (*comedienne*), and indeed, Eliante appears throughout the novel in a series of remarkable fashions mimicking the many costume changes of a thespian. Her metaphorical performances of self are echoed in several staged appearances before actual audiences, spectacles including a knife-juggling act at a party and a Spanish dance for a small group of guests. The symbolism of Eliante's costuming may have resonated particularly well with Rachilde, who had first fashioned herself as the scandalous cross-dressing author of *Monsieur Vénus* but then found herself playing a number of challenging – possibly incompatible – new roles in the 1890s, including wife, mother, publisher, playwright, and benefactor.

Rachilde's use of space is theatrical as well, for Eliante's house, where most of the plot-driven chapters take place, reproduces the architecture of a stage. The mansion is divided into two distinct wings that correspond to the two sides of a theatre stage, which were labelled *côté cour* (courtyard side) and *côté jardin* (garden side);[32] the residence is thus, as Hawthorne suggests, a type of "domestic theater."[33] On the public side of the mansion where visitors are received in the côté cour Eliante enacts her bourgeois widow character, saving the private wing of the côté jardin for intimate, yet liberating, performances of her sensual and erotic self.[34] The côté jardin location echoes the garden in Act II of *Madame La Mort*, associating this setting in *La Jongleuse* with death through the play's titular "Mort," the slim woman in black that Eliante portrays in the novel.[35]

A staircase scene opens *La Jongleuse*, setting the stage for the metaphor of the theatre that will imbue the text and for fashion's role in shaping the woman performer. Eliante, sheathed in a high-necked black silk dress, departs early from a dinner gathering, descending a staircase that is deserted save for Léon, who follows her. After catching sight of him behind her in a landing mirror, Eliante continues down the flight of stairs, stopped momentarily by Léon when he treads upon the long train of her gown. Arriving at the first-floor coatroom, Eliante envelops herself in an oriental wrap, "a violent stole, an adventurer's stole, like a firework"[36] ["une écharpe violente, une écharpe d'aventurière, comme un feu d'artifice"[37]], and mounts her waiting carriage. To Léon's surprise, the coach stops before him and Eliante invites him to accompany her, thus permitting the young man and the reader access to the decadent narrative that will then unfold.

In Hawthorne's description of the plot structure, this opening scene is an "exception," falling out of the rubric of the domestic theatre chapters because it does not occur in Eliante's stagelike mansion and thus disrupts the unity of place important to classical drama.[38] The point is apt, but to my mind the staircase lead-in to the narrative is also consistent with the logic of the late-nineteenth-century theatre in architectural terms for, much like the grand escalier of Garnier's Opéra, it serves as an entrance that is designed not only to direct viewers to the ostensible performance within but to provide as well a space for spectacle itself. As Rops's painting reinforces, steps, as opposed to the stage, are often where the "real" moments of drama occur, the force of their ability to arouse emotion evidenced by the intense reactions of the spectators in the background of Rops's composition. The staircase in Eliante's case is a threshold, one in which performance occurs but is not constrained by the formal limitations of the theatre. It is an architectural manifestation of possibility, one that anticipates in its very design the electrifying collisions – echoed sartorially in the "fireworks" of Eliante's oriental shawl – that can take place when different registers of performance meet, from the quotidian performance of identity to the choreographed production of the theatre.

Right away, then, fashion connects Eliante to the potential of the staircase to construct and destabilize both identity and conceptions of space. The opening phrase establishes the protagonist's union with her clothing and with the area through which she navigates: "This woman let her dress trail behind her like a queen trailing her life"[39] ["Cette femme laissait traîner sa robe derrière elle comme on peut laisser traîner sa vie quand on est reine"[40]]. That the train is described as "her life" binds Eliante to a garment that, in fact, seems to be attacking her, a dress that is described as "tightening around her throat as if to strangle her" ["lui serrant la gorge à l'étrangler"[41]]. But the garment also offers her the capacity to transform her environment, for, as she walks, the train of her gown creates a wave ("formed a wave around her, undulated"[42] ["roulait une vague autour d'elle, ondulait"[43]]), modifying the ground beneath her through a water metaphor that converts the trailing fabric into "the same moiré circles that are seen in deep water in the evening, after a body has fallen"[44] ["les même cercles moirés que l'on voit se former dans l'eau profonde, le soir, après la chute d'un corps"[45]]. This phrase has been interpreted to augur Eliante's eventual suicide, as "her dress threatens to swallow her up, to engulf her … [and] ultimately destroy her."[46] Although it is true that the protagonist's gown is meant to symbolize a dangerous threat to its wearer, when the sentence is reconsidered in spatial terms one notes that her black silk dress also makes possible Eliante's transformation of the building from a location of "monotonous official evenings"[47] ["monotones soirées officielles"[48]] into a space of decadent delectation characterized by the sensuality of water, the tantalizing mystery of shadowy darkness, and the sublimeness of death (called up by the image of the falling body).

In any case, the staircase remains a location of performance, for Eliante, stopping at the first landing, glances into a mirror not in order to view her own image but to glimpse her audience: Léon. Seeing through the mirror's reflection, which imposes Léon's desires back upon her, Eliante knows by reading her spectator that she is being pursued by a man whose ultimate wishes will be to remove her clothing in order to dominate her. As if anticipating her audience's desire to gain mastery over her, Eliante has come prepared in a protective garment, a "hermetic dress"[49] ["robe hérmetique"[50]] that conceals her body from prying eyes and fingers. In this opening passage, which sets the tone for the rest of the novel, Rachilde's rendering of Eliante's tight clothing reflects ambivalence about what clothing does to and for the female body. On the one hand, the writer underscores the violence inflicted on the woman performer by her own costume: Eliante is strangled and bitten ["mordait"[51]] by her collar, squeezed ["pressant"[52]] by her long gloves, and moulded ["moulée"[53]] by her close-fitting garments and accessories. On the other hand, these descriptions of clothes that assault the body imply at the same time the masochistic element of dress as fetish, whereby the pain of physical discomfort heightens a simultaneous pleasure.[54] The masochism associated with fetishistic garments is articulated, for example, in the paroxysm of joy that Eliante later conveys as her juggling knife strikes her in the neck and kills her, an apparently pleasurable cutting of skin that she experiences all the while wearing a large belt that, in the manner of bondage wear, "tightly encircled her thighs" (translation modified)[55] ["lui sanglait les cuisses"[56]]. In *La Jongleuse*, Rachilde complicates the intersection of costuming and performance, highlighting the exceptional woman's ability to transform her space and gain pleasure through fashion. At the same time, she critiques a society in which women must constantly defend themselves from the threat of masculine aggression and denounces the pain suffered by way of the very instruments – garments – that Eliante deploys to strategize self-preservation and identity formation alike.[57]

"Skirt and Bodice Floated on Her": Eliante as Loie Fuller

Rachilde's ambivalence towards Eliante's costumed performance crystallizes on the staircase. If, as we saw above, garments function to cover the body, as she continues to descend and Léon steps on the hem of her dress, Eliante is not concealed but revealed:

> On the second landing, at the point where a second marble servant lifted her spray of light while smiling a white sugary smile, the black woman let out a cry, the light cry of someone nervous who is provoked, but without turning round: her dress had just pulled tight suddenly from the train to the neck, the whole fabric had stiffened into an iron bar and the decorous costume, the chaste sheath, detached itself bit by bit from the woman,

giving her up to the electric lights more naked, despite her blackness, than the marble statue. Skirt and bodice floated on her.[58]

[Au second palier, à l'endroit où une seconde servante de marbre haussait sa gerbe de lumière en souriant d'un sourire de sucre blanc, la dame noire poussa un cri, un léger cri de nerveuse, qu'on impatiente, mais sans se retourner: sa robe venait de se tendre subitement de la traîne au col, toute l'étoffe se roidissait en barre de fer et le costume correct, la gaine chaste, se détachait peu à peu de la femme, la livrant aux transparences électriques plus nue, malgré sa noiceur, que la statue de marbre. Jupe et corsage flottaient sur elle.[59]]

Rachilde's images of the dress are vividly tactile: the garment is described as an "iron bar" that pulls at the back of Eliante's neck and the fabric seems to detach from her body, calling up the thought that she is being skinned alive. These metaphors highlight the violent corporeal manipulations that pose a threat to the woman performer whose costuming is, in part, a defensive strategy in reaction to male aggression, here enacted by Léon when he steps on her train. The fashion metaphor evokes the larger threat of masculine violence, which is represented in another passage through Léon's frustrated thought of raping Eliante. In this later moment, Léon is prevented because, he reasons, he is dressed in formalwear and must abide by the decorum that his garments require: "He obeyed mechanically *because he was wearing a suit*; if he had been in an ordinary jacket he would undoubtedly have raped her"[60] ["Machinalement, il obéit *parce qu'il était en habit*; s'il avait été en veston, il l'aurait sans doute violée" (original emphasis)[61]]. Rachilde's reference to rape in this remark should be read partly as one of her typical sardonic asides, for Eliante clearly dominates and manipulates Léon throughout the novel rather than the other way around. Nonetheless, the startling phrase points both to the penetrability of Eliante's costume and to the fact that the functions and meanings of clothing are inconsistent. Indeed, on the staircase landing, Eliante is not protected but betrayed by her shadowy gown's sudden inability to conceal her body. For a split second she appears more "nude" than the white statue of a smiling naked woman, the alabaster exhibitionist inverse to Eliante's modest dark elegance. Two conditions related to fashion make the exposure of Eliante's body possible. First, she is detached from her shielding costume, which "floats" over her body rather than sheathing it in close protection. Second, electric light shines through the thin fabric, allowing Léon to view the body that is otherwise safely encased.

To understand the nuances of these two details, it is important to situate the passage in its cultural context. For turn-of-the-century readers, it is possible that this moment of visual spectacularity by way of powerful electric lights would have evoked the staged performances of the famed dancer Loie Fuller, whose innovative technique of using electric lights to illuminate her seductive modernist dances earned her the monikers "Electric Salomé" and *la fée électrique* or "the electric fairy."[62] Fuller was an American who arrived in France in 1892 and almost immediately took the Parisian entertainment scene by storm, pioneering a new style of dance that involved the creation of original, specialized costumes. Sewing excessive amounts of fabric to her dancing attire, in particular to her sleeves, Fuller would then attach these extra yards of cloth to handheld rods. Training strong, sometimes coloured electric lights onto herself during her wildly popular dance performances, Fuller manipulated her body and costume to create enormous abstract geometric forms that enthralled audiences, who found the shapes to be an entrancing marriage of technology and the organic human body, all the more beautiful for their ephemerality (see figure 2.2). Her performances created a sense of the otherworldly, giving her fleeting tableaux the character of "un-dreamt-of places," as an enthusiastic Mallarmé would describe them.[63]

In 1900, the year that *La Jongleuse* was published, Loie Fuller was featured as one of the star attractions at Paris's World Exposition, an international fair that ran from mid-April through mid-November and whose visitors numbered over fifty million, a staggering figure. While one cannot be certain that Rachilde's description of Eliante's "performance" on the staircase landing is a direct reference to the prominent dancer, Fuller's dazzling popularity throughout the last decade of the century and especially at that year's World Exposition suggests she may have been an intertext. Eliante's episode on the stairs shares several important aspects of Fuller's dancing. From the point of view of fashion, the "iron bar" created by the tautly pulled cloth of Eliante's dress simulates the stiff rods that Fuller attached to her costume sleeves and that constituted one of her most iconic sartorial inventions. What is more, the airy silk "floating" over Eliante's skin echoes the buoyant suspensions of fabric created around Fuller's body as she danced. There are also technological similarities, including the electric lights that illuminate both women and accentuate the movement of their bodies.

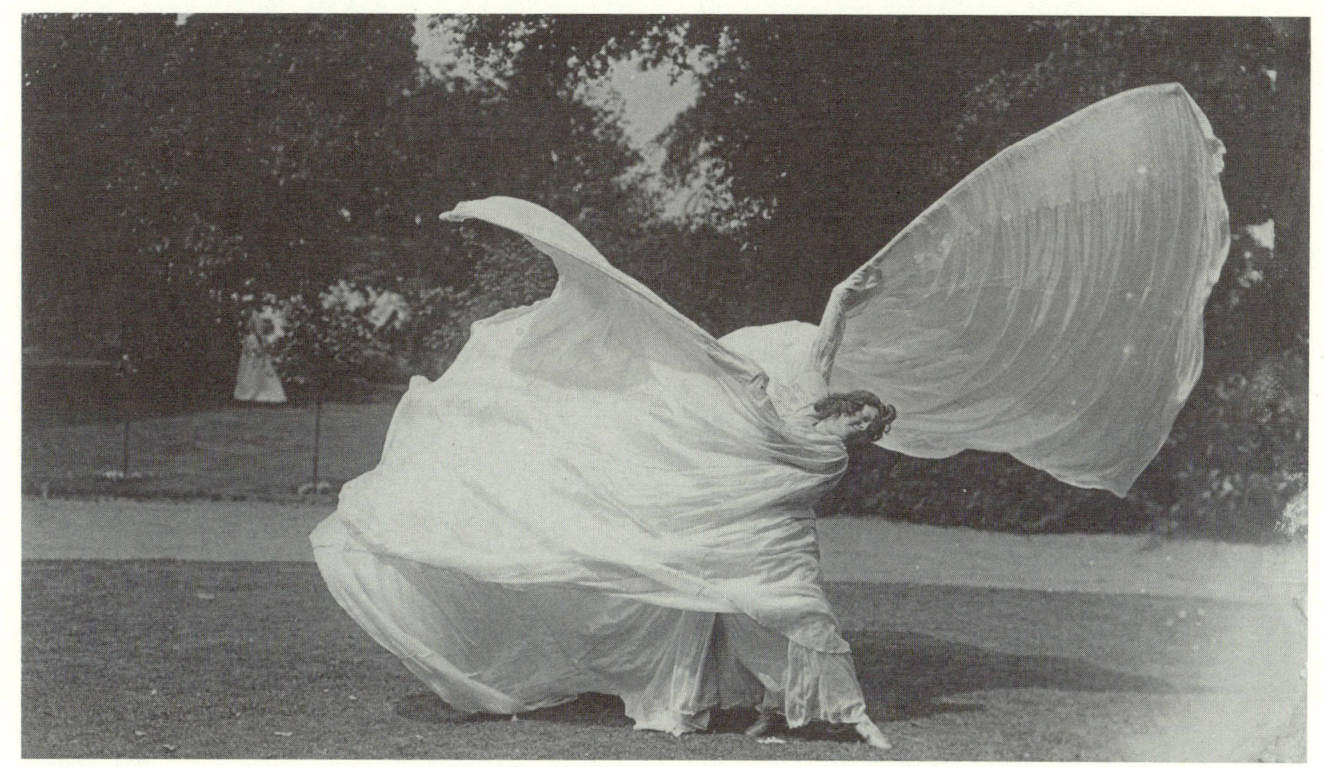

2.2 Samuel Joshua Beckett, [*Loie Fuller Dancing*]. Photograph, c. 1900. Image copyright © The Metropolitan Museum of Art. Image source: Art Resource, NY.

Rachilde emphasizes her protagonist's graceful gestures as, undaunted by Léon's clumsy foot, Eliante gathers up her train "with one sweeping gesture"[64] ["d'un seul geste arrondi"[65]], her movements especially noticeable for being "so supple"[66] ["si flexible"[67]]. Eliante's flexibility and the roundness of her "sweeping gesture" – the term "arrondi" meaning "round" or "curved" – might have reminded readers of the giant smooth circles of silk that Fuller created through the graceful contortions of her pliant body. Paradoxically, the electric beams that illuminate Eliante's dress also give the appearance of arrested motion. Not unlike the theatre floodlights in Degas's paintings of dancers, or, to cite a subsequent version of light technology, flash photography,[68] the electric beams for Rachilde and Fuller both record the fixity of bodies in motion. Rachilde's textual "photograph" of Eliante is a single impression of a woman caught in time, one that may have been, too, a nod to the staggering proliferation of photographic images that were made, copied, and sold of Fuller dancing.

Finally, in both instances, electric lights are key to expressing the modernity of the spectacle and of the space in which it occurs. The modern quality of the staircase is clarified when the opening of the novel is examined against the one juggling performance of the novel that Eliante offers on a properly defined stage several chapters later. This juggling demonstration takes place during a ball hosted in the "public" wing (*côté cour*) of Eliante's mansion, a large gathering of guests including her niece Missie's boisterous young friends and Eliante's older, more conservative acquaintances. Absent at the start of the gathering, Eliante suddenly appears dressed as a juggler in a skin-tight leotard and wielding a set of heavy steel knives, which she begins to juggle before her seated audience. Artfully tossing her blades with the elegance and skill of a professional juggler, Eliante captivates the crowd through the riskiness of her routine and the obvious pleasure she experiences in performing it. This scene has been analysed by Catherine McGann, who approaches it through the lens of Bakhtin's theory of the carnival. Eliante's juggling act is, for McGann, consistent with Bakhtin's notion of the carnivalesque in that it is a joyful celebration for a mixed-class audience that simulates the festive spectatorship of the popular street square.[69] The juggling exhibition occurs on a stage, but one that has no footlights to separate performer from crowd, so that at the conclusion of the demonstration, Rachilde writes that the audience "stormed the stage"[70] ["escalada la scène"[71]]. McGann argues that the absence of footlights is an important aspect of the performance's carnivalesque dynamic, citing Bakhtin's statement that "carnival does not know foot-lights, in the sense that it does not acknowledge any distinction be-tween actors and spectators. Footlights would destroy a carnival, as the absence of footlights would destroy a theatrical performance."[72] The juggling scene in the novel thus stages the classic Bakhtinian carni-valesque, even down to the detail of absent footlights. Consequently, though, it lacks the electric lights that would code it as a *modern* spec-tacle and thus the juggling display more fully expresses Bakhtin's Rabelaisian mode of performance – one steeped in the tradition of Renaissance acrobatic troupes – rather than the pioneering, technology-driven dances of Loie Fuller that were all the rage in 1900. The electric lights that provide the "spark" of modernity are not on the stage but on the stairs, a space on which, as we have seen, fashion and the woman performer are most dazzlingly illuminated.

Recently, the historian James H. Johnson has posited a transforma-tion in attitudes surrounding carnival-like occasions in the nineteenth century.[73] Focusing on the trope of masks in works by Paul Verlaine, Jean Lorrain, Remy de Gourmont, and Rops – men from Rachilde's decadent circle and related groups – Johnson grounds these texts in social history. As the century progressed, Johnson notes, social roles in France became increasingly more static such that, by the last decades of the 1800s, people could no longer imagine the same kind of radical class mobility that had once seemed plausible. Reflecting this change, carnivalesque dressing-up, which operates in part to call social stability into question, occurred less frequently. Late-century masked balls became characterized by relative homogeneity and conformity in costume, imbuing these occasions with what Johnson terms an "anti-carnivalesque imposture" (20:10) that contradicted the genuine social mobility that disguises of the 1830s and 1840s had once projected. Johnson's discussion may highlight a gendered difference in attitudes towards the relationship between (productive) insubordination of car-nivalesque and dress that Rachilde's novel illustrates. For if the works of creative men from her era suggested a loss of belief in the subversion of disguise, linking masks more to madness and other signs of psycho-logical degeneration than true social change, as Johnson convincingly shows, then *La Jongleuse*, featuring a frequently "masked" and cos-tumed female protagonist, seems in contrast to indicate some lingering faith in dressing-up as a strategy, if not for men then for women. As Johnson asserts, "inequality encourages masking" (20:29), perhaps a subtext of a novel written by an author accustomed to being relegated to a position of subordination by her gender and searching for ways to thwart such discrimination.

Deeply ingrained with the nostalgic, aristocratic attitude of nineteenth-century decadence, Rachilde created numerous portraits of female protagonists such as Eliante Donalger and Raoule de Vénérande who shunned conformity to any accepted code of expression or desire. Preferring to see herself as an exceptional elite, Rachilde distanced herself from contemporaries who might have embraced her, such as late-century feminists whose movements were grounded in collectivity, and thereby remaining, in some ways, aloof from some currents in the gender politics of her day. Thus, as her disdain for Eliante's progressive, bloomer-wearing niece Missie implies, it is likely that Rachilde would have been loath to use the word "modern" to describe heroines with whom she clearly empathized. Yet, her books are filled with proud female leads, protagonists whom she self-consciously modelled on herself and who foreshadowed things to come. For instance, Raoule de Vénérande, with her cropped locks and masculine attire, is a prototype for the *garçonne*, the boyish, car-driving, cigarette-smoking gamine who would become the face of feminine modernity in the following century.

Even more significant for our purposes is the fact that Rachilde's manipulations of dress and space evince a preoccupation with women's experience in the modern urban landscape. Eliante Donalger, although the inverse in many ways of Missie's "modern woman," skilfully deploys dress on the fin-de-siècle staircase, a space that exemplifies the performance-driven spectacularity of late-nineteenth-century modernity but is also problematized through Rachilde's exposure of the limits such spaces placed on women. As such, her texts are consistent with those of other early Third Republic writers, those authors who did not focus exclusively on public Haussmannian spaces as the primary sites of cultural production in which new relationships had emerged between Parisians and their city. Joining other writers of her day, Rachilde turned to the dislocations of servant stairwells and deserted staircase landings, showing these to be inherently connected to, but distinct from, the public spaces that had been built to serve as and represent locales of the modern. Her fiction, which privileged metaphors of theatricality and highlighted the importance of costuming to a woman's successful navigation of the metropole, points to the gendered challenges women faced and to the skills of performance they developed to meet them. Women were the city's constant performers, Rachilde's works seem to suggest, whether to their ultimate benefit or detriment.

Plunging Perspectives: Caillebotte's Vertical Views

The paintings of Gustave Caillebotte (1848–1890), today embraced as highly emblematic of modern – and early postmodern – Parisian bourgeois experience,[74] provide useful pictorial intertexts through which to read the final two staircases analysed in this chapter: those in *Bel-Ami* (1884) by Guy de Maupassant (1850–1893) and *Sapho* (1885) by Alphonse Daudet (1840–1897). During his lifetime, Caillebotte was best known as a prominent collector of Impressionist artwork and as a wealthy patron to the painters of this artistic movement. In recent decades, however, scholars have recognized Caillebotte as a major artist in his own right, with most interest directed at his 1876 *Le Pont de l'Europe* and 1877's *Rue de Paris; Temps de pluie*.[75] As in these paintings of well-dressed urbanites strolling on boulevards and bridges, many of Caillebotte's depictions of social interactions among city dwellers convey a paradox of fragmented isolation and interconnectivity that is informed by his wide-angle representations of Haussmannian boulevards and by the modern buildings imposed across his canvases. Karin Sagner's remark, that "of all the Impressionist painters, Gustave Caillebotte came nearest to the Haussmannesque aesthetic," bears witness to the strong associations now made between the city and his work.[76] One hallmark of this "Haussmannesque aesthetic" is Caillebotte's use of perspective to elongate Haussmann's buildings and to emphasize their appearance of lengthening horizontally and far off into the distance.[77] Among other things, by way of this distortion, he suggested in visual terms the extended "reach" of Second Empire urban planning and the imperialist attitudes of those behind it. Recent interest has focused on how Caillebotte attended not only to horizontal lines but also to the verticality of Parisian edifices and the ways in which they offered an elevated vantage point of the streets below.[78] This perspective provided a visual trope for expressing new spatial configurations of modern life in the city. Painting often from the fourth-floor vantage point of his own apartment located in the elegant neighbourhood of Garnier's Opéra,[79] Caillebotte chronicled these views in canvases such as *Un Balcon* (1880) and *Le Boulevard vu d'en haut* (1880), works that suggested a new preoccupation of looking at the city from far above. As Michael Fried notes in his analysis of the steeply falling lines in the bird's-eye-view painting *Jeune homme à la fenêtre* (1876), during this period "plunging perspectives of this sort are a recurrent feature of Caillebotte's art."[80] Repetition of this theme during the 1870s and 1880s implies that, for the painter, the practice of gazing down on Paris had become generalized, a result, perhaps, of the increased ubiquity of tall bourgeois homes being erected on a mass scale to serve as middle- and upper-class housing.[81]

The Caillebotte fortune derived in part from the textile business that the painter's father had inherited; it is perhaps fitting, given his family's historical connection to fabric, that fashion is so pervasive in Caillebotte's images of everyday urban life.[82] Masculine dress in particular reinforces the sense of elevation in Caillebotte's city buildings and the emerging modern viewership with which he was fascinated. In many of his works, such as *L'Homme au balcon, boulevard Haussmann* (1880), elongated tailored frock coats worn by sharply dressed men peering at treetops and streets below create strong perpendicular lines that mimic the imposing sense of height that Haussmannian architecture sought to achieve (see figure 2.3). Verticality is further emphasized by a profusion of top hats, one of Caillebotte's favourite accessories. Tellingly named "chapeaux haut-de-forme," literally "high-formed hats," these quintessential signs of bourgeois masculinity further extend body length upward, serving as a sartorial symbol for the lofty position, both social and spatial, that these men of wealth and status held in France's capital.[83]

Invisible but implied in Caillebotte's images of verticality are the interior staircases that many city dwellers were required to climb in order to attain these soaring heights. Such staircases appear in Maupassant's *Bel-Ami* and in Daudet's *Sapho* and allow both authors to meditate on the meanings of these vertical views as well as on the metaphor of ascension and its inverse, decline. The texts were written in the early 1880s, the same years when Caillebotte was painting tall buildings, spectators on top-floor balconies, and bird's-eye perspectives of Paris streets. What they provide are literary representations of the climb through interior space that are implicit in the painter's images. Viewing the city from above was not a new theme in literature of the nineteenth century.[84] What sets the texts by Maupassant and Daudet apart from earlier works is their intense interest in how characters reach high positions and where key moments in their ascents occur. For both authors, dislocated staircases are spatial metaphors for the moral decline hidden behind men's rise to the pinnacles of surface elegance and spectacle characterizing late-nineteenth-century society.

Published only one year apart and featuring somewhat similar plot lines, *Bel-Ami* and *Sapho* had, nonetheless, quite different trajectories, as have their authors. In the 1870s, Daudet was a prominent literary

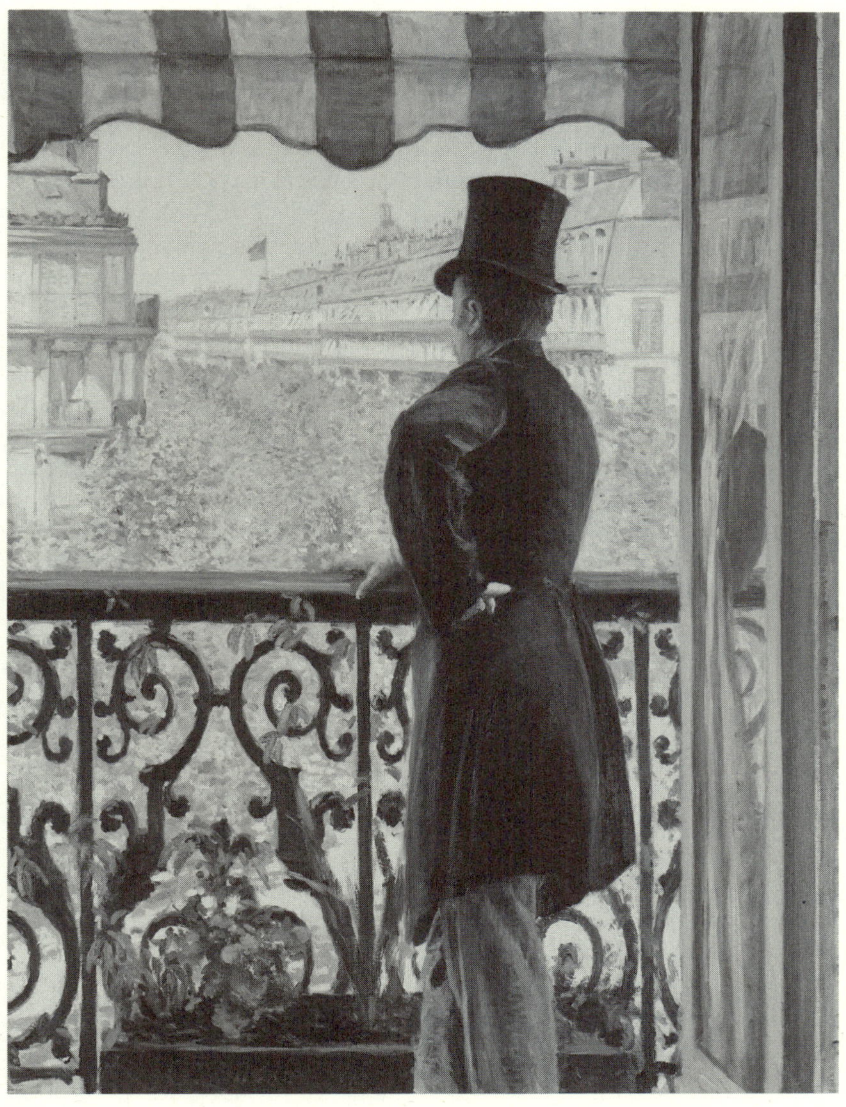

2.3 Gustave Caillebotte, *L'Homme au balcon, boulevard Haussmann*, 1880. Oil on canvas. Private collection. Reproduced by permission of the Bridgeman Art Library.

figure, well known for his novels, short stories, and plays. Among his most memorable portraits of Paris in the 1880s is *Sapho*, a novella loosely based on his own life that later served as the subject of an 1897 opera by celebrated composer Jules Massenet. However, following the author's death that same year, *Sapho*, and Daudet more generally, faded into relative obscurity, both popular and critical. In contrast, as is well known, Maupassant was exceedingly prolific during the 1870s and 1880s, enjoying a meteoric rise to fame before dying prematurely in a mental asylum at the age of forty-two. *Bel-Ami*, in addition to some of his celebrated short stories including "Boule de Suif" (1880) and "Le Horla" (1887), are fixed firmly in the canon of late-nineteenth-century French letters, in contrast with Daudet, whose works today are far less studied.[85] These differences notwithstanding, *Bel-Ami* and *Sapho* are both reflections on urban space and fashion that plot in textual form some of the same visual concerns put forth in the paintings of Caillebotte. In the manner of typical bildungsromans, the two works centre on young men from the provinces who arrive in Paris where they seek their fortune, all the while engaging in sexual liaisons with various archetypes of Parisian women. Georges Duroy, protagonist of *Bel-Ami*, and Jean Gaussin, the male lead of *Sapho*, are neither sympathetic central characters nor obvious villains. Rather, like many late-century figures of modernity, they are "heroes of non-heroism" ["héros du non-heroïsme"[86]], to borrow a phrase from Bernard Urbani. Significant to the present discussion is the fact that *Bel-Ami* and *Sapho* feature scenes in staircases that occur early in their respective narratives and are key to establishing the up/down trajectory of their main characters. Moreover, in both cases, fashion is called upon to foretell the course of the protagonists' experience of the city and to criticize bourgeois preoccupations with diversion and pleasure that seemed to epitomize, for both writers, Paris in the 1880s.

Appearing as Being: Maupassant's *Bel-Ami*

In the famous staircase episode that opens the second chapter of *Bel-Ami*, Maupassant highlights men's garments and Duroy's trip of self-discovery up three flights of steps to foreshadow the young man's rise to the top of the glittering world of wealth and power that the remainder of the novel records. Arriving at a dinner party where he will be introduced to the influential men and women whom he will eventually eclipse or dominate by seduction, Duroy enters the Forestiers' apartment building at street level and is told by the concierge to take the stairs to the flat on the third floor. As the protagonist trudges slowly up the first flight, the reader learns that Duroy has never before worn a formal suit. Required to rent one for the occasion, he is anxious about the effects of an outfit that seems to him "defective" ["defectueuse"[87]] because he is wearing ordinary dull boots as opposed to shiny patent leather, a dickey that is already creased, and trousers that are slightly too big for him ["les bottines non vernies," "le plastron trop mince se cassait déjà," "son pantalon, un peu trop large"[88]]. However, at the first landing, Duroy catches sight of a handsome man in a full-length mirror and experiences a shock: "Duroy recoiled with a start and then stood dumbfounded: it was his own reflection in a tall wall-mirror on the first floor landing which produced the effect of a long gallery"[89] ["Duroy fit un mouvement en arrière, puis il demeura stupéfait: c'était lui-même, reflété par une haute glace en pied qui formait sur le palier du premier une longue perspective de galerie"[90]]. So astonished is he by the successful appearance of his smartly clad body that it takes the protagonist a moment to realize that the stylish man in the reflection is none other than himself.[91]

It is in this passage describing the first staircase landing that Maupassant evokes the metaphor of garments-as-costume only to complicate it. Enjoying the head-to-toe reflection accorded him by the full-length mirror, Duroy begins practising a variety of gestures and expressions "like an actor studying his part"[92] ["comme font les acteurs pour apprendre leurs rôles"[93]]: he smiles, offers up his hand to shake, and pretends to flirt with imaginary women. However, despite Maupassant's nod to the vocabulary of performance, he does not describe Duroy's comportment throughout the novel in the manner of an actor's artificial simulation of emotions and intentions. Rather, Duroy's rise in society, doubled here by his literal ascension up the stairs, will be navigated primarily by way of the callous ambition that comes quite naturally to him and that he rarely, if ever, dissimulates. That is, despite Maupassant's use of the word "actor," Duroy will find that he does not, in fact, need to play a part. This is because in a society that privileges exterior appearance over interiority, he simply *is* what others see when they look at him in fine clothes. Forestier suggests the crucial importance of appearances in remarking, not entirely facetiously, "In Paris, you realize it's better to be without a bed than not to have evening clothes"[94] ["A Paris, vois-tu, il vaudrait mieux n'avoir pas de lit que pas d'habit"[95]]. Analysing Maupassant's thematizing of exterior appearance versus interior self, Claudine Giacchetti insightfully declares that in *Bel-Ami* "appearance ... becomes a new way of being" ["paraître ... devient un nouveau mode d'être"].[96] This "new way of being" is endemic to the modern social milieu of which Duroy will become "king," as his name portends. Through fashion, then, Duroy begins to understand that he is not a rumpled imposter but rather the attractive man in the fine suit that he meets in the first-landing mirror. In Mary Louise Roberts's words, the character is "all costuming, all wardrobe ... all artifice – a surface play of roles and images."[97] As the novel progresses Duroy will learn that he is no different from the other superficial people he encounters except insofar as he is the most adept at existing as his own appearance; he will become the king, that is, of negotiating modernity's "new way of being."

The staircase in which Duroy encounters his well-dressed appearance is highlighted in this passage, inviting the reader's attention. Michel Foucault's discussion of *heterotopias* provides a critical apparatus for reading Maupassant's treatment of the relationship between the well-heeled image that Duroy sees in the mirror – his appearance, or *paraître*, to cite Giacchetti – and the staircase in which the reflective surface hangs. The term "heterotopia," in Foucault's formulation, is a reconfiguration of "utopia," a place that, by definition, is not real. Heterotopias, in contrast, are "places that do exist and that are formed in the very founding of society – which are something like countersites, a kind of effectively enacted utopia in which the real sites, all the other real sites that can be found within the culture, are simultaneously represented, contested, and inverted."[98] Not surprisingly, given his work elsewhere on the expansion of regulatory institutions in the 1800s, Foucault dates the emergence of modern heterotopian spaces – "the very founding of society" – to the nineteenth century, which brings his discussion to bear on Maupassant's literary construction of the Third Republic. In particular, Foucault's examination of mirrors helps to illuminate Maupassant's critique of modernity's turn to privileging appearance over being and the novelist's understanding of this turn as spatially determined.

The staircase in *Bel-Ami* fits well into Foucault's description of the fifth principle of heterotopias: "the heterotopic site is not freely accessible like a public place ... to get in one must have a certain permission and make certain gestures."[99] These conditions are present as Duroy ascends from the public street to the exclusive rooms above that have, heretofore, been off limits. To enter the private building, he must first be granted permission by the concierge, and the accessibility of the staircase depends on his making the appropriate gestures, including dressing correctly for the occasion. However, the focus here is not on the staircase as a heterotopia but rather on the *mirrors*, also heterotopian spaces, that exist on its landings. As Stirling Haig has remarked, the mirror appears throughout the novel as an "insistent gauge of Duroy's rise"[100] and a symbol of "the codes of the artificial"[101] that facilitate his ascent. Attending to Maupassant's depiction of staircase mirrors is useful because they describe the nature of the modern urban spaces in which they are located.[102]

For Foucault, a mirror is a heterotopia in that it both represents and inverts the real spaces around it, including the space in which it is situated. He notes that a mirror "makes *this place that I occupy at the moment when I look at myself in the glass* at once absolutely real, connected with all the space that surrounds it, and absolutely unreal, since in order to be perceived it has to pass through this virtual point which is over there" (emphasis added).[103] In *Bel-Ami*, the staircase, the place that Duroy occupies at the moment that he looks at himself, is both real – a physical location with steps and banisters – and unreal, since a virtual example of itself also exists in its own reflection. Foucault's meditation suggests a reading of Maupassant's text whereby the staircase, like other spaces of Haussmannian modernity, are as virtual as they are real. That is, despite their intended symbolisms – among them, Second Empire permanence, power, and monumentality – what is built into these constructions is their own contestation, the possible inverse of these very meanings. It is this tension between the virtual and the real nature of modernity's urban spaces that Maupassant, like other early Third Republic writers reacting to instabilities including Haussmannization, war, and the Commune, addressed in their fiction.[104] As we will see, though, Duroy's reception of the virtual character of the staircase and, by extension, a city filled with similar spaces, is largely positive. In this way, it differs radically from the far more critical stance of Maupassant himself.

Through the mirror's reflection, Foucault writes, "I discover my absence from the place where I am since I see myself over there."[105] By way of this reasoning, one might say that what Duroy discovers in the mirror is not his presence but his absence on the staircase, the replacement of his *être* (ridiculous and poorly clad in a rented suit) with his *paraître* ("a man about town whom at first glance he had thought extremely smart and distinguished-looking"[106] ["un homme du monde, qu'il avait trouvé fort bien, fort chic"[107]]. What is striking about this moment of realization is that for Duroy, the substitution of his appearance for himself is a moment of extreme happiness: "he was overjoyed as he realized how much better he looked than he could possibly have believed"[108] ["un élan de joie le fit tressaillir tant il se jugea mieux qu'il n'aurait cru"[109]]. Duroy's elated reaction to his virtual situation in modern space contrasts with Foucault's declaration that "the anxiety of our era has to do fundamentally with space."[110] Far from producing anxiety, the awareness that Duroy is what his clothes make him to be, that the spaces of modern urban life facilitate the surrender of his self to his virtual self, is joyous news. His delight compounds as he then races up to the second landing where he encounters his reflection in another mirror and is filled with "an inordinate self-confidence"[111] ["une confiance immodérée en lui-même"[112]] that "looking as he did, surely he would succeed"[113] ["il réussirait avec cette figure-là"[114]]. Crossing before the second mirror, "he slowed down to watch himself as he went by. It seemed to him that he looked really elegant"[115] ["il ralentit sa marche pour se regarder passer. Sa tournure lui parut vraiment élégante"[116]]. This sartorial detail, that Duroy pauses to admire not himself but the effect of his clothing, is significant, for the virtual – the elegance of his outfit – again takes the place of the real, or the dishevelled "defectiveness" of cheaply rented eveningwear. Maupassant's description of Duroy's ascent up the staircase presages the character's eventual rise to power, which will occur in part by way of his seductive good looks. Yet, it does more, for it calls attention as well to the staircase of the bourgeois apartment building as a dislocation where appearances supersede all else, just as they do on analogous staircases of public spectacle such as Garnier's Opéra.

Like Foucault, Maupassant does not share Duroy's joy at the prospect of an urban milieu centred on appearances. On the contrary, the novelist counterbalances Duroy's ascension with the character's moral decline in order to denounce the fall of the protagonist and Third Republic society alike. Duroy's decline manifests itself in several ways, including his preoccupation throughout the text with his own death and his descent into immoral behaviour for personal gain. Numerous passages in which Duroy gazes down on ominous images from vertiginous heights underscore this. For example, Duroy's fifth-floor apartment on the rue Boursault is among the most elevated locations described in the novel. However, rather than according Duroy a horizontal panoramic view of scenic Paris, Maupassant emphasizes the vertical drop from Duroy's window which overlooks "a sort of deep abyss, the immense cutting of the railway" (translation modified)[117] ["un abîme profond, sur l'immense tranchée du chemin de fer"[118]]. As in Caillebotte's paintings, Duroy's point of view derives from the extreme height of his apartment building. What he sees out of his window, however, are not Caillebotte's boulevards, buildings, and high treetops but rather profound obscurity: the "black pit"[119] ["trou sombre"[120]] of the tunnel into which trains disappear.[121] This dark hole of oblivion recurs with some frequency in reference to Duroy's visions of his own demise. For instance, when Duroy is languishing in Jacques Rival's gloomy cellar and distressed by the possibility of dying in an impending duel, he pictures the shadowy hollow of a basement as "the grave"[122] ["un tombeau"[123]]; later, in his apartment the night before the gunfight, he imagines the pistol pointing at him, zeroing in on "the little dark aperture of the barrel which was about to discharge a bullet"[124] ["ce petit trou noir et profond du canon dont allait sortir une balle"[125]]. Paradoxically, it is from the highest location in the text – his fifth-floor apartment – that Duroy reflects with terror on the lowest condition imaginable, which is his own death. The higher the rise, Maupassant may have been warning, the greater the potential fall.

Duroy's anguished pessimism in these moments of dread is replaced in the end by his sentiment of invincibility, which comes to fruition in the final paragraph of the novel on the staircase of the Madeleine church. The rapid fall into darkness that Duroy fears earlier in the text never materializes and is replaced instead by his deliberate and glorious descent of the grand church's exterior staircase: "Slowly he went down the steps between the two lines of spectators"[126] ["Il descendait avec lenteur les marches du haut perron, entre deux hais de spectateurs"[127]]. Maupassant's cynical use of this location is highly symbolic: intended as a self-tribute to Napoléon I and designed to resemble a Roman temple, the Madeleine church in the heart of Haussmann's Paris is one of the nineteenth century's greatest monuments to empire. The author makes much of the imperial undertones of Duroy's victorious march down the steps, noting that, like a conquering sovereign, the protagonist has now set his sights, literally and figuratively, on the Palais-Bourbon across the Seine, a seat of France's central government and a former abode of the royal Bourbon dynasty. At the same time, Maupassant underscores the visual pomp of this staircase moment, drawing parallels between the Garnier *grand escalier* and the Madeleine church stairs where a crowd of aptly named "spectators" has amassed to witness Duroy's post-wedding processional in all its glamour. Backed by a host of fashionable silk-clad invitees and a wedding party attired in attractive pink, Duroy is the very picture of sartorial elegance, as summarized by the narrator, who notes, "he looked very smart in his morning coat"[128] ["il portait bien son habit"[129]]. Tellingly, fashion hints at the dark truth beneath Duroy's handsome exterior, for his one accessory, a newly acquired ribbon marking his (ironic) induction into the Legion of Honor, is ominously red "like a spot of blood"[130] ["comme une goutte de sang"[131]]. Nonetheless, the promise that Duroy's well-heeled appearance will lead him to triumph, a lesson learned on the Forestiers' staircase, reaches its fulfilment on the monumental stairs of the Madeleine church in a passage that symbolizes the replacement of an old monarchist empire with the new regime of bourgeois arrivism that Duroy represents.

The Madeleine stairs and the Forestiers' staircase close and open the novel, suggesting the importance of this dislocation to the architecture of the text more generally. One final example proves significant both to this discussion of *Bel-Ami* and to this chapter's concluding analysis of Daudet's *Sapho*. This is the working-class staircase in Duroy's apartment building that carries him up to his fifth-floor plunging view. Let us return to the novel's opening. After enjoying his initial success at the Forestiers' party and setting into motion his plan to ascend to their status, Duroy makes his way home where the shabbiness of his apartment building contrasts with the elegance of the space from which he is just returning. As he trudges up to his flat, Duroy's distaste for his current living conditions projects onto the malodorous, soiled stairwell on the rue Boursault where he lives:

> as he went upstairs … the dirty steps littered with pieces of paper, cigarette-ends and kitchen garbage, he was seized by a feeling of disgust and nausea and a desire to move out of there as quickly as possible, to go and live like the rich in clean homes with carpets on the floor.[132]

> [il éprouva, en montant l'escalier … les marches sales où traînaient des bouts de papier, des bouts de cigarettes, des épluchures de cuisine une écoeurante sensation de dégoût, et une hâte de sortir de là, de loger comme les hommes riches, en des demeures propres, avec des tapis.[133]]

Clearly, not all staircases in the novel are the same. This is not a grand staircase of Parisian modern splendour but one that Duroy hopes will soon be his past. It is a space bereft of modernity's motion: there is no rapid sprint up the stairs by the energetic future journalist, nor the formal march of the wealthy empire builder into which he transforms. Instead, there are things that linger with no chance of movement, such as the "stale smell of filth and decaying walls"[134] ["odeur stagnante de crasse et de vieille muraille"[135]] that permeates it. It is a place without lights or mirrors, where appearances are irrelevant. And tellingly, it is a staircase without fashion, for although Duroy is still in his rented eveningwear, upon reaching his flat his eyes fall on the garments he normally wears, "his everyday clothes ... limp, empty, and worn, as squalid as the tattered clothes in the mortuary"[136] ["ses habits de tous les jours ... vides, fatigués, flasques, vilains comme des hardes de la Morgue"[137]]. These sad rags evoking emptiness and death are not the high-fashion clothes that he now knows he needs, and they disturb him because they remind him of his reality – his *être* – while what he craves is to be his appearance. The only way in which he can make this happen is to exist in spaces of *paraître*, where he can be the virtual man in the mirror. Maupassant expresses his biting critique of Third Republic hypocrisy, superficiality, and ostentation by suggesting that Haussmannian spaces, reflections of the society that produces them, will be Duroy's greatest ally in this ultimately successful endeavour. For, as Duroy finds, the city, like the Forestiers' staircase, will welcome him and alter him permanently into Bel-Ami, the handsomely dressed image he meets in the heterotopian mirror.

What this examination of the staircase in *Bel-Ami* reveals is the prominence of dislocated parts of the urban landscape in Maupassant's censure of the middle and upper classes. The major role that a minor but ubiquitous city space like the staircase plays in the author's famously unconcealed pessimism has been rather overlooked; drawing notice to it helps illuminate a spatial crossover in the literary production of other authors of his day, including Daudet, as we will presently see, as well as Rachilde, whose *Monsieur Vénus* appeared in 1884, the same year as *Bel-Ami*. Thus, we can posit a more generalized interest among writers of this period to explore spaces that define and trouble notions of the modern in ways that, for instance, boulevards and parks do not. Maupassant's virulent disapproval of most of the characters in his Parisian fictions is directed not only at them but at the locations that accommodate them and that both replicate and facilitate all that is duplicitous and shallow in humanity. His pessimism resonates with Foucault's offering that, in modernity, heterotopias are everywhere:

when the mirror gestures to the virtual nature of the space in which it hangs, it is also gesturing to the many other virtual spaces around it. In *Bel-Ami*, where appearance trumps all else, what is at stake (and lost) through the Haussmannian appropriation of urban space is a modernity wherein anything beyond the virtual can thrive.

To return to the works of Caillebotte, although it is important to avoid overly literal correspondences between them, connections can be teased out between the painter's 1880s vertical view canvases and *Bel-Ami*. In *L'Homme au balcon, boulevard Haussmann*, for instance, the smart figure in the top hat, one hand confidently set against his waist, could easily represent the future Duroy, elegantly surveying his boulevard empire, symbol of the larger modern city. Similarly, the contemporaneous *Un Balcon, Boulevard Haussman* might depict two Duroys, the stylish gentleman in the middle distance eagerly leaning over the rails to inspect the urban topography that he has conquered or will conquer, while the more shabbily dressed man in the foreground evokes the earlier Duroy, more hesitant before his sartorial transformation and lingering at the back of the balcony, but with his gaze still trained intently on the built landscape below.[138] The point to be gleaned is not that the works of Caillebotte and Maupassant intentionally illustrate one another, but that such visual and textual overlap implies a larger discourse on dislocated urban spaces that was shared by artists and writers of the day. If the staircase is more explicitly referenced by Maupassant while remaining "off" the canvases of Caillebotte, both narratives invite reflections on how – literally and figuratively – these men of power arrive "at the top" and what (dubious) implications their personal ascents project for modern society.

Sapphic Steps: Daudet's *Sapho*

In *Sapho*, Daudet takes up the themes of ascension and decline that we have been exploring above, framing this juxtaposition, like Maupassant, in the context of an interior apartment building staircase. Reminiscent of the stairwell that leads to Duroy's home, this is a multistorey flight of steps that ends at the top of the building, at protagonist Jean Gaussin's humble student quarters on the fifth floor. The staircase in *Sapho* incorporates similar elements from Rachilde's novels, in particular her notion of the theatre-house in *La Jongleuse*, which is anticipated in Daudet's treatment of a Parisian home used exclusively for performance. The titular character of *Sapho* is Fanny Legrand, courtesan and muse to

Paris's avant-garde artists. Daudet's novella chronicles the tempestuous love story between Fanny and Jean, a destructive affair marked by a pattern of cohabitation and rupture during which the two characters find they can live neither with nor without each other. Their years-long liaison has them dwelling together first in a modest Parisian studio and then in the countryside on the outskirts of Paris, where Jean ends up miserable residing with Fanny and her son from a previous affair with an incarcerated counterfeiter. Jean falls in love with Irène, the niece of a doctor, and decides to marry her, but is unable to sever ties with Fanny and breaks off his engagement. Fanny agrees to meet Jean in the southern port city of Marseilles and to follow him abroad to live in Peru. The text closes on the day of the ship's departure, with a letter from Fanny informing Jean that she has decided to leave him forever and remain in Paris with the father of her child.

As Urbani notes, the treatment of space is a veritable preoccupation in Daudet's novel.[139] As in *Bel-Ami*, *Sapho* takes the reader to multiple locales both in the provinces and within the city limits. Passages set in Paris highlight a variety of locations, from the mansions of the wealthy to the opulent homes of kept courtesans to lower-class apartments and public streets. The opening chapter, which ends with a scene on the stairs, demonstrates Daudet's self-conscious mapping of three distinct milieus. Presaging the first chapter of *La Jongleuse*, *Sapho* begins at an evening fête, moves next to the street and a brief carriage ride, and ends at a residence where the first intimate encounter between the protagonists takes place.

Like Rachilde, Daudet establishes early on the importance of the metaphor of theatricality to the overall text. Jean and Fanny meet at a masked ball where both are in costume, Fanny dressed as an Egyptian peasant – Daudet's version of nineteenth-century seductive orientalist fantasy – and Jean as an alpine fife player, an allusion to his simple provincial roots. The masquerade party is thrown by the wealthy engineer Déchelette, who spends two months of the year in Paris transforming his atelier into a celebration of sensorial pleasures for a diverse crowd from high society, the art world, and the demi-monde. Here Rachilde's metaphor of Eliante's home as a theatre is made literal, for the sole purpose of Déchelette's former residential space is to accommodate these lavish twenty-four-hour revelries. Using vocabulary of the stage, Daudet describes Déchelette's arrival in the capital every summer as the rising of "a theater curtain" ["un rideau de théâtre"][140] that heralds the start of a season of festivities. The popularity of Déchelette's soirées signals a new vogue of urbanites opting to remain in Paris during the hot and humid summer months, rather than following the tradition of retiring to historically fashionable vacation sites like the seaside. The space in which Jean and Fanny meet, like Garnier's Opéra, is thus a location of extreme theatricality that also represents the most modern of social trends.

The first nine lines of the text are spoken as though words in a play, a dialogue between Fanny and Jean that sets the novella's theatrical tone. The drama then unfolds against a backdrop that Daudet terms a "spectacle,"[141] which he encapsulates in an extravagant, paragraph-long sentence:

The studio – the hall rather, for little work was ever done there – extended to the roof, making one enormous room, and its light and airy summer draperies, its shades of fine straw or gauze, its lacquered screens, its multi-colored glassware, and the cluster of yellow roses which embellished the opening of a high Renaissance fireplace, were illuminated by the variegated, bizarre reflections of innumerable Chinese, Persian, Moorish, and Japanese lanterns, some in perforated iron carved like the door of a mosque, others in colored paper shaped like different fruits, others like open fans, flowers, birds, and serpents; and flashes of electricity, of a bluish tinge, would suddenly pale all those thousands of lights, and cast a frosty gleam, like a ray of moonlight, on the faces and bare shoulders, on all the phantasmagoria of dresses, feathers, spangles, and ribbons, jostling one another in the ballroom, and sitting in tiers on the Dutch staircase, with its massive rail leading to the galleries on the first floor, which were overtopped by the long necks of the double basses, and the frenzied flourishes of the conductor's baton.[142]

[L'atelier, le hall plutôt, car on n'y travaillait guère, développé dans toute la hauteur de l'hôtel et n'en faisant qu'une pièce immense, recevait sur ses tentures claires, légères, estivales, ses stores de paille fine ou de gaze, ses paravents de laque, ses verreries multicolores, et sur le buisson de roses jaunes garnissant le foyer d'une haute cheminée Renaissance, l'éclairage varié et bizarre d'innombrables lanternes chinoises, persanes, mauresques, japonaises, les unes en fer ajouré, découpées d'ogives comme une porte de mosquée, d'autres en papier de couleur pareilles à des fruits, d'autres déployées en éventail, ayant des formes de fleurs, d'ibis, de serpents; et tout à coup de grands jets électriques, rapides et bleuâtres, faisaient pâlir ces mille lumières et givraient d'un clair de lune les visages et les épaules nues, toute la fantasmagorie d'étoffes, de plumes, de paillons, de rubans qui se froissaient dans le bal, s'étageaient sur l'escalier hollandais à large rampe menant aux galeries du premier que dépassaient les manches des contre-basses et la mesure frénétique d'un bâton de chef d'orchestre.[143]]

Daudet's kaleidoscopic passage is a cipher for late-nineteenth-century modernity itself, replete with fashion accessories, the abrupt shock of electric lights, exoticized furnishings and a staircase on which all meet in a multisensorial "phantasmagoria" of display. Urbani's description of Jean's integration into the space recalls the ocular mechanisms at work on Garnier's grand escalier where fashionable Paris went to see and be seen: "The space is a stage on which the young student sees, watches, and is observed" ["Cet espace est une scène où le jeune étudiant voit, regarde et où il est observé"].[144] For Urbani, theatricality in *Sapho* is linked to insincerity; thus, Daudet's passage underscores the fickle unreliability of the society in which Jean finds himself: "The assorted and strange lights reflect off the exotic décor and give it a magical appearance. But they are artificial, like the place, the party and the guests, fleeting and inconsistent, paled by the electric beams" ["Les lumières variés et étranges se reflètent sur le décor exotique et lui donnent un aspect féerique. Mais elles sont artificielles, comme le sont le lieu, la fête et les invités, évanescents et inconsistants, pâlis par les jets électriques"].[145] Society's artificiality, metaphorized in the frosted, non-natural pallour cast on human skin by electric beams, informs the space itself. Yet, Daudet's attitude towards this "fleeting and inconsistent" milieu is contradictory since, on the one hand, like Maupassant, he is critical of a city that the courtesan Fanny emblematizes, a city driven primarily by whim and the desire for immediate pleasures. On the other hand, as the paragraph above attests, he seems equally enthralled by these very same elements of modern urban life, which he celebrates, perhaps in spite of himself, in passages of stunning narrative "phantasmagoria."

Fashion and the Senses

This fantasy world is, in part, one of visual spectacle, but sight is not the only sense at work. Visual stimulation joins other forms of sensory perception, especially sound and touch. The evening is filled with noise. There is deafening laughter, frenetic dance music, calls of streetwalkers, and simulations of the shrill cries of "girls of the Orient"[146] ["filles d'Orient"[147]] to add exotic flavour. Bodies interact through physical contact: Jean is jostled on the crowded dance floor and couples caress each other as the night fades to morning. Daudet links these sensations to garments, expressing through clothing the multisensory impressions of this night of fashionable debauchery. Various costume accessories are particularly suggestive of touch, sound, and smell: a houndsman's whip evokes the snap and scent of a leather strap; steel knives plunged into a geisha girl's chignon imply the cutting of flesh; a Spanish bride's bouquet of flowers fills Jean's nose with the heady perfume of white jasmine.

Fanny's costume exemplifies Daudet's evocation of multiple sensations through fashion:

> From the long sheath of blue woolen stuff, in which her full figure swayed with an undulating motion, emerged two round and shapely arms bare to the shoulder; and her little hands laden with rings, her wide-open gray eyes increased in apparent size by the curious iron ornaments hanging from her forehead, formed a harmonious whole.[148]

> [Du long fourreau de lainage bleu où sa taille pleine ondulait, sortaient deux bras, ronds et fins, nus jusqu'à l'épaule; et ses petites mains chargées de bagues, ses yeux gris larges ouverts et grandis par les bizarres ornements de fer lui tombant du front, composaient un ensemble harmonieux.[149]]

Fanny's Egyptian outfit is a collection of textiles and ornaments that marry the suppleness of softly waving fabric with the hardness of metal jewelry.[150] Her headdress, made of "curious iron ornaments," appeals especially to Jean's various senses. Visually, it harmonizes with the rest of her outfit and has the optical effect of amplifying her wide-open eyes. Jean also experiences the accessory aurally when Fanny turns abruptly and he is met "with the clicking sound of her barbaric jewels" ["avec le cliquetis de sa parure barbare"].[151] Finally, as we will see, when they move later to Jean's staircase, sight and sound give way to a haptic connection that occurs through the intermediary of Fanny's costume.

Leaving behind the sensory overload of Déchelette's masked ball, the couple arrives in the early morning greyness at the young man's apartment building where Jean, with naive gallantry, offers to carry Fanny up the four flights of stairs to his modest lodging. En route to the first floor he is pleased by the feel of her weight in his arms, but on the second flight she grows heavy and her headdress begins to dig into his skin: "Her iron pendants, which at first caressed him with a pleasant tickling sensation, sank slowly and cruelly into his flesh" (translation modified)[152] ["Le fer de ses pendeloques, qui d'abord le caressait d'un chatouillement, entrait peu à peu et cruellement dans sa chair"[153]]. Jean staggers, breathless, up the next two floors, the staircase appearing to grow larger and to turn "in an interminable spiral"[154] ["une interminable spirale"[155]]. By now an unbearable burden that Jean can barely hold, Fanny is described as a dreadful, dehumanized, choking encumbrance: "It was no longer a woman that he was carrying, but something heavy, ghastly, which suffocated him, and which he was momentarily tempted to drop, to throw down angrily at the risk of crushing her brutally"[156] ["Ce n'était plus une femme qu'il portait, mais quelque chose de lourd, d'horrible, qui l'étouffait, et qu'à tout moment il était tenté de lâcher, de jeter avec colère, au risque d'un écrasement brutal"[157]].

Despite the violence of this last image, Daudet recounts the scene with some humour: Jean is likened to a piano mover (the slight Fanny in the absurd role of a piano), and when they reach their destination Fanny's regretful sigh "Already ..." (translation modified)[158] ["Déjà ..."[159]] is countered comically by Jean's relieved thought to himself: "At last!"[160] ["Enfin!"[161]]. Nonetheless, the chapter's ironic last line makes explicit the sobering symbolism of the couple's trip up the stairs: "The ascent of those stairs in the melancholy grayness of the morning was an epitome of their whole history"[162] ["Toute leur histoire, cette montée d'escalier dans la grise tristesse du matin"[163]]. Like Maupassant describing Duroy's staircase ascent in *Bel-Ami*, Daudet calls up the dichotomy of moving up while sinking downward.[164] The rise to heights of pleasure that the couple will experience in Jean's apartment is marked by the sensation of a terrible heavy load that Jean cannot bear and that he wishes already to hurl down. However, Jean's weighted-down ascension is more tactile than Duroy's visual encounter of himself in the landing mirrors. Daudet's depiction of costume is what makes this evident, for it is through Fanny's accessory that her "cruelty" to Jean is foreshadowed in palpable terms. The iron pendants that imbed progressively into the young man's skin, and his powerlessness to remove them, foreshadow a union based on Jean's suffering at the hands of a woman that Daudet, in the style of many writers of his day, renders as a seductive but dangerous femme fatale. The surface appearances of clothing in *Bel-Ami* manifest in *Sapho* as garments that dig spitefully below the surface, cutting irreparably into Jean's body just as Fanny will cut mercilessly into his life.

Daudet's treatment of Fanny's headdress in the staircase represents urban space somewhat differently from the elegant surface treatments of Caillebotte and Maupassant. For Daudet, spaces of modernity seem characterized by sensory overload, initially akin to the spectacular fashions worn in them and personified by the captivating courtesan Fanny. They are a "phantasmagoria of dresses, feathers, spangles, and ribbons, jostling one another in the ballroom," spaces that entrance newcomers through the various senses. Yet, the heady spectacle of Déchelette's home-turned-debauchery hall does not predict the "whole story" of Fanny and Jean. Rather, that task is reserved for the staircase, where the fantasy of the senses becomes instead an endless, weighty, cutting reality for Jean, victim of woman, modernity, and urban space alike.

The open ending of *Sapho* further sets the novella slightly apart from the other texts examined here. Eliante's suicide at the conclusion of *La Jongleuse* sounds a death-knell on Raoule de Vénérande's attempts in *Monsieur Vénus* to live in a patriarchal society that rejects her non-normative desires, while Duroy's triumph over Paris in *Bel-Ami* expresses Maupassant's dark pessimism about urban space's fostering of hypocrisy and greed. In contrast, *Sapho* concludes with Jean situated in a space of possibility: a boat at the port city of Marseilles can lead him to new beginnings, both sentimentally and geographically, should he carry through with his plans to become vice consul in Arica.[165] It is noteworthy that Jean's destination is Peru,[166] for by choosing a South American location relatively unencumbered by France's rising colonial strife, Daudet creates what might be understood as a new frontier of freedom and possibility for Jean. The city name "Arica," by its very similarities to the word "Afrique," might have been an intentional signal that Jean is going to a place that is *not* Africa.[167] One hesitates to call this ending optimistic, for Jean may not board the awaiting ocean liner at all, opting instead to return to his spiral of self-destruction in Paris with Fanny. This outcome seems in some ways probable, given that the unending cycle of despair is the "whole story" of the couple, as we learn in Jean's belaboured stagger up the stairs. Moreover, reading Daudet's choice of Arica through the contemporary lens of postcolonialist critique, Jean's embarkment to Peru, a country that in the early 1880s was weathering a territorial war with Bolivia and Chile, seems consistent with France's empire-building impetus to insinuate itself in politically destabilized overseas territories that were rich with natural resources and ripe for exploiting.

If the ending of *Sapho* thus testifies to differences among the works of Maupassant, Rachilde, and Daudet, one notable similarity remains, and that is their universal use of the staircase dislocation to express distrust at what modern urban space had become through the manipulations of Haussmannization. This distrust is distinct from Baudelaire's nostalgic mourning over the lost city and his melancholic fascination with urban changes as they were coming to fruition in the Second Empire. Yet, they are also related through the metaphor of fashion, in whose dialectic of ephemerality and permanence Baudelaire envisioned modernity itself.

Conclusion

In his analysis of the rituals of barricade building, Mark Traugott writes:

> Such ceremonial activities served to separate the state of everyday political existence, with its presumption of stasis or continuity, which most of us take to be "normal," from the insurrectionary situation, which, even in the context of nineteenth-century Paris, remained exceptional and was perceived to hold both the potential for sudden violence and the promise of meaningful change. In other words, the construction of barricades was an act that *invited people to question the presumption of normalcy* (emphasis added).[168]

Barricades, I hope to have shown earlier, are not as far removed from the grand staircases of Haussmannization as they might at first seem. If the building of barricades that ushered in the Third Republic "invited people to question the presumption of normalcy" by way of the "abnormal" conditions that they created, it may be that the frequency of the staircase theme in literature of the period stands for a shared question: what would "normal" life be in Third Republic modernity? For Zola, the question finds its answer on the staircase of the Bonheur, symbol for "modern activity" that is erected on the bones of Mouret's first wife, Mme Hédouin, herself a symbol of a respectable but outdated mode of commodity culture. Zola's modernity, unable to escape its founding on the blood of the Commune, has no recourse but to build constantly upon itself. Rather than stone and rubble, it finds a new debris – lace, gloves, fans, lingerie – fashions that seem ever-growing, magnified by endless description and piled in mountains upon the ruin under the stairs. For Rachilde, the staircase points first to the possibility of a gendered paradigm shift that later gives way to a more pessimistic view that new urban spaces have simply reproduced former conditions relegating women to multi-attired performances rather than agents of their own identities. In the texts of Maupassant and Daudet, modern city life is a virtual surface of fashionable appearances or a costumed phantasmagoria; one can either conquer it in the manner of Duroy or leave it behind like Jean might.

As we have seen, authors of the early Third Republic took up Baudelaire's metaphor of fashion as a code for modernity, but they had a different set of concerns from the poet, who died in 1867 without ever witnessing the Commune or the exponential rise of commodity infrastructures that Zola, in particular, sought to document. The writers examined here were not immune to the allures of wealth, spectacularity, and monumentality that Paris had come to represent in France and abroad; indeed, they were among the most adept at reproducing this very image of the fashionable city. At the same time, their treatment of modern life's dislocations exposed uneasy truths about the razed areas upon which grand public monuments had been built. As the recurrence of staircases in their works suggest, the future outcomes for "normal life" in the city that authors predicted were far less clear than Haussmannization had sought to project.

PART TWO

The Antechamber

3 Waiting for Change: Zola's *Au Bonheur des Dames* and *Nana*

Studies of Paris during the Third Republic typically view the period through the lens of various forms of dynamic change, transformation, growth, and motion.[1] Rather in contrast, then, this chapter on the antechamber dislocation begins by evoking the notion of an opposite force: waiting. Waiting is, perhaps, not the intended subject matter of Edgar Degas's 1873 painting *L'Absinthe*, nor does the image depict a proper antechamber, as an early version of the title, *Dans un café*, or "*In a café*," would assert. On the other hand, Degas's melancholy representation of two urban dwellers seated side-by-side on a café bench is not, either, an image of the act of imbibing the painting's titular absinthe, since the two people are not touching the glasses on the table. Rather, Degas's painting can be read as a portrait of waiting, of two immobile figures caught between sips of greenish liquid or puffs on a pipe. Degas's depiction of inactivity in the post-Haussmannian city, communicated by what T.J. Clark calls the "almost catatonic quality of the sitters and their expressions,"[2] is made poignant by the viewer's realization that there may be no purpose behind such stagnation. Perhaps the two figures wait for someone or something but, as is more likely, they are in a state of late-nineteenth-century ennui that derives from waiting for nothing (see figure 3.1). Seen in this light, Degas's café represents a waiting room in the context of everyday life, a space in which all action is suspended and sensations dulled by alcohol or the fog of world-weariness. It is a visual depiction of spleen, the paralyzing mood of the century that Baudelaire and other writers from the previous decades so frequently articulated.

This chapter's interest in the stasis of modernity is inspired, in part, by recent work on paralysis as a recurring motif in French writings that

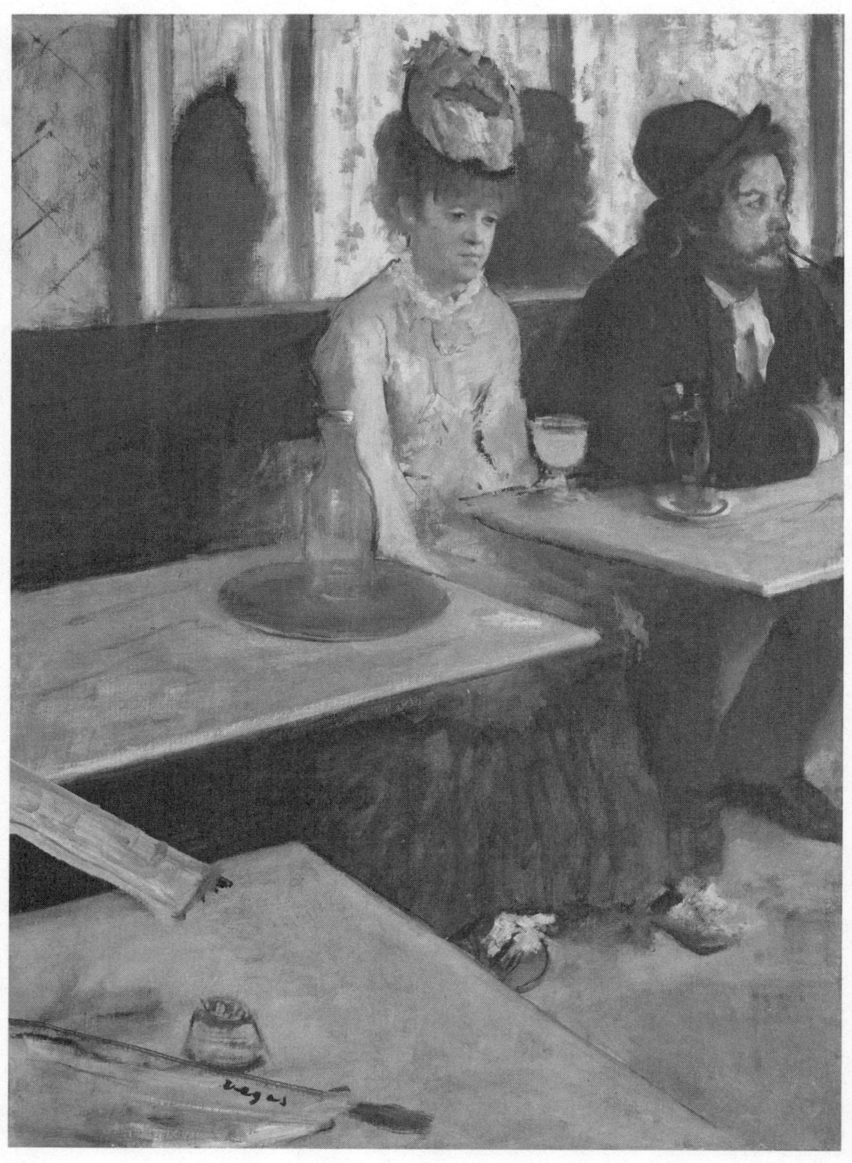

3.1 Edgar Degas. *Dans un café*, also called *L'Absinthe*, 1873. Musée d'Orsay, Paris. Reproduced by permission of the Bridgeman Art Library.

prefigure postmodernity. In *Paralyses: Literature, Travel, and Ethnography in French Modernity* (2011), John Culbert dates early narratives of fixity, impasse, and frustration to mid-nineteenth-century texts, particularly those by Baudelaire, Gautier, and Fromentin. Paralysis, which Culbert defines as the negation of travel or motion,[3] expresses a moment of crisis in the period arising from "anxieties about spatiotemporal displacements within the lived present of the modern metropole."[4] My examination of the urban antechamber resonates with this analysis, particularly with the argument that paralyses are aporetic and thus undermine the very impasses upon which they are structured. In a similar spirit, Part II will consider the ways in which antechambers in literature are informed, on the one hand, by the inertia of waiting and, on the other, by animation and change, where fashion is the nexus of this tension.

For example, to return to Degas's painting, the trancelike lethargy of both people and space is complicated by fashion, which expresses a disparity between the scene's inertia and its subtle sense of change. For, in fact, dynamism and movement *are* to be found in *L'Absinthe*, specifically in Degas's depictions of sartorial adornment.[5] Splashes of white pigment representing the woman's shoe ribbons, ruffled collar and earring, and her neighbour's shirt and cuff trigger eye motion for the viewer, whose gaze bounces across the canvas among these small patches of white. These glints of brightness, shimmering against the sallow greys, greens, and yellows of Degas's café, also represent temporal transformation, demonstrating the Impressionists' ambition to capture the passing of time in a single image. The painter's quick brushstrokes, which produce the frothy texture of the woman's skirt flounces and the decorative bows on her shirt, echo the ephemeral treatment of tulle fabric in Degas's scenes of ballerinas, lending the sense of a dancer's weightlessness and lyrical motion to the work. The woman's spectacularly upright hat works against the defeated slump of her shoulders, amplifying her lived presence in space. In particular, the white cloth crowning her hat sweeps into a plump oval that hints at a sense of movement and seems to counteract, in part, her otherwise deflated, static body.[6]

Through its treatment of fashion and space, Degas's painting thus summarizes these concomitant forces of stagnation and transformation, nuancing the stereotypical image of Third Republic Paris as a time and space in perpetual motion. As we will see, fixity and change also inform the depictions of antechambers in literary works of the period. This dialectic of waiting and changing in late-century writings is important to distinguish from Baudelaire's earlier descriptions of both modernity and fashion as the paradox of the eternal and the ephemeral. The Third Republic iteration of Baudelaire's famous dictum may indeed derive, to a degree, from the conception of modern urban living that the poet of *Les Fleurs du mal* often expressed through metaphors of garments and accessories. However, for the next generation of city writers, concerns had shifted from viewing the "eternal" (or "Beauty" as Baudelaire also termed it) as a nostalgic ideal, as something irrecoverable that needed to be inscribed in literary memory. Likewise, "transitoriness" was no longer an "evil" (*mal*) of an urban environment in which only the poet could still discern the exquisite "flowers" (*fleurs*) of modern experience. Unlike texts from this previous generation, the works by Baudelaire's successors studied here codify delays and transformations as ever-present conditions of the present and future urban landscape. For these authors, primarily prose writers associated with naturalism and decadence who expanded on Baudelaire's theories linking *mode* with *modernité*, change, mobility, and motion were not necessarily associated with the loss of a treasured way of life, that which was "temporary" and vanishing to Baudelaire. Instead, later writers viewed the notion of change in terms of the possibility of paradigm shifts, especially in areas of class, gender, and national identity. At the same time, the suspensions, hesitations, and extended periods of waiting also inherent to their brand of modernity suggest that doubts existed whether such shifts could – or should – truly occur.

The fact that authors of this era evoked delay and transformation when writing about antechambers is logical in light of the two primary functions of this space. The *Trésor de la langue française* clarifies these two purposes, defining antechambers both as waiting rooms and as rooms to be passed through en route to another part of a building.[7] Fashion adds a layer of complexity to the antechamber's functionality, for this was also the room intended for the removal, donning, or temporary storage of various forms of outerwear, such as coats, or accessories meant for use out of doors, such as hats, parasols, and canes. In fiction, these seemingly inconsequential moments of sartorial transformation or accumulation take on discursive importance, charged as they often are with broader meanings about lived experience in the city. We will see that literary texts feature passages in which antechambers are used against or beyond their intended functions, these "improper" uses of the space exposing larger disturbances to systems of social regulation, including class hierarchy and bourgeois sexual propriety. In paintings of the period, Hollis Clayson argues, the threshold space was depicted as a location of permeability, one that was "literally 'on edge' – both unclear and a site of inherent tension because of its composite identity."[8] Antechambers in literature amplify destabilizations to identity, which were simultaneously manifesting themselves in the realm of fashion.

An example from Rachilde's *Monsieur Vénus* illustrates this last point. Using an antechamber, Rachilde points out that social identities, which had once relied upon the signals imparted by clothing, were experiencing considerable slippage. In this passage, Marie Silvert, Jacques's prostitute sister, arrives at the entryway vestibule of Raoule's mansion splattered in mud from the street where she has been walking and asks to see the mistress of the house. When she is received informally by the household staff due to her filthy appearance, Marie haughtily refuses to take a seat in the vestibule, declaring, "I don't hang about in antechambers"[9] ["Je ne pose pas dans l'antichambre, moi"[10]]. Because she will not be seated in preparation for a possible long wait in the entry room like a service person, Raoule's page then mistakenly believes that she must be "someone of influence"[11] ["quelqu'un d'influent"[12]]. Reasoning through his "error," the servant reflects to himself, "under the Republic, clothes mean less and less all the time"[13] ["les costumes perdent de plus en plus leur signification sous la république"[14]]. In point of fact, the page is *not* at fault in judging Marie as a member of the lower street-walking classes. However, he realizes that it is possible to make an initial mistake about her station because outfits "mean less and less all the time." Garments, which historically functioned as visual indicators of a person's place in society, were no longer to be trusted during the Third Republic as fixed signs of social standing. The ambiguity inherent to antechambers – spaces not limited to one defined rank of society – along with the unreliability of garments as signs of class, allow Rachilde to stage Marie's subversion of identity to the prostitute's advantage.

If, as Rachilde here demonstrates, an antechamber is a space of uncertainty, what are its definable characteristics? Turning again to the *Trésor*, one finds that the French term *antichambre* derives from the Latin root "ante," meaning "prior," and "chamber," an enclosed room.[15] Etymology thus shows that an antechamber is implicitly transitional, that it is encountered "before" another room and is not an ultimate destination, since there will be an "after" space that implies transference from one location to the next. This implication of movement in the word's prefix contrasts with the notion of a "chamber," which describes a space in an edifice where one is meant, relatively, to linger and which implies an act that typically took place in antechambers: waiting. Synonyms for antechambers include "vestibule" and "entrance" (*entrée*), although, as we will see, antechambers are not always located at a building's point of arrival. In this section, for example, we will examine theatre foyers, interior dressing rooms, and other types of small, enclosed salons in which waiting and transition are implied and fashion plays an important role in catalyzing frictions therein.

One focus here will be the way in which symbolic meanings of antechambers are informed by notions of class that are brought to the fore in contexts related to garments. As with the term "wait" in English, one definition of the French word *antichambre* refers to the notion of servitude, designating a "waiting room at the entrance of a private mansion where servants charged to receive and introduce visitors stand ready" ["Pièce d'attente à l'entrée d'un hôtel particulier où se tiennent les domestiques chargés de recevoir et d'introduire les visiteurs"].[16] Tellingly, according to another definition, the term *antichambre* could also mean "a group of servants in a house" ["ensemble de domestiques d'une maison"],[17] the term operating as a metonymy for the wait staff itself. Indeed, servants were often called to antechambers to assist their employers with the final touches of dressing, or to tend to the outer garments and accessories of arriving and departing visitors. Thus, the location was a space where the working class and activities related to clothing collided. In *Au Bonheur des Dames*, Zola plays with these intersections of class, space, and fashion to call attention to broader instabilities arising as a result of changing social dynamics. As we will see, Zola uses the classed connotations of the antechamber to illustrate a climax in the novel's social and sentimental tensions, deliberately staging the scene during a key fashion moment: the fitting of an overcoat gone dramatically awry. We will read the important overcoat chapter through the larger lens of "liberal democracy," a social order that Zola seemed both reluctant and keen to advance in his novel, and one that will be explained in detail below.

A second emphasis in this section will be the antechamber as a space of desire, wherein the gratification of sexual pleasure is delayed, heightened, and facilitated. For this we will turn to Zola's *Nana* and examine the author's treatment of garments in the novel's antechambers, particularly in relation to Zola's expectations about the future of naturalism. In my reading, *Nana* is not (only) a reaction to the fall of the Second Empire, as it has often been understood, but is also an articulation of

Zola's hopes about how approaches to writing would develop in the following years of the Third Republic. Chapter 4 begins with an analysis of the waiting room and suspensions of time in Maupassant's "La Parure," a short story in which the author deploys the titular necklace as a tool of revenge on bourgeois vanity. We will then return to Maupassant's *Bel-Ami*, this time not to the male protagonist but to the outfits worn by Duroy's lover Clotilde de Marelle. This analysis centres on a metaphorical antechamber and the author's critique of colonialism and of the growing presence of overseas imperialism infecting life in the French capital.

"Let Her Wait!": Delaying Denise

In *Au Bonheur des Dames*, Zola dramatizes the antechamber's dual purpose as waiting room and changing room in a chapter located not in the department store but rather in Henriette Desforges's luxurious apartment on the rue de Rivoli. This climactic passage, which features two important antechambers, thus takes place well outside the department store walls but, as is characteristic of dislocations, the grand space of modernity that the Bonheur epitomizes continues to infiltrate the smaller problematic versions in Mme Desforges's home. The two waiting rooms studied here reproduce some of the hierarchies present in the department store even as they challenge them in ways that would have been impossible in the Bonheur. Yet the store is not entirely absent, for the garment that serves as a catalyst for the scene's disruptions to class and gender originates there. In this episode, Mme Desforges arranges for Denise to come to her home under the pretense that an overcoat, purchased at the department store, is in need of tailoring. Suspecting rightly that Mouret is in love with Denise, and still desperate to rekindle his fading affections, Henriette orders the young woman to arrive during her weekly salon when Mouret and her circle of middle- and upper-class friends will converge. After being made to wait humbly in the entryway antechamber, where her working-class status is put on display before the curious stares of arriving guests, Denise is finally admitted to the apartment's dressing room to tailor the overcoat to Mme Desforges's body. Hoping to expose their affair, the latter summons Mouret to her private dressing room. Here she forces the young woman to get on bended knee before her to pin the overcoat and demeans Denise's work while Mouret looks on, helplessly. Suddenly, and uncharacteristically, Denise retaliates for the abuse, insulting her tormentor in furious resistance. Flinging the coat and pins aside, the two women face each other, enraged.[18] Henriette, already mortified by Denise's affront, is further humiliated when Mouret comes to his employee's defence. The episode concludes with Mouret ushering the young heroine to the door and then returning to admit that he loves Denise to a despondent Mme Desforges.

On one level, the passage serves as a turning point in the novel's romantic intrigue in that Mouret announces his true feelings, paving the way for his eventual union with Denise. However, the focus here will be on how the dichotomy of waiting and changing allows Zola to comment on fluctuations in urban class hierarchies, and on the way in which modern space and fashion could both reinforce and threaten formerly rigid social stratifications. In the entry room, the first of the chapter's two antechambers, Mme Desforges obliges Denise to wait as a spiteful reminder of the existing social order that accords her, the wealthy mistress of the house, implicit superiority over a department store salesclerk.[19] Through the leitmotif of arriving guests, Zola reinforces the fact that Denise waits, both in the sense of service and delay. As visitors appear, each asks about the young woman standing in the antechamber, giving Mme Desforges opportunity to reiterate that Denise is in a state of stasis: "'That's a very charming young lady in the antechamber. Who is it?' 'Oh, no one,' Madame Desforges replied in a nasty voice. 'A shop girl who is waiting'"[20] ["Il y a une bien charmante jeune fille, dans l'antichambre … Qui est-ce? – Oh! personne, répondit Mme Desforges de sa voix mauvaise. Une demoiselle de magasin qui attend"[21]]. When Mme Marty encourages her hostess to tend to the overcoat, Mme Desforges's remark, "'Oh, any time. There's no hurry'"[22] ["– Oh! tout à l'heure, rien ne presse"[23]] further prolongs Denise's paralysis in the antechamber. The repetition of these inquiries at regular intervals in the opening pages of the chapter underscores the passing of time, reminding the reader of the long wait that Denise endures in the dark entryway.

Meanwhile, Denise's low rank in society is called up by Mme de Boves, whose innocent inquiry whether Denise is a new maid invites Henriette's snide reply, "'Isn't that right? All these shop girls look like chambermaids'"[24] ["N'est-ce pas? toutes ces filles de boutique ont l'air de femmes de chambre"[25]]. Zola underscores Denise's inferior status by merely referring to her rather than providing her perspective during this scene, treating the heroine narratively in the manner of the salon guests who quickly forget about her once they are settled in the next room. In particular, Zola prohibits her participation in the first third of the chapter, the section of the text in which discussions about developments in the modern city and the recent growth of the department store remain the privileged purview of the company in the salon. Through this narrative exclusion of Denise, Zola illustrates her marginalization from upper-class modernity more broadly.

Yet, Denise's introduction into the antechamber also heralds an unravelling of the very social inequity that Mme Desforges desperately wishes to preserve. This is first suggested in a dialogue between Henriette and a servant, who asks where Denise should be installed:

> "'Let her wait!'…
> "'Should I show her into Madame's dressing room?'
> "'No, no, leave her in the antechamber!'" (translation modified)[26]

> ["Qu'elle attende!
> – Faut-il la faire entrer dans le cabinet de madame?
> – Non, non, qu'elle reste dans l'antichambre!"[27]]

The imperative mode of the command that Denise "wait" (*attende*) highlights Mme Desforges's power to compel the young woman to do as she says, while the directive that she stay in the antechamber relegates Denise to a space associated with servitude. At the same time, Henriette's words are launched with the force of "the pain of her jealousy"[28] ["souffrance jalouse"[29]], thereby revealing her painful suspicion that Denise has already undermined her authority by possessing Mouret's love, which is an implicit challenge to the wealthy woman's social superiority (as well as a personal affront). In the exchange between Mme Desforges and her servant, the location specified is not arbitrary because the antechamber is a room intended to immobilize Denise in lower-class inferiority. What Henriette fails to recognize is that it is also a room anticipating change, one that sets the stage for a shift in the balance of power as symbolized by the levelling of class differences that takes place next in Mme Desforges's dressing room.

On Pins and Needles

The disturbances to traditional social standings subtly implied by Denise's wait in the entryway hall erupt dramatically in the subsequent antechamber of the chapter, the literal and figurative "changing room" in which the tailoring of the overcoat takes place. Attempting to sustain Denise in a state of social immobility, Mme Desforges demands a complete refitting of the garment, making the chore as lengthy and tedious as possible: we read that the pinning "took a long time: [Denise] had to go from one shoulder to the next"[30] ["dura longtemps: il lui fallait passer d'une épaule à l'autre"[31]]. However, conditions in the antechamber favour instabilities, as evinced by a second reversal that then occurs, this time to traditional gender roles. Remarkably, this upset to gendered hierarchies involves the most dominant, seemingly all-powerful masculine figure of the novel: Octave Mouret. Upon his arrival in the changing room, the typically virile Mouret is made to assume the sartorial tasks of a chambermaid, tasks by which he is both feminized and humbled. First he is called in to assist with the fitting; then he is sent to fetch extra pins, which he holds obediently.[32] To prolong the chore for Mouret and for Denise alike, Mme Desforges takes the pins slowly, one by one. Finally, after the two women fling the pins and the garment aside in rage, Mouret retrieves the castaway overcoat, folds it, and hands it to Denise, all the while ushering her respectfully to the door in the manner of a servant tending to the outerwear and departure of a social superior.

While it is true that at other points Mouret adopts feminized mannerisms, including a high flutelike voice and graceful gestures, he does so as a business strategy in order to charm his female clientele and arouse their desires to purchase goods at the Bonheur. Here, in contrast, in the destabilizing space of the second antechamber, Mouret's feminization is a disadvantage imposed upon him that relegates him to a submissive position and forces him to experience, if only temporarily, the compliance that patriarchy traditionally demands of women. The tailoring pins that Denise uses to alter the coat are symbolic objects in this disruption to Mouret's masculine authority. In her analysis of pins in late-nineteenth-century French fiction, Mary Donaldson-Evans notes that these sharp metal implements were typically associated with women because household activities such as sewing and embroidery were commonly their designated assignments.[33] Yet, even while pins evoked such chores that linked women to domestic confinement, in works of literature these pointed fasteners also became figurative weapons wielded by potentially dangerous women. Pins thus conjured up notions of feminine subversion, suggesting that male authors of the period harboured, as Donaldson-Evans offers, "a fear of a feminist revolt, a fear that with the apparently modest means at their disposal, women will literally 'stick it' to the male and thereby overthrow the power that has for so long kept them spinning and sewing by the hearth."[34] The pinning episode in Zola's novel exemplifies the types of narratives to which Donaldson-Evans refers. Mouret's helplessness before the two women in the second antechamber and his demotion from dynamic department store owner to paralysed pin holder suggests the author's underlying apprehension that Third Republic women were indeed presenting ever-increasing challenges to former conventions of male dominance.

The tailoring pins are also a testament to the importance of fashion to Zola's troubling of social roles in the charged atmosphere of the antechamber. Using these tools of fashion as sartorial metaphors, he implies that hierarchies assigned by birth and wealth had once been held strictly in place, not unlike fabric tightly secured by pins. Yet, like two pieces of cloth that come undone once the pins anchoring them are removed, such social configurations can unravel. Initially, the pins are also used to underscore Denise's inferiority through physical suffering, one plight of the working class. Distressed by Henriette's spiteful allusions to past intimacies with Mouret, Denise twice sticks pins into her own palm, her pricked flesh a corporeal manifestation of Mme Desforges's injurious performance of social supremacy. However, when the function of the pins switches from poking through fabric to pricking Denise's skin, social tensions reach their climax and tenuous class distinctions rupture, punctured like the young woman's pierced flesh. As the two women fling aside their respective sartorial objects, they deploy pins and overcoat no longer as instruments of fashion but instead as expressions of their fury:

> The pair of them, face to face and trembling, stared at one another. They were no longer lady and shop girl, merely women, as though made equal by their rivalry. One had violently torn off the coat and thrown it on a chair; while the other flung the last pins remaining in her hand on to the dressing-table without looking where they were going.[35]

> [Toutes deux, face à face, frémissantes, se contemplaient. Il n'y avait désormais ni dame, ni demoiselle de magasin. Elles n'était plus que femmes, comme égalées dans leur rivalité. L'une avait violemment retiré le manteau pour le jeter sur une chaise; tandis que l'autre lançait au hazard sur la toilette les quelques épingles qui lui restaient entre les doigts.[36]]

Zola's intention to showcase this fashion outburst as a climactic disruption to power dynamics between upper and lower classes is made transparent by his declaration that the two women are now "equal," " no longer lady and shop girl." Moreover, through impersonal references to "one" woman and "the other," Zola renders it difficult to discern which of the two characters throws the pins and which removes and then violently hurls the coat. Ambiguities expressed through fashion objects grammatically cement the indistinguishability between Denise and Henriette, underscoring the antechamber's momentary levelling of class distinctions.[37]

"And Still She Did Not Move": Waiting for Liberal Democracy

Beyond providing space for shifts in social hierarchies, Mme Desforges's antechambers can be connected to Zola's larger predictions for the future of consumer-based society, which are expressed through the dialectics of delay and transformation. This discussion relates to the conflicted outlook on capitalism that *Au Bonheur* communicates more broadly, and Denise's crucial role in helping Zola mitigate, perhaps only partially, his own misgivings about it. Zola's ambivalence about mass industrialization might be summarized as follows: although he is highly critical of Mouret's large-scale monopoly because of the brutal suffering that it causes to its workers and to traditional family-run enterprises, at the same time Zola marvels at the department store for its enthralling spectacularity, innovative drive, and progressive spirit. Zola makes his heroine benevolent, pure, and logical, and assigns her the task of arguing that Mouret's callous brand of capitalism is both inevitable and, in spite of its ruthlessness, a positive step in the development of modern society. The sympathetic Denise is thus central to Zola's absolution of the negative impacts of capitalism that his novel, paradoxically, also seeks to expose. This is because Zola's (not untroubled) viewpoint – that capitalism is an overall benefit to society – requires for its justification the selflessness that Denise personifies, an altruism that offsets the self-interestedness that implicitly drives Mouret and high capitalism alike.

The novels' closing union between Denise and Mouret thus has clear economic implications, but goes beyond them, for it relates, too, to Zola's projections for the future of the nation in sociopolitical terms. This future, as Peter Starr argues, is for Zola a "liberal democracy," or "a social order [that is] both democratic *and* capitalist" (original emphasis).[38] The antechamber episode calls particular attention to a quality that Denise possesses – one that has gone disregarded in other analyses of the novel – that is essential to the flourishing of liberal democracy that Zola envisions. This is her ability to wait. Denise's unflagging patience is cited throughout the novel,[39] but nowhere does she display it more than in Mme Desforges's foyer, where she demurs, unmoving, in the shadows:

> Every time the door opened, you could see a dark corner of the antechamber, lit only by its ground glass windows. There in the darkness a vague shape could be seen, *motionless* and *patient*. Denise was standing. There was a leather-covered bench, but pride forbade her to sit on it. She realized that she was being insulted. She had been there for the last half hour, *without a gesture* or a word. The ladies and the Baron had stared at her as they went past, and now the voices from the drawing rooms reached her in faint snatches. All of this pleasant luxury assaulted her with its indifference; yet *still she did not move* (emphasis added).[40]

> [Chaque fois que la porte s'ouvrait, on apercevait un coin obscur de l'antichambre, éclairée seulement par des vitres dépolies. Là, dans le noir, une forme sombre apparaissait, immobile et patiente. Denise se tenait debout; il y avait bien une banquette recouverte de cuir, mais une fierté l'en éloignait. Elle sentait l'injure. Depuis une demi-heure, elle était là, sans un geste, sans un mot; ces dames et le baron l'avaient dévisagée au passage; maintenant, les voix du salon lui arrivaient par bouffées légères, tout ce luxe aimable la souffletait de son indifférence; et elle ne bougeait toujours pas.[41]]

Tellingly, Denise's suspension – repeatedly emphasized here by the phrases "motionless," "without a gesture," and "still she did not move" – is anything but paralyzing. On the contrary, her steadfastness allows her to endure hardship, serves as a silent revolt, and foreshadows the disruptions soon to take place in Henriette's changing room. Denise's endurance distinguishes itself from patience alone, which does not portend success in the modern world as evidenced by her cousin Geneviève, who wastes away, "exhausted by waiting"[42] ["usé dans l'attente"[43]] for a marriage to Colomban that never takes place.

In contrast to her cousin's morbid perseverance, Denise's patience is a forward-thinking version of waiting that sets its sights on the future rather than dwelling on the suffering of the present or becoming mired in nostalgia for the past. For Denise, waiting, paradoxically, results in productivity, a fact that is exemplified by her steady approach to effecting changes in the Bonheur that increase both humane treatment of workers and profits.[44] Denise's manner of waiting is the Third Republic reply to the paralysis of Second Empire ennui, the latter represented by Mouret's splenetic schoolmate Paul, who notes that his life is one of "stagnation and emptiness"[45] ["l'immobilité et le néant"[46]]. Paul's pessimistic description of his own inertia is the inverse of Mouret's anti-immobility stance, expressed in the latter's impassioned assertion that "action contains in itself its own reward. Doing, creating, struggling against harsh realities and either defeating them or being defeated – all of human joy and health are there!"[47] ["l'action contient en elle sa récompense. Agir, créer, se battre contre les faits, les vaincre ou être vaincu par eux, toute la joie et toute la santé humaine sont là!"[48]]. Paul, morose and inert, is the foil that enables Zola to frame Mouret's contrasting ode to modernity's dynamism in a favourable light, suggesting his own admiration for his protagonist's progressive drive.[49]

The placement in the novel of this exchange between Paul and Mouret is significant, for it occurs directly following Denise's escape from Mme Desforges's dressing room. The antechamber passages described above are thereby bookended by two descriptions of modernity's activity. That is, before Denise arrives and during her long wait in the first antechamber, it is the department store, symbol of vigorous growth and a future consumerist society, which dominates the conversations of the guests in the salon. Then, after Denise departs from Henriette's changing room, Mouret delivers his above tribute to modern action. In this way Zola models the dialectics of waiting and changing not in the Bonheur department store, but rather in Mme Desforges's dislocated antechambers, where Denise actively waits for the social and economic transformations that she senses on the horizon and that are expressed by Mouret at the end of the chapter.

Like Denise, Zola's reflections on modern existence are as much contemplations of a society yet to come as they are of their Second Empire "present."[50] As argued in chapter 1, the novelist seemed not to have fully exorcised past traumas such as the Commune in this, his "poem to modern activity." Nonetheless, as Starr notes, "Zola's *Bonheur* looks to the future as the sole moment at which the promise of democracy (specifically liberal democracy) might be fully realized."[51] In the final two sentences of the antechamber chapter, Zola posits the importance of actively waiting to this future capitalist democracy. In these closing lines, Baron Hartmann, gazing in admiration at Mouret, suddenly has this sight replaced with a vision seen earlier of Denise waiting in Henriette's foyer: "He had a mental image of the modest profile of the young woman he had seen as he came through the antechamber. There she was, patient, alone, and formidable in her gentle sweetness"[52] ["Et il crut revoir le profil modeste de la jeune fille, qu'il avait aperçue en traversant l'antichambre. Elle était là, patiente, seule, redoubtable dans sa douceur"[53]]. Hartmann, himself an obvious allegory for the architect of modernity Baron Haussmann, "comes through" the antechamber space, enacting the progressive motion and transformation associated with his flesh-and-blood analogue Haussmann and which is performed throughout the novel by Mouret. At the same time, however, the Baron sees that Denise, too, is "formidable," juxtaposing his recollection of advancing through the antechamber with the recognition of Denise's powerful aptitude to remain "patient" as she waits in the entryway. In anticipation of the final paragraph of the novel, which joins Mouret and Denise in matrimony, Zola closes this chapter with Hartmann's image of a new era symbolized as a union of Denise's gentle patience and Mouret's ever-adapting vitality.

We have been analysing how fashion objects and metaphors are key to Zola's observations about modern experience and his forecast for the last decades of the nineteenth century. For it is by way of a coat, sharp pins, and a failed clothing alteration that Zola predicts a future of liberal democracy, one that he represents as a productive marriage of Mouret's philosophy of commercial innovation and change with Denise's patience and compassion. Significantly, this waiting and changing episode takes place not in the Bonheur, but rather in a pair of antechambers, seemingly minor spaces outside of the department store walls in which major symbolic delays and transformations occur. Although Mouret's cathedral of consumption is unquestionably the primary site of Zola's novel, it is not here that modernity's dialectic is most pointedly staged. Rather, it is to antechambers – dislocations of the modern department store – that Zola turns for the task.

Waiting for Nana: Fashioning Naturalism

In 1878, one year before the first serial instalment of *Nana* appeared in the newspaper *Le Voltaire*, Zola published a collection of three of his recent works for the theatre: a stage version of the novel *Thérèse Raquin*, a comedy entitled *Les Héritiers Rabourdin*, and a farce called *Le Bouton*

Rose. Rather than adopting a celebratory tone, however, Zola opened the preface to his collection with a blunt observation: "The three plays that I am assembling in this volume had no success at all" ["Les trois pièces que je réunis dans ce volume n'ont eu aucun succès"].[54] Although Zola's curt description of the public's poor response to his works might have seemed to some readers the exaggeration of a writer well known for (melo)dramatic declarations, in this case the assessment was quite accurate. Written and performed between 1873 and 1878, all three of Zola's plays had been utter failures at the box office: *Les Héritiers Rabourdin*, the most popular of the trio, had offered up a dismal seventeen performances and the other two had fared even worse. For this author who was "famous for being famous, or for wanting to garner fame in literary history,"[55] as Emily Apter puts it, Zola's frustration was hardly a surprise. Neither was the characteristic defiance with which he responded to such disappointment, concluding his preface with a fiery promise and prediction:

> I am publishing my booed plays and am *waiting* … When there are around twenty of them they will be able to attain respect. What I am *waiting* for is an evolution in our dramatic literature, the public's and critics' appeasement in my regard, a more clear and fair appreciation of what I am and what I want … My novels have ended up being read, my plays will end up being heard" (emphasis added).

> [Je publie mes pièces sifflées et *j'attends* … Lorsqu'il y en aura une vingtaine, elles sauront se faire respecter. Ce que *j'attends*, c'est une évolution dans notre littérature dramatique, c'est un apaisement du public et de la critique à mon égard, c'est une appréciation plus nette et plus juste de ce que je suis et de ce que je veux … On a bien fini par lire mes romans, on finira par écouter mes pièces.[56]]

Of interest in this passage is the verb *attendre*, a term that the author repeats twice and that I have translated above as "waiting." Yet, as the *Trésor de la langue française* indicates, the verb *attendre* can also connote "hope" for a particular outcome, or, even more decisively, "expectation" of a given result. Given the polemical tone of Zola's preface, it is reasonable to read his use of the term to include these nuances, and to amend the second *j'attends* in particular to an expression of Zola's hope ("*j'attends*" = "I hope") that his plays would eventually be as successful as his novels. The future tense of the verb *finira* in the last phrase might then mark an evolution from hope to expectation. We can read the end of Zola's preface as a flourishing declaration about the future: as in the case of his novels, he announces, the public *will* take notice of his plays.

This discussion of fashion and the dislocated waiting room in *Nana* thus begins with Zola's acute sense of anticipation, once coinciding with an especially crucial moment in his career. This was the period in the late 1870s when the novelist was attempting to delineate the methods and importance of naturalism, the narrative approach that, for him, provided the most apt method for chronicling modernity. In the citation above, Zola's anticipation is expressed by way of the eventual success that he foresees happening – or, perhaps more accurately, *hopes* will happen – once writing for the theatre has "evolved" enough for readers to gain, in his words, "appreciation of what I am and what I want." Not coincidentally, I submit, waiting in eager anticipation in antechambers is also a central theme in *Nana*. It will be argued that the novel echoes in narrative form two of Zola's interrelated hopes: (1) his hope for a future positive reception of his undervalued plays of the 1870s and (2) his hope that the public would learn to appreciate, to paraphrase, "what he was and what he wanted" as a writer more generally.

As is well known, Zola outlined these two concepts – the type of author that he was and how he wished for his writing to be understood – in *Le Roman expérimental*, translated as *The Experimental Novel*, his treatise on naturalism in which he sought to define an evolved form of nineteenth-century realism. This didactic essay first appeared in France in 1879, concurrent with *Nana*, which itself appeared shortly after the 1878 publication of Zola's three failed plays. The temporal convergence of these works, and the fact that Zola was working on them in close succession or simultaneously, invites us to consider them in relation to one another. By way of a brief summary, *Le Roman expérimental* suggests that literary production can and should be modelled after the theories put forth by scientist Claude Bernard in his 1865 text (*Introduction à l'étude de la médecine expérimentale* [*Introduction to the Study of Experimental Medicine*]). In this study, Bernard had championed the scientific method – an approach based on observation, data gathering, and experimentation – and had advocated adopting these techniques in his own field of medicine. Zola's suggestion to transfer Bernard's concepts from the physical sciences to fiction was, from the start, highly controversial, receiving criticisms from a mostly hostile press, and even from his own close friends.[57] The actual content of *Le Roman expérimental* has been a subject well covered by others, as has the theme of garments, especially in their relation to the prostitute's body, in *Nana*.[58] But the way in which Zola's treatment of fashion relates his courtesan novel directly to his development as a naturalist writer has yet to be examined. The following analysis will draw attention to Zola's highlighting in *Nana* of a defining element of modern fashion: its ability both to create and to express anticipation. In this way, it reconsiders the novel with respect to the author's hopes for his recent theatrical writings as well as within the larger context of Zola's expectations for literary naturalism.

Nana can be described as a series of extended periods of waiting for the novel's protagonist, a text saturated with characters in a constant state of delay. Zola often sets these episodes in antechambers, rooms in which male clients hang about for hours, waiting expectantly for their turn with the lovely blonde Venus. The opening chapter, which begins and ends in the foyer of the Théâtre des Variétés, establishes the recurring pattern of eager anticipation that will permeate the text. The reader, like the characters of the novel, is introduced to Nana not by her corporeal appearance but by way of the tantalizing, albeit vague, reputation that precedes her. As a result, the theatre foyer is a space of high anticipation, one in which ticket holders linger impatiently to enter the hall for the ingénue's debut. Their curiosity is incited by the sound of the name "Nana" that reverberates, enticingly, throughout the room:

> A stream of people was crowding around the box-office, and there was a din of voices, in the midst of which Nana's name sounded with all the lilting vivacity of its two syllables. The men standing in front of the playbills spelt it out aloud; others uttered it in a questioning tone as they passed; while the women, at once uneasy and smiling, repeated it softly with an air of surprise. Nobody knew Nana. Where had Nana come from? ... A fever of curiosity urged it forward, that Parisian curiosity which is as violent as a fit of brain-fever.[59]

> [Une queue s'écrasait au contrôle, un tapage de voix montait, dans lequel le nom de Nana sonnait avec la vivacité chantante de ses deux syllabes. Les hommes qui se plantaient devant les affiches, l'épelaient à voix haute; d'autres le jetaient en passant, sur un ton d'interrogation; tandis que les femmes, inquiètes et souriantes, le répétaient doucement, d'un air de surprise. Personne ne connaissait Nana. D'où Nana tombait-elle? ... Une fièvre de curiosité poussait le monde, cette curiosité de Paris qui a la violence d'un accès de folie chaude.[60]]

In the waiting room lobby, a dearth of information about the enigmatic actress feeds the public's "fever of curiosity" to see her. This agitated desire escalates into disorder that Zola registers through fashion: "Everyone wanted to see Nana. A lady had the flounce of her dress torn off; a man lost his hat"[61] ["On voulait voir Nana. Une dame eut le volant de sa robe arraché, un monsieur perdit son chapeau"[62]]. Sartorial disturbance to the patrons' skirt and hat set up the subsequent arrival of two courtesans, Lucy Stewart and Blanche de Sivry, who further disrupt the foyer by impeding circulation with their enormous dresses:

> One of them in blue, the other in pink, they blocked the way with their flounced skirts … by this time Nana's name was echoing more loudly than ever *to the four corners of the foyer*, in the midst of a *desire sharpened by delay* (emphasis added, translation modified).[63]

> [Elles bouchaient le passage de leurs jupes chargées de volants, l'une en bleu, l'autre en rose, et le nom de Nana revenait sur leurs lèvres, si aigu, que le monde les écoutait … comme un écho, Nana sonnait *aux quatre coins du vestibule* sur un ton plus haut, dans un *désir accru par l'attente*.[64]]

The obstruction that the courtesans present with their clothing in this crowded space mirrors the disruption that the two women represent to the larger bourgeois social order. For by sleeping with men from diverse backgrounds and all levels of economic means, carrying disease across social strata, and facilitating infidelity, they pose a threat to the stability, health, and morality of the middle and upper classes. Zola signals the courtesans' impact on Parisian society through a double reference to fashion: their billowing gowns impede movement in the theatre foyer at the very same moment that damage and mayhem are occurring to the skirt and hat of the lady and gentleman in the lobby. The two prostitutes and their dress predict the eventual arrival in the text of Nana, also a woman of chic fashionability who will wreak havoc on society.

Indeed, Lucy and Blanche find themselves joining the others eagerly awaiting Nana in the theatre lobby, a space that seems designed for the very purpose of inciting anticipation. Zola's description that sounds in the lobby reach "to the four corners of the foyer," can be read as a variant of the common idiom, "to the four corners of the world" (*aux quatre coins du monde*). With the substitution of the term "foyer" for "monde," then, Zola's theatre waiting room seems to take on exaggerated dimensions, as though it is not merely a foyer, but a one-room symbol of the larger world. Yet, the lobby, which serves as a conduit to other destinations as do all antechambers, does not, in fact, comprise the entire world, for there are other "worlds" around and beyond it that the author highlights. On one side, for example, is the main hall where the performance takes place, both in the sense of the staged musical act in which Nana appears and in terms of the audience members' display of themselves for the visual consumption of other spectators. On the other side of the theatre, flanking the waiting-room foyer is the boulevard, observable through the lobby's wrought-iron doorways: "Through the three open gates could be seen the vibrant life of the swarming boulevards, ablaze with light in the fine April night"[65] ["Par les trois grilles ouvertes, on voyait passer la vie ardente des boulevards, qui grouillaient et flambaient sous la belle nuit d'avril"[66]]; "the dense night of the boulevard beyond was dotted with lights above the vague mass of an ever-moving crowd"[67] ["au-delà, la nuit épaissie du boulevard se piquait de feux, dans le vague d'une foule toujours en marche"[68]]. This vantage point from the theatre entry hall emphasizes the fact that the vestibule is an intermediary space, neither the main hall nor the boulevard but the area that lies between these two "worlds" and built to be traversed by modernity's crowds. The foyer is a spatial manifestation of Nana herself, both epitomizing high fashionability and high permeability. It is a room, moreover, that heightens eager anticipation by temporarily frustrating spectators' desires and forcing them to wait. Their tense excitement seems to render the waiting room more compelling than the boulevard "beyond" or even the performance hall itself, implying that, for Zola, it is in the antechamber dislocation that the interesting action of modernity truly occurs.

Other antechambers in the novel similarly lead to and from worlds, from the "world of pleasure" that sex with Nana represents to what might be thought of as the "everyday world," a banal existence of public respectability. The former is the place that her many lovers are so desperate to reach that they drive themselves to disgrace, ruin, and even death. It is also a place to which their access is routinely delayed. Over the course of the novel, men wait for Nana in three key locales: the assorted rooms of her homes, the theatre during her performances, and the street below the hotel in which she dies. We will return to the third case later, beginning here with Zola's deployment of fashion to express anticipation in the first two types of waiting rooms.

Nana's homes, like their owner, are spaces of circulation, subject to the constant infiltration of men arriving from various locales across the city. Yet, they are also ad hoc waiting rooms, for once her visitors gain admittance into Nana's house they are forced to wait in spaces reappropriated solely for this purpose. The second chapter of the novel illustrates this well. As numerous suitors arrive in hopes of connecting with the blonde courtesan, they are one by one delayed in a range of areas throughout the flat. Because the true antechamber of the apartment is already occupied by Nana's many creditors, Zoé, the clever maid, instals the young Georges Hugon in an unfurnished storage room,[69] the banker Steiner in "the little sitting room"[70] ["le petit salon"[71]], and the would-be count Valaque in "la chambre à coucher"[72] or the bedroom. Lacking rooms for the overflow of men that continue to arrive, the maid finally directs them to wait in "a queue on the stairs"[73] ["une queue dans l'escalier"[74]]. The reiteration of the verb "to wait" (*attendre*) in Zoé's reminder that "there are some people waiting to see you"[75] ["il y a du monde qui attend"[76]] and Nana's impatient reaction that "they could wait"[77] ["le monde pouvait attendre"[78]] summarizes the fact that the protagonist's ostensible lodgings actually serve as a series of waiting spaces. Indeed, in Nana's eyes, suitors and their respective holding rooms seem to be somewhat synonymous; when referring to the men stashed about the apartment, she simply gestures to "the adjoining rooms"[79] ["les pièces voisines"[80]] as though the spaces themselves represent her clientele. When, later in the novel, the young woman moves to a mansion in the wealthy parc Monceau neighbourhood, this building, too, functions essentially as a waiting room for male callers. To accommodate this growing pool of visitors, the normal waiting space with which the mansion comes equipped must be expanded. To this end, the vast entryway vestibule is filled with sofas, stuffed chairs, and a tray of visiting cards, eventually rendering the entire first floor of the mansion not a true living area but, in Zola's words, "an antechamber" ["une antichambre"][81] in and of itself.

Not by coincidence, both of Nana's homes are in locations strongly associated with modernity and fashionability. The former is on the chic boulevard Haussmann in a structure designed by the street's namesake, one representing a building style that became in these years the quintessential modern lodging for Paris's middle and upper classes.[82] The latter is an opulent mansion, newly erected, in a fashionable district populated by the most well-to-do of the nouveaux riches. By deliberately choosing these symbolic locales, Zola links Nana to sites of the urban landscape that were associated with stylish modernity. At the same time, he problematizes the meanings of these spaces, in particular by depicting them as distortions of the bourgeois home. As Nana relocates numerous times throughout the novel, she perpetuates the alienation that some feared was caused through Haussmannization by turning her living quarters into an assorted collection of impersonal waiting rooms. Garments in these spaces suggest Zola's cynical attitude about the decline of the urban home, as city lodgings became less characterized by comfort and privacy and more by the constant impersonal appropriation of anonymous men. In the mansion near the parc Monceau, Nana's first-floor antechamber is a space "where men's overcoats and hats were always lying around"[83] ["où trainaient toujours des pardessus et des chapeaux d'homme"[84]]. Accessories represent the well-dressed suitors who enter wearing these items and "make themselves at home" while they wait, abandoning jackets and hats in the foyer as though they have arrived in analogous rooms in their own houses where they store their outerwear. At the same time, the discarded garments demonstrate both the men's absence and their anonymity, since the hats and coats have clearly been worn but we do not know the identities of the bodies now missing from them. Cast-off clothing items attest to the hastiness with which wearers eagerly depart the antechamber once they are summoned, at long last, to find pleasure with Nana. Fulfilment in these perversions of the home is not instantaneous, then, but delayed. In this way, Zola's depiction of Nana's homes as waiting rooms pessimistically evokes a metropolis driven primarily by the pursuit of sensual, but impersonal, gratification. To gain entry into this modern city, Zola seems to imply, is first to wait.

Anticipation in the Theatre Loge

The Théâtre des Variétés where Nana performs, much like her Parisian homes, is represented as a series of waiting rooms. These include the dressing compartments in which Nana and her fellow performers wait to be called to the stage, as well as other behind-the-scenes areas that, through function rather than design, are spaces of delay and anticipation. One such location is the backstage loge of the concierge Mme Bron, an entryway where flowers and mail are delivered for the actors. Zola's sketches of the actual Théâtre des Variétés on which he based his fictional version include the "loge du concierge" and his notes making reference to its unique placement between two sets of staircases attest to the author's interest in precisely how it was positioned backstage.[85] Significantly, although not built for such a purpose, this room in the novel becomes a spot where suitors linger in hopes of being chosen to spend the evening with Nana (or, in her absence, with another of the actresses). In particular, the loge is a space expressing tensions between elements that belong and those that do not. The room is untidy: dirty dishes lie forgotten on the table and the room smells of strong alcohol and stale cooking, yet it is populated with wealthy men, whose smart clothing indicates that they are out of place in their sordid surroundings: "In the midst of this filth and disorder, immaculately dressed, white-gloved men of the world sat with patient, submissive expressions on the four straw-bottomed chairs, turning their heads sharply every time Madame Bron came downstairs from the theater with a reply to some message or other"[86] ["Au milieu de ce désordre de soupente mal tenue, des messieurs du monde, gantés, corrects, occupaient les quatre vieilles chaises de paille, l'air patient et soumis, tournant vivement la tête, chaque fois que Mme Bron redescendait du théâtre avec une réponse"[87]]. The men are described as "patient," resigned to waiting despite the unpleasant shabbiness of the environment, but they eagerly anticipate, too, a visit with Nana, as the rapid and expectant swings of their heads imply. The gentlemen's fine garments – impeccable white gloves and formal eveningwear – signal a surface disparity between their high standing in society and the far less respectable "filth and disorder" of the theatre backstage.

However, the room, partitioned off by two walls of glass, is also described as "a huge transparent lantern"[88] ["une grande lanterne transparente"[89]], a metaphor that affords Zola the opportunity to critique upper-class hypocrisy. The waiting room "lantern" seems to illuminate and make "transparent" a certain reality: the men's lust for Nana and her fellow demimondaines is so powerful that they will abase themselves, sitting awkwardly on uncomfortable straw chairs next to other (not very) "respectable" members of society who will eventually take pleasure from the very same corrupted women. Despite the moral purity that the whiteness of their gloves implies, Zola suggests, these well-heeled suitors are no less squalid on the inside than Mme Bron's grimy loge. This dissonance between fashion and space enables Zola to illustrate that the men are as morally unclean as the room in which they find themselves. Moreover, as in the case of Nana's parc Monceau mansion, the theme of waiting reiterates that such frustrating delays had become a condition of life, one, paradoxically governed by modern simulants and pleasures.

La Faloise's Foppish Fashions

Let us return to the proposal with which this examination of *Nana* began, which is that the novel should be read bearing in mind a particular discursive context. In accordance with David Baguley, who notes, "Zola's ideas [in *Le Roman expérimental*] belong very much to the context of the reception of his works,"[90] the discourse that we will consider includes *Le Roman expérimental*, which was published simultaneously with *Nana*, and will also involve Zola's 1878 preface to the collection of his three disastrous plays. The circumstances surrounding the production of these three texts are important because, when considered in tandem, they suggest new ways of reading *Nana* as well as Zola's approach to promoting naturalism. In what follows, the sartorial elements of Mme Bron's waiting room will be linked both to the state of hopeful anticipation evinced in Zola's preface and to his essay on naturalism. We will tease out this connection by examining the author's depiction of an often-overlooked character: Hector de La Faloise.

La Faloise, one of the finely attired gentlemen in Mme Bron's loge, is a character in whom comic relief and fashion collide. Freshly arrived in Paris from the provinces in order to (euphemistically) "complete his education"[91] ["achever son éducation"[92]], La Faloise is at first bewildered by the life of pleasure available to him in the capital city but later adapts, transforming from a naive newcomer to a pompous, ridiculously dressed fop. La Faloise becomes such a slave to following Paris's showy trends, wearing ostentatious garments and adopting an affected manner of speaking, that, eventually, he begs to be ruined by Nana, perversely thinking this to be the period's ultimate fad. The scene in the theatre loge takes place relatively early in La Faloise's "education" when the young man has learned to dress properly for the theatre but is still only confident enough to court chorus girls. Already, though, he is a target for Zola, who pokes fun at the gangly youth by surrounding him with a family of fighting kittens as he waits, awkwardly, backstage:

> La Faloise was sitting on one of the chairs at the back of the room, between the table and the stove. He seemed set on passing the entire evening there, yet he looked uneasy, and kept tucking up his long legs because a whole litter of black kittens were pestering him, while the mother cat sat staring at him with her yellow eyes.[93]

[La Faloise était sur une des chaises, au fond, entre la table et le poêle; il semblait décidé à passer la soirée là, inquiet pourtant, rentrant ses longues jambes, parce que toute une portée de petits chats noirs s'acharnaient autour de lui, tandis que la chatte, assise sur son derrière le regardait fixement de ses yeux jaunes.[94]]

As La Faloise nervously adjusts his lanky legs to avoid the kittens, a nearby actress identifies him to Mme Bron by the fact that the mother cat is inhaling the scent of his pants: "It's the thin one next to the stove – the one whose trousers your cat's sniffing at"[95] ["C'est le maigre, à côté du poêle, celui dont votre chatte sent le pantalon"[96]].

Three elements in this episode bear highlighting. First is a possible similarity between La Faloise and Zola himself, which is that both men appear determined to wait for what they want. For La Faloise, this is a night of pleasure with a woman; for Zola, as he describes it in his 1878 preface, this is the public's understanding and recognition of his works for the theatre and of his writing philosophy more generally. Both men also display perseverance: even after he is dismissed, La Faloise slips back into the loge in order to resume waiting on his old, uncomfortable chair. Zola, we recall, notes that time will likely pass before the public truly appreciates his works. It may take years, the time to write a total of twenty plays, he declares, before this hoped-for end comes to pass. He writes, "I am publishing my booed plays and am waiting," we recall, as though acknowledging that waiting is simply a part of the process. To wait for what one desires is therefore both a narrative theme in *Nana* and a condition that Zola seems to accept as part of the modern authorial experience.

Second, the inclusion of the humorous clothing detail in this passage – the cat sniffing the pant leg of an ill-at-ease La Faloise – invites us to think about the ways in which fashion and comedy or diversion coincide in the text. For this, it is useful to take up a more detailed sartorial examination of this amusing character, for whom garments are an important distinguishing feature. As noted above, La Faloise eventually blossoms into an absurd dandy and Zola will ridicule him for, among other things, his preference for modish garments. When La Faloise arrives at the Grand Prix de Paris horserace, one of the most stylish events of the season,[97] Zola notes his sartorial transformation:

Since he had come into his inheritance, he had become terribly *chic*. He was wearing a wing-collar and a suit of light-coloured cloth which clung to his narrow shoulders. His hair was in little curls and he affected a weary sway of the body and a gentle drawl, with slang words and phrases which he did not take the trouble to finish (translation modified).[98]

[Depuis qu'il avait hérité, il était devenu d'un chic extraordinaire. Le col brisé, vêtu d'une étoffe de couleur tendre qui collait à ses maigres épaules, coiffé de petits bandeaux, il affectait un dandinement de lassitude, une voix molle, avec des mots d'argot, des phrases qu'il ne se donnait pas la peine de finir.[99]]

As he puts on airs, La Faloise's attention-grabbing behaviour renders him what Zola, in full irony, refers to as extraordinarily "chic." This, Zola would have known, was a loaded term. According to the *Trésor de la langue française*, the word *chic*, perhaps a derivative of the German *schicken* meaning "to make happen or arrange," was employed by authors including Balzac, Flaubert, and Gautier in the first half of the nineteenth century to invoke subtlety, finesse, and elegance.[100] However, around mid-century, such positive connotations seem to have destabilized, as demonstrated most famously by Baudelaire in "Du chic et du poncif," a section of *Le Salon de 1846* in which the poet described "chic" as an "awful and bizarre word" ["mot affreux et bizarre"][101] that implied artificiality or falseness. According to Baudelaire, these inferior epithets described paintings offered by second-rate artists capable only of copying "vulgar and banal ideas" ["des idées vulgaires et banales"][102] through gestures owing more to muscle memory than to true artistic creativity. In line with Baudelaire, Zola describes La Faloise as "chic" to comment on his lack of originality, which informs the young man's naive devotion to the latest styles, no matter how ridiculous they make him appear. His gaudy attire is case in point: rather than appearing in sombre colours, he stands out in "light-coloured clothes" corresponding more to the bright hues worn by eighteenth-century libertines than to the dark tones favoured by elegant nineteenth-century bourgeois men. Moreover, in this era of relatively short male hairstyles, La Faloise wears his locks long in a curled, sweeping look of which Zola seems to disapprove, likely associating such tresses with romantic-era affectation. Yet, the item of attire perhaps most laden with problematic meanings for the author is La Faloise's *col brisé*, his turnover shirt collar.

The *col brisé*, literally a "broken collar," also known as a *col cassé*, was a high neckband featuring points that folded down, which opened at the neck and was often detachable.[103] The accessory would eventually develop into the Arrow collar, a tall, stiff neckband with small points that was worn with formal dress and that was popularized especially in the early decades of the twentieth century.[104] Collars, clothing historians agree, were extremely important menswear accessories in terms of what they could convey symbolically and aesthetically. Alan Flusser notes, for instance, that as the style and shape of the masculine dress shirt became standardized over the course of the nineteenth century, "the collar became its most distinguishing and fashion-sensitive feature."[105] As is true of most garments, however, the wearers and meanings of the collar could be varied and contradictory.[106] The high collar was adopted by the wealthy, likely to confer their own status and prestige through its blinding whiteness and impressive height on the neck. The 1891 dictionary, *Slang and Its Analogues Past and Present*, records that *col-cassé* was also used in the vernacular as a synonym for "dandy," which emphasized a relationship between the accessory and men who were exceptionally concerned with dress and appearance.[107] Yet, the style appealed as well to the rising middle class, for whom the detachable high collar addressed the problem that white neckbands were generally quick to show dirt and perspiration. The col cassé neckband (like all detachable collars) was therefore ideal for its practicality, since it could be removed from the rest of the shirt to be laundered and supported good hygiene practices, which were increasingly important as signs of proper bourgeois taste and respectability.[108]

Other examples in Zola's works imply that, for him, the *col brisé* had only negative connotations that opened up its wearer to teasing, or even full-out ridicule. For instance, the col cassé is specifically mentioned in *La Curée* as a fashion worn by M. de Mussy,[109] a stuffy bureaucrat whose comic rigidity is communicated by the stiffness of his high, unbending collar. In *Nana*, Zola also cites the collar as an accessory worn by two elaborately primped young men, who erupt into a ludicrous, yet humorous, shouting match over Nana's on-stage debut: "In the passage two young men, spick and span with curled hair and turned-down collars, were quarrelling. One of them kept repeating the words 'Beastly, beastly!' without giving any reasons; the other replied with the words 'Stunning, stunning!' and also disdained all argument"[110] ["Dans le couloir, deux jeunes gens, frisés au petit fer, très corrects avec leurs col cassés, se querellaient. L'un répétait le mot: Infecte! Infecte! sans donner de raison; l'autre répondait par le mot: Épatante! Épatante! dédaigneux aussi de tout argument"[111]]. The finicky dress and overly primped hairstyles of the two young men and their inane debate render them precursors for what the vain, overdressed La Faloise will eventually become.

Building on this earlier image of the arguing fops in the theatre, towards the end of *Nana*, Zola cements clear links between La Faloise's attire and his preposterousness. As he sinks deeper into financial woes and overgroomed preciousness alike, La Faloise is described as follows:

> His debts were crushing him, all he had left was an income of a hundred francs a year, and he could see himself being compelled to go to the provinces to live with a finicky uncle; but that didn't matter, because he had made his mark – the *Figaro* had printed his name twice. And with his scraggy neck sticking out between the turn-down points of his [false] collar, and his waist squeezed into an excessively short jacket, he would swagger about, uttering parrot-like exclamations and affecting the weariness of a puppet which has never felt a single emotion (translation modified).[112]

> [La dette l'écrasait, il ne possédait plus cent francs de rente, il se voyait forcé de retourner en province vivre chez un oncle maniaque; mais ça ne faisait rien, il était chic, *Le Figaro* avait imprimé deux fois son nom; et le cou maigre entre les pointes rabattues de son faux col, la taille cassée sous un veston trop court, il se dandinait, avec des exclamations de perruche et des lassitudes affectées de patin de bois, qui n'a jamais eu une émotion.[113]]

Spending his entire inheritance on Nana and being absurdly delighted because his name appears twice in the papers as a result, La Faloise's transformation from inexperienced provincial to ruined urban dandy is complete. His col brisé is once again called upon to confer his droll, foppish tastes, but this time Zola specifies that the collar is detachable or "false" (*faux*), the term signifying doubly La Faloise's slavish adherence to damaging fads and the artificiality of his demeanour and character. The notion of the detachable collar, an accessory designed to be changed frequently, also enables Zola to connect La Faloise to fickleness, and to imply that his morals shift as easily as a collar can be discarded and replaced. What is important to take from this discussion is that, whatever their connotations, La Faloise's col brisé and accompanying garments create opportunities for characters in the novel and readers alike to be amused at his expense. As Zola first establishes in the waiting room loge while the cat sniffs suspiciously (hungrily? amorously?) at his pants, La Faloise is a comedic character, whose humour will be communicated in large part through the sartorial.

Nana vs. *Le Roman expérimental*

The third and final point involving La Faloise brings us back to our initial premise about Zola's anticipatory state of mind at the end of the 1870s. I would like to argue that *Nana* and *Le Roman expérimental* represent two dramatically different approaches that Zola undertook in order to achieve what he ultimately desired, which was acceptance and appreciation of naturalism (and therefore his life's work more generally). As we noted above, in the preface to his plays he suggests that these are things for which he is resigned to wait. Yet, the next two major works he produced implied otherwise: that he was, in fact, eager to hasten the pace and garner the public's approval as quickly and decisively as possible. Like the impatient ticket holders waiting for Nana's debut in the theatre antechamber, Zola seems little interested in enduring a prolonged delay. There is an urgency to *Le Roman expérimental* that implies not the patience to wait but rather the great need to convince readers to quickly join him in adopting a new literary model based on Bernard's scientific method. A polemic, the essay is argumentative and aggressive, representing a "literary battle" ["bataille littéraire"] as Zola would call it in his introduction to the fifth bound edition.[114] His rhetorical strategy thus involves hostility, in particular towards, in his words, "critics who have mocked my scientific pretentions" ["critiques qui se sont moqués de nos prétentions à la science"].[115] He goes on to condemn fellow authors, in particular romantics, poets, and philosophers, those "idealistic writers" ["les écrivains idéalistes"][116] who, he suggests, have only contributed "stupidities" ["sottises"][117] and "follies" ["folies"][118] to the project of understanding humanity. This kind of impoverished writing, he snaps in disgust, has left society (*nous*) "rotting in lyricism" ["pourris de lyrisme"].[119]

On the contrary, in *Nana*, Zola adopts very different techniques to convince his readers of the merits of naturalism. Such divergence in approaches can be explained in part by the (obvious) fact that the two texts represent separate genres, that the first is a didactic essay and the second a work of fiction. Still, the two texts are connected, since *Nana* is very much a naturalist project that incorporates the main elements that Zola spells out in his treatise. In keeping with the data-gathering philosophy of naturalism, for instance, the novel is based on months of observation of the theatre backstage and other locations connected to the demimonde. Moreover, the text explores a primary concern of nineteenth-century scientific discourse, namely, the dynamics of the social and genetic influences on modern human behaviour. However, rather than deploying the argumentative tone of *Le Roman expérimental*, Zola's methods of persuasion in *Nana* depend more on what are also primary subjects of the plot: seduction, entertainment, and, most importantly for our purposes here, fashion.

Of all of the *Rougon-Macquart* novels, including *Au Bonheur*, *Nana* is to my mind the most concerned with not just the meanings of worn garments but also with the workings of fashion in society, that is, with what makes someone or something appealingly fashionable. Nana *is* fashion, as Zola states in so many words: "Thereupon, Nana became a woman of fashion"[120] ["Alors, Nana devint une femme chic"[121]]. As has been examined elsewhere, one source of Nana's fashionableness is that her clothing choices are impulsive and often surprising, as exemplified by the pleasingly "bold"[122] ["hardie"[123]] skirt silhouette that she debuts at the Longchamp races.[124] Like the garments she wears, Nana is alluringly unpredictable, inciting excitement and anticipation whenever she appears. Rather than representing refined elegance, however, her looks derive from the poorer disreputable quarters of the city from which she, too, hails, and are informed by her occasionally vulgar tastes. Offering the titillation of dressing in street-inspired style to the upper class, she becomes a cutting-edge trend setter featured in newspapers and storefronts as the embodiment of the latest style.[125] As Zola puts it,

> Her photographs were displayed in the shop-windows, and her remarks were quoted in the papers. When she drove along the boulevards in her carriage, people would turn round and tell one another who she was, with all the emotion of a nation saluting its sovereign, while she lolled back in her flimsy dresses, smiling gaily under the rain of little golden curls which fell around the blue of her made-up eyes and the red of her painted lips.[126]

> [Ses photographies s'étalaient aux vitrines, on la citait dans les journaux. Quand elle passait en voiture sur les Boulevards, la foule se retournait et la nommait, avec l'émotion d'un peuple saluant sa souveraine; tandis que, familière, allongée dans ses toilettes flottantes, elle souriait d'un air gai, sous la pluie de petites frisures blondes, qui noyaient le bleu cerné de ses yeux et le rouge peint de ses lèvres.[127]]

Turning heads wherever she goes, Nana is so compelling a fashion icon that women in high society, even those who would not choose for reasons of proper etiquette to associate themselves with a "painted-lip" prostitute, wait to see what Nana wears first and then seek to emulate her. In Zola's words, "She set the fashion, and great ladies imitated her"[128] ["Elle donnait le ton, de grandes dames l'imitaient"[129]]. The ultimate arbiter of the latest look, Nana's attractive "gay" smile and tantalizingly "flimsy" dresses are tools of her daring, but still charming, seduction.

Fashion, as both metaphor and phenomenon, enables Zola to construct a novel that, echoing its protagonist, seduces, surprises, attracts, and entertains. As we have seen with La Faloise, for instance, symbolic sartorial objects give Zola access to humour. This injection of comedy supports one of his main objectives, which is to point out and critique flaws of human character, but it does so while still amusing readers. Moreover, as Henri Mitterand notes, the actress/*cocotte* was itself "a fashionable theme" ["un thème à la mode"[130]], the subject of many popular novels, operettas, and paintings in cultural production of the 1860s and 1870s that focused on "ladies of the night" ["les dames de nuit"].[131] The prostitute was, likewise, a recent trend in the "high" literary circles with which Zola associated. In 1876, for instance, just three years before *Nana* began appearing in the *Voltaire*, Joris-Karl Huysmans had published *Marthe, histoire d'une fille*; the year following Edmond de Goncourt's *La Fille Élisa*, also a novel about a prostitute, had appeared.[132] By writing about a courtesan, a character type that was especially in vogue, Zola presented his readers with a fashionable subject that, he surely sensed, was likely to appeal to them.

We should note here that Nana's capriciousness, conveyed through her pleasing sartorial unpredictability, is really a euphemistic metaphor for the disruptions, and eventually the very real damage, that Zola has her inflict upon society. For, as he writes in his preliminary outline for the novel, Nana ultimately ends up "becoming a force of nature, a ferment of destruction" ["devenant une force de la nature, un ferment de destruction"].[133] Tellingly, though, there is a crucial detail in Zola's notes that is worth highlighting, which is that the novelist immediately hastens to add "but this without meaning to be" ["mais cela sans le vouloir"],[134] an insertion that seems to pardon Nana's effects of devastation and even underscore her innocence. The same description and absolution from Zola's notes is preserved almost verbatim in the final version, which appears in the novel as part of Fauchery's newspaper article, entitled "La Mouche d'Or," or "The Golden Fly," a thinly veiled allegorical depiction of Nana: "She had become a force of nature, a ferment of destruction, without wanting it herself" (translation modified)[135] ["Elle devenait une force de la nature, un ferment de destruction, sans le vouloir elle-même"[136]].

Thus, despite the fact that Zola renders Nana the agent of colossal damage, especially to the finances of her lovers, from his earliest to his final depictions of her she is also, to an extent, forgivable for the harm that she causes. Zola's apparent sympathy for his character may relate to her difficult childhood as the impoverished daughter of alcoholics, which Zola documents earlier with great pathos for the family's suffering in the novel *L'Assommoir*. In any case, it was clearly important to him that Nana be, in spite of it all, likable. In his preparatory notes, Zola declares that Nana is to be "very cheerful, very gay" ["très rieuse, très gaie"],[137] instilling her with appealing traits that do indeed characterize her throughout the novel. Nana's cheerfulness and gaiety especially imbue passages in the text about fashion and anticipation, such as the Longchamp chapter in which the display of stylish garments, the suspense of the horserace, and the term "gaiety" ["gaieté"] are leitmotifs throughout.[138] Perhaps in his impatience for naturalism to be accepted, Zola rightly sensed that the "gais" and fashionable charms of *Nana* would be more effective in convincing the public than a rhetorically charged polemic. For indeed, *Nana* was a runaway success: correctly anticipating high sales, the novel's publisher Charpentier printed 55,000 copies of the bound volume to be sold in the first edition of 1880;[139] by September of 1881 the novel was in its 106th printing.[140] On the other hand, although *Le Roman expérimental* also received its share of interest, this attention was overwhelmingly negative, and likely did little to accord Zola, as he hoped for in his 1878 preface, "a more clear and fair appreciation of what I am and what I want."

Conclusion

We have been examining how *Le Roman expérimental* and *Nana* might both reflect Zola's hopeful anticipation that he, and naturalism, would be understood and appreciated. The author implies in the 1878 preface to his three plays that he is willing to wait for this desired goal, leaving the public to decide his fate. However, as the multiple meanings of the verb *attendre* suggest, Zola's attitude while drafting his subsequent two works may have fluctuated across some combination of waiting for, hoping for, and, perhaps, at times, expecting eventual accolades. His pointed explanatory essay on a controversial literary philosophy was one manifestation of his mindset in the late 1870s; *Nana*, a novel about the pleasures of Parisian modernity that offered the public diversion, enjoyment, and titillation, was another. In the latter text, as we have seen, Zola's sense of anticipation is dramatized through the recurring motif of the antechamber waiting room, wherein fashions signal the disruptive changes and frustrated delays that seemed to be, for him, increasingly typical of modern experience.

It is not necessarily the case that Zola intended for these three texts of 1878 and 1879 to resonate so closely with one another. It is, in contrast, far more certain that he planned for Nana to serve as an allegory for the doomed Second Empire, the period from 1852 to 1870 that endured the first wave of Haussmannization and that, for him, was characterized by the same vulgar, ostentatious allure as the Golden Fly. Zola's deliberate foregrounding of the novel's historical context, especially in the final chapter, demonstrates how the concept of waiting goes beyond informing the plot of the novel to suggest as well conditions of life in an urban landscape on the brink of tumult. In the novel's last pages, Nana dies, hideously disfigured by smallpox, her inner corruption finally displayed openly on her face in a symbol of Napoléon III's regime, whose internal degradation had, for Zola, long been hidden behind its glittering exterior. Nana's death coincides with the start of the Franco-Prussian War, a conflict that France would lose disastrously and that would lead directly to the horrors of the Commune. Earlier, I alluded to one final waiting room of sorts, that of the street below the room where Nana expires, which is described in the last paragraphs of the novel. In this passage, the male characters collect in the boulevard to wait for Nana's death, forming a stagnant group whose inertia contrasts with the mobilized soldiers who march naively towards a future defeat at the hands of the Prussians. By deliberately concluding *Nana* on the verge of the Franco-Prussian War, Zola invites his readers to meditate on the infamous drawn-out wait that subsequently took place in Paris immediately following France's defeat. I am referring to the Siege of 1870–71.

As is well known, during this terrible winter, Haussmann's capital found itself surrounded by the Prussian army. Unable to receive provisions from the provinces, Parisians starved and died, trapped in an urban landscape that had promised the dynamic movement and changes of modernity but in which many could do little more than wait, for months, for the siege to end.[141] John Milner observes that, during this time of imposed fixity, eyewitness accounts implied that "the strains of siege in a modern city were producing a desperation intense enough to spark rebellion; repression, revolution and civil war. As [the author Jules] Claretie noted succinctly in his journal for Sunday 22 January, it was on the 128th day of the siege that Frenchmen had begun killing Frenchmen."[142] The dire effect of this period of waiting was the civil war of the Commune, which erupted after almost four long months of rising tensions in the confined and beleaguered capital city.

As the men at the end of *Nana* linger together in the public street, suspended in anticipation of the protagonist's demise, Zola's readership may have been reminded that, during the Siege, Paris as a whole became like a giant waiting room, a city-sized antechamber, the outlets of which had been sealed off. The novel thus concludes as it starts, in anticipation that something imminent will occur. In the opening chapter of the text, located in the theatre antechamber, it is the arrival of the gay, already fashionable Nana, which lies ahead. In contrast, readers of the last chapter of the narrative who knew the city's impending fate would have recognized that what awaited the apprehensive characters in *Nana* was not the glory of a victorious military campaign, but rather a long and bitter wait broken only by political polarization and violent civil strife. Part cautionary tale and part epitath, *Nana* concludes with this dark truth, one temporarily clothed in an engaging and fashionable narrative but eventually stripped bare like the courtesan's decomposing body.

4 Maupassant, Transformation, and the Unexotic Exotic

"And They Lived Like This for Ten Years": "La Parure"

Dresses with interchangeable bodices are more in demand than ever, and this is understandable; they assist, without inconvenience, with no waste of time, in completely transforming an outfit. So, let us say that a lady went out with a black taffeta dress with a triple skirt or one with three flounces, with a winter bodice, very high-necked, very warm; upon returning home, she finds company that she did not expect; she must immediately preside over dinner or go to a show; in two minutes, she has removed her hat, replaced it with a little hair accessory, made of a fringe of black silk lace held together with black gemstones; she has abandoned her day-time city bodice in order to slip on a low-cut black taffeta one with short sleeves, draped with crepe of the same color with a jet-black fringe; there she is, decked out.

[Les robes à corsages de rechange sont plus demandées que jamais, et cela se conçoit; elles aident, sans dérangement, sans perte de temps, à une transformation complète dans le costume, ainsi, admettons qu'une dame soit sortie avec une robe de taffetas noir à trois jupes ou à trois volants, avec un corsage d'hiver, bien montant bien chaud; en rentrant chez elle, elle trouve des visites qu'elle n'attendait pas; il lui faut immédiatement présider le dîner ou se rendre au spectacle; en deux minutes, elle a retiré son chapeau, l'a remplacé par une petite coiffure montée, formée d'une barbe de blonde noire, agrafée de jais; elle a quitté son corsage de ville pour en passer un de taffetas noir, décolleté, à manches courtes, drapé de crêpe de même couleur avec frange de jais; la voilà parée.][1]

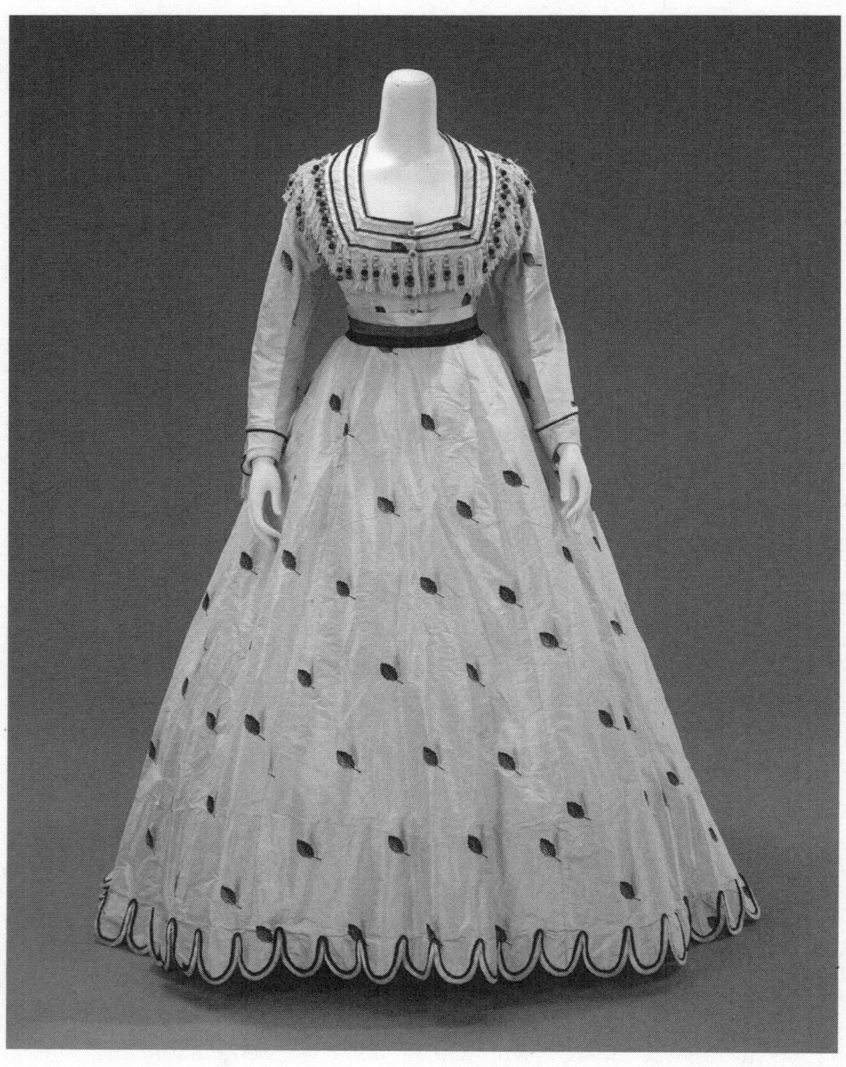

4.1 Texier St Engley, Coordinates, Evening, c. 1875. Brooklyn Museum Costume Collection at the Metropolitan Museum of Art. Gift of the Brooklyn Museum, 2009. Gift of Joanne Johannes Polster. Photographed by Lea Christiano.

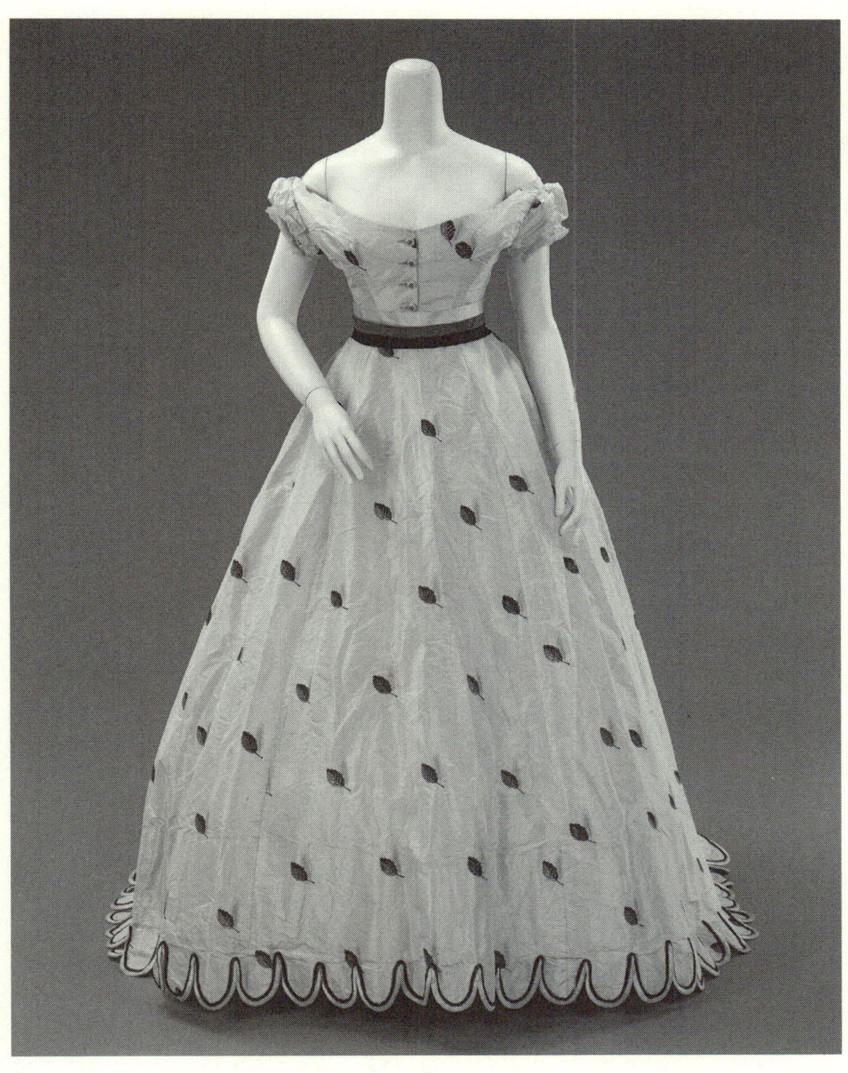

4.2 Texier St Engley, Coordinates, Evening, c. 1875. Brooklyn Museum Costume Collection at the Metropolitan Museum of Art. Gift of the Brooklyn Museum, 2009. Gift of Joanne Johannes Polster. Photographed by Lea Christiano.

The breathless enthusiasm with which the fashion editor of *Le Conseiller des dames et des demoiselles* describes what she calls "dresses with interchangeable bodices" – in essence a single skirt with several matching tops – may reflect the fact that, in 1854 when the report appeared in the journal, this exciting trend was still relatively new. Unlike many fads, however, this one actually took hold, as this circa 1875 example of a dress with two contrasting tops demonstrates, and even increased in popularity well into the Third Republic (see figures 4.1 and 4.2). The enduring success of the *robe à transformation*, as it became commonly called, is not surprising, for, as the correspondent for the *Conseiller* suggests, the ability to match several bodices with the same skirt simplified some of the complicated rituals of dressing with which women of the period were faced. The numerous names for the countless categories of dresses that existed attest to some of these complexities. There were, for example, *robes de jour*, *robes de visite*, *robes de réception*, *robes de ville*, *robes habillées*, and *robes de soir*, not to mention garments meant for specific activities such as the *robe de bal*, the *costume de promenade en montagne*, the *toilette de courses*, the *costume pour le chemin de fer* or the *robe pour la plage*, to name a few.[2] Moreover, depending on her social status and lifestyle, a stylish woman could be expected to change clothing several times a day. In the morning, she might wear a loose peignoir around the house, then change into a daytime dress appropriate for a range of leisure occupations, such as visiting friends in their homes, shopping in the city, or riding or walking in the park. If she went horseback riding, she would don an *amazone*, a tailored, masculinized ensemble complete with top hat and riding pants under her long skirt. If the genteel sport of bird hunting were on the day's agenda she would switch to the shortened skirt, nature-coloured fabrics, sturdy boots and feathered hat appropriate for this stylish activity (see figure 4.3). In the late afternoon, she might change into a diaphanous tea gown for entertaining at home, or if dining or going to the theatre, she would adopt an evening outfit, which was more ornamented than her day dress and would often feature short sleeves and a lower-cut neckline. For a very formal ball, her ensemble could include a plunging décolletage, opulent jewelry, and a gown made of fine silk.

This overwhelming list of garments and costume changes does not necessarily represent the typical experience of a middle- or upper-class woman, for normally, clothing would not need to be changed quite so frequently all in one day.[3] However, it does illustrate the reality that in the late nineteenth century different activities and times of day

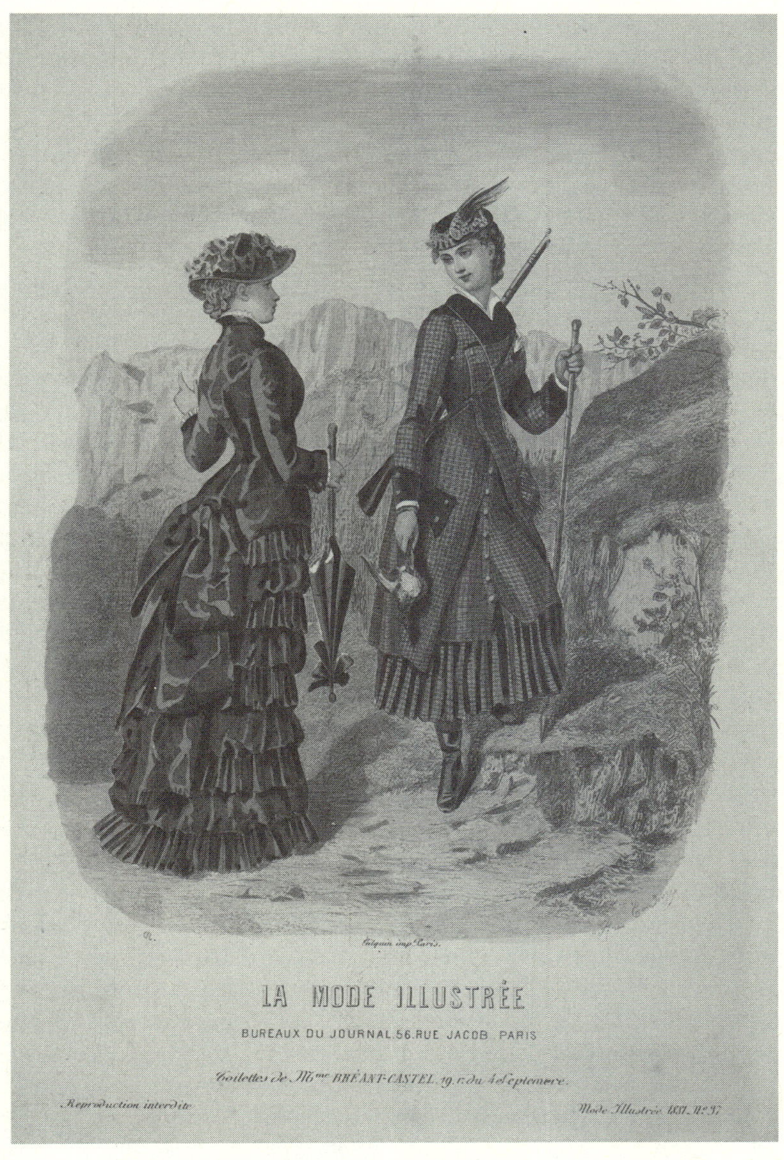

4.3 Adèle-Anaïs Toudouze, *A Lady in a Hunting Costume with a Lady in Walking Costume on a Mountain Path*, from *La Mode Illustrée*, 1881. Hand-coloured lithograph. Image copyright © The Metropolitan Museum of Art. Image source: Art Resource, NY.

required that fashionable women change into a new outfit. The robe à transformation responded to the need to go, in particular, from day-time pursuits to evening occupations and to do so quickly, or "in two minutes," as the reporter declares.

Costume historians aptly point out that the robe à transformation is both a material reaction to and a reflection of late-nineteenth-century modernity itself.[4] Its emphasis on rapidity and conversion, for example, rendered it a sartorial manifestation of speed, movement, and transition, all concepts associated with the period of Haussmannization. In what follows, I will argue that the dress style is also an expression of the waiting room/changing room dynamic that Maupassant illustrates in his short story, "La Parure." As mentioned above, garments can themselves be thought of as spaces in which the clothed body exists and operates. Maupassant's texts are particularly alert to this quality, as shown in his frequent juxtapositions of fashions with interior décors. Thinking about Maupassant's work in relation to the robe à transformation helps to call attention to the importance of place in narrations about urban life in the late 1800s that deliberately took characters to different locales of the cityscape. Indeed, part of the reason that the garment "transformed" was in order to respond to new environments. Thus, as the *Conseiller* implies, a "winter bodice, very high-necked, very warm," which was appropriate for walking on an open boulevard on a chilly day, would not be suitable for an evening in a restaurant or theatre, where a bodice that was "low-cut, with short sleeves" would be more fitting, both for the formalness of the occasion and for a space that could be crowded and stiflingly hot.

With its unique capacity to change (several bodices) while remaining static and unchanging (one skirt), the robe à transformation is a textile representation of the textual space of the antechamber, where waiting (staying in one place) and transforming (moving from one place to another) occur. As we will see, the antechamber figures prominently in Maupassant's "La Parure," both literally and figuratively, and references to the space coincide with crucial fashion moments. By tracing the themes of delay and transformation in the text and their relationship to space and garments, one can arrive at a reading of the tale's conclusion that nuances typical interpretations of Maupassant's biting critique of middle- and upper-class society. I will submit, instead, that the ending of "La Parure" might indicate a degree of optimism with respect to modern city dwellers, one usually left unrecognized in studies of Maupassant's works.

In brief, "La Parure," or "The Necklace" centres on Mme Loisel, a dissatisfied middle-class wife who dreams of a life of luxury that her husband, a government worker with a modest income, cannot provide. When M. Loisel receives an invitation to a formal ball, his vain wife, anxious to appear more affluent than she actually is, asks first for a new outfit and then, having secured this, borrows a diamond necklace from her wealthy friend, Mme Forestier, to complete the look. The ball is the highlight of Mme Loisel's life: she is admired and envied, just as she has always desired. Upon returning home, however, she discovers that she has lost the necklace. In order to repay the debt that they incur in replacing the diamonds, the Loisels spend the next ten years in poverty doing menial labour. After the debt has been paid, Mme Loisel encounters Mme Forestier, who does not recognize her after her years of physical toil. The story ends with Mme Forestier's dramatic revelation that the necklace that Mme Loisel had borrowed from her was a worthless fake.

"La Parure" is marked by a tension between changing and waiting that relates to the particularities of the literary genre that Maupassant famously pioneered: the short story. A short story by its very parameters must cover a great deal of narrative ground in a relatively small amount of text. "La Parure," at a trim 2,600 words, does this admirably, but Maupassant complicates the conciseness of the story with a major temporal extension in its plot. We note, for example, that the story takes place over the course of more than ten years. This long duration is at odds with the brevity of the text itself, which creates a friction that Maupassant enhances narratively. To take the most striking example, in the phrase, "And they lived like this for ten years"[5] (translation modified) ["Et cette vie dura dix ans"[6]], the author distils an entire decade into one terse sentence that, to enhance the effect, is an independent paragraph unto itself. The phrase, along with the plot more generally, duly expresses rapid change (in the abrupt shortness of the sentence) and the delayed pause of the ten-year interval during which time the Loisels must wait before they can hope to regain their middle-class lifestyle. However, to complicate any return to their former life, Maupassant equally implies that Mme Loisel is irrevocably altered, as evinced by her friend's inability to recognize her and Mme Forestier's exclamation, "how you've changed!"[7] ["comme tu es changée!"[8]].

Like the robe à transformation, which, according to the fashion reporter for the *Conseiller*, promises "a complete transformation of an outfit," Mme Loisel is completely transformed by the story's conclusion (albeit not as she had intended). Yet, well before Mme Forestier provides confirmation of Mme Loisel's conversion, Maupassant links her to the notion of change. From the beginning of the story, Mme Loisel dreams of her life transforming from the dull existence that she detests to a fantasy of "a life of refinement and luxury"[9] ["toutes les délicatesses et tous les luxes"[10]]. Dissatisfied by her simple bourgeois lot, she yearns to alter her living quarters, the food that she eats, and, most of all, the clothes that she wears. Later, during her decade-long interval as a labourer, she returns to the idea of transformation, this time reflecting on the capriciousness of human existence and musing to herself, "Life is so strange, so fickle [changing]!"[11] ["Comme la vie est singulière, changeante!"[12]]. The changes that Mme Loisel contemplates are like those that the robe à transformation illustrates. On the one hand, they are radical transformations, fundamental alterations to an entire outfit or to Mme Loisel's daily lifestyle. On the other hand, they are superficial, performed on the exterior body in the case of the robe à transformation, and related to surface and appearance, like the showy dinners and opulent surroundings that Maupassant's protagonist craves.

Fashion, then, symbolizes exceptionally well the changes to which Mme Loisel aspires, and also those to which she must submit. For, as the title implies, it is the necklace that is the catalyst for change, as the loss of the accessory is the impetus for the gross interruption to the Loisels' bourgeois trajectory and the dramatic new direction their lives then take. Yet, fashion is an apt metaphor, too, for other important mechanisms at play in Maupassant's tale, namely, those of suffering and longing for what one does not have. As Mary Donaldson-Evans observes, "The two verbs which figure most prominently in this story are *souffrir* and *songer*."[13] These two terms could equally apply to a paradox of fashion, which causes suffering (of the manipulated body, for example) while simultaneously feeding and providing a point of access to dreams of a life that is not one's own. "Fashion acts as a vehicle for fantasy," submits Elizabeth Wilson in her aptly named study *Adorned in Dreams*.[14] This is the case for Mme Loisel, whose list of things for which she "daydreams" (*songer*) culminates in fine garments and jewels, or, to be more precise, her lack thereof: "She had no fine dresses, no jewelry, nothing. And that was all that she cared about; she felt made for it" (translation modified)[15] ["Elle n'avait pas de toilettes, pas de bijoux, rien. Et elle n'aimait que cela; elle se sentait faite pour cela"[16]]. As part of the fantasy that fashion can generate, Mme Loisel believes that these items of adornment can lead to what, it turns out, is her true dream: to have and to be what others want. Maupassant continues, "She would so much have wanted to be pleasing, envied, seductive, and desired" (translation modified)[17] ["Elle eût tant désiré plaire, être enviée, être séduisante et recherchée"[18]].

In symbolizing the life of which a young Mme Loisel dreams, however, elegant clothing and accessories also represent her suffering, since there is no indication that she will ever acquire them, a fact that causes her great pain. After Mme Loisel visits a wealthy friend who appears to have all that she herself desires, we read, "Sometimes, for days on end, she would weep tears of sorrow, regret, despair, and anguish"[19] ["Elle pleurait pendant des jours entiers, de chagrin, de regret, de désespoir et de détresse"[20]]. Garments and jewelry might even be said to increase Mme Loisel's affliction, for dress and fine jewels are the two obstacles that (initially) prevent her from attending the ball, compounding her consternation.[21] In short, Mme Loisel falls prey to the fantasy that the report on the robe à transformation perpetuates: that to be happy she must be fashionable, and to be fashionable she "must" ["il lui faut"] continually transform herself according to fashion's exigencies. Contemplating clothing items that she does *not* possess, fantasy garments that exist only in her dreams, leads to her bitter suffering, emphasized by the phrase "sorrow, regret, despair and anguish." The necklace itself can be considered an object of suffering in the sense that it is the instrument with which Maupassant takes revenge on Mme Loisel, a character who incarnates the pettiness, hypocrisy, and vanity of the middle classes that the author so frequently attacked in his writings.

The role of the necklace in inflicting punishment on Mme Loisel brings us to the antechamber, specifically the waiting-room salon in which the necklace may have been lost. At the end of the protagonist's glorious evening at the ball, we find that M. Loisel has been waiting for her for four hours, so long, in fact, that he has fallen asleep: "Since midnight her husband had been dozing in a small, empty side-room with three other men whose wives were having an enjoyable time"[22] ["Son mari, depuis minuit, dormait dans un petit salon désert avec trois autres messieurs dont les femmes s'amusaient beaucoup[23]]. Along with his delayed and slumbering companions, M. Loisel has turned the side room into a waiting room, a space in which to pass the time from midnight until four in the morning. Yet, to serve as a location for waiting is not the drawing room's sole role in the narrative, for it is also the site in which Mme Loisel's vanity is most condemnably enacted. Embarrassed by the plainness of her coat, Mme Loisel flees the room rather than waiting for a carriage and taking the risk that her outerwear will reveal to others the reality of her social and economic condition. The scene develops as follows:

> [M. Loisel] threw on her coat which he had fetched when it was time to go, a modest, everyday coat, a commonplace coat violently at odds with the elegance of her dress. It brought her down to earth, and she would have preferred to slip away quietly and avoid being noticed by the other women who were being arrayed in rich furs. But Loisel grabbed her by the arm: "Wait a sec. You'll catch cold outside. I'll go and get a cab." But she refused to listen and ran quickly down the stairs (translation modified).[24]

> [Il lui jeta sur les épaules les vêtements qu'il avait apportés pour la sortie, modestes vêtements de la vie ordinaire, dont la pauvreté jurait avec l'élégance de la toilette de bal. Elle le sentit et voulut s'enfuir, pour ne pas être remarquée par les autres femmes qui s'enveloppaient de riches fourrures.
>
> Loisel la retenait:
>
> "Attends donc. Tu vas attraper froid dehors. Je vais appeler un fiacre."
> Mais elle ne l'écoutait point et descendait rapidement l'escalier.[25]]

Maupassant never specifies that the necklace falls off in the antechamber, but it seems fitting that a chief site of Mme Loisel's prideful behaviour might also be the location of the loss of the jewels that leads to her punishment. Sartorially, it makes sense as well, since M. Loisel "throws" the garments on her shoulders and, perhaps, in so doing, jars loose the accessory. Or it could be Mme Loisel herself who causes the diamonds to fall. When M. Loisel questions her about the last time she had the necklace, she remembers feeling it in the antechamber: "I remember fingering it in the minister's vestibule" (translation modified)[26] ["je l'ai touchée dans le vestibule du ministère"[27]]. Perhaps it is her own anxious "fingering" that sends the jewels to the floor.

In any case, what is important is that Maupassant uses both the antechamber and fashion to expose Mme Loisel's shortcomings of character. As Donaldson-Evans observes, "Madame Loisel's social pretense ... had caused her to borrow the necklace and perhaps even to lose it (for had she not been ashamed of her modest outer garments she would have waited at the ball while her husband went in search of a fiacre instead of leaving with him so that she would not be seen)."[28] Donaldson-Evans is correct to call attention here to Mme Loisel's "modest outer garments" because these are the very objects that Maupassant draws on to depict and criticize his protagonist's flaws. To develop this point in spatial terms, one notes that Mme Loisel's pride culminates specifically in a waiting room, leading to the suggestion that her crime of vanity is made manifest because she does not, in fact, wait. If she had not been so hasty in her shame and had only *waited*, Maupassant might be implying, someone at the ball could have seen the jewels fall. If his wife had not been in such a hurry, M. Loisel might have had the time to find a proper carriage; the necklace might not have been dropped on the street or in a seedy night cab, two other possibilities that the text advances. As a space made crucial to the narrative through fashion (plain outerwear is thrown on, wealthy women slip on furs, possibly the necklace is lost), the antechamber represents for Maupassant a dislocation in which both waiting (by M. Loisel) and major changes (to the Loisels' lifestyles) collide.

We noted above that, regardless of the pettiness of her reasoning, Mme Loisel suffers in the antechamber and that clothing – her shabby everyday wear – is the catalyst of her distress. Recalling fashion's paradox of causing both suffering and dreaming, we see that antechambers are the loci of not just pain, but of her fantasies as well. At the beginning of the story, Maupassant provides this description from Mme Loisel's imagination:

She dreamed of silent antechambers hung with oriental tapestries, lit by tall, bronze candelabras, and of two tall footmen in liveried breeches asleep in the huge armchairs, dozing in the heavy heat of a stove. She dreamed of great drawing-rooms dressed with old silk, filled with fine furniture which showed off trinkets beyond price, and of pretty little parlours, filled with perfumes and just made for intimate talk at five in the afternoon with one's closest friends who would be the most famous and sought-after men of the day whose attentions were much coveted and desired by all women.[29]

[Elle songeait aux antichambres nettes, capitonnées avec des tentures orientales, éclairées par de hautes torchères de bronze, et aux deux grands valets en culotte courte qui dorment dans les larges fauteuils, assoupis par la chaleur lourde du calorifère. Elle songeait aux grands salons vêtus de soie ancienne, aux meubles fins portant des bibelots inestimables, et aux petits salons coquets parfumés, faits pour la causerie de cinq heures avec les amis les plus intimes, les hommes connus et recherchés dont toutes les femmes envient et désirent l'attention.[30]]

Madame Loisel's dream includes several types of antechambers: luxury entry halls where uniformed doormen nap, and private salons where exciting flirtations – or more – with sought-after men occur. These antechambers, exotic and opulent, are the antithesis of her actual lodgings, "the run-down apartment they lived in, the peeling walls, the battered chairs, and the ugly curtains"[31] ["la pauvreté de son logement … la misère des murs … l'usure des sieges … la laideur des étoffes"[32]]. One might argue that all antechambers are "luxury" spaces in the sense that, unlike a bedroom or a kitchen, an antechamber is non-essential and supplemental. It is thus logical that Mme Loisel's fantasy would include lavish antechambers, since such "luxury" rooms inherently represent the extra indulgences that she and her simple, utilitarian, middle-class apartment lack. What is notable is that Mme Loisel's dream home includes *primarily* this category of room, for two of the three spaces mentioned in her fantasy are antechambers and parlours.

"A Complete Transformation": Maupassant the Optimist?

Perhaps the most cruel (and compelling) element of "La Parure" is the incompatibility between the Loisels' ten years of waiting to pay off the debt, and the closing line, Mme Forestier's devastating admission, "Oh! my poor Mathilde! But it was only an imitation necklace. It couldn't have been worth much more than five hundred francs!"[33] ["Oh! ma pauvre Mathilde! Mais la mienne était fausse. Elle valait au plus cinq cents francs!"[34]]. It is here that the reader abruptly receives the stunning news that, as Donaldson-Evans puts it, the ten years of "intense activity" that follow the loss of the necklace is marked by its own "futility."[35] In some respects, it is true that the Loisels' decade of labour seems rendered pointless by the final phrase. Yet, Maupassant may equally be implying that the turn of events is actually "a fortuitous event in Madame Loisel's life," as Donaldson-Evans also suggests.[36] There is the possibility, for example, that Mme Loisel has emerged from her punishment of menial labour "transformed" into a better, less shallow person, one who will no longer take the pleasures of a modest but comfortable life for granted. The open ending, which leaves the reader with no indication of what will next occur, may allow for this hopeful interpretation.

However, the character who provides the strongest case that the notoriously cynical Maupassant may have had more faith in modern urban society than typically thought is not Mme Loisel but rather the wealthy Mme Forestier, to whom Maupassant accords a scant, but powerful, few sentences at the end of the story. Indeed, Mme Forestier speaks the final phrase, a textual place of honour that suggests that her contribution to the tale is particularly important. But what, precisely, is this contribution? I would argue that what Mme Forestier provides is true compassion, an empathy that she instinctively feels in reaction to her friend's misfortune. We read, for example, that Mme Forestier becomes "very upset"[37] ["fort émue"[38]] and clasps Madame Loisel's hands, thereby connecting with the parts of the body – hands – that have suffered and now define Mme Loisel as a "manual" labourer. The fact that she touches Mme Loisel's hands at all is remarkable, since toiling has turned them unappealingly old and red, the opposite of the porcelain white skin cherished as a sign of upper-class gentility. The dialogue similarly points to Mme Forestier's sympathy for Mme Loisel's plight: of the seven lines that she utters, two include the exclamation "My poor Mathilde" [ma pauvre Mathilde"].[39] In this repeated phrase the term "poor" emphasizes Mme Forestier's dismayed pity for the woman whose hands she holds, while her use of Mme Loisel's first name indicates intimacy and friendship. The numerous exclamation points at the ends of Mme Forestier's spoken lines reiterate that her concern and pity for Mme Loisel are involuntary and uncalculated emotions.

Floriane Place-Verghnes, commenting on Mme Forestier's final revelation, notes that the ending invites us to reassess the entire narrative from the range of viewpoints of the different characters: "Because she or he is disoriented by the final clause, the reader must reconsider after the fact its implications from the point of view of the Loisels, of Mme Forestier, and finally of him or herself as reader" ["Parce qu'il est dérouté par la proposition finale, le lecteur doit reconsidérer *a posteriori* les implications du point de vue des Loisel, de celui de Mme Forestier, et enfin du sien en tant que lecteur"].[40] Rereading the text with Mme Forestier's viewpoint in mind, one can posit that Mathilde's plight inspires honest and heartfelt sympathy from her more fortunate friend. Although it may be stretching the point to suggest that Mme Forestier is thus heroic, at the very least she displays traits at the end that render her more estimable than the prideful Mme Loisel or the well-meaning but oblivious M. Loisel.

Maupassant's vast body of work does include a few admirable characters: one thinks, for example, of the courageous fishermen of "Deux Amis" or the self-sacrificing protagonist of "Boule de Suif." However, it is rare that an upper-class Parisian woman would appear commendable in a Maupassant story, especially in light of the author's many disparaging tales about the moral deficiencies of the urban bourgeoisie. There is, however, at least one other character that comes to mind, one that shares the same name with the compassionate woman of "La Parure": *Bel-Ami*'s Madeleine Forestier. Madeleine, an intelligent and able journalist, is arguably the most respectable character in *Bel-Ami*, a novel that otherwise features a host of weak, cruel, and shallow protagonists. The scholar (and coincidentally named) Louis Forestier offers that Madeleine may have been modelled after a secretary for whom Maupassant felt "a tender friendship" ["une tendre amitié"];[41] the author's affection for this woman may have influenced his relatively positive portrait of Madeleine. It is not certain why Maupassant chose the same name for his two characters, but perhaps the most logical explanation is the simplest one. Maupassant began writing *Bel-Ami* the summer of 1884.[42] Having published "La Parure" in February of that same year, the name may have been fresh in his mind, and, due to the fact that the tale appeared during a period in which Maupassant wrote a number of short stories in rapid succession, he may not have noticed using it a second time. As I will discuss in the last part of this chapter, especially for the plot of *Bel-Ami*, which the author deliberately linked to political events of the day, Maupassant was in need of a generic moniker like "Forestier" that would read as typically French but would not be associated with an actual person appearing in newspaper headlines.[43] It is possible that, in searching for a suitable name for the respectable Madeleine Forestier in *Bel-Ami*, Maupassant drew subconsciously on the humane Jeanne Forestier of "La Parure."

Perhaps the identical names are simply an unintended coincidence, but the uncommonly sympathetic portrait of Madeleine Forestier supports the interpretation that the similarly named Jeanne Forestier of "La Parure" represents a favourable side to modern urban society that the author perceived alongside his deep pessimism about it. The final line of the story, Mme Forestier's exclamation of pathos, presents the possibility of a metropolis populated not (only) with superficial malcontents like Mme Loisel, but also those who feel some connection to the pain of others (whether or not, in the end, they can do anything to alleviate it). By the conclusion of the tale, Mme Loisel is "dressed like any working-class woman"[44] ["vêtue comme une femme du peuple"[45]], far removed from silk gowns, diamond necklaces, and even the simple theatre dress that, through vanity, she refuses to wear to the minister's ball. Others have noted that, for the reader, the dramatic power of "La Parure" lies, to an extent, in Maupassant's mastery of the realist strategy to create recognizable tropes for characters and situations, what Roland Barthes famously called "the reality effect" or "l'effet de réel." Indeed, Mme Loisel is not unlike Emma Bovary from a previous generation, a dissatisfied, fashion-hungry, middle-class housewife that readers quickly understand as an archetype, a particular case representing bourgeois society more generally.[46] "La Parure" is thus an individual story representing global vanity and shallowness, traits that Maupassant, in most other cases, suggests were typical of the bourgeoisie in 1880s Paris. Here, however, in what I am reading as momentary optimism – unexpected for Maupassant – the author accords the final word not to the character taken in by the fantasies and superficial urgencies that the robe à transformation maintains, but rather to the compassionate upper-class woman who sees through Mme Loisel's shabby clothes and chafed hands to embrace her in a moment of empathy and shared human suffering. As though himself undergoing a rapid and "complete transformation," trading his dark cynicism for this glimmer of hope, Maupassant may have been adopting, however temporarily, an entirely new point of view, one as transformative to our reading of the text as multiple bodices can be to a single skirt.

"Algiers, That Antechamber to the Deep Mystery of Africa": Fashioning Exoticism in *Bel-Ami*

In France the 1870s were a decade that comprised two very significant *spatial* movements or events. It was the decade that saw the formation of a consciousness conducive to producing a colonialist, expeditionary class. The speed and mathematical directness with which the railroad proceeds through space, joining together previously inaccessible places as coordinates in a systematized grid, had already begun, within Europe, to make space *geographic*. Throughout the 1870s France prepared to accelerate that movement into a geopolitical one, to expand and project onto a global scale Haussmann's intraurban "fantasy of the straight line." France strengthened what would become its major role in the European transformation of space into colonial space, and in the establishment of an international division of labor. And second, on another but no less important scale, there occurred the spatial event of the Paris Commune, what in the 1960s was proclaimed by many to be the first realization of urban space as revolutionary space. (Original emphases)

– Kristin Ross, *The Emergence of Social Space:*
Rimbaud and the Paris Commune[47]

Kristin Ross's examination of 1870s urban and geopolitical space through the lens of Rimbaud's revolutionary poetics focuses specifically on Paris during the Commune. But, as Ross rightly maintains in the passage above, the "spatial event" of the Commune should also be understood within the larger context of France's vigorous politics of colonial expansionism at work during this period. Like Ross's study, my own discussion of the staircase in chapter 1 centred on the Commune space in literature and, in particular, drew parallels between the barricades and discourses of fashion in Zola's *Au Bonheur des Dames*. It is Ross's other point that I address here, turning to late-century connections between the Parisian metropole and the colonial spaces to which France was ever more aggressively laying claim in these years. This approach centres on sartorial objects and the metaphor of the antechamber in Maupassant's *Bel-Ami*. In particular, the focus will be on the ways that garments reveal Maupassant's critique of France's expansionist politics by highlighting what he depicts as the harmful effects of colonization to France itself, as opposed to abroad. We begin with *Bel-Ami*'s treatment of orientalism, which, to borrow a formulation from Susan Hiner, can be characterized as "the domestication of the exotic."[48]

Hiner's phrase derives from her work on the *cachemire*, a highly fashionable shawl having Eastern origins that inscribed it with orientalist exoticism. Her focus, like mine, is on texts set in the urban capital, fiction in which colonial expansion from Europe to the colonies works in tandem with the importation of goods, such as the cachemire, which travelled in the opposite direction, moving away from points abroad and into France. Hiner uses the cachemire to posit the role of fashion accessories in a general "domestication" of objects derived from conquered lands. One compelling phenomenon surrounding these items was that while imports continued to retain some of the allure of the foreign, over time they could likewise be divested of it through their appropriation into Western culture. Hiner explains this process as follows: "When the symbol of conquest comes home to France, it is taken up by the fashion system and apparently seamlessly incorporated into a domestic economy ... the garment is quickly converted from exotic signifier to domestic currency."[49] Implicit in Hiner's study is the crucial notion that colonization should not be thought of as occurring solely in territories far remote from the French Hexagon. Rather, through urbanites' consumption of commodities exploited abroad, overseas imperialism operated in its own complex manner within the city limits of Paris itself. She notes, "Part of colonialism's staying power within the metropole lay in the colonizing culture's assumption of oriental goods into its own signifying systems – the goods became domesticated, that is, converted into an appealing and consumable form of domination over western women and their bodies."[50] Hiner's work, which treats texts from throughout the nineteenth century, reveals that the fashionableness of garments associated with exoticism, whether they were produced in the colonies or in France itself, could diminish over time. In the case of the cachemire, for example, the fact that shawls from the early 1800s were hand-made, rare, and appealingly unfamiliar like their countries of origin conferred distinction upon the items and their wearers alike. By the end of the century, however, mass production had increased the availability of the chachemire to women of the middle and lower classes, stripping it of some of its allure. As Hiner submits, "These objects only retained their power inasmuch as they continued to refer to the exotic/erotic."[51] The shawl, by then somewhat banal, had lost some of its exoticism, along with much of its fashionable cachet.

The notion that accessories could lose their ability to connote fashionability and that, moreover, this was related to a perceived loss in their exoticism, is illustrated in *Bel-Ami* through Maupassant's complication of fashion, urban dislocation, and colonial space. As discussed elsewhere, in the novel, the exotic/erotic is associated with Duroy's lover Clotilde de Marelle and manifests materially in the garments that she wears.[52] Tellingly, though, Maupassant's representation of Clotilde as "the Orient" seems deliberately overdetermined. One could argue that, by the 1880s when *Bel-Ami* was penned, orientalism was a trope that had become, through massive overexposure in literature, art, and commercial culture, as de-exoticized as a late-century cachemire shawl. Clotilde's constant practice of donning orientalized fashions – clichéd "Eastern" attire including a Japanese kimono and a "Spanish outfit"[53] ["costume espagnol"[54]] – thus make her a banal version of recognizable orientalist tropes rather than a truly foreign presence. Maupassant's use of fashion to evoke Eastern stereotypes connects him to an established yet shifting tradition in French letters. In 1845 Gautier had celebrated the rising vogue of Eastern-styled garments in Paris – "scarves once used by harem slaves, woven through with gold, multicoloured in a thousand hues … the camelhair burnous … the tarbouch" ["des écharpes tramées d'or, bariolées de mille couleurs qui ont servi aux esclaves du harem … le burnous en poil de chameau … le tarbouch"] – and declaring his orientalist fantasy that, in time, "France will be mahometanized" ["La France sera mahométane"].[55] A few decades later, however,

Mallarmé altered Gautier's tone in *La Dernière Mode* by featuring articles "written" by a host of exotic others such as "a Creole lady"[56] ["Une dame créole"[57]], "Zizy, a mulatto maid from Surat"[58] ["Zizy, bonne mulâtre de Surate"[59]], and "Olympe, a negress"[60] ["Olympe, négresse"[61]]. That these "foreign" personae were tongue-in-cheek feminine pseudonyms suggests that Mallarmé deployed them more for comedic effect and titillation than to praise them in the apparently sincere, albeit orientalist, manner of Gautier or to convey the genuinely alien or mysterious.

This decline in orientalism's power to connote the exotic in fashion is echoed in a strikingly spatial phrase in *Bel-Ami* in which Duroy, by way of the narrator, refers to the capital city of Algeria as "Algiers, that antechamber to the deep mystery of Africa" (translation modified)[62] ["Alger, cette antichambre de l'Afrique mystérieuse et profonde"[63]]. Louis Forestier understands this colonial-architectural metaphor – Algiers standing in for an antechamber – as a reflection that, by the mid-1880s, the exotic connotations of capital cities in the Maghreb had largely diminished. In Forestier's words, "around 1885, there was a miragelike vision of Africa in the French mentality. Algeria as a department of France and Tunisia as a protectorate both were, to everyone, a part of the familiar landscape even taught in schools" ["Autour de 1885, il y a un mirage de l'Afrique, dans la mentalité française. L'Algérie départementalisé, la Tunisie sous protectorat font partie du paysage familier, scolaire même, de chacun"[64]]. The familiarity of North Africa, Forestier implies, contrasts with the mysteriousness of points further south and west in the continent, areas that Duroy envisions as "the Africa of Arab nomads and strange negroes, an Africa unexplored and alluring"[65] ["l'Afrique des Arabes vagabonds et des nègres inconnus, l'Afrique inexplorée et tentante"[66]]. This latter construction of a deeper region in Africa, one populated with animals so implausible that they seem to originate in fairy tales, is an entirely different locale from the Mediterranean city of Algiers because it retains the "unexplored" and "alluring" qualities that, according to Forestier, had faded for Maupassant's readers with respect to the North, a *concept*, though certainly not a place, seemingly more familiar to a French readership.

Forestier's point might benefit from a slight nuance. For although it is convincing that, after half a century of official colonization, the *idea* of the Maghreb had become partly banalized in the French imagination, it seems equally likely that evocations of Algeria would have retained *some* of their exoticism (as they do today). In any case, though, Forestier's position that the North African territories had by the 1880s lost a degree of their power to signify the exotic in France also seems supported by the ubiquity of orientalized referents in paintings, decorative objects, photographs, and travel narratives that urban dwellers of the period encountered regularly in their everyday lives. Diminished exoticism is reinforced as well in Clotilde de Marelle's garments, which readers would have *recognized* as "exotic", ironically, due to their familiarity with the trope. Attired in Spanish- and Japanese-inflected clothing, Clotilde thus represents a character type – the orientalized Western woman – that was fully identifiable to late-century Parisians. Although her style of dress and Clotilde herself continue to symbolize the *erotic* in the text, like the late-century cachemire and the Maghrebi capitals, her fashions lose some of the charge making them wholly *exotic*. Simply put, Clotilde *signifies* the exotic through dress rather than embodying it.

Clotilde's exoticism is further mitigated by another category of femininity that she represents: the chic Parisienne. As Ruth Iskin argues, the chic Parisienne became a discernible symbol of urban femininity in the last decades of the nineteenth century. A modern, stylish, sometimes coquettish icon of the metropolis, she represented the "authentic" city dweller. Clotilde, with her "little birdlike head"[67] ["petite tête d'oiseau"[68]] matches the physiognomy of the chic Parisienne, who was distinguishable by her pert upturned nose and petite head.[69] Iskin explores how this construction of French femininity was marketed as a fashionable model, not just of Paris but also of the nation at large; tellingly, when the archetype was exported, it was directly connected to discourses of colonialism. Iskin shows, for instance, that through its dissemination in international media and at events like the Universal Expositions seeking to reiterate France's cultural and political dominance in the world, the Parisienne was used to represent the superiority of the Third Republic to the rest of the globe.[70] That Maupassant has Clotilde don traditional dress from countries that would have been considered non-Western suggests not only her appropriation of these cultures via their garments but also that, with the innately expert style of the Parisienne, she wears them "better" than women in their countries of origin. As Iskin suggests, "In her elegant fashionability, *La Parisienne* was established as French and superior. She was modern and 'civilized' in contrast to 'other' cultures, which were presented as archaic or exotic."[71] Following Iskin, we can read Clotilde's sartorial mastery to stand in for the more general imperialism that France was imposing upon territories abroad. Closer to home, within the capital city, her stylish and appealing outfits have just the right touch of flamboyance to exhibit both the flair of the chic Parisienne and the safe mystique of recognizable orientalism. In a sense, Clotilde relies on this touch of the exotic in order to be fashionable, a fact that draws attention to the ways in which modernity itself, metaphorized in fashion, was contingent upon exoticism. On the other hand, to remain unthreatening, her otherness must be deracinated and made readable through the context of Western modernity that the chic Parisienne epitomized.

Behind the Veil: Domesticating Colonization

What I am calling Clotilde's "unexotic exoticism" is underscored especially in episodes from the novel in which she wears a veil. Like the cachemire, this accessory well exemplifies fashion's domestication of exoticism since it was associated, on the one hand, with its Eastern origins, yet was rendered familiar to French wearers through its assimilation into traditional Gallic wardrobes. As Marni Reva Kessler notes in her study of the complex cultural meanings of the veil in the second half of the nineteenth century, the veil's status as a fashion object linked it to a system of colonialism that was enacted in daily urban life. Kessler argues that "the persistent fashionability of the French veil was actually an integral part of the structure of imperialism itself, and therefore a subtle mechanism of international politics taking place on a local and quotidian level."[72] Moreover, the stylishness of the veil could assuage lingering fears of colonized subjects, whom the French continued to mistrust. In Kessler's words, "By translating the Muslim veil into French, certain cultural clichés associated with the colonies [that their people were brutal, violent, and irrational] could be smoothed over and perhaps contained."[73]

For Maupassant, in contrast, it was not the colonized subjects who were brutal and violent but rather the French, whose methods he had witnessed firsthand in 1881 when he was sent by the newspaper *Le Gaulois* to report on a rebellion fomenting in Algeria. In July of that year he wrote, "Nothing can give an idea of the intolerable situation in which we are putting the Arabs. The principle of French colonization consists of making them starve to death" ["Rien ne peut donner une idée de l'intolérable situation que nous faisons aux Arabes. Le principe de la colonisation française consiste à les faire crever de faim"].[74] Later, in 1884, he levied additional criticisms of the brutality of French imperialism, again including himself with the perpetrators by way of the pronoun "we" ["nous"]: "We have remained clumsy, brutal conquerors, infatuated with our own preconceived notions. The lifestyle we impose, our Parisian houses, our customs are offensive on this soil, like crude mistakes of art, wisdom and understanding" ["Nous sommes restés des conquérants brutaux, maladroits, infatués de nos idées toutes faites. Nos mœurs imposés, nos maisons Parisiennes, nos usages choquent sur ce sol comme des fautes grossières d'art, de sagesse et de compréhension"].[75] The same callous qualities that Maupassant identifies with the French resurface in *Bel-Ami* to describe Duroy during a key moment in which the protagonist remembers, with a cruel smile, stealing food from and killing three Arab men while stationed as a soldier in the Maghreb.[76] As we will see, Duroy's clumsiness, brutality, and self-interestedness – qualities that render him similar to the colonizing nation – are especially highlighted in his first encounter alone with a veiled Clotilde.

In this passage, Mme de Marelle, wearing a veil, arrives at Duroy's apartment where they will consummate their affair.[77] The episode calls attention to Clotilde's transparent accessory by passing over descriptions of her other garments, a rare occurrence for a character whose dress Maupassant typically portrays in detail. The scene unfolds thusly:

> He took her in his arms and was feverishly kissing her hair through her veil between her forehead and her hat.
>
> An hour and a half later, he went with her to the cab-rank in the rue de Rome.[78]

> [Il l'avait prise dans ses bras, et il baisait ses cheveux avec emportement, entre le front et le chapeau, à travers le voile.
>
> Une heure et demie plus tard, il la reconduisit à la station de fiacres de la rue de Rome.[79]]

In this encounter, the veil metaphor and Duroy's rough possession of Clotilde work together to echo practices of colonialism. The "feverishness" (*emportement*) with which Duroy embraces Clotilde, awkwardly kissing her veil rather than her face in his haste to arrive at sexual ownership of her body, mimics what Maupassant describes as the "clumsy" colonial aggressions of an occupying nation keen to exploit its territories abroad. The verb *emporter*, which can also mean "to conquer" or "to steal," further nods to Maupassant's critique of the French imperial enterprise. When Duroy masters Clotilde sexually, she becomes an allegory for that which is conquered, the personification of the colonized

Orient that her clothing evokes. This symbolism is apparent in the contrasting ways in which Duroy, at a later moment, covets her and her opposite, Madeleine Forestier. In the case of Madeleine, the quintessentially elegant Frenchwoman, he feels "an urge to kneel at her feet or kiss the dainty lace around her neck and slowly breathe in the warm, fragrant scent which was surely wafting from between her breasts"[80] ["le désir de se coucher à ses pieds, ou de baiser la fine dentelle de son corsage et d'aspirer lentement l'air chaud et parfumé qui devait sortir de là, glissant entre les seins"[81]], while for the latter, "his desire was more brutal and more direct, a desire which made his hands twitch as he saw her lifting breasts beneath their flimsy covering of silk"[82] ["il sentait en lui un désir plus brutal, plus précis, un désir qui frémissait dans ses mains devant les contours soulevées de la soie légère"[83]]. The term "brutal" and Duroy's eagerly twitching hands underscore the physicality of colonial violence that the aptly named Duroy, symbolic "king" of the empire, inflicts on the body signifying the exotic other. His rough possession of Clotilde differs from the much more gentle, passive seduction that he imagines enacting upon Madeleine, a cipher for France. Although both women are eventually "occupied" by Duroy in confirmation of his masculine dominance over the feminine, the brutality of Duroy's mastery over Clotilde can be read to imply Maupassant's censure of France's acts of cruelty in North Africa.

It is on this last point that we will linger with the goal of exploring what, precisely, may have been the impetus for Maupassant's critique of colonization. This is because I believe that the answer is more complex than the author's simple abhorrence for the starvation tactics of the French that he had observed in Algeria. For this discussion, we will turn to Maupassant's treatment of the urban home space and fashion, two themes in the novel where his depictions of orientalism are especially revelatory. To revisit the example of Clotilde's veil, in the citation above, care has been taken to reproduce the way in which the text appears in the original, with a paragraph separation between the two lines. This typographical element is important because it illustrates how the sartorial object in question – the veil – informs the textual rendering of the sexual encounter itself, an act of intimacy that takes place in this unnarrated space between the two phrases.[84] From a pragmatic standpoint, the fact that the intercourse between Duroy and Clotilde is left undescribed is not surprising, since any overly suggestive prose may have rendered the text too sexually explicit to print in *Le Gaulois*, a mass-circulation newspaper marketing itself as serious and "respectable."

Yet, when read through the clothing accessory that Maupassant is highlighting in the passage, the intimate encounter can be understood as "veiled," shrouded within the blank space situated between the two short paragraphs. This detail may echo Maupassant's judgment that the violence of colonialism, like Duroy's aggressive "taking" of Clotilde, was being kept out of sight from the general French population, concealed as if by a covering of fabric. In the early 1880s when the novel appeared, Maupassant may have believed that these realities were being "veiled," in particular, behind political rhetoric that had been actively circulating as politicians like Prime Minister Jules Ferry and other powerful government officials vigorously called for increased French development in the Maghreb.[85] Summarizing this expansionist platform, Forestier notes that "between 1880 and 1885, Jules Ferry extolled colonization on economic grounds – France needed markets – on military grounds and for reasons of prestige" ["entre 1880 et 1885, Jules Ferry prônait la colonisation pour des motifs économiques – la France avait besoin de marchés –, militaires et de prestige"[86]]. However, it was an uphill battle to convince the rest of France – a country recently wounded by war with Prussia and the loss of the territories of Alsace and Lorraine – to enter into another long and costly military campaign. Situating the veil within this historical and political context, Kessler observes that "the rising popularity of the Parisian veil from the 1850s to the 1880s coincides with the government's struggle for the expansion and maintenance of the French Empire in North Africa as it confronted the dwindling of public support for many imperialistic practices."[87] Understood in this light, Clotilde's domesticated veil points to the author's anti-Ferry stance and his denunciation of the hidden malevolence of colonization, which was occurring abroad physically but which was generated domestically in France through political manoeuvring taking place in the urban capital.

Examining the domestic workings of imperialism invites us to study closely the location in which the veiled sexual incursion between Duroy and Clotilde occurs, a space that is quite literally domestic for it is Duroy's home. Ashamed because his apartment is so shabby, Duroy tries to hide its cosmetic flaws, orientalizing the space by decorating it to resemble the inside of an Eastern-inspired paper lantern:

He hit on the notion of pinning tiny Japanese decorations all over the walls and he went out and bought for five francs a whole collection of pieces of coloured silk, little fans and small screens which he used to hide the more obvious stains on the wallpaper. On the window-panes he stuck transparent pictures of boats on rivers, flocks of birds flying across red skies, women of all the colours of the rainbow standing on balconies and processions of little black figures on plains covered in snow (translation modified).[88]

[Il eut l'idée d'épingler sur les murs de menus bibelots japonais, et il acheta pour cinq francs toute une collection de crépons, de petits éventails et de petits écrans, dont il cacha les taches trop visibles du papier. Il appliqua sur les vitres de la fenêtre des images transparentes représentant des bateaux sur des rivières, des vols d'oiseux à travers des ciels rouges, des dames multicolores sur des balcons et des processions de petits bonshommes noirs dans des plaines remplies de neige.[89]]

Once again, like Clotilde's stereotyped "Japanese" and "Spanish" garments, orientalism is here overdetermined, exaggerated by the high accumulation and clichéd "Easternness" of Duroy's decorative transformations. Moreover, the items he acquires are cheap knick-knacks that he has purchased "for five francs," inexpensive knock-offs of more valuable art objects and available to anyone with pocket change. They are "exotic" items that have lost their exoticism to all but those with the questionable low tastes of Duroy and Clotilde, both of whom appreciate the décor.

Spaces of overdetermined orientalism are a recurring theme in this relationship. Later, for example, the couple meets in an apartment that Clotilde rents for the sole purpose of facilitating their tryst, a flat located on the evocatively named "rue de Constantinople."[90] Through these orientalized apartments, Maupassant thus phrases the domestication of the exotic not only sartorially but in spatial terms as well. These terms are equally political, for, as Nicholas White has argued, in *Bel-Ami*, "the decor of domestic space represents foreign policy."[91] Following White, I believe Maupassant's attention to the urban space of Duroy's flat can be connected to the metaphor cited earlier of Algiers as the "antechamber" to Africa. Let us return, then, to the meaning of the architectural metaphor as Louis Forestier explains it above. For Forestier, we recall, by the time Maupassant was writing *Bel-Ami*, the Maghreb was a concept as familiar in France as any others taught to French schoolchildren. To this readership, Algeria would have been an "antechamber" in the sense of a mere entry hall that allowed admission to the deeper, still exotic, recesses of the rest of the continent. This attitude is reflected in

Maupassant's second report for *Le Gaulois*, which he wrote while in Algeria in 1881, in which he notes that arriving in the northern Maghreb only provokes in him a deep desire to advance ever more into Africa: "As soon as you have set foot on African soil, a singular need seizes you. The need to go farther, to the south" ["Dès qu'on a mis le pied sur cette terre africaine, un besoin singulier vous envahit. Celui d'aller plus loin, au sud"].[92] Like a foyer, Algiers in *Bel-Ami* seems merely the conduit leading to a new space, a room of transition that itself holds less interest than the tantalizing and mysterious parts of Africa that lie beyond.

The theme of the antechamber entryway, understood in these terms, underscores France's colonial entrance and expansion into Africa as well as Duroy's "admission" into the realm of shady politics and finance in Paris that, like a colonizer, he exploits and dominates later through cruel and fraudulent means. As Culbert puts it, "The symbolic capital of Bel-Ami's colonial experience, however ineptly managed on his part, enables his entry into this world of corruption."[93] Duroy's apartment can be read as an urban cipher for the conduit "antechamber" that Algiers represents for the rest of Africa, for his dubious rise to power rests on the sexual encounter that takes place in this space. Indeed, his orientalized flat reproduces the dialectic that we have been examining here in antechambers, namely, that of waiting and changing. After Duroy prepares his domicile for the arrival of his soon-to-be mistress, for instance, he experiences a delay: "Then he waited"[94] [Puis il attendait"[95]]. Duroy's wait for Clotilde frustrates him, as demonstrated in the forceful embrace that he imposes upon her before she even has the chance to remove her hat and veil. Waiting provokes his will to alter not merely his apartment but everything about his situation – his poverty, obscurity, and access to sexual conquests – things he is able to change subsequently thanks, in part, to advantageous connections made through Clotilde. Duroy's impatience in his flat mirrors Ferry's keenness to wait no longer and to colonize further into Africa and beyond, an eagerness to dominate that Maupassant critiques. The waiting and changing dynamic enacted in Duroy's Parisian home thus illustrates the mechanizations of colonialism on a citywide scale that gestures towards acts on a global scale.

The question might now be posed: if Clotilde's clothing and Duroy's efforts at interior design have been "domesticated" and no longer connote the exotic beyond surface caricature, why does Maupassant include them in the text? What, in other words, are the functions in the text of an exotic orientalism that is not really exotic? I would like to suggest that an answer lies in the antechamber metaphor, a space in which two opposite types of transitions are possible. That is, an antechamber permits a double movement: one can both exit and enter through it. Bearing this in mind, let us return to the phrase in question: "Algiers, that antechamber to the deep mystery of Africa,"[96] or, in the original, "Alger, cette antichambre de l'Afrique mystérieuse et profonde."[97] Logic tells us to translate the preposition *de* here as "to," because it is the most plausible option, and one that echoes the movement colonization makes in extending away from France and *to* Africa. But, technically, the word *de* also means "from," thus, grammatically speaking, the return motion can also be implied in the phrase. The sentence reflecting this change would then be: "Algiers, that antechamber [leading] *from* Africa." In this second version there is the ghost of a reference to something moving *from* Africa, through the intermediary of Algiers, and (back) to France.

What is it that France might be importing *from* Africa and allowing to enter into its own domestic space? One thinks first of goods, such as the fashions described above, that were modelled after constructed visions of the Orient and also materially exploited from peoples abroad. But in divorcing these items from their exotic charge – clothing Clotilde and decorating Duroy's flat with unexotic exoticism – Maupassant seems to suggest that this is a red herring, that there is a further, more profoundly insidious, importation at work. I would argue that *Bel-Ami* is Maupassant's anxious expression that the "clumsy" and "offensive" brutality that he had witnessed in Algeria was no longer characteristic behaviour of colonization abroad but rather colonization at home. To play with Hiner's formulation, it is not merely the domestication of the exotic that fashions in the novel represent but, additionally, the domestication of colonization that is brought back to Paris. This process is illustrated by Duroy himself – in the ways that he transforms over the course of the novel and in what he ultimately becomes. As Susan Barrow argues, by the end of the text Duroy is like a savage animal, a predator capable of ugly barbaric behaviour that deeply contrasts with the exterior beauty for which he, "Bel-Ami," is ironically nicknamed. She notes, "In what may be termed the revenge of the Orient, *Bel-Ami* illustrates how French society has been irreversibly altered by the experience of colonialism through the internalization of primal behaviors."[98] This influx of animal-like behaviour, Duroy's conversion to beast that Barrow provocatively labels "the revenge of the Orient," is, I believe, at the base of Maupassant's critique of colonization, which is that what is being imported through the process of engaging in overseas imperialism is the savageness of the colonizer, which entrenches itself not only in faraway lands but internally, as well, in spaces as nearby as Parisian home apartments. For Maupassant, movement through the antechamber from the colonies to France is dangerous, not for the reasons that immigration is feared by some today, but because the brutality learned through colonization (re)enters to infect and epitomize modern urban life.[99]

For Barrow, Duroy comes to represent the West's stereotype of Africa as a place of primal savagery and incivility. She writes, "Duroy 'becomes' Africa by internalizing the code of the wild experienced through his military service."[100] I would amend this to suggest that Maupassant ascribes Duroy's savagery not to his exposure to Africa, but rather his exposure to *colonizing* Africa. Duroy's savageness, which is learned and internalized through the acts of cruel violence that he commits in the Maghreb, is especially important in light of the paradox that he incarnates as a representative of both the exceptional and the universal. That is, in one sense, Duroy is an extraordinary man who experiences a unique trajectory from obscurity to the pinnacle of Parisian society. At the same time, it can be argued that he is Everyman, a typical urban subject who symbolizes what all of the city and nation might ultimately become.[101] Clothing reinforces Duroy's Everyman status: his sober black suits and regularizing top hats form the standardizing uniform of nineteenth-century bourgeois masculinity, rendering him an archetype for French universality.[102] My reading of this novel implies that the impetus for Maupassant's sharp criticism of colonization is not what it does to the colonies, but rather what it might do to French society more generally as such brutal practices, personified by Duroy, are domesticated, normalized, and eventually imitated by the rest of Paris, symbolized by the admiring crowds gathered to witness his post-wedding triumph at the Madeleine.

One final example summarizes Maupassant's problematizing of space and fashion in the antechamber and its relationship to his critique of colonization. Above we have seen that Clotilde signifies exoticism without being exotic, for she is as knowable as the chic Parisienne who simply masquerades as an exotic other. Maupassant's handling of Clotilde's garments in relation to the space in which she lives further nuances her symbolic role in the text. Arriving for an intimate tête-à-tête at Clotilde's house, Duroy is asked to wait for her in the salon, a wait that turns out to be a lengthy one: "Duroy sat down and waited. He waited a long time"[103] ["Duroy s'assit et attendit. Il attendit longtemps"[104]]. This extended wait, emphasized here by the repetition of the verb *attendre*, affords Duroy the time to inspect Clotilde's salon-turned-waiting room, which, he notes, is filled with old, worn furniture and shows signs of neglect. Duroy is surprised by Clotilde's apparent indifference to interior décor because it contrasts greatly with the attention that she clearly pays to her elegant and carefully crafted outfits. When he returns to Clotilde's home several days later, Duroy's surprise at the disconnect between her attractive gown and the room turns to uneasiness:

> She was wearing an alluring and provocative dark red dress that fitted tightly round her waist and hips and over her breasts and arms; and Duroy had a strange feeling of surprise and almost embarrassment which he found it hard to explain at the discrepancy between such tasteful, well-groomed elegance and her obvious indifference towards the place where she lived.[105]

> [Elle portait une robe marron foncé, qui moulait sa taille, ses hanches, sa gorge, ses bras d'une façon provocante et coquette; et Duroy éprouvait un étonnement confus, presque une gêne dont il ne saisissait pas bien la cause, du désaccord de cette élégance soignée et raffinée avec l'insouci visible pour le logis qu'elle habitait.[106]]

Calling attention to Duroy's "discomfort" that Clotilde's living room does not match her attire, Nicholas White rightly calls this a "decontextualisation," a lack of symmetry "between character and space" that Duroy "simply cannot understand."[107] Why Duroy would be troubled at all by an absence of cohesion between place and garments, curious in and of itself, is rendered even more puzzling by the fact that Maupassant never truly explains Duroy's mysterious discomfort. My interpretation is that Duroy's anxiety in this episode relates to Maupassant's mapping of colonization onto both fashion and the domestic space of the urban capital. In my reading it is a subtle echo of Maupassant's own worry – a worry the origins of which he, like Duroy, may not have understood himself – of the more profound and dangerous problem of the domestication of colonization to humanity at home. As *Bel-Ami* illustrates, for Maupassant it is not in locations of imperial grandeur such as the late-century Universal Expositions or Orient-inspired department store buildings where such anxieties manifest.

Rather, he sets the passage in the dislocated space of the antechamber, a micro-locale in which clothing and space problematically collide to symbolize macro-problems of global imperialism.

Conclusion

In *Paralyses*, John Culbert argues that doubt in the "historical mission" of colonization, which appears prevalently in French literature of the twentieth century, actually originates in the nineteenth century when such misgiving began to dominate authors' works.[108] In agreement, I have been arguing that this doubt is well present in *Bel-Ami*, particularly through the expression of the exotic that Clotilde's fashions provide in the literal and metaphorical antechambers populating the novel. It might seem counterintuitive to examine the operations of colonization in a novel that is "about" fashionable Parisian high life, but as Hiner notes of urban texts by Balzac, Flaubert, Zola, and Proust, "These novels, although squarely set in Paris and offering complex portrayals of distinctly Parisian society, offer a view into the structures of power elucidated and maintained by colonialism."[109] Maupassant joins other writers who were using the capital city as a setting for literary interventions on overseas expansionism. This network of texts might be thought to constitute an uneasy response to France's growing tendency to view the colonies primarily as an area to territorialize, or what Ross terms "the late-nineteenth-century European construction of space *as* colonial space."[110]

In some ways, this reading of *Bel-Ami* as a critique of a rising culture of empire building in the 1880s might seem to run counter to this chapter's earlier analysis of the conclusion of "La Parure." That is, we have been focusing here on the familiarly cynical Maupassant, whereas the first analysis highlights what I interpret as his optimism about human compassion. Yet, these two viewpoints are not necessarily mutually exclusive, for it is reasonable to believe that Maupassant, like Zola, may have fluctuated between pessimism and optimism about modern existence. What this chapter thus reveals are tensions inherent to Maupassant's own views on modernity, which were articulated both in flashes of hopefulness as in "La Parure," or in more drawn-out censure, as in the case of his anti-hero Georges Duroy. To further nuance the matter, I read *Bel-Ami* as a *warning* of the looming catastrophe of the domestication of colonization rather than condemnation of a fait accompli. Even as the novel foreshadows in negative terms what actually *did* take place in the last years of the century, as France forcefully imposed itself further into Morocco, Tunisia, and Algeria,[111] it simultaneously suggests that humanity might prevail through sentimental connections felt by even the most cold-hearted of modern urban subjects. This is exemplified in the final phrase of *Bel-Ami*, which describes Duroy's vision not of the National Assembly building that he seeks to occupy but rather of Clotilde, before a mirror, fixing her hair. To be sure, the image can be read as Maupassant's closing indictment of Duroy's lust for women and general desire to conquer; support for this interpretation of Clotilde as a sexualized conquest includes the sensual and intimate detail that she always arranges her hair in this manner when she is "getting out of bed" ["au sortir du lit"].[112] However, the sentence is complicated by the sensitivity of Duroy's recollection, in his endearing memory of the "little kiss-curls on her temples" (translation modified)[113] ["petits cheveux frisés de ses tempes"[114]]. Thus, the physical closeness in the image certainly gives it sexual undertones but the memory is also not without fondness, signalling to my mind the protagonist's possible affection, even tenderness, for the only woman of the novel that he might be said to love (in his own way), a woman who represents the chic Parisienne or a cipher for Paris itself. As in "La Parure," for Maupassant, cynicism about modern life and the future of the urban metropolis seems equally mitigated by these occasional glints of human connectivity.

Part II has focused on how fashion illuminates the dialectic of waiting and changing occurring in literary and visual depictions of late-century antechamber dislocations. Degas's *L'Absinthe*, a painting of a waiting room in the context of everyday life, gave us a visual point of departure for Zola's treatment of Denise's hallway delay and Mme Desforges's dressing-room fitting, where charged spatial and sartorial metaphors illustrate the class instabilities that were increasingly characteristic of late-century urban experience. These are also the locations in which Zola demonstrates his broader endorsement of high capitalism and his prediction of its future success in France's developing liberal democracy. The chapter on *Nana* situated the novel in the context of the author's literary development, understanding the text as a reflection of Zola's anticipatory state of mind as he waited for the public's response to naturalism. It discussed male garments by way of the dandified style of the fop La Faloise, whose wait in a backstage theatre loge for the fashionable Nana connects to Zola's two very different efforts to promote naturalism, a literature through which, he believed, the most faithful narrations of modernity could be achieved. In Part III, we will return to Zola, this time to *La Curée*, his first novel on fashionable high life. As we will see, Zola's tragicomic depiction of the haute couture fashion designer and the space in which he works shares elements with similar figures and locales in Georges Feydeau's play *Tailleur pour dames* and Rops's painting *Le Muscle du grand couturier*. It is to this last image that we now turn.

PART THREE

The Fashion Atelier

5 Places and Spaces of Haute Couture: Feydeau's *Tailleur pour dames* and Zola's *La Curée*

Félicien Rops's watercolour, *Le Muscle du grand couturier* or *The Muscle of the Great Designer*, a provocative image of a tailor on one knee measuring a nearly fully undressed woman, signals a rising interest in a new urban space of late-nineteenth-century modernity that was linked to the emergence of the *grand couturier*, a figure who would come to dominate both the world of high fashion and representations of it (see figure 5.1). I call this space the "fashion atelier" and define it as a location in which some manner of fashion creation occurs. The fashion atelier appears in texts of the era under a number of forms. These include the haute couture fashion house, the tailor's workshop, and the garment factory sweatshop, as well as other spaces that are not ateliers per se but are transformed in key narrative moments into areas of garment design or production, including dressing rooms, boudoirs, and, even in one case that we will examine, a scientific laboratory. Rops's image permits us a view into his voyeuristic version of the fashion atelier and simultaneously points to some of the dislocation's implicit complexities.

Le Muscle du grand couturier

In the painting, a woman wearing only stockings and shoes, her dress in a crumpled pile at her feet, stands before a man who takes her measurements with the aid of his *mètre* or tape measure. The woman's casual nudity indicates that she is most likely a prostitute or courtesan, one of Rops's favourite subjects to illustrate. The title of the piece identifies the man as a *couturier*, a word that historically referred to "a person whose profession is sewing" ["personne dont le métier est la couture"][1] and seems to apply to the male figure whose act of measuring

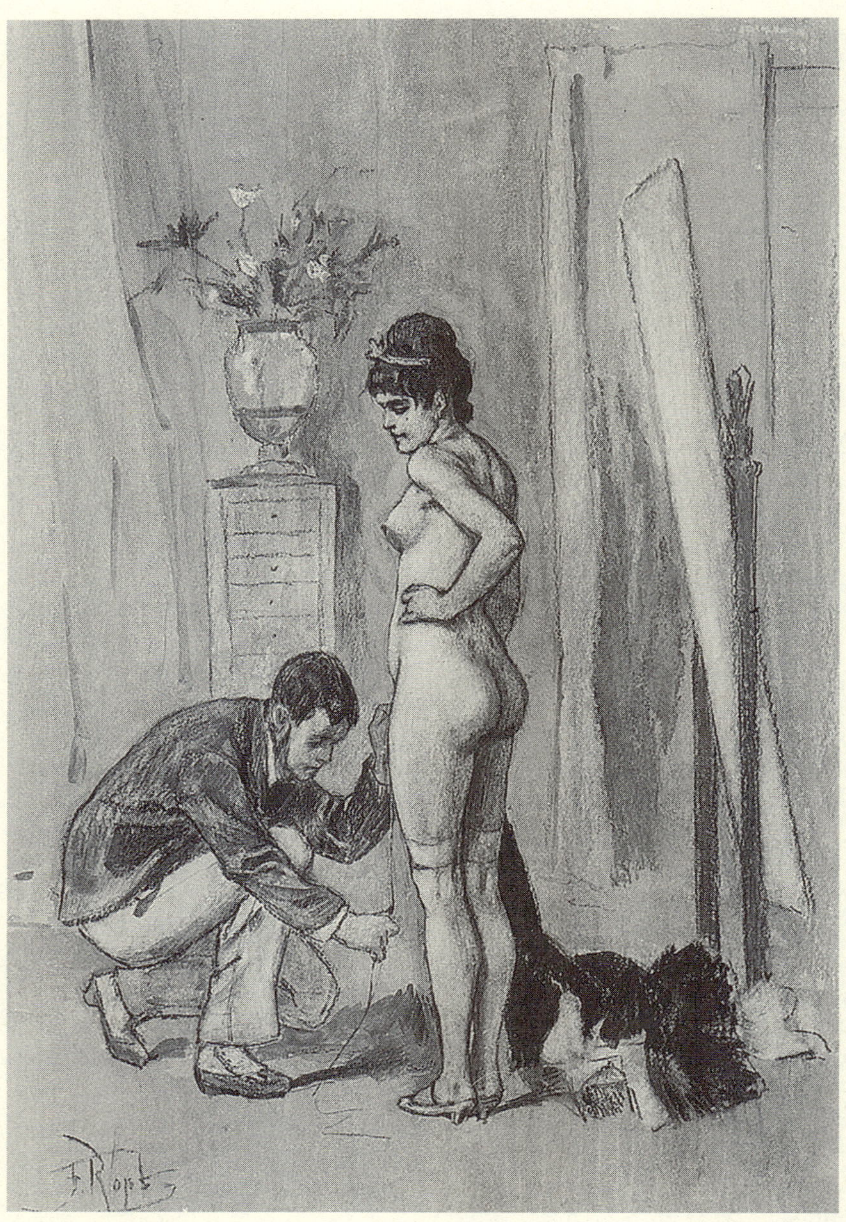

5.1 Félicien Rops, *Le Muscle du grand couturier*, 1878–81. Collection J.P. Babut du Marès, Namur. Reproduced courtesy of Jean-Pierre Babut du Marès.

suggests he is a tailor. However, in this period the term *couturier*, particularly when qualified by the adjective "grand" as in Rops's title, was increasingly associated with high-fashion clothing designers who created, but did not necessarily sew, one-of-a-kind garments, especially for the very wealthy. This shift in meaning away from sewing and towards designing is reflected in the 1863 designation of the term in Emile Littré's *Dictionnaire de la langue française*, which defines the couturier as "a person who directs a fashion house, who creates designs" ["personne qui dirige une maison de couture, qui crée des modèles"].[2] This definition de-emphasizes the production of garments in favour of not only the artistic and creative but also the commercial and entrepreneurial aspects of the occupation, which were growing in importance as French fashion continued to rise as a major national industry. Since Rops's painting dates to the late 1870s when the artist was actively involved in the fashion industry (see chapter 1), he was surely aware of the changing meanings surrounding the designation of *grand couturier*, a moniker rendered at times even more confusing since it was frequently shortened to simply "couturier." Rops's insider knowledge of the players at work in high fashion likely informed his ambiguous portrait of the man on bended knee, for it is not entirely clear from the image whether it depicts a traditional tailor – a man who sews – or a *grand couturier*, who concerns himself with creating the ideas for garments rather than with the task of stitching them together. Although the figure is clearly at work in the manner reminiscent of a tailor, his gleaming white shoe covers (*guêtres*), a style associated more with men of means than with tradespeople, might seem to indicate that he is (or wishes to appear) in a class separate from the common needleworker.

As is typical of works by Rops, the title of the watercolour is a play on words functioning on a number of levels. The Latin word for the French phrase *muscle couturier* is "Sartorius," a term deriving from the same root as the word "sartorial," meaning "related to clothing." The *Sartorius*, commonly known as "the tailor's muscle," is an anatomical designation for the longest anterior muscle of the thigh. The *Trésor de la langue française* explains that the *muscle couturier* may be so named because, when contracted, it allows one to sit cross-legged, the traditional posture of tailors. In Rops's painting, the *Sartorius* is the section of the woman's leg that the man is measuring, providing one explanation for the term "muscle" in the work's title. But one can also read *Le Muscle du grand couturier* as a tongue-in-cheek reference to the courtesan herself, a crucially important client to haute couture because of her unparalleled influence on the fashion system. As we saw in chapter 3, in the 1800s the alluring woman-for-hire had the ability to create demand and stimulate dress sales, for just by exhibiting garments on her body the stylish courtesan could transform them into the height of vogue. Thus, like her fictional sister Nana, the prostitute in Rops's image might be thought of as the titular "muscle" that powered much of the late-century high-fashion industry. To add another meaning to Rops's title, the courtesan's tools of the trade included not simply her clothing but, naturally, her body: the flesh and muscles inside the fabric. By featuring the woman's sensuous gluteus maximus prominently in the centre of the composition, Rops draws attention to this provocative "muscle" of the courtesan's body, contrasting the potency of this corporeal instrument of seduction with the relative feebleness of the couturier's slim, nearly invisible, measuring tape.

One interpretation of the left side of the composition, then, is that the *grand couturier*'s bowed posture, downturned gaze, and limp implement make him appear deferential, desexed even, a stoic figure mechanically going about his job with no apparent sign of arousal. Yet, the inclusion of the titillating, nearly unclothed figure on the right, and the placement of his left hand close to the nubile young woman's genitals, invite a more suggestive interpretation of the male subject. His right leg, for example, conspicuously bent upward and aiming at a point between the woman's thighs, might imply the underlying vigour of his own *"muscle couturier,"* now a euphemism for an erect phallus.[3] This interpretation is supported by the fact that phalluses frequently – almost obsessively – appear in many of Rops's works, yet it is likewise complicated because, unlike in his other images, the sex organ here is far less literally rendered. Considered within the context of Rops's larger corpus, then, the figurative as opposed to literal suggestion of a phallus, coupled with the tailor's inert measuring tape and relative indifference to the nude prostitute, might actually call into question his virility instead of confirming it.

We can highlight two readings of Rops's ambivalence regarding the masculinity of the *grand couturier* and the painting's lack of clarity vis-à-vis the uncertain sexual rapport between the man and the woman. First, the painting illustrates rising gendered tensions that were impacting late-century garment trades, and, second, these tensions were related to spaces of work. For the watercolour is deliberately set in a behind-the-scenes dislocation in which the tailor can fit the prostitute with the uniform of her street profession, uniting two types of interdependent labour and urban locales in the nexus of the fashion atelier. Training his ironic wit on a dislocation connecting the new "man of fashion" and the "working girl," two charged figures of late-century haute couture, Rops calls attention to a number of themes also present in the texts that are to be examined in this section: Georges Feydeau's play *Tailleur pour dames*, Zola's *La Curée*, the article "Robes et Manteaux" and novel *En Ménage* by Joris-Karl Huysmans, and a selection of Rachilde's novels from the late 1800s consisting of those already studied above as well as *Nono* (1885), *La Marquise de Sade* (1887), and *L'Animale* (1893). To analyse these texts from a deliberately spatial point of view we will engage with geographer Yi-Fu Tuan's influential theories on space and place with respect to Feydeau's play, as well as Michel de Certeau's critical work on strategies and tactics in connection with Rachilde's fiction. The complexities in *Le Muscle du grand couturier* initiate this discussion of overlapping concerns in literature that will include the troubling status of the couturier and his workspace, the interplay between dark comedy and clothing, the gendering of various forms of work in the production of fashion, and women's use of clothing to navigate the city.

To address the first point, as Rops's composition illuminates, the space in which garments were invented and constructed could be an ill-defined one. The viewer notes, for example, the indeterminacy of the painting's location: it is not clear whether the fitting is taking place in a shop, a boudoir, a living room, a dressing room or the couturier's atelier, to name some possibilities. The composition's few pieces of furniture, including a full-length mirror, a narrow chest of drawers, a vase filled with flowers, and the suggestion of a curtain over a window or doorway, do little to shed light on this question. As this chapter will demonstrate, in his three-act comedy *Tailleur pour dames* (1886), Georges Feydeau takes advantage of the inherent ambiguity of a *couturière*'s workshop to multiply the humorous cases of mistaken identity that take place therein. Comedic touches are employed as well in *La Curée* as Zola lampoons the figure of the designer all the while revealing his more sinister undertones, using these to comment on fashion's role in the simultaneous rise and ruin of the urban cityscape.

Meanings of the spaces in which fashions were created in the late-nineteenth century were complicated in part by the fact that divisions separating those working in the range of professions related to garments – tailors, designers, seamstresses, and embroiderers, to name a few – were becoming increasingly blurred. This occurred as clothing companies mass industrialized and began to subsume multiple types of workers under one centralizing roof, thus minimizing their importance as artisan specialists. On the other hand, the period was characterized as well by an *increase* in specification about one garment worker in particular, as demonstrated by the practice of naming this profession to reflect not just the person's trade but also his status in the commerce of clothing. This is what took place with the term *couturier*, a word that came to point both to the changing social status of a rising elite working in clothing and to a new direction in the overall gendering of the garment industry. Since at least the eighteenth century, clothing in France that was destined for women of means had been primarily designed and sewn by *marchandes de mode* or *couturières*, the feminine form of the masculine noun *couturier*.[4] The legendary example in French history is Rose Bertin, eighteenth-century clothier to the infamous trend-setting monarch Marie Antoinette.[5] In contrast, during the late nineteenth century, as the divide widened between what would become defined in this period as *haute couture* – a single outfit made by hand for one person – and *la confection*, or the mass-produced ready-to-wear industry, the elite couturier became masculinized in both name and practice. To cite the most prominent example, the English transplant and renowned "father of haute couture" Charles Frederick Worth has been credited as the first man to proclaim himself a "couturier" in the 1860s.[6] Other men, including Jacques Doucet and Paul Poiret, soon followed, constructing themselves into highly recognizable public figures associated with haute couture as well as with art, theatre, and other forms of "high" culture.[7] It was at this time that new terms, including the aforementioned "grand couturier" and "tailleur pour dames" or "ladies' dressmaker" came into use to distinguish traditional tailors who had customarily made menswear, from the rising class of privileged men who worked on clothing – sewing, designing, or a combination of both – for an international clientele of wealthy women.[8]

"My Vast Ateliers": Feydeau's *Tailleur pour dames*

We will turn in earnest to the vexed circumstances created for women as a result of the (re)gendering of fashion labour in chapter 6. This present chapter will focus instead on the newly named male professional, the "tailleur pour dames," as he is depicted first in Feydeau's 1886 comic farce of the same name and then in Zola's novel *La Curée*. *Tailleur pour dames*, Feydeau's first full-length play, includes three acts, the second of which is set entirely in an abandoned *couturière*'s atelier.[9] That the play was a highly successful debut for an unknown first-time playwright – it enjoyed an impressive seventy-nine performances in its initial run at the Théâtre de la Renaissance[10] – implies the public's interest not only in Feydeau's work but also in the figure and space of the haute couture tailor.

The intrigue of the play revolves around the protagonist, Doctor Moulineaux, and his attempts to facilitate an extramarital tryst with the attractive Suzanne while hiding his indiscretion from a host of other characters: his naive wife Yvonne, her meddling mother Mme Aigreville, Suzanne's volatile husband Aubin, and Aubin's mistress Rosa, who had once been Moulineaux's lover. Moulineaux arranges to meet Suzanne in a flat that was once a dressmaker's studio and, when they are caught, he pretends to be her tailor in order to hide the affair. The play, in the typical style of Feydeau, is a near-chaotic romp filled with deceptions and mistaken identities and in which comedic tension repeatedly arises because the truth – Moulineaux's infidelity – threatens to be exposed at any moment. Act II is no exception, its confusion and volatility augmented by the fact that each character in the play save one makes an appearance at some point in the *couturière*'s atelier. Continual disruptions perpetrated by these numerous performers increase the instances of comedic moments by complicating Moulineaux's lies and his indiscretions (and those of other characters with secrets to hide), which eventually compound into an elaborate, seemingly intractable, web of dissimulations. As befits a comedy, however, all is resolved during Act III, as Moulineaux successfully negotiates the genre's requisite "happy ending" by convincing Yvonne that he is a loving and faithful husband. Despite the fact that the conclusion is based almost entirely on lies fabricated by Moulineaux and the play's other philanderers, the work finishes literally with a laugh, the punchline of a joke serving as its final sentence.

Because *Tailleur pour dames* is a work of theatre, the importance of garments, or costumes, to be more specific, would seem implicit. And yet, interestingly, Feydeau generally did not provide much in the way of written instructions about the items of clothing that he wished for his actors to wear on stage. This is in stark contrast to his keen interest in the interactions between his characters and the spaces into which he wrote them. As a rule, Feydeau was highly attentive to setting and to spatiality more generally. The mise en scène, or the placement of his characters on the set, was one of his major preoccupations, as demonstrated by the meticulous stage directions and extensive descriptions for actors' locations in his scripts.[11] *Tailleur pour dames* is no exception. In the *didascalie*, or stage directions, Feydeau takes great pains to indicate where characters should be placed, going so far as designating by way of numbers following their names where they should be positioned in relation to one another. This almost obsessive quality of such precise stage directions suggests the extent to which spatiality was one of Feydeau's primary concerns.

Because Feydeau provided very few remarks about costumes, one might infer that staging was a more important concern than his performers' attire. And yet, as we will see, dress is a vital matter in *Tailleur pour dames*, as the reference to clothing in the title implies. To begin with, garments contribute importantly to the *quiproquo*, or the misunderstandings that lead to multiple cases of mistaken identity in the play and that help to drive its humour. Hilarity erupts, for instance, when a character puts on an outfit that he or she normally does not wear, setting off a chain of events whereby an unsuspecting observer misidentifies that person to comedic effect. Often these moments represent temporary reversals of social norms, such as in Act I when the butler Etienne is taken for Moulineaux, a doctor above his station, because Etienne has misunderstood a directive and has donned his employer's bathrobe.[12] This sartorial misstep causes Aubin to believe that Etienne is the man of the house and Moulineaux is his butler. The error will later allow Moulineaux to pass himself off as the play's titular "tailor for ladies," which triggers the elaborate and fast-paced mirth of Act II. This example illustrates how manipulations of fashion and farce go hand in hand, for such uproarious moments that are an integral element of the genre are facilitated especially effectively by way of garments.

And yet, although the humorous aspects of Feydeau's play are enhanced by dress, fashion's more sobering implications and complex operations are revealed when the reader turns away from the comedic. Or, to be more precise, when the reader recognizes the far darker undertones of Feydeau's brand of humour. As Norman Shapiro has argued, "one does not have to look far into a typical Feydeau comedy to perceive an undercurrent of pessimism regarding the human condition."[13] In his plays, Feydeau's pessimism is frequently directed towards those like Moulineaux, likable people who do, nonetheless, cheat and lie in order to keep their errors in judgment from being discovered. For Shapiro, Feydeau's condemnation of such comportment is expressed in the ways that he constantly, sometimes relentlessly, "punishes" offenders for their less-than-admirable behaviour. Since Feydeau's works are comedies and not tragedies, the "sufferings" that his characters endure manifest in what might be thought of as minor afflictions, such as stress, humiliation, or confusion. And yet, the many seemingly trivial entanglements and embarrassing situations in which characters find themselves actually attest to what Shapiro rightly deems Feydeau's "comic cruelty,"[14] whereby minor discomforts that elicit laughs stand in for the deeper hardships that humans also suffer.

In Act II, Feydeau's "comically cruel" punishment of Moulineaux involves placing him in an unyielding series of potentially harmful situations. The greatest physical danger is represented by an apparently violent Aubin, who, Suzanne insists, will kill Moulineaux if he finds out about their affair.[15] Moulineaux's motivation to fabricate lies is thus a twofold fear: fear of injury by Suzanne's jealous husband Aubin and fear of what Peter Parshall terms "a ruined reputation."[16] On the one hand, this second fear might appear inconsequential relative to the first, for the threat of bodily harm or death seems infinitely more dire than the risk that one's reputation be harmed. Moreover, since Moulineaux is a man, his reputation would not be greatly harmed by taking a mistress, in contrast with a married woman caught with a lover, who, in addition to being shamed, could risk tangible sanctions such as losing property and dowry according to the patriarchal laws of the day. However, this anxiety of a relatively minor consequence for Moulineaux – a destroyed reputation – in fact symbolizes more profound fears plaguing the characters of Feydeau's plays.

For instance, Moulineaux's superficial embarrassment at having to assume the identity of a modest *tailleur pour dames* can be read as an expression of deeper anxiety at the thought of sustained and real social abasement. Moulineaux's petty humiliation conceals a larger fear that the classed social system with which he is familiar, in which medical doctors enjoy privileges that servants and most tailors do not, might be under threat. Danger to Moulineaux's social status is paralleled by the constant threat hanging over the stability of his marriage, which is menaced throughout the play by the exposure of his secret affair. Moulineaux's discomfort at the thought of finding himself relegated to an inferior status is illustrated when he forgets at one point that he is supposed to be a producer of garments and is offended by the suggestion that he should fabricate a dress for a new customer. The moment occurs when Aubin arrives at the *couturière*'s flat with the news that he has invited a woman friend to the atelier to purchase some new garments. "You think that I have nothing better to do than [to make dresses]" ["Vous croyez donc que je n'ai que ça à faire"],[17] Moulineaux snaps at a bewildered Aubin, who is confused because he thinks he is doing Moulineaux "the tailor" a service by providing a new client. A further indication that Moulineaux's anxiety relates to his social status is the fact that he follows up his retort with the exasperated question, "And my medical practice?" ["Et ma médicine?"][18] Mounting stress causes Moulineaux to slip up and reveal, temporarily, his true occupation, a moment of candour indicating a wish that his "normal" identity as a doctor be restored.

On one level, Moulineaux's desire to be connected to his real profession is understandable because occupations in Feydeau's plays are associated with stability and orderliness.[19] As Act II of *Tailleur pour dames* devolves towards ever greater instability, Moulineaux's need for the general sense of order that his occupation signals is therefore logical. Another subtext of this desire is Moulineaux's investment in maintaining a hierarchical social system that protects the privileges of doctors over tailors and that, in the chaotic environment of the *couturière*'s flat, is called into question.

Indeed, preserving his class distinction is such a priority to a prideful Moulineaux that he later attempts to improve his *fictitious* status as fashion worker by aligning himself not with the lowly tailor but with the high-end couturier. He does so in a number of ways, which include specifying that he is not a mere needleworker but a "grand" couturier, suggesting that his prices are triple those of others as befits a sought-after designer, and making reference to owning "vast ateliers" elsewhere. The scene takes place at the beginning of Act II as Moulineaux attempts to seduce Suzanne by wooing her on bended knee. Aubin suddenly enters, and, seeing a man kneeling before his wife like the couturier of Rops's painting, concludes that a fitting must be taking place:

AUBIN. – You were in the middle of taking my wife's measurements. I saw it!

SUZANNE, *seizing the opportunity*. – Perfectly so! Monsieur was at the waistline.

MOULINEAUX, *floundering*. – That's right! … the waist … around the waist, … one hundred ten around the waist.

SUZANNE, *sharply*. – What, one hundred ten! … Fifty-two, come on!

AUBIN, *laughing*. – Yes, fifty-two!

MOULINEAUX, *trying to regain composure*. – Perfectly so! … Only, I'm going to tell you, this, it's a custom of *grand couturiers*. Everything is counted double.

AUBIN. – Even the bills?

MOULINEAUX. – Ah! No, bills are tripled! … yes, that's what distinguishes us from low-ranking couturiers, eh! Plus, you know, like this, without a measuring tape … eyeballing it …! Um, you … you wouldn't have a measuring tape on you?

AUBIN, *laughing*. – I don't believe so! But you, you don't have one?

MOULINEAUX. – No! … Um! that is yes …I have too many! Only they are at the atelier … in my ateliers! … My vast ateliers.

[AUBIN. – Vous étiez en train de prendre les mesures à ma femme. J'ai vu ça!

SUZANNE, *saisissant la balle au bond*. – Parfaitement! Monsieur en était au tour de taille.

MOULINEAUX, *barbotant*. – En effet! … la taille, … le tour de taille, … cent dix de tour de taille.

SUZANNE, *vivement*. – Comment, cent dix! … cinquante-deux, voyons!

AUBIN, *riant*. – Oui, cinquante-deux!

MOULINEAUX, *tâchant de reprendre contenance*. – Parfaitement! … Seulement, je vais vous dire, ça, c'est une habitude des grands couturiers. Tout est compté double.

AUBIN. – Même les factures?

MOULINEAUX. – Ah! Non, les factures, c'est le triple! … oui c'est ce qui nous distingue des petits couturiers. Eh! Puis, enfin vous savez, comme ça, sans mètre … à vue d'œil …! Euh! Vous … vous n'auriez pas un mètre sur vous?

AUBIN, *riant*. – Je ne crois pas! Mais vous n'avez pas ça, vous?

MOULINEAUX. – Non! … Euh! c'est-à-dire si … j'en ai trop! Seulement ils sont à l'atelier … dans mes ateliers! … Mes vastes ateliers.][20]

Here, despite the distracting worry of being caught nearly *in flagrante delicto* with Aubin's wife, Moulineaux aggrandizes himself as a high fashion couturier. He aligns his work with the artistry and skill of the talented designer by implying that he can measure Suzanne by "eyeballing" her body without the aid of a tape measure. The suggestion that his fees are "triple" those of other dressmakers, like those of the most elite designers, is further evidence of his status as an upper-echelon fashion creator.[21] Finally, he alludes to a separate workspace ("the atelier"), a location that seems to grow ever grander as it evolves from one single studio to multiple spaces and finally a collection of "vast" ateliers, all apparently belonging to him ("*my* ateliers").

Yi-Fu Tuan's "Space" vs. "Place"

If Moulineaux's attempts to exaggerate the prestige of his (non-existent) "vast ateliers" reflects a more profound dread that he forfeit his advantageous rank in society or, worse, that society cease to be governed by the class divisions that he has come to count on, it is important to note that these fears are implicitly related to anxiousness about space and location. What might Moulineaux's self-aggrandizing reveal about the nature of his true fears and how they relate to the space of the tailor's studio? Human geographer Yi-Fu Tuan's thoughts on the distinction between "space" and "place" help to elucidate an answer. As Tuan has influentially argued, "space" can be thought of as "a symbol for openness and freedom,"[22] something that people "long for."[23] "Place," on the other hand, represents the security to which humans are "attached."[24] In the modern urban world, place can be exemplified by what Tuan terms "architectural space" or "the built environment" which, as one of its functions, "clarifies social roles and relations."[25]

Tuan's discussion relates to Parshall's notion cited above that what is most often under threat for the upper-class characters of Feydeau's plays is their reputations. Recasting the idea of a person's reputation in spatial terms and within the context of *Tailleur pour dames*, one can think of Moulineaux's reputation as a manifestation of his "place" in society, an indication of where he is located in the highly stratified social system of Paris in the late nineteenth century. For Tuan, who seeks to understand spatiality through human encounters with their environments, "places" are "centers of felt value"[26] or, as he puts it more succinctly, "security."[27] In this light one can read Moulineaux's concern that he might lose his "place" in society as echoing a more deep-seated fear of a threat against a core sense of security. Feydeau articulates Moulineaux's fear through a chaotic mapping of both space and place in Act II, as his protagonist finds he is unable to control or navigate the atelier dislocation and loses all feelings of security. As the Act progresses, to borrow Tuan's phrase, the "built environment" of the urban fashion atelier devolves into a setting in which social roles and relations are not clarified but, rather, endlessly transform and become hopelessly confused. Feydeau's numerous stage directions demonstrating his keen interest in spatiality, along with the fact that many of his plays are set in Paris and include allusions to well-known locations – famous nightclubs and restaurants, for example – explicitly link his literary production to the built environment of the capital city. Feydeau's problematic treatment of location in *Tailleur pour dames* thus suggests that his characters harbour reservations about their metropolitan surroundings, reservations that his audience, composed of the same middle- and upper-class population, may in turn have shared. By marking the fashion atelier with confusion and ambiguity, Feydeau creates a dislocation that symbolizes in microcosm the same ambivalence that the macrocosm of the metropolis might have engendered in its inhabitants.

Uncertainty about the function and meaning of the *couturière*'s abandoned atelier is fostered by the fact that, over the course of Act II, the location is understood to be numerous different spaces by the play's various characters. The atelier is first named by Moulineaux, who, disgruntled upon arrival at the condition of the apartment where he hopes to have his tryst with Suzanne, declares that the flat is one of "the completely broken-down apartments" ["des appartements tout disloquées"] that the building's proprietor, Bassinet, rents out. Fittingly, for our purposes, the term *disloquées*, here literally meaning "broken," is also a synonym for "dislocated." When Moulineaux describes the atelier as "broken-down," it is in reference to the lock on the front door, which is broken and no longer latches, a condition that, we will see, has important spatial repercussions. Like some of the other dislocations discussed in this book, Feydeau's atelier is a "space" in Tuan's sense of the term, where liberty from constraints (e.g., Moulineaux's extramarital affair) is a possibility. But it is a space, too, where this liberty threatens to advance into chaos, as exemplified by the fact that the atelier itself undergoes a constant redefinition of purpose.

For example, Moulineaux wishes for the atelier to serve as a getaway for his amorous liaison with Suzanne but, unbeknownst to him, the atelier also remains for some characters the former shop of Mme Durand, the real *couturière* who once worked there. The location's previous identity as an actual facility in which to buy a dress brings about the sudden entrances of Mme Durand's former customers, Mlle Pomponette and Mme d'Herblay, neither of whom knows that Mme Durand has abandoned the premises. The arrival of these two women at unexpected moments throughout the act adds to the disordered atmosphere of the space, much to Moulineaux's dismay. Asking for garments and alterations and disrupting Moulineaux's attempts to court Suzanne, Mlle Pomponette and Mme d'Herblay contribute to Moulineaux's franticness as he tries to hide the infidelity from his and Suzanne's families. As if the situation is not confusing enough, the atelier is inscribed with an additional name and layer of functionality by the proprietor, Bassinet, who agrees to rent a flat to Moulineaux's mother-in-law, Mme Aigreville. It is thus that Mme Aigreville arrives abruptly in the middle of Act II, thinking that she is in the mezzanine apartment ["l'entresol"][28] that Bassinet has promised her, thereby providing another label – mezzanine apartment – for the atelier. When Mme Aigreville finds Moulineaux compromisingly alone with Suzanne, he quickly formulates the lie that the space is actually a lodging, Suzanne's "home" ["maison"],[29] and that he is on a medical house call to an ill patient. Thus he marks the atelier with still another identity, that of Suzanne's alleged domicile. Finally, spatial confusion reaches its pinnacle of absurdity when Bassinet leads Aubin to believe that Mme Aigreville is the Queen of Greenland who has come to see her couturier (Moulineaux "the tailor") for a gown fitting. As the older woman sweeps past Aubin, in deference to "her majesty" Aubin bows down before her, exclaiming "the court!" ["la cour"],[30] symbolically transforming the atelier into the metaphorical space of "the crown" that members of the monarchy theoretically embody wherever they go.

This confusion as to what, precisely, the atelier represents, stands in to suggest a larger uncertainty about how emerging spaces of the city like the fashion atelier could, should, and would be used. The myriad functionalities of Mme Durand's atelier – broken-down apartment, *couturière*'s atelier, mezzanine, bourgeois home, the court – echo the depiction of space in Rops's painting, in which the setting of the tailor's fitting session is defined in part by its vagueness. In this way, both text and image generalize how such newly created urban locations resisted definition. In the play, the ambiguity of the dressmaker's studio is displayed in the way that Feydeau's characters accept, or partially accept, the first explanation that they are given about the space because there are no defining features about it to suggest otherwise. Thus Mme Aigreville half believes the story that the atelier is Suzanne's home and Suzanne the lady of the house while retaining some of her initial suspicions to the contrary. The fact that dressmakers sometimes went to clients' homes for fittings, combined with the detail that the flat is located in a neighbourhood filled with middle-class homes, renders

Moulineaux's explanation plausible, yet not completely certain.[31] The undercurrent of unreliability in the tailor's studio is demonstrated likewise by Aubin, who believes on first sight that Moulineaux is Suzanne's dressmaker, despite the fact that a man kneeling before his wife clutching her waist would be highly improper in another spatial context. On the one hand, the space is convincing to Aubin, such that he sees a version of Rops's indifferent, unaroused tailor rather than the reality of Moulineaux's licentious intentions. On the other hand, Aubin's primary function in the play is to call into question the validity of Moulineaux's claims to being a tailor and thus the validity of the space itself, his suspicion serving as a necessary catalyst for the farcical moments to occur.

This lack of clarity about the dislocated space of the tailor's atelier in turn points to the idea that traditional rules of identity and comportment within it could equally be in flux. As Feydeau likely sensed, the couturier was the perfect character type to illustrate unpredictabilities in behaviour, because, as a newly emerging figure himself, his comportment had not yet been well defined. In *Tailleur pour dames* the playwright exploits this to comedic effect, forcing his protagonist into sartorial situations in which he is completely inept but is forgiven for his erraticisms because these are assumed to be the traits of a high fashion designer. A comic exchange ensues, for instance, when Moulineaux, who knows nothing about women's attire, must describe to Aubin the dress that he is purportedly making for Suzanne:

> AUBIN. – Say, what are you doing for[32] my wife?
>
> MOULINEAUX, *fervently.* – Me? … nothing! Don't believe…
>
> AUBIN. – What do you mean … nothing?
>
> MOULINEAUX, *recovering himself.* – That is, yes I am! … A … a coat-gown with an overskirt … in tulle … with shirred bands … in fur, ornamented with onyx … on the pants.
>
> AUBIN. – What pants?
>
> MOULINEAUX. – What pants? … The pants underneath. You can't see them.
>
> AUBIN. – That must be strange, this combination. Shirred bands in onyx on pants! … You must be careful of being eccentric, Suzanne … (*To Moulineaux.*) Do you have a sample model?
>
> MOULINEAUX. – A sample model? … yes, yes, I have masses of them. But you can't see them. They are in my ateliers … in my ateliers, my sample models. You understand, there are rival designers! One would only have to breathe a word about these looks …

AUBIN. – So we can't choose them? …

MOULINEAUX. – Choose them? Yes you can, but you can't see them!

[AUBIN. – Dites-moi, qu'est-ce que vous faites à ma femme?

MOULINEAUX, *vivement*. – Moi? … rien! … Ne croyez pas …

AUBIN. – Comment … rien? …

MOULINEAUX, *se reprenant*. – C'est-à-dire si …! Une … une polonaise … en tulle … avec des bouillonnés … en fourrure, ornés de jais … le pantalon.

AUBIN. – Quel pantalon?

MOULINEAUX. – Quel pantalon? … Le pantalon du dessous. On ne le voit pas.

AUBIN. – Ça doit être curieux, ce mélange-là. Des bouillonnées en jais, sur le pantalon! … Défie-toi de l'excentricité, Suzanne … (*A Moulineaux*.) Vous n'avez pas un modèle?

MOULINEAUX. – Un modèle? … si, si, j'en ai des masses. Mais on ne peut pas les voir. Ils sont dans les ateliers … dans les ateliers mes modèles. Vous comprenez, la concurrence! … On n'aurait qu'à les souffler? …

AUBIN. – Alors on ne peut pas les choisir? …

MOULINEAUX. – Les choisir? si, mais pas les voir!][33]

At first, Aubin is rightly suspicious of the disastrous garment that Moulineaux struggles to articulate, since it would be difficult to imagine an attractive outfit composed of the chaotic amalgamation of fabrics and accessories that Moulineaux randomly cites. However, Aubin does not conclude, as he should, that the outfit is utter nonsense, but rather that it is "eccentric," a quality that he will then assume applies equally to its creator. As the act progresses, Moulineaux's curious behaviour, especially with respect to articles of clothing, continues to be explained by way of the alleged eccentricity of the couturier. After she is rudely sent away by a panicked Moulineaux, for example, Mme d'Herblay returns several scenes later in need of an alteration. Moulineaux, who suddenly finds it necessary to prove that he is, indeed, a couturier, welcomes her back with a gallantry that prompts her to remark in surprise, "Well! [Now] he is friendly!" ["Tiens! Il est aimable"].[34] Moulineaux's temperamental treatment of his client, first abusive and then gracious, appears not to contradict but rather to reinforce that he must be a true *tailleur pour dames*. This is evidenced by Mme d'Herblay's display of trust in him during the cringe-inducing scene that follows. Here, a distressed Moulineaux advances towards the woman's jacket with scissors in hand, forced to attempt an alteration in front of Aubin and Mme d'Herblay despite his total lack of tailoring skills. At the last minute, he is spared, but not before his bizarre behaviour with the scissors appears in the eyes of those watching to strengthen his standing as an unpredictable – and thus probably authentic – couturier.

As we will presently see, Zola similarly exploits the couturier's eccentricity, also with comic results, in his portrait of Worms, the high fashion designer of the novel *La Curée*. What is important to remark about Feydeau's play is that this lack of definitive knowledge about how, precisely, a *tailleur pour dames* might be expected to act is augmented by the atelier itself, which remains equally ill-defined as it undergoes the multiple identities that we have noted above. Turmoil in the atelier is exacerbated by the fact that the front door lock is broken, which means that all the characters that Moulineaux tries to avoid can and do enter and exit the space as they please. Several times in the act, Moulineaux blocks the door with a chair, attempting to control the flow of humanity that disrupts identities both of and in his location. Tuan might call this a reflection of his desire to "clarif[y] social roles and relations" in his "built environment." However, Moulineaux's makeshift blockade proves ineffective in this regard, as first Aubin[35] and then Bassinet[36] break through and allow others to follow suit. Moulineaux's vain endeavours to keep at bay outside threats to his security (as upper-class doctor) contribute to the overall chaos of the act. For, ultimately, he is unable to prevent the stream of undesired visitors from penetrating into a location that he had hoped would be a tranquil retreat – a "place," in Tuan's sense, of social predictability over which he is master – for the "space" of sexual freedom that his affair also represents.

Couture Contamination

In Act II, rotating spatial identities are limited to the atelier where the action takes place. However, in Act III, the possibility of negative repercussions outside of the atelier arises, as Feydeau gestures towards a breach of containment whereby the disruptions of the *couturière*'s atelier begin to infect the former safety that the home, traditionally a secure "place," represents. Feydeau genders this dangerous infringement upon the sanctity of the bourgeois home, framing it through the figure of the fallen woman. As the play reaches its climactic dénouement, Moulineaux's wife Yvonne encounters Rosa in her living room, a woman whom she believes is her husband's mistress but who is really Aubin's lover (and, to add further complications, the wife of Bassinet).

Yvonne, a forgiving soul who has earlier decided to pardon Moulineaux for what she thinks may have been a momentary dalliance, suddenly erupts, accusing Moulineaux of bringing his mistress to their place of residence: "Ah! That's too much, sir! All that was missing was that you bring your *"couturières"* to the conjugal home!" ["Ah! C'est trop fort, monsieur! Il ne vous manquait plus que d'amener vos couturières au domicile conjugal!"].[37] What is problematic to Yvonne is not so much that Moulineaux is having an affair, which she now appears to accept, but that he allow it to infiltrate her home, the "place" in which she, a domestic housewife, is likely most secure. As Leonard Pronko points out, in many works by Feydeau, the areas inhabited by the respectable middle-class woman seem constantly menaced by the prostitute. He notes, "There are two major facets to Feydeau's picture of life: one is that of the bourgeois household, but the other is that of the demimonde, and even when we are within the confines of a well-regulated middle-class home, the threat offered by the attractive women of the half-world is always present."[38] In one sense, Yvonne uses the term *"couturière"* to describe Rosa because the two initially met at the atelier and Yvonne associates her with a dressmaker. But Yvonne is also using the word as a euphemism for a loose woman, her term inscribing both the figure of the *couturière* and the space in which she works with morally suspect connotations.

Ironically, Yvonne is not incorrect in her accusations of unfaithfulness: Rosa *did* sleep with Moulineaux in the past and *is* having an affair with the married Aubin. Moreover, the *couturière*'s atelier *is* being used for illicit liaisons, both those of Moulineaux and Suzanne, as well as Aubin and his mistress Rosa. These truths notwithstanding, by rendering the collision of the home and her husband's rendez-vous location intolerable to Yvonne, Feydeau suggests that it is not infidelity per se but rather spatial confusion of home and urban dislocation that is most disturbing. The unsettling blurring of the home space and the *couturière*'s atelier is introduced earlier by Suzanne, who describes the atelier as "the former lodging of a *couturière*" ["l'ancien logement d'une couturière"],[39] thereby pointing to an uncertainty about Mme Durand's own use of the space. Was it her "lodging," in the sense of "dwelling," that is, the home in which she lived? Was it a boutique where garments were displayed and sold? Was it a workshop for dress construction? A combination of all three?

These questions are left unanswered, for Mme Durand never appears in the play, remaining to the end an unknowable presence whose abandoned "lodging" seems to inherit her same indecipherability. It is the careful reader who discerns that Feydeau likely wishes to hint that the space is indeed one of impropriety, not only because of Moulineaux and Aubin who both seek to use it for extramarital affairs, but also because of the women who circulate through it more generally. The dubious identities of Mme Durand's two female clients encourage this reading. For example, the name of Mme Durand's first customer "Mademoiselle Pomponette" evokes the term *pompon*, which, as in English, refers to a tufted ball-shaped ornament. It calls up as well the related verb *pomponner*, which means "to finish or dress someone with a great deal of care and coquetry."[40] The character's name, rendered informal and girlish by the *-ette* suffix, brings to mind the flirtatiousness (or "coquetry") of dance hall girls, many of whom had stage names ending in "ette."[41] By alluding to a sartorial embellishment, Mlle Pomponette's name also evokes the "extreme care in dress" associated with the fashionable high-class prostitute. These charged evocations imply, then, that Mlle Pomponette is not really a "respectable" woman. As it happens, she is not the only one. There is a subtle implication that Mme d'Herblay, too, might be involved in illicit sexual comportment, which she hints at by informing Moulineaux (the tailor) that her altered jacket should be delivered to a new address situated one floor above her previous location. This very slight change in address seems a peculiar detail, until one begins to imagine that, for instance, Mme d'Herblay might be hiding something from *Monsieur* d'Herblay. Could she be having an affair with the neighbour upstairs? Or, perhaps, even having liaisons with several men in the same building? No matter the precise meaning, this rather minor insertion of a new delivery address for the jacket seems a nod towards more major questionable behaviour related to dress (or undress) facilitated by the *couturière*, behaviour that would not be consistent with that of a reputable housewife. In this way, the stylish yet morally suspect characteristics of Mme Durand's clientele instils the former lodger, her workspace, and the goings on within, with an undercurrent of unseemliness.

In *The Structural Transformation of the Public Sphere*, Jurgen Habermas addresses this subject in a discussion of what he calls the "institution" of the mistress, which underwent dramatic changes following the rise of the bourgeois class in France's capital.[42] As Habermas explains it, the "playful intimacy" that had formerly been available when pre-bourgeois society accepted the role of the mistress was transformed through the development of new middle-class mores into a threat to the system that was replacing it: that of the nuclear family. He writes, "A playful intimacy, where it managed to arise nevertheless, was distinct from the permanent intimacy of the new family life."[43] Naturally, "playful intimacy" with Suzanne is just what Moulineaux wishes to gain for himself, but he knows it must remain separate from his private home life. His challenge is to find a space to conduct his affair in a city that seems spatially unreceptive to it. Habermas, studying living conditions of the rising middle class, argues that the increase in bourgeois privatization and rising emphasis on home life under modernity coincided with changes in architectural structures of the urban environment. Rooms in dwellings became entirely organized around home life, "a private life that had assumed institutional form in the enclosed space of the patriarchal conjugal family"[44] and that did not favour uses – such as entertaining a mistress – outside of this system. Reading Moulineaux's dilemma through Habermas implies that the protagonist's plight is inherently connected to spatial changes occurring in the Parisian cityscape. The recurring intersection of the fashion atelier and women of ill repute also seen earlier in Rops's image is a subject to which we will later return when we focus on reinforcements of the trope by Zola and Huysmans as well as Rachilde's contestation of it.

Sartorial Seriousness

For the audience, the result of such utter confusion of space and identity in *Tailleur pour dames* is a raucously funny play. Yet, the underlying message of Feydeau's work, I have suggested, is more sobering if the play is taken as an allegory for modern life in the urban capital. As some have argued, Feydeau's farces, which are always on the brink of complete pandemonium, reveal a pessimistic view that life itself is absurd and, possibly, even meaningless.[45] His early vaudevillian comedies, of which *Tailleur pour dames* is the first, thereby anticipate his later plays, which have been described as "atrociously cruel farces under their burlesque appearance" ["farces atrocement cruelles sous leur apparence burlesque"].[46] Thus, although known for its inherent silliness and humour, Feydeau's body of work has also been seen to predict the endeavours of twentieth-century surrealists and existentialists, writers and artists who grappled with the meaning of life in the face of the later traumas of war and alienation through which they were living. Shapiro points out that, like works by these twentieth-century thinkers, Feydeau's theatrical exploration of human existence is based on a tension between chance and destiny, where the characters appear to be at the whim of chance but are actually being carefully controlled by their creator Feydeau:

> The very essence of Feydeau's theater [is that] seeming chance is really a well-regulated creation of the author. The playwright, like a master puppeteer, assumes a god-like role, creating around his helpless characters a universe of seeming absurdity in which their efforts to resist their destiny are frantic but fruitless. Some, consequently, are tempted to see in such a universe an embodiment of the absurd, finding in Feydeau's merciless and often gratuitous imbroglios a foretaste of the existentialist view of the human condition. As such, Feydeau's theater is eminently cruel … Feydeau's characters are often the victims of a relentless whimsy which delights in recreating, in a comical dramatic fiction, the absurdity and inexplicability of real life.[47]

Those who "take Feydeau seriously" generally concur on Shapiro's last point,[48] crediting the playwright's ability to illustrate the inexplicability of life to the paradox of controlled chaos that he dramatized so adroitly. Feydeau's mastery at staging movement, at playing with misunderstandings inherent to homophonic language, and at maintaining throughout a sense of realism in the face of the absurd, all contributed to this end.[49] I would add another item to this list of Feydeau's talents, namely, his flair for expressing anxiety about life's absurdity in directly addressing new locales produced by the modern cityscape. The location of the *tailleur pour dames* exemplifies this type of carefully crafted, yet absurd, site, in which characters' very core identities are called into question so repeatedly that they no longer know who they are or how to behave in the space.

A case in point is Moulineaux, who finds himself at a loss when Aubin asks him, "the tailor," for his name. Put on the spot, Moulineaux awkwardly adopts the moniker *Machin*, a nonsensical slang word approximating the term "whatsit" that in colloquial language is used as a placeholder for a forgotten or inaccessible word. Naming himself for something that means nothing, Moulineaux assumes an absurd label that gestures towards his increasing lack of selfhood. His identity is further shaken when Aubin asks him point blank whether he is a tailor:

AUBIN. – Look, are you a couturier, yes or no?
MOULINEAUX, *reaching stage left*. – Eh! Me, yes, I do believe I am a
   couturier!

[AUBIN. – Enfin, êtes-vous couturier, oui ou non?
MOULINEAUX, *gagne l'extrême gauche*. – Hein! Moi, oui, je crois bien que je
    suis couturier!][50]

The audience understands that Moulineaux does not really think that
he is a garment worker and is simply saying so to conceal his infidelity.
However, his false admission equally implies Moulineaux's reluctant
acceptance that his once fixed identity as a doctor of high social standing is no longer stable. It also indicates that this disruption is related to
the ambiguous space in which the character finds himself.

This link between the couturier's studio and the protagonist's shaky
identity grows as Moulineaux begins, in spite of himself, to take ownership of Mme Durand's former space. Absentmindedly referring to it as
"my place" ["chez moi"],[51] Moulineaux symbolically replaces his actual
home (the typical meaning of the phrase "chez moi") with the fashion
atelier and its intrinsic absurdity. The problem is that the location that
he now claims as his own is not a "place" in Tuan's sense of the term,
for, as we have seen, he can have no security in it. Moreover, the
couturière's studio, far from clarifying social roles and relations, actually
confounds the very system, over which he, a privileged man with high
status, had once unquestionably exerted power. Furthermore, as
Moulineaux's fruitless attempts to seduce Suzanne demonstrate, the
workspace of the *tailleur pour dames* is not a "space" either, for the tryst
that represents freedom from the constraints of marriage never materializes. Rather, in the atelier, the protagonist is imprisoned in a space
where he is at the mercy of outside forces that render his existence absurd. To put it in terms used by the surrealists a generation later,
Moulineaux is in the "infernal machine," to which the site gives rise.[52]
Neither "place" nor "space," the fashion atelier is a dislocation of urban
modernity where, in the cruel judgment of absurdist works, life may
very well have no meaning. It is no wonder that, when Suzanne asks at
the start of Act II whether he is happy, Moulineaux can only stammer
repeatedly "What!" [Comment donc!"],[53] as though the very question
of happiness is meaningless in this space.

Perhaps the most important markers of the play's (il)logic are fashions themselves. We have seen, for instance, that the ridiculous dress
that Moulineaux "designs" for Suzanne is a chaotic mess of garment
fragments and incompatible fabrics such as fur and tulle, an outfit composed of elements that would be devoid of sense if they were assem-
bled into an actual dress. Later, when Aubin inquires about the status of

the outfit in front of Yvonne, Moulineaux must invent another incongruous sartorial object as an explanation for his confused wife, who remains ignorant that Aubin believes her husband to be a couturier. This time Moulineaux concocts a garment that he calls "a health dress" ["une robe de santé"],[54] a preposterous item that he describes as "a homeopathic robe … with electricity inside" ["une robe homéopathique … avec de l'électricité dedans"].[55] Noting that the robe functions through "science,"[56] a realm of knowledge traditionally open only to men, Moulineaux implies that Yvonne, as a woman, is not likely to understand it. His hopes are that this nod to his authority as a man of medicine will induce his wife to believe the ruse. In fact, though, part of the absurdity of the invented garment resides in the very "scientific" incompatibility of its parts. For, as an invasive treatment applied to the body's exterior, the notion of electrical shock therapy contradicts the very tenets of homeopathy, which encourages the body to heal itself by producing antibodies from within.[57] The outfits that Moulineaux dreams up in *Tailleur pour dames* are the very material expressions of incongruity and meaninglessness that the space generates.

It is possible to imagine that, for Feydeau, the idea of a site without meaning was more palatable than the notion of an inimical place: the overindustrialized, alienating urban environment hostile to human life that the newly reconfigured Paris represented to its critics. (The name of Moulineaux's mother-in-law – "Aigre-ville," literally, "sour city" – seems to motion towards the latter.) These two possible versions of the city – either meaningless or unwelcoming – were both disquieting in their own way and may have been why humour was Feydeau's chosen genre. Supplying comedies to a Parisian audience so desirous of distraction that it was prepared to laugh even at its own expense can be understood as one strategy to mitigate anxieties over changing social roles and questions of identity in the modern cityscape that Feydeau's audience, and Feydeau himself, may have shared. His dark humour had the power to activate a laughter that Noëlle Benhamou has called "black but liberating" ["grinçant mais libérateur"],[58] evoking both the bleak pessimism and need for cathartic release that early Third Republic Paris invoked for some. The point here has been to examine how Feydeau's portrait of the couturier and his space of work illuminates the playwright's ambivalence about the unstable meanings and absurdities inherent to Haussmannized Paris. In the following discussion of Zola's *La Curée* we will continue to explore the figure of the haute couture tailor and his relationship to problematic spaces of fashion.

La Curée: **Haussmann's réseau**

La Curée (1871), Zola's dazzling account of speculation, Haussmanization, and Second Empire fashion, ends with the somewhat abrupt juxtaposition of death and the haute couture designer: "Next winter, when
Renée died of acute meningitis, her father paid her debts. Worms's bill
came to two hundred and fifty-seven thousand francs"[59] ["L'hiver sui-
vant, lorsque Renée mourut d'une méningite aiguë, ce fut son père qui
paya ses dettes. La note de Worms se montait à deux cent cinquante-sept
mille francs[60]]. Zola's choice to make the last two sentences of the novel
about Renée's death and to mention it in conjunction with Worms, her
high-fashion tailor, invites us to examine the relationship between these
two elements of the novel in greater detail, particularly as they intersect
with the space of the fashion atelier.

Although some work will be necessary to unpack the couturier's key
role in the text and Zola's connection of tailor's atelier to Renée's demise, the reference to death itself should come as no surprise given the
novel's title. *La Curée* has been translated as *The Kill*, the English version
of the title aptly alluding to the death of a targeted victim. Renée is perhaps the ostensible "kill" in the novel, but she is not the only one, since
the plot explicitly allegorizes the Second Empire, a political regime that
fell in 1870, the year prior to the novel's publication in volume form, the
"death" of which Zola was also referencing. A chronicle of excess, luxury, pleasure, and greed under the reign of Emperor Napoléon III, *La
Curée* is a pointed critique of what Zola portrays as the fraudulent economic forces at work behind the physical construction of the city's new
boulevards, monuments, parks, and buildings. As his title implies, the
newly rebuilt city inherited by the early Third Republic was indelibly
marked by the "killer" instincts of its mid-century planners. In particular, the rapid expansion of this glittering yet corrupt metropolis is facilitated by the shady speculation practices perpetrated by Zola's ruthless
anti-hero Aristide Saccard. Saccard's desire to dominate urban space
informs the plot's overall development, making spatiality one of the
novel's subtexts. Indeed, Saccard marries Renée primarily for the large
property adjacent to Paris that she will inherit and that he knows will
be developed under Haussmannization. Like a hunter stalking his prey,
Saccard patiently manipulates his wife into signing this property over
to him so that he alone can profit from its subsequent development.
Renée is killed by meningitis, but the reader understands her illness
as resulting from deep unhappiness about her meaningless existence,

which revolves around the pursuit of physical pleasure and the purchase and corporeal display of inordinately expensive garments.
Meanwhile, like the ancient myth of Phaedra upon which it is loosely
based, *La Curée* stages an incestuous and tragic love affair between
Renée and Saccard's son from a prior marriage, the effete dandy
Maxime. Through their incest and the blurring of their respective gender roles, Zola renders the couple of Renée and Maxime a symbol of
sexual deviance pointing to the overall "killing" of social morals during
this period. Losing Maxime provokes the despair that finally kills the
female protagonist, this rupture having sartorial undertones since
Maxime had been both Renée's lover and a fellow lover of fashion.

In addition to this trio of protagonists, one of the most vital characters to the novel's successful portrayal of modernity is Renée's haute
couture dressmaker, a man known simply as "Worms." With the exception of one key scene, Worms seems not to be a prominent character in
the text. In fact, however, the *grand couturier*'s formidable influence is
exerted throughout. His name is repeatedly mentioned at key moments,
as exemplified, we have seen, by his presence in the final phrase of the
novel. Worms also appears in a crucial passage at the mid-point of the
novel where Saccard's stealthy appropriation of Renée's inheritance
unfolds.[61] In this section, which includes no less than six references to
Worms, Renée's deep concern about her debt to the clothing designer
"torments" ["tourmente"][62] her so greatly that her husband is able to set
in motion his plan to swindle her out of the Charonne property. This is
the plot of land adjacent to Paris that Saccard knows will be a source of
enormous profit when the metropole, through Haussmannization, ex-
pands beyond the former city limits. Renée's anxiousness about her
clothing bills ("Renée, who was very worried about Worms's bill"[63] ["la
jeune femme, que le mémoire de Worms inquiétait beaucoup"][64] is the
catalyst for the eventual surrendering of her land, the last of her fortune, to Saccard. This passage, located near the midway point of
the novel, suggests the couturier's central role in Renée's downfall.[65]
Beyond these literal references to Worms, the novel contains numerous
descriptions of extravagant garments worn by Renée[66] and others in her
circle of well-heeled society ladies. These gowns are part of a sustained
sartorial discourse that runs throughout the work, making of Worms,
and the high fashion world that he epitomizes, an omnipresent element
of the urban Parisian backdrop that Zola creates.

That haute couture and Worms are leitmotifs in the novel suggests
the significance of women's fashion and the couturier to its narrative

arc.[67] The three main characters of the story allegorize the domains of modernity that Zola wished to explore in the novel, namely, corruptive forces behind the construction of modern Paris (Saccard), inner degradation hidden behind ostentatious beauty (Renée), and degeneration, especially in areas of gendered and sexual conduct (Maxime). Tellingly, these three spheres are intricately linked through fashion. In addition to an incestuous bed, for instance, Maxime and Renée share a passion for chic clothing and fashionable high life. Yet, their flamboyant taste in dress is far more than a shared character trait: the young man's fine attire feminizes him and renders him a symbol of sexual deviance, while Renée's impulsive consumption of costly attire is integral to Saccard's rise to economic dominance in the new capital. For it is only when Worm's exorbitant clothing bills plunge Renée into insurmountable debt that Saccard can "go in for the kill" as the novel's title implies, seizing her land in order to further his spatial appropriation of Paris through the construction of new zones of the city.

Taking into account the interconnected network formed by the Renée-Saccard-Maxime triad, I will read *La Curée* as Zola's vision of how the privileging of haute couture fashion, and the nouveau riche attitude that it symbolized during the Second Empire, informed the very growth and eventual layout of the rapidly evolving city. For indeed, the novel is preoccupied with urban space; as Brian Nelson translating Claude Duchet puts it, "*The Kill* is 'less a study of characters placed in a particular milieu than a study of a milieu placed in particular characters.'"[68] Spatial concerns of the novel in turn are connected to fashion, since Saccard's development of the modern landscape depends on Renée's frivolous purchasing of garments for which she cannot pay, and, moreover, on her desire to show off her beautiful clothing, an impetus with which the display-oriented architecture of the period colludes. In fact, luxury fashion seems so central to *La Curée* that the metropole ends up resembling a series of haute couture houses, wherein the commerce and exhibition of exquisite clothing are defining features.

To understand Zola's Paris in these terms, as a metaphorical set of interconnected *maisons de couture*, allows for new insights into the author's attitude towards the ideologies of city planning under Napoléon III. For, although much of the *Rougon-Macquart* represents Zola's overall critique of the principles associated with Haussmannization,[69] in *La Curée*, the author paradoxically implies that citywide moral downfall is due not to the principles of Second Empire urban planning themselves, but rather to an unintended consequence of their successful execution.

This consequence relates to the Haussmannian impetus to order space, one that Paul Rabinow citing Françoise Choay describes as a drive towards overall "regularization."[70] Haussmann's approach to the regularization of Paris was informed especially by the intertwined notions of circulation[71] and, to use a term frequently cited both then and now, the *réseau* or "network" structuring it.[72] Prendergast summarizes this ideology well: "Control the network of circulation, said the earlier reformers, ensure the orderly flow of traffic, waste and bodies, and the rational city will emerge."[73] As is well known, in order to enact major improvements to the city's circulation that were mindful of its growing population and emerging modes of transportation, Haussmann reconfigured an infrastructure of wide navigable boulevards, bridges, avenues, and smaller street connections.[74] This massive network was one of the most recognizable characteristics of Haussmannian regularization, and, for some later critics, is a key spatial feature of early Third Republic modernity that would impact urban conditions in the century to follow. Foucault, writing that "the anxiety of our era has to do fundamentally with space," specifies that modern space should not be thought of as discrete sites in isolation but rather as "relations of proximity between points or elements," or, more succinctly, as "relations among sites."[75] Foucault's understanding of space as a network – as the relations themselves connecting sites to one another – is anticipated a century earlier by Zola, whose depiction of Paris in *La Curée* is an illustration of the regularized paths of movement among locations that helped to define the Haussmannian city.[76]

This chapter will suggest that it was not the implementation of urban regularization per se that was problematic for Zola. Rather, it was the contagion resulting from Haussmannization's successful network of spatial connectivity that engendered the novelist's distrust, one that would erupt a decade later more obviously in *Nana*'s subtext of urban infectivity. In *La Curée*, Zola uses the fashion house to suggest that a theoretically beneficial regularization of city space is problematized by dislocations, which compromise healthy circulation because they encourage instead a citywide cross-contamination of modernity's flaws. To examine the dubious meanings of the *maison de couture* for Zola this discussion begins with the author's portrait of the haute couture designer and his place of work, reading this figure and his atelier within the context of contemporaneous journalistic depictions. It then analyses the Saccard mansion as a metaphorical fashion house exemplifying the harmful *réseau* inadvertently brought about by Haussmannization.

This system of linked urban spaces, which facilitates a dangerous spreading of fallen morals across Paris, culminates in the eventual effacement, or "killing off," of its agent: the fashionable woman.

Worms-Worth: The Fashion Designer

As his readers would have instantly surmised, the character of Worms in Zola's novel is the author's winking nod to the flesh-and-blood couturier Charles Frederick Worth (1825–1895), the most influential designer of prestige women's wear of the late nineteenth century, and a man, we recall, often referred to as "the father of haute couture." That said, another less frequently cited but plausible inspiration for the character may have been the painter Jules Worms (1832–1924),[77] an artist of nostalgic romantic canvasses that were exhibited throughout the 1860s and 1870s at the Paris Salon. Jules Worms's paintings, which were at times fashion laden, might have equated him in Zola's eyes with artists that the novelist ridiculed as "painter-couturiers" (*peintre-couturiers*)[78] for their inclination to overprivilege garments in works that he likened, disparagingly, to commercial fashion plates. In 1868, the year that Zola wrote passionately in favour of Manet and Courbet, painters that he deemed had been unfairly overlooked by the Salon and the public alike, two of Jules Worms's canvases were purchased by the French government, one destined to be mounted in the Musée du Luxembourg and the other finding its way eventually to the Musée d'Orsay where it hangs today. When Zola was drafting *La Curée* shortly after 1868, he may have been criticizing such honours bestowed on Jules Worms and other *peintre-couturiers* in his novel's unflattering portrait of the high fashion designer, while simultaneously poking fun at the artistic pretenses of couturiers more generally.

The possibility that Jules Worms was a model for Zola's couturier character notwithstanding, the most probable inspiration for the figure in *La Curée* was surely Charles Frederick Worth, whose real-life story was well known to Third Republic readers. An Englishman who moved to Paris in 1845, Worth worked first as a draper in the fabric industry before starting a luxury dressmaking company with his partner Otto Bobergh in 1858 on the city's elegant rue de la Paix. Quickly Worth rose to fame for the sumptuous gowns that were the specialty of his *maison*, and for dressing not only glamorous society women and royalty, such as the renowned trend setters Princess de Metternich and the Empress Eugénie herself, but also high-profile and somewhat disreputable figures including the Countess de Castiglione, mistress of Napoléon III. Taking sole control of the business in 1870, he renamed the house Maison Worth and worked there until his death in 1895, when his sons, Gaston and Jean-Philippe, took over the thriving family business.[79]

As Nancy J. Troy argues, Worth's success as the first elite male couturier was due in part to how he promoted himself as an exceptional artist and his fashions as masterpieces.[80] I would like to focus on how the position of "artist" that Worth claimed for himself was related to the space in which he worked. This was the *maison de couture* on the rue de la Paix that bore his name and in which it was he, rather than his wealthy customers, who exerted an artist's authority. Peter Wollen points out that, as a sign of his artistic pretentions "Worth was able to get his clients to come to his house, rather than the other way round, just as a patron might visit an artist's studio.[81] In this Worth was rather unusual, for, as Susan North indicates, other fashion houses with similar standing, such as the highly successful British firm Redfern, opened numerous shops outside their home base in England and their representatives habitually travelled to Europe and North America, going directly to their clients. In contrast, North notes, "Worth had no branch outlets in the nineteenth century, in part because he felt he did not need the business and also because it would have diluted his position as the highest authority of taste: the Worth customer had to travel to Paris."[82] These observations by Wollen and North suggest that the notion of circulation was an important element of the haute couture designer's presence in social space: not only did Worth have the unique ability to displace powerful fashion icons from across the city's landscape (not to mention other countries and continents), but his formidable influence then extended from his atelier to the world beyond, as these women in turn circulated his elegant garments across the capital city, France, and nations abroad.

In *La Curée*, Zola satirizes the notion of the *grand couturier* as genius artist by way of an ironic episode describing Worms at work in his fashion house. In this passage, Zola indulges in a sardonic portrait of the flamboyantly erratic couturier, offering another model of the eccentric fashion designer that is reminiscent of Moulineaux "the tailor" in Feydeau's *Tailleur pour dames*:

When the great Worms finally received Renée, Maxime followed her into the consulting room … [Worms] made Renée stand before a mirror which rose from the floor to the ceiling, and pondered with knit brows while

Renée, overcome with emotion, held her breath so as to remain quite still. After a few minutes the master, as if gripped by inspiration, sketched in broad jerky strokes the masterpiece he had just conceived, exclaiming in short phrases: "A Montespan dress in pale-grey faille …, the skirt describing a rounded basque in front …, large grey satin bows to bring it up on the hips …, and a puffed apron of pearl-grey tulle, the puffs separated by strips of grey satin (translation modified).[83]

[Lorsque le grand Worms recevait enfin Renée, Maxime pénétrait avec elle dans le cabinet … [Worms] faisait mettre Renée debout devant une glace, qui montait du parquet au plafond, se recueillait, avec un froncement de sourcils, pendant que la jeune femme, émue, retenait son haleine, pour ne pas bouger. Et, au bout de quelques minutes, le maître, comme pris et secoué par l'inspiration, peignait à grands traits saccadés le chef-d'œuvre qu'il venait de concevoir, s'écriait en phrases sèches: "Robe Montespan en faille cendrée …, la traîne dessinant, devant, une basque arrondie …, gros nœuds de satin gris la relevant sur les hanches …, enfin tablier bouillonné de tulle gris perle, les bouillonnés séparés par des bandes de satin gris."[84]]

Here Zola ridicules high-society women like the breathless Renée, who willingly suffer discomfort and anxiety at the hands of their dressmakers, while simultaneously lampooning the idea that the man is an artist, overstating this analogy with the terms "master," "sketched," "inspiration," and "masterpiece." To extend the satire, Zola exaggerates Worms's unpredictable behaviour, such that the process of making fashions renders Worms's mannerisms particularly erratic. When inspiration strikes, for example, Worms describes accessories "with a triumphant facial contortion of a Pythoness"[85] ["avec un grimace triomphante de pythonisse sur son trépied"[86]]; when inspiration is lacking, his eyebrows contort, he holds his head in his hands, collapses melodramatically on an armchair, and dismisses Renée, theatrically declaring, "No, no, not today … I can't relate to you this morning"[87] ["Pas possible, pas possible, chère dame, vous repasserez un autre jour … Je ne vous sens pas ce matin"[88]]. As Priscilla Parkhurst Ferguson aptly puts it, Worms is "almost a caricature of the romantic artist [who] keeps all the women in thrall, makes his customers wait for hours, and produces an outfit only when truly inspired."[89] Like Feydeau's Moulineaux, Zola's Worms is not a serious artist but a comedic character with humorously, and exaggeratedly, strange behaviours.

Ironically, Zola's very impulse to caricature Worms renders him consistent with descriptions of the elite fashion designer appearing in numerous non-fiction reports of the period. In a 1901 article signed by a reporter called "Intime," the British monthly *The Lady's Realm* supported Zola's rendering of the hierarchical imbalance between couturier and client, declaring that "fashion is ruled not by the customer but by the *costumier* [sic]."[90] Another telling example is Hippolyte Taine's 1867 *Notes sur Paris*, which includes the portrait of a temperamental designer who tyrannically dictates what society women should wear, all the while proclaiming himself "a great artist" ["un grand artiste"].[91] The latter text is especially relevant to this discussion because Zola's vision of naturalism was heavily influenced by Taine's philosophies on the nexus of literature, science, and contemporary society. Taine's *Notes sur Paris*, a satirical account of modern Parisian ways of life, was published just four years before the appearance of *La Curée*. Given Zola's keen interest in Taine's writings, it is reasonable to expect that he derived inspiration for Worms from this text. Although Zola's Worms is more playful than the damning version scripted by Taine, *Notes sur Paris* includes many similarities, such as the couturier's authoritarian manner with women and his self-proclaimed status as artist. Taine wrote:

Women bow down in order to be dressed by him. This black, dry, nervous little being, who has the appearance of a monstrous runt scorched in the fire, receives them wearing a velvet smock, superbly spread out on a divan, a cigar at his lips. He says to them: "Walk forward, turn; good; come back in eight days, I will create for you the outfit that is appropriate for you." It is not they who choose, it is he … Several of them, his favourites, come to have him inspect them, before going to a ball; he gives little tea parties at ten o'clock. To people who are surprised he responds, "I am a great artist, I have the colour mastery of Delacroix and *I paint*. An outfit is worth as much as a painting."

[Les femmes font des bassesses pour être habillées par lui. Ce petit être sec, noir, nerveux, qui a l'air d'un avorton roussi au feu, les reçoit en vareuse de velours, superbement étalé sur un divan, le cigare aux lèvres. Il leur dit: "Marchez, tournez-vous; bien; revenez dans huit jours, je vous composerai la toilette qui vous convient." Ce n'est pas elles qui choisissent, c'est lui … Plusieurs d'entre elles, les favorites, viennent se faire inspecter par lui, avant d'aller au bal; il donne de petits thés à dix heures. Aux gens qui s'étonnent, il répond: "Je suis un grand artiste, j'ai la couleur de Delacroix et *je compose*. Une toilette vaut un tableau"] (original emphasis)[92]

As this example demonstrates, the *grand couturier* as "great artist" who "composes" garments and declares that his dresses are more valuable than works by celebrated painters such as Delacroix was not a satire perpetuated by Zola alone. Taine's text highlights as well the motif of the couturier as high ruler, one that Zola seems to have borrowed for his portrayal of Worms. In Taine's version, the tailor reclines sultan-like on a plush sofa and compels women to "bow down in order to be dressed by him." Zola's portrait of Worms as the couturier "to whom the great ladies of the Second Empire bowed down"[93] ["devant lequel les reines du second Empire se tenaient à genoux"[94]] echoes Taine's depiction of Worth, down to the image of kneeling women and elements of interior décor, such as the lush upholstered sofas upon which both "kings of fashion" lounge.[95]

Genius artist and supreme sovereign are not the only metaphors that Zola uses to describe Worms.[96] More provocative still is the novelist's transformation of Worms into a facilitator of ladies' tea parties where sexual transgression is an implicit undercurrent. Tellingly, Zola reproduces the couturier's own dubious extravagance through the very location in which he works and receives his clients:

The great man's showroom was huge and square, and furnished with enormous divans. Maxime entered it with religious emotion. Dresses undoubtedly have a perfume of their own; silk, satin, velvet, and lace had mingled their faint aromas with those of hair and of amber-scented shoulders; and the atmosphere in the room had the sweet-smelling warmth, the fragrance of flesh and luxury, that transformed the apartment into a chapel consecrated to some secret divinity. It was often necessary for Renée and Maxime to wait for hours; a queue of at least twenty women sat there, waiting their turn, dipping biscuits into glasses of Madeira, helping themselves from the great table in the middle, which was covered with bottles and plates of cakes. The ladies had made themselves at home, talking freely, and when they ensconced themselves around the room, it was as if a flight of doves (*lesbiennes*) had alighted on the sofas of a Parisian drawing room.[97]

[Le salon du grand homme était vaste, carré, garni de larges divans. [Maxime] y entrait avec une émotion religieuse. Les toilettes ont certainement une odeur propre; la soie, le satin, le velours, les dentelles, avaient marié leurs arômes légers à ceux des chevelures et des épaules ambrées; et l'air du salon gardait cette tiédeur odorante, cet encens de la chair et du luxe qui changeait la pièce en une chapelle consacrée à quelque secrète divinité. Souvent il fallait que Renée et Maxime fissent antichambre pendant des heures; il y avait là une vingtaine de solliciteuses, attendant leur tour, trempant des biscuits dans des verres de madère, faisant collation sur la grande table du milieu, où traînaient des bouteilles et des assiettes de petits fours. Ces dames était chez elles, parlaient librement, et lorsqu'elles se pelotonnaient autour de la pièce, on aurait dit un vol blanc de lesbiennes qui se serait abattu sur les divans d'un salon parisien.[98]]

Scholars note Zola's surprising inclusion of the term *lesbiennes* in Worms's salon and have interpreted it as an overdetermined connection between the haute couture fashion house and transgressive female sexuality.[99] In this way, Zola joins Rops and Feydeau in depicting the fashion atelier as a location linked to women representing sexual deviance. Zola's metaphor of the couture house as a "chapel" filled with eroticized odours of incense mixing with the hair and flesh of women further moves the description in the direction of exaggerated feminocentric sensuality, whereby the atelier is less a space of garment manufacture and more one of profane and hypersexualized female comportment.

Despite such liberties taken in service of literary symbolism, however, Zola's version of Worms's *maison de couture* does correspond in some ways to less licentious period depictions of the high fashion houses of Worth and his contemporaries. In 1894, M. Griffith, a reporter for the British *Strand Magazine*, paid a visit to Worth and to several of his Parisian rivals. Griffith's report illuminates how Zola's rendering of the designer's space exaggerates some elements to support his critique of modern society, even as it conforms in other ways to period descriptions of actual late-century couturier houses. One example is Zola's treatment of the luxurious décor chez Worms, which matches Griffith's account of the opulent rooms inside the top Parisian *maisons de couture*, but not, interestingly enough, those of Paris's most well-known designer. For, although Griffith's readers may have expected the facilities of the famous father of haute couture to be the most exquisite in the city, surprisingly the reporter found Maison Worth to be relatively simple, restrained, and "plainly furnished."[100] Instead, the interiors that caught Griffith's eye, and for which he saved his greatest enthusiasm, were the "beautiful salons"[101] of Félix, a couture house in the affluent Faubourg St Honoré located not far from Worth's establishment.[102] Praising the space's sumptuous décor, Griffith reproduced the rooms of Maison Félix in lavish textual detail:

> One salon is in the style of Louis XVI. [*sic*], with panels of green brocaded velvet, alternating with console tables, surmounted by long mirrors, made on the models of those in Trianon: the decoration is white and gold; the couches and chairs are covered with green striped velvet and satin, and huge pots filled with ferns and palms stand on pedestals. A gallery leading from the first salon to a second has four large panels, painted by Louise Abbéma, representing Sarah Bernhardt in "Ruy Blas," Croizette in the "Caprices of Marianne," Ada Rehan in the "School for Scandal," and a fancy costume of the period of Louis XV. These panels are exquisitely painted, and illustrate some of M. Felix's choicest designs in fancy dress. The Grand Salon has panels of old tapestry, coloured glass ceiling, draperies of plush, and long mirrors framed in mahogany. Every room is lighted with electric light, and the groups of palms, screens, and harmonious colouring of carpets, furniture, and walls make delightful surroundings for trying the effect of beautiful gowns and fabrics.[103]

Griffith's glowing review of Félix's[104] premises accentuates the locale's aristocratic connotations (Louis XVI décor and Trianon-inspired furnishings), its connection to high art (paintings by noted salon artist Louise Abbéma), its lushly upholstered divans, and its vast size, all elements that Zola incorporates into Worms's fashion house in *La Curée*. The images in Griffith's article prominently featured these rooms, reflecting his readers' interest in these luxury spaces that were typically off-limits to the general public. Griffith's report included five half-page illustrations based on photographs of Félix's showrooms, which were entitled, respectively, "The Young Ladies' Room," "The Fashion Hall," "The Grand Salon," "The Entrance to The Grand Salon" and "The Entrance to The Trying-On Rooms" (see figure 5.2).[105] Although the titles of the rooms pointed to some differences in terms of clientele and function – young women versus more mature clients, trying on versus displaying – the images also depicted the spaces as uniformly majestic,

---

5.2 (opposite) Anonymous, *The Grand Salon – M. Felix's Establishment*, in *The Strand Magazine: An Illustrated Monthly*, ed. George Newnes (London: George Newnes Ltd, 1894), 749. Print from a photograph. Reproduced by permission of the General Research Division, the New York Public Library, Astor, Lenox, and Tilden Foundations.

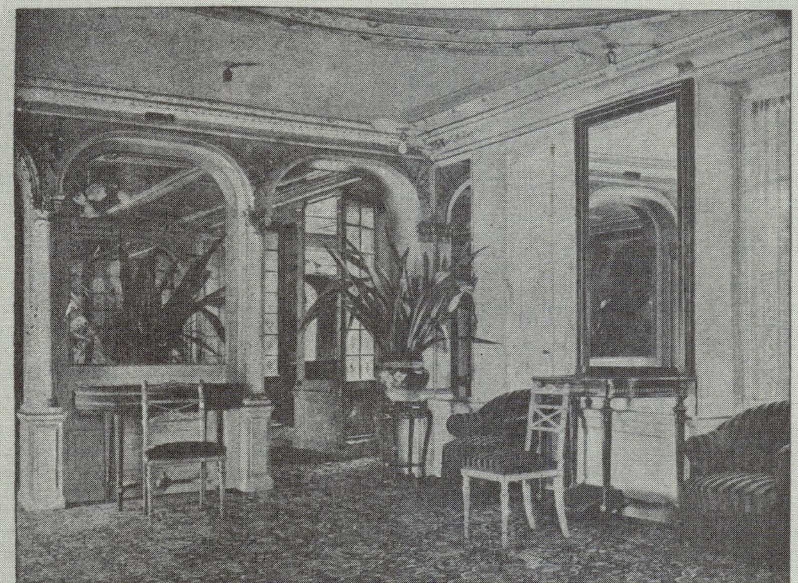

PARIS DRESSMAKERS.   749

From a]   THE FASHION HALL—M. FELIX'S ESTABLISHMENT.   [*Photograph.*

makers. Mme. Carnot, who took a great interest in this charity, was present, and the fine show-rooms looked lovely, filled with all kinds of pretty satchels, cushions, and a thousand and one dainty trifles made from odds and ends, and looking so fresh and

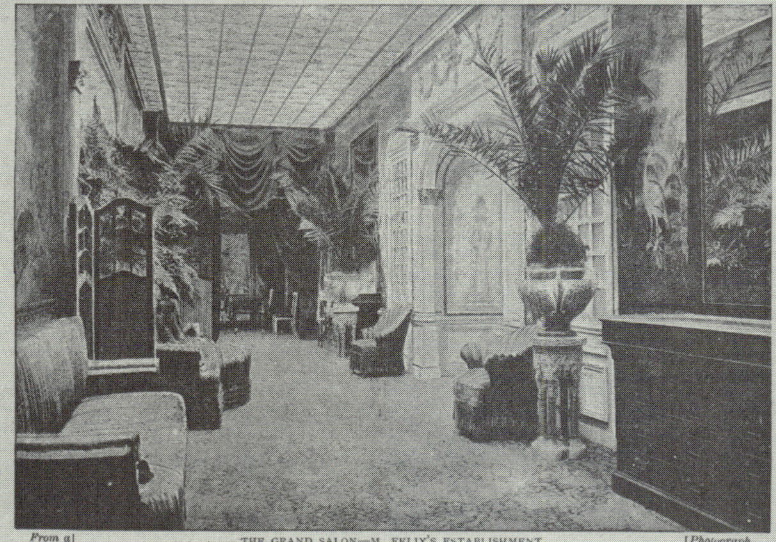

From a]   THE GRAND SALON—M. FELIX'S ESTABLISHMENT.   [*Photograph.*

drawing attention to the stuffed couches and armchairs, heavy drapes, armoires carved of exotic woods, tall mirrors, and lush plants that decorated all of the rooms. In privileging these aspects of décor at the Maison Félix, Griffith's report bears witness to more than just a late-century fascination with the extravagant spaces where haute couture was created. His remark that Félix's establishment constituted "delightful surroundings for trying the effect of beautiful gowns and fabrics," suggested the crucial importance of a suitable environment for the display of fashions that the physical premises of the couture house both provided and reinforced. This link between space and clothing calls to mind the approach of architect Charles Garnier, who took into consideration the sumptuous outfits that would be worn in his Opéra while he was designing the building's famous staircase (see chapter 1). In their own ways, then, the writings of Griffith, Garnier, and Zola all imply that fashion spaces of the city, from the Opéra to Félix's couture house and Worms's establishment, exemplified an impetus of Haussmannian modernity to plan new urban locations in part with the display of garments in mind. They posit, moreover, the inherent interconnectivity among these sites associated with high fashion, an urban network that, we will see, Zola appears to distrust for facilitating the circulation of damaging social and moral behaviours.

Another point of similarity between Griffith's account of the interiors of elite couture firms and Worms's location is the importance of spatial layout. Although the Maison Worth was not as lavish as the facilities of M. Félix, Griffith noted that both businesses separated spaces according to function. The areas serving Worth's clients, for example, included both "reception and fitting rooms,"[106] an arrangement that segregated waiting areas from the workrooms themselves. In similar fashion, the room titles in Félix's establishment assigned them different purposes, from the "Trying-On Rooms" where garments were donned to test fit and appearance to the "Grand Salon," a long and narrow hall likely used as a waiting room by clients before and after appointments. In *La Curée*, Zola evokes just such divisions by partitioning off Worm's *cabinet* or office, separating the space where Renée is accorded a private audience with the designer from the luxurious waiting room. This highlights not only the exclusivity of Worms's private office but also the fact that the function of Worms's grand salon is different from that of his personal atelier. That is, the latter space is where Worms conjures up garments while the former exists to provide the women who populate it with the comforts of their opulent homes (to make them feel "chez elles"). For, as Zola makes clear, in the salon, the order of the day is not to produce garments, but rather to enjoy cakes and wine, idle conversation, and nestling on couches.

If in literal terms the couturier's private atelier is more a space of clothing design than the waiting chamber, in narrative terms the salon is just as crucial a location of fashion creation. This is because it is by way of the sumptuous *grand salon*, rather than Worms's personal chamber, that Zola weaves symbolic meaning into the garments that he wishes for them to evoke. Gowns that bear the Worms label might not be designed or sewn in the grand salon, but this location enables Zola to "make" them through luxurious textual descriptions into material signs of the modern society that he seeks to condemn. Informed by space, the dresses in *La Curée* thus come to symbolize deviant female sexuality, the profanation of the sacred, and overindulgence, all characteristics present in Zola's description above of the couture house salon. One might argue that the author's intention is to imply that it is women who carry these traits *to* the salon, and who then infuse these qualities into their "home away from home." But we note that there is also a continuation to this process, a dissemination of these damaging characteristics throughout the city. Contagion circulates as women in fine garments exit the salon of the *maison de couture*, an epicentre for social, sexual, and moral degradation, and these same features, facilitated by the network of Haussmann's infrastructure, are transported by Worms's sharply clad clientele into other areas of the urban landscape.

Renée's garments exemplify such articles of clothing that are imbued with the extravagance and sexual deviance of the spaces in which they are made. One such outfit is a brand-new dress that Renée wears home from Worms's atelier on the day that Maxime arrives to live at the Saccard mansion. The meeting takes place years before the first sexual encounter between Renée and her stepson, when the young man is still but an adolescent of fourteen and Renée is newly married to his father. Maxime and Renée are immediately drawn to one another over a mutual flair for fashion. The seeds of their future incest are planted as Renée is "returning from her dressmaker" ["revenait de chez son tailleur"],[107] a spatial detail that ties her garments to the location where they were just produced. Zola describes Renée's outfit as follows:

> She wore a delightful skirt of blue faille, with deep flounces, and over that a sort of guard's coat in pale grey silk. The flaps of the coat, lined with blue satin of a deeper shade than the faille of the skirt, were boldly caught up and secured with ribbon; the cuffs of the flat sleeves and the broad lapels of the bodice stood out wide, trimmed with the same satin. As a crowning

touch, as a bold stroke of eccentricity, two rows of large buttons, made to look like sapphires fastened in blue rosettes, adorned the front of the coat. It looked both ugly and entrancing.[108]

[Elle portait une délicieuse jupe de faille bleue, à grands' volants, sur laquelle était jetée une sorte d'habit de garde française de soie gris tendre. Les pans de l'habit, doublé de satin bleu plus foncé que la faille du jupon, étaient galamment relevés et retenus par des nœuds de ruban; les parements des manches plates, les grands revers du corsage s'élargissaient, garnis du même satin. Et, comme assaisonnement suprême, comme pointe risquée d'originalité, de gros boutons imitant le saphir, pris dans des rosettes azur, descendaient le long de l'habit, sur deux rangées. C'étaient laid et adorable.[109]]

In Renée's outfit, Zola frames his portrait of the "ugly" and "entrancing" elements of her character, as well as those of the modernity that she allegorizes. On the surface, the skirt is "delightful" but the garment's chic "ugliness" is a sign of hidden degradation: the sexual and moral corruption that Renée will eventually engage in through incest. The symbolism of Renée's dress applies equally to built space in the newly modernized city. Her gown, like the buildings constructed to display Second Empire grandeur, hides its criminality behind its stylish façade. The surplus of ornamentation on the dress underscores the excessive, and thus transgressive, sexuality of its wearer. It is a sartorial rendering of the Saccard mansion itself, where exaggerated embellishments on the outside of the building and in its opulent interior chambers materially represent the sexual transgressions that take place within it between Renée and Maxime. The trimmings on Renée's dress – flounces, flaps, cuffs, lapels, and buttons – are folds and fasteners that open, hinting at a similar permeability of the body that they clothe. This porous quality extends to the Saccard home, an architectural exemplar of Haussmann modernity in which "there was a slamming of doors all day long"[110] ["les portes y battaient toute la journée"][111] and its "new and dazzling luxury was continually traversed"[112] ["le luxe neuf et éclatant en était traversé continuellement"[113]]. Like the mansion doors, perpetually open to all, the buttonholes and hooks of Renée's dress suggest her constant state of penetrability.[114]

Tellingly, during this first encounter the illicit sexual partnership between Renée and Maxime is foregrounded by a spontaneously occurring partnership in fashion design. Renée, peering at herself in a mirror and being slightly dissatisfied by an asymmetrical fold on her bodice, asks Maxime for ideas on improving the look of her dress. Suddenly revealing his innate talent for sartorial styling the youth suggests an idea for the outfit that Renée finds delightful: a necklace featuring a large cross. First, though, he runs his finger over the offending crease, his hand lingering for a moment at her bosom. Later, after they have begun their liaison, Maxime reminisces about this first meeting: "'Do you remember, the day I arrived in Paris?'… 'You were wearing such a funny dress, and I drew an angle on your chest with my finger … I felt your skin under your blouse, and my finger went in a little … It was very nice"[115] ["Tu te souviens, le jour où je suis arrivé à Paris … tu avais un drôle de costume; et, avec mon doigt, j'ai tracé un angle sur ta poitrine … je sentais ta peau sous la chemisette, et mon doigt enfonçait un peu … C'était très bon"].[116] Through fashion Maxime and Renée display their irreverence, trivializing the cross by transforming this sign of religious devotion into another frivolous accessory on an already over-embellished outfit. Moreover, the soft fold of cloth on Renée's dress and Maxime's finger are standins for their genitalia: pleasurable penetration is simulated as the young man pushes into her blouse. Incest, the great sexual crime of the novel that parallels the general degeneration of upper-class society as a whole, is first mediated through contact across Renée's dress, a garment marked by the overindulgence and sexually deviant environment of the *maison de couture* where it originates.

The Saccard Maison (de Couture)

Maxime and Renée demonstrate during their first encounter at the Saccard mansion that Worms is not the only clothing designer in *La Curée*, for the two lovers are fashion creators in their own right. Following his successful debut styling Renée's "entrancingly ugly" outfit, Maxime embarks on a period of intense study of the finest clothiers, hat shops, perfumers, and sellers of toiletries in Paris,[117] turning himself into an expert in modern chic and becoming his stepmother's trusted style adviser. We read that, despite his young age, "Renée consulted him seriously about her gowns"[118] ["Renée le consultait gravement sur ses toilettes"[119]], allowing the blossoming dandy a role in generating the haute couture looks that she then parades throughout the city. Renée, too, has a hand in the creation of her garments. In fact, she is as much a "maker" of Second Empire fashion as Worms, because the success of his creations depends both on her body to give life to his gowns and, importantly, on her ability to make his frequently risky looks appear chic and attractive. As it does for Nana, sartorial audacity accords Renée a major role in inventing cutting-edge styles that she alone can pull off. These include her daring gown decorated with vivid scenes of a deer hunt[120] and the flesh-coloured nudelike body suit that she boldly dons during the novel's climax. Renée is not simply muse and willing mannequin, then, but fashion innovator as well. As Ferguson points out, in the case of some of the most memorable outfits of the novel, "the ideas come from Renée – the 'prodigiously original and graceful dress' that she wears to the Tuileries is *her* 'real discovery' that comes to her one sleepless night" (original emphasis).[121] Indeed, Zola specifies that the gown is "faite" by Renée, employing the verb *faire* meaning "to do" or "to make," emphasizing grammatically that it is Renée, not Worms or Maxime, who creates the garment.

Renée's location when she dreams up this dress – her home – reinforces the connection between the place where fashions are typically made (Worms's fashion house) and the Saccard mansion, the novel's other troubled arena of sartorial creation. The process that Renée undertakes to create her ball gown likens her to Worms and the real-life designers on whom he is modelled: those heads of couture houses who staffed others to do the actual cutting and sewing and to produce material objects representing their artistic revelations. After Renée has a vision of the garment, we find that "three of Worms's assistants had come to her house to work on [it] under her supervision" ["trois ouvriers de Worms étaient venus [l']exécuter chez elle, sous ses yeux"].[122] Adopting the role of the male designer, Renée compels others to displace themselves at her convenience, just as Worth, playing the role of a great artist, required customers to come to him rather than the other way around. Like Worms and Worth, Renée does not fabricate the dress; rather, she oversees its production. However, in Renée's case, garment design takes place in what is literally her *maison* – the house where she lives – which seems spontaneously to transform into an ad hoc *maison de couture*. The polysemy of the word *maison* points to connections between Renée's home space and Worms's atelier, two different types of "houses" that are, nonetheless, embedded with similar brands of glamour and fashionability. That they are also spaces instilled with sexual and moral deviance suggests Zola's critique of the Haussmannian network that links them together, a spatial framework that may have been intended to regularize and improve circulation but that results instead in a dangerous flow of corrupt desires.

The Saccard mansion shares key characteristics with the fashion house as Zola and journalists of the day described it. Both are temples to the ostentatious aesthetics of the Second Empire, which, as noted above, Zola highlights by describing the grand home as an impromptu fashion atelier. We read that when Saccard is away:

> The house belonged to Renée and Maxime: they took possession of the father's study; they unpacked the tradesmen's parcels there, and articles of finery lay about among the business papers. Sometimes people had to wait for an hour at the study door while the schoolboy and the young married woman discussed a bow of ribbon, seated at either end of Saccard's writing-table.[123]

> [La maison appartenait à Renée et à Maxime. Ils s'emparaient du cabinet du père; ils y déballaient les cartons des fournisseurs, et les chiffons traînaient sur les dossiers. Parfois des gens graves attendaient une heure à la porte du cabinet, pendant que le collégien et la jeune femme discutaient un nœud de ruban, assis aux deux bouts du bureau de Saccard.[124]]

Here fashion objects – spilling fabrics and ornamental bows – are ciphers for excess and frivolity that forge an implicit connection between Worms's atelier and the Saccard home. Renée and Maxime are the agents who infect the mansion with the same superficiality and transgressive desires of the haute couture house. The Saccard mansion is filled with the comings and goings of a population in perpetual motion: it is "continually traversed by a flood of vast, floating skirts, by processions of tradespeople, by the noise of Renée's friends, Maxime's schoolfellows, and Saccard's callers"[125] ["traversé continuellement par des courses de jupes énormes et volantes, par des processions de fournisseurs, par le tohu-bohu des amies de Renée, des camarades de Maxime et des visiteurs de Saccard"[126]]. This continuous stream of humanity, a simulacrum for the movement of crowds traversing city streets, is Zola's suggestion that the Saccard home is as public as the boulevards.[127] Less obviously, the metaphor also likens the mansion to late-century *maisons de couture*, for in both fashions were displayed through a similar type of spatial navigation. Late-century descriptions of elite fashion houses indicate that it was common for female staff members to model various styles of a designer's garments and to walk them about the premises. When M. Griffith visited Worth, for example, he was enchanted by the attractive women employees whose job it was to stroll around the atelier as live mannequins. He noted that "several young ladies are dressed in the latest style of morning, visiting, dinner, and reception toilettes, and are paraded in turn, this way and that, before clients, to enable them to judge of the effect of the garments when worn."[128] In 1901, "Intime" of *The Lady's Realm* described a similar scene at the establishment of Félix, where "living models, tall, graceful young ladies with perfect figures, who not only know how to wear a dress well, but how to move about with ease and elegance" were to be found "trying on gowns over their tight-fitting alpaca or silkdresses [*sic*] and walking at different speeds up and down the showrooms before a customer."[129] In an 1870 article appearing in the popular newspaper *La Vie parisienne*, a writer reporting on the premises of "Monsieur Chose" (a thinly veiled allusion to Worth) took note as well of models in the *maison de couture*, suggesting that this phenomenon was already in vogue during the years that Zola was writing *La Curée*. Zola's version of urbanites streaming through the Saccard mansion shares elements with this account from *La Vie parisienne*, the latter including this description of models opening doors and striding purposefully through the couture house:

> To the left and the right the doors were wide open, and lovely, bareheaded girls walked to and fro, rather extraordinary silhouettes dressed in the day after tomorrow's fashions, coiffed in original chignons. Frightfully up to date, they escorted customers to the door while taking leave of others and greeting still others … They walked about the salons in model dresses, living examples of the celebrated What's-His-Name's art.[130]

The Saccard mansion, like the fashion atelier described above, is characterized by the constant motion of people who move "to and fro" and are dressed to represent a heterogeneous population of walkers in the city. Zola calls up this similarity by highlighting the crowds, this diverse "world" ["monde"][131] of Parisians that he describes, tellingly, in terms of their clothing: "silk gowns, dirty skirts, workmen's blouses, dress-coats"[132] ["robes de soie, jupes sales, blouses, habits noirs"].[133] Citing garments-in-motion as a metaphor for the urban masses, Zola evokes the early versions of catwalk performances contemporaneously taking place in haute couture ateliers.[134] Rather than relying on a locale such as the boulevard to portray bodies traversing the urban milieu, however, Zola chooses the Saccard abode, a structure performing as more fashion atelier than home, and in which the sheen of luxury garments gives way to the corruption of "dirty skirts."

Renée's *Cabinet de toilette*

If the ground floor of the Saccard mansion echoes the larger metropole through its staging of fashions' movements through space, in terms of the *creation* of garments, it is the second floor that contains the novel's most critical site: Renée's *appartement particulier*, or her private suite. Described earlier in excessive detail, thereby foregrounding its importance as a narrative location, the suite reappears in the penultimate chapter as the site of the heroine's dramatic psychological breakdown. The *appartement*'s position on the second floor follows the model of the city's most elegant fashion houses, where showrooms were often situated above ground level.[135] The multiroomed suite, which includes a boudoir, a bedroom, a walk-in closet, and a dressing room, further echoes the variety of spaces typically found in the haute couture *maison*.[136] We recall that the gown that Worms's employees construct for Renée is conceived "one sleepless night (*insomnie*)"[137] ["dans une nuit d'insomnie"[138]], the term "insomnie" implying that the moment of inspired creation takes place in her bedroom as she attempts to sleep. In this room, sumptuous décor and luxury fabrics symbolize sexual transgression and the female body. Renée's bedroom is "a nest of silk and lace, a marvel of luxurious coquetry"[139] ["un nid de soie et de dentelle, une merveille de luxe coquet"[140]]. Its walls are "hung with … a heavy pale-grey silk"[141] ["tendus d'une étoffe de soie mate gris de lin"[142]], "furnished with chaises-longues"[143] ["garnie de chaises longues"[144]], and curtains "of Venetian lace over a silk lining"[145] ["en guipure de Venise, posée sur une doublure de soie"[146]]. It is fitted with a massive bed that resembles "a woman's dress, rounded and slashed and decked with puffs and bows and flounces"[147] ["une toilette de femme, arrondie, découpée, accompangée de poufs, de noeuds, de volants"[148]] and a canopy "like a skirt"[149] ["pareil à une jupe"[150]] that calls to mind "some tall amorous girl, leaning over, swooning, almost falling back on the pillows"[151] ["quelque grande amoureuse, penchée, se pâmant, près de choir sur les oreillers"[152]]. The bed, on which Renée leaves the warm imprint of "the perfume of her body"[153] ["le parfum de son corps"[154]], is likened to a "sanctuary"[155] ["sanctuaire"[156]], a "chapel"[157] ["chapelle"[158]], dimly lit in a "religious semi-darkness"(translation modified)[159] ["demi-jour religieux"[160]]. Silk, lace, plush furniture, women's dress, languid female desire, odours of bodies, the sacred made profane: these elements in Renée's private suite mirror those in Worms's atelier salon cited earlier in this chapter. Not only is Renée's apartment cut from the same transgressive cloth as the haute couture atelier, it is an architectural manifestation of the same qualities – luxurious beauty and sexual vice – that Renée herself embodies. Thompson notes that in this passage "the metaphors of room-as-woman, room-as-fabric and fabric-as-woman become all but indistinguishable from one another."[161] By personifying the bed as the ornamented woman who sleeps in it, and describing the rooms as though they are dressed in the same opulent fabrics used to make gowns, Zola conflates Renée's body with the space itself.

This intersection of female embodiment, fashion, and space is concretized during the novel's climax, which takes place on the night of a costume ball at the mansion. Persuaded to ascend to his wife's second-floor apartment by his sister Sidonie, who has been slighted by Renée and seeks revenge on her, Saccard enters the suite and walks in on his wife and Maxime in a sensual embrace. Saccard's initial fury about his wife's infidelity with his son dissolves into triumph as he collects the deed that she has signed that will give him control of her land, and father and son descend the stairs together to rejoin the ball below. Serving first as the charged site of Saccard's discovery, Renée's chambers then provide the spatial framework for her subsequent breakdown, helping to illustrate her shocked realization of having been little more than a beautiful luxury object for the two men, both of whom, she sees, had used and discarded her primarily in pursuit of their own desires.

Still wearing her party costume, which is little more than a transparent blouse and flesh-coloured body suit,[162] Renée is left stunned and alone, her absence of dress a symbol for the lack of power that she all at once understands she possesses. The disarray of the dressing room, which is strewn with undergarments, beauty implements, and open perfume containers, conveys her disordered psychological state. Peering at herself in the mirror and suddenly ashamed by the outfit that had allowed her guests to scrutinize the intimate contours of her body, Renée sees herself as though nude. The narrator, adopting her point of view, wonders, "Who had stripped her naked?"[163] ["Qui l'avait mise nue?"[164]]. Repeating this query for several pages, Zola uses this fashion refrain to signal the fissuring of his protagonist's emotional and mental stability, what he terms the "destruction (*craquement*) of her brain"[165] ["craquement cérébral"[166]]. This turn of phrase reiterates a connection between Renée's unravelling state of mind and her clothing, for we learn earlier that Renée has prudently ordered several identical bodysuits and that, in fact, her maid Céleste has already "split"[167] ["fait craquer"[168]] one of the duplicates due to its delicate fabric. Using the same verb *craquer* to refer to Renée's *maillot* and to her psyche, Zola calls upon fashion to presage the protagonist's fragility and subsequent cracking-apart or "madness"[169] ["folie"[170]].

Theorists who study fashion argue that garments can function as signals of unclear boundaries between oneself and one's surroundings. Elizabeth Wilson suggests, "If the body with its open orifices is itself dangerously ambiguous, then dress, which is an extension of the body yet not quite part of it, not only links that body to the social world, but also more clearly separates the two. Dress is the frontier between the self and the non-self."[171] In this passage of *La Curée*, Zola evokes Wilson's uncertain "frontier between the self and the non-self" through Renée's delicate *maillot*, which marks a separation between her body and the environment around her but connects them, too, by conflating her flesh with the nudity that her garment and dressing room artificially simulate. Divested of her usual finery, Renée imagines that her rosy nakedness is embodied also in the room's flesh-coloured décor, "the pink bath, the pink skin of the hangings, the pink marble of the two tables"[172] ["la baignoire rose, la peau rose des tentures, les marbres roses des deux tables"[173]]. Rather than seeing beauty, however, Renée observes an overwhelming "orgy of lust"[174] ["débauche de voluptés vivantes"[175]], and is driven towards madness by the fact that the nudity of her body is reflected in the room's furnishings.

Effacing the Woman of Fashion: The Gaping Hole

Zola's treatment of Renée's dressing room thus parallels her evolution in the novel from a dazzling force of fashionable overindulgence to a devastated sartorial absence. Her garments, excessively ornate for most of the text, are replaced in the end with the unadorned, ripped, and discarded body suit that is a metaphor for Renée's barren and destroyed life. The dressing room demonstrates this same trajectory towards absence in spatial terms. Decorated with ornamental elements highlighting ephemerality – transparent chiffon fabric ["mousseline"],[176] flower motifs, and pale pastel hues – the room has, as Jean Borie describes it, "an overloaded but fragile décor" ["un décor surchargé mais fragile"].[177] Borie's term "fragile" is applicable on a number of levels, for it is precisely at the moment of Renée's deepest sartorial and psychological fragility that the ornate room gives way to reveal a black empty space concealed within it. Overwhelmed by the room's abundant décor, Renée turns her gaze to "the gaping hole of the staircase, down which she had just watched the father and son disappear" (translation modified)[178] ["le trou béant du petit escalier, dans lequel elle venait de voir disparaître les épaules du père et du fils"[179]]. The dark void becomes a narrative focus through Renée's fixation; we read that "she could not take her eyes away from the well" ["elle ne pouvait détourner les yeux de ce trou"].[180] Brian Nelson rightly observes of these pages that Renée's "self-disgust is intensely associated with the decoration and the profusion of artefacts and discarded clothes in her dressing room,"[181] but it is important to note that her despair is additionally trained upon the converse of such luxury: the abyss that it conceals. In this, the novel's climax, Zola replaces the gilded, fabric-laden, luxuriously upholstered quarters of Renée's apartment and the *maison de couture* that it mirrors with the nothingness represented by empty space (the "gaping well") and absent fashion (Renée's nudity). The black cavity into which Saccard and Maxime disappear symbolizes the dark and corrupt emptiness masked behind the dazzling opulence that both Renée and the modern city superficially embody.

To return to the notion of fashion and surface appearance discussed in chapter 2, we might posit that Renée's alienating experience in her fashion atelier-bedroom signals a rupture between what she is and what the trappings of dress make her appear to be. Her crisis occurs when she learns that when the signifier that once represented her – fashionable clothing – is removed, what is left is nothing. Anne Anlin Cheng's observation that dress points to the erasure of the stylishly clad woman implies that Renée's effacement is a condition of the female fashion icon more generally:

> The truly stylish woman, like fashion itself, is the one who announces herself by erasing herself, whose originality lies in her capacity to be copied and to be transferable ... this blankness, furthermore signifies the interplay between nothing and everything that conditions the possibility of social value ... with the explosion of capitalism and commodity culture in the nineteenth and twentieth centuries, this delicate balance between worthing everything and nothing will evolve into seemingly irreconcilable opposition.[182]

The traumatic, "irreconcilable opposition" of this moment in *La Curée* lies in the fact that Renée comes face to face in the mirror with the realization of her own ultimate effacement – her own death. Thus we return to the relationship between Renée's demise and the *grand couturier* with which this discussion of *La Curée* began. I have endeavoured to show that what might appear at first an enigmatic, abrupt conclusion to the novel is, in fact, a subtext woven profoundly into the plot. Renée's death at the text's close is the ending that the novel predicts throughout in its connected treatments of fashion spaces and dress. Of *La Curée*'s morbid conclusion Borie notes, "Renée is killed not by her sin nor by her 'blood' nor by Venus. She is killed because she suddenly understands that history, *her* history … is in reality thoroughly empty, hollow, inert, solitary" ["Renée n'est pas tuée par son péché, ni par son 'sang,' ni par Vénus. Elle est tuée parce qu'elle comprend soudain qu'une histoire, *son* histoire … est en vérité toute vide, creuse, inerte, solitaire"] (original emphasis).[183] Zola registers Renée's "emptiness" through metaphors that confound fashion and space: her hollow discarded bodysuit; the chasm of debt to Worms that she is unable to fill; the gaping black void that her dressing room conceals within it. The final two sentences of the novel, in which Renée's death is mentioned in conjunction with the couturier Worms, thereby connect by way of the city's network linking the haute couture fashion atelier, the Saccard mansion, and the stunning but ultimately empty garments created in them.

Conclusion

Zola's descriptions of Worms's atelier emphasize similarities with Renée's *cabinet de toilette*: in both locales clothing is created, donned, and removed; both include sumptuous furnishings and luxury interiors; both are spaces of illicit sexuality, Worm's premises marked by an undercurrent of transgressive lesbianism and Renée's suite characterized by the incest that she engages therein with Maxime. The novel's portrayal of rising architectural modernity underscores the extent to which fashion might have played a role in informing the construction of the Haussmannized city, a space built for a population whose navigation of the urban landscape echoed the movements of live mannequins traversing the haute couture atelier. The point we have been building to is that the fashion house in *La Curée* is a metaphor for a network of circulation in which order and control are compromised by a simultaneous threat to containment inherent to the urban environment. For Zola, the result is a destructive spreading of social ills – sexual degeneration, wastefulness, superficiality – all epitomized in modern fashion and its system of distribution. Read together, Renée's gowns and the *réseau* of spaces in which they are made (Worms' studio, the Saccard mansion, her *cabinet de toilette*) comprise Zola's critique of an inborn weakness in the spatial ordering put into place through Haussmannization.

As suggested by the controlled deliberateness of Haussmann's engineering plans, the intention for the new infrastructure of circulation was for it to be systematized and orderly, the well-oiled machine or industrious hive that in the later novel, *Au Bonheur des Dames*, the department store symbolizes in microcosm.[184] It seems not to be the plans themselves that Zola condemned, at least in the early years of the Third Republic, for although he was critical of the Baron's methods, he also praised them as "more or less good, more or less legal and prudent" ["plus ou moins bons, plus ou moins légaux et prudents"].[185] The problem, as *La Curée* implies, was that the successful implementation of Haussmann's interconnected network did not result in the healthy circulation of people and goods but rather the unhealthy spread of modern vice, greed, and frivolity. In the novel, the rise of the city coincides with the rise of fashion, both engendering their respective forms of destruction. By emphasizing the resemblance between the two primary *maisons* of the text – the mansion and the haute couture establishment – Zola draws attention to the fact that Saccard (a cipher for Haussmann) and Worms, the masters of both "houses," are two sides of the same coin, both building intertwining empires on the backs of women who will ruin or "efface" themselves purchasing gowns that, ultimately, serve to increase the wealth and power of men. Although it would be a mistake to infer a feminist undercurrent in Zola's point of view, his commentary is, in fact, implicitly gendered, as Renée, the novel's titular "prey," represents countless other female victims of a fashion system masculinizing itself through the rise of the male couturier and shifting its power to men at women's expense. The chapter that follows directly addresses the question of gender in late-century representations of the fashion atelier by focusing on the spaces of garment manufacture in which it was women, rather than men, who were the primary creators.

6 A Woman's Work(space): Dressmaking Ateliers in Huysmans's *En Ménage* and Rachilde's Late-Century Novels

Among the many remarkable garments in the archives of Le Musée Galliera, Paris's museum of historic and contemporary fashions, there is an especially noteworthy specimen: a chocolate-coloured ladies' dress jacket, hand-embroidered with a rich pastel plant motif of pink blossoms, shimmery yellow flowers and graceful green leafy stems (see figure 6.1).

A stunning example of haute couture finery, the coat well reflects the curved bustle and torso-hugging style that came into favour during the early decades of the Third Republic. Indeed, as explained in the catalogue notes of an exhibition held at the Grand Trianon in Versailles in 2011, the jacket was likely worn by an upper-class woman in the 1870s or 1880s.[1] Despite its obvious beauty, though, to even the casual viewer standing before the garment it is apparent that something is amiss. The first sign might come from an awkward dart over the *jaquette*'s right bosom, which inelegantly cleaves whole petals off a large pink rose. Or it might be the clumsy mismatched vertical patterns lining the front panels of the coat that stand out as its primary flaws. In any case, for an object made of costly fabrics and featuring labour-intensive, hand-stitched decorations, these failures of cut and fit seem incongruous with respect to the garment's otherwise high level of craftsmanship. That is, until the catalogue description is consulted and facts about the jaquette's provenance are revealed. For here one learns that the dress waistcoat was "transformed" (*transformé*) in the late 1800s and actually began its life three-quarters of a century earlier; moreover, it was not originally a woman's top at all, but rather an *"habit d'homme"*[2]: a frock coat worn by a man.

Although present-day onlookers might be surprised to learn that the jaquette was modified from a man's body to a woman's, it was not, in

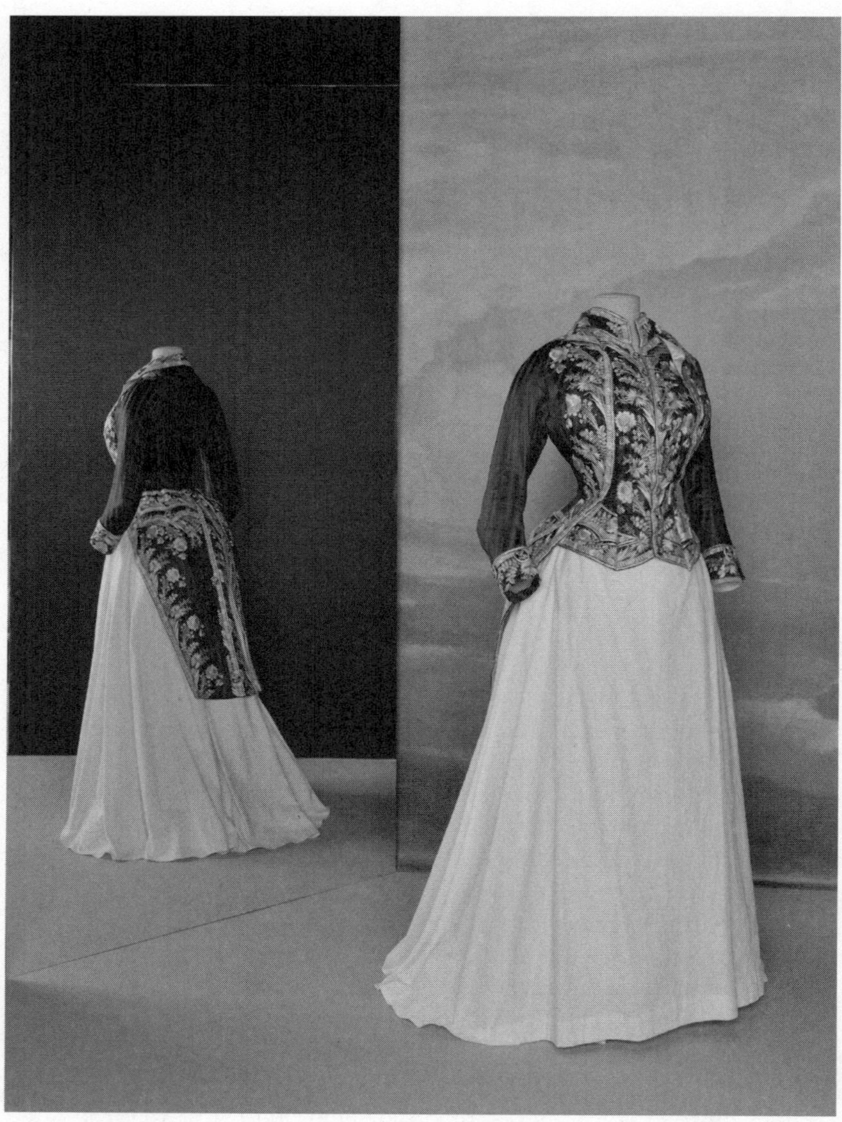

6.1 *Habit d'homme transformé en jaquette de robe*, made 1804–14, modified c. 1877–82. Musée de la mode de la ville de Paris. Image in *Le XVIIIe au goût du jour: Couturiers et créateurs de mode au Grand Trianon*, ed. Olivier Saillard (Paris: Art Lys Eds, 2011), 27. With the kind permission of the Chateau, the Museum, and the National Domain at Versailles.

fact, uncommon for women of the nineteenth century to reappropriate menswear from previous eras, particularly fine objects of clothing that had belonged to wealthy aristocratic ancestors. The archives of the Musée Galliera include dozens of such men's waistcoats and jackets from the eighteenth and early nineteenth centuries that were refashioned in later generations to fit women.[3] Representing a practice of sartorial regendering, the dresscoat is a fitting symbol for some of the themes to be treated in the chapter that follows. As clothing made for a man and later claimed by a woman, it is a metaphor for frictions and transformations taking place in early Third Republic gender politics. It documents the rise of masculinized styles in womenswear during this period,[4] which paralleled uneasy attitudes as women became increasingly involved in areas of social life – such as working outside the home – that had been the traditional arenas of men. The modified item of clothing also evokes a regendering in manufacturing that took place as tailors of menswear, who were skilled at working with traditional suit fabrics such as wool and flannel, increasingly found themselves employed as dressmakers by a female clientele that embraced the new masculine-inspired looks coming into vogue. As we will see, this shift was not without controversy, since male couturiers could fall under suspicion for the intimate proximity to women's bodies that such tailoring occasioned. Finally, the gender of the jaquette's eventual wearer serves as a reminder of the fact that it was women, not men, who formed the backbone of clothing production. For although this was the period coinciding with the reign of the male haute couture designer, it was women who left their homes in overwhelming numbers to be the seamstresses and the "little hands" (*les petites mains*) – the decorators (*garnisseuses*), embroiderers (*brodeuses*), and pin girls (*arpettes*) – who would meet the era's growing call for mass-produced clothing made in small- and large-scale factories.

The various levels of regendering occurring in the fashion industry resonate with complex attitudes about modern city space as they were represented in the texts and images to be examined here. As a counterpoint to the discussion of the male couturier in chapter 5, this final chapter focuses on the figure of the woman garment maker and her relationship to her atelier. The study begins with a series of paintings of *modistes* by Degas, which centre on the female hatmaker. It then juxtaposes Degas's images with two texts by Joris-Karl Huysmans: "Robes et Manteaux," a short article from 1880 depicting women at work in a ready-to-wear garment factory and Huysmans's expanded version of the article, published the following year as the novel *En Ménage*. To a degree, these representations illustrate the woman fashion worker in a positive light, Degas by likening the milliner's construction of ladies' bonnets to the noble work of a painter creating a canvas and Huysmans by celebrating the lively camaraderie fostered in the Parisian workspaces of female labourers. However, ultimately, Huysmans upholds period connections between women who worked in clothing ateliers and transgressive sexuality that echo the portraits of fashionable women studied in chapter 5 in the texts of Zola and Feydeau. Although Degas avoids this stereotype, he joins Huysmans in painting female garment workers favourably not for their own laudable qualities but rather for the way in which they support masculine artistic production.

To examine a bold challenge to this practice, the chapter will conclude with a study of the fashion atelier space in several late-nineteenth-century novels by Rachilde. Focusing on the spatial concerns underpinning Rachilde's fiction, I interpret her novelistic response to the male-authored texts of her day as an expression of Michel de Certeau's later writings on tactics and strategies in urban space. As though taking a man's jacket, cutting it, and restitching it into one fit for a woman, the heroines in Rachilde's works refashion the trope whereby women are relegated to supporting, secondary roles to men. In particular, they appropriate the high position of male couturier within spaces of garment creation in order to emphasize and celebrate the ingenuity and aesthetic talent that women hold independently of men. In this way, Rachilde addresses prevailing gender prejudices by advancing a feminist critique of misogynist attitudes, both about women working in fashion and creative women more generally.

In socio-economic terms, this chapter is a discussion of two very different experiences: the first section treats depictions of the female working class, while the second part examines fictional accounts of women from privileged ranks who were spared from many of the economic concerns plaguing their less affluent sisters. Nonetheless, representations by men of these two types of women overlapped in several important ways. First, the productivity of women who created objects of ladies' *toilettes*, from seamstresses to ad hoc designers with high social standing, was often devalued with respect to work undertaken by male counterparts. Second, regardless of their social class, whether they designed garments like Worth or stitched them together with thread and needle, women's efforts were shown to be valued primarily insofar as they supported the artistic endeavours of men. As we will see, the ways that women are depicted in the spaces in which they create sartorial objects illustrates a patronizing attitude about women's cultural production more broadly. It is this patriarchal outlook that Rachilde's stylish femme fatales determinedly oppose through their strategic appropriation of impromptu fashion ateliers that serve as ciphers of the larger cityscape.

As we examined in chapter 5, the late nineteenth century was an era when Worth and other male couturiers claimed power and prestige by marketing themselves as haute couture artist-designers. Meanwhile, the far less glamorous world of *la confection*, or the mass-production of ready-to-wear garments, became the destiny of labouring women. An 1897 article in *Le Monde Illustré* citing statistics from France's Office du Travail indicated that there were, at that point, 500,000 female factory workers (*ouvrière couturières*) in France, with 90,000 in Paris alone. This excluded women who made menswear and female heads of fashion boutiques who themselves sewed garments; to include them, reporter Guy Tomel submitted, the number would rise to one million. This staggering figure prompted Tomel to conclude, "There is thus no other profession that ... has a social importance comparable to that of the couturière" ["Il n'y a donc pas de métier qui ... ait une importance sociale comparable à celui de la couturière"].[5]

The feminizing of the fashion-manufacturing workforce did not take place without controversy. Male tailors reacted with alarm, suggesting that women would only produce inferior products compared with those fabricated by the skilled hands of men.[6] Opposition to seamstresses on the part of tailors intensified as styles for women became increasingly masculinized from the 1860s onward, for this was a period in which suitlike riding habits and dresses inspired from military uniforms became all the rage. For instance, the famous British fashion empire Redfern, which opened a branch in Paris in 1881, developed the instantly popular *costume tailleur*, consisting of a tailored jacket and skirt cut from wools and using methods that had been developed for menswear by master tailors.[7] Nancy Green describes the resulting tensions as "a long struggle between highly skilled custom tailors and ready-to-wear garment workers."[8] She notes that "the more highly skilled and articulate mid-nineteenth-century tailors defended their craft by identifying their mode of production with art and relegating ready-to-wear to an artless, industrial production. They castigated putting out and homework as fragmenting the work, demeaning the worker's labor, and lowering taste."[9] Such rhetoric can be explained, in part, as tailors' perceptions that seamstresses were invading their occupation and posing a threat to their livelihood.[10] Still, since putting out, homework, and ready-to-wear were often the purview of seamstresses, to devalue this type of work was implicitly to devalue women.

This fearful opposition arose despite the fact that the women working in nineteenth-century garment ateliers led far from an enviable existence. De Marly notes that "the clothing industry has a dreadful history of exploitation, particularly in mass production and in the small firms making ready-to-wear."[11] The exploitation of factory seamstresses in these "sweatshops"[12] – a term in use even then – included their being subjected to long and strenuous hours, unsafe working environments, constant unhealthy inhalation of particles and toxic fumes, and very little pay.[13] As de Marly summarizes it:

> The conditions suffered by the hundreds of seamstresses involved in this industry did not much concern couture houses in the early days … the rates of pay were undeniably bad … The average Parisian dressmaker's in 1867 might employ between four and forty seamstresses, who were paid on a daily basis, although some were paid by the piece. Their average wage was 2 francs 25 centimes a day, the men in the industry averaging 5 francs a day. This was at a time when an embroidered shawl could cost 300 francs, and a ready-made gown up to 400 francs.[14]

Wages could be so meagre that some women, unable to subsist on pay alone, reportedly resorted to paid sex work to survive.[15] To add to the precariousness of their existence, each year seamstresses faced the *morte-saison*, the dead season when employers' need for their labour waned and many were let go. As Green notes, this cycle of unemployment was characteristic of the garment industry, in part, because its products were driven by seasonality. Its negative impact was felt especially by women, since they comprised the majority of the fashion workforce.[16]

Degas's *Modistes*

Degas's interest in the female garment worker centred on milliners – women who constructed, fitted, or sold hats to middle-class and wealthy customers. The painter's fascination with hatmakers and their spaces of production and consumption was sustained over his career, as demonstrated by the twenty-two pieces on them that he created from the early 1880s through at least the end of the century and possibly the first decade of the twentieth century.[17] In recent years, scholarship has called increased attention to the millinery pieces, which for years were sidelined in favour of Degas's images of dancers and horse races, the only two subjects that eclipse in numbers those of his hatmaker paintings. Of particular interest to us is a recent argument that Degas's milliners are ciphers for the artist himself. As Scott Allan puts it, "however much [Degas] may have been interested in millinery as a trade in its own right, his interest in it also had a great deal to do with [his] own studio craft … it would have been easy for him to identify his practice as an artist with millinery."[18] This identification is suggested in Degas's interpretation of "the modiste as absorbed artisan,"[19] of hatmaking as a reflective act that involved concentration, inspiration, and revision – all elements of the artistic process for which Degas himself was known.[20]

Like other women garment workers from the labouring class, *modistes* were sometimes depicted as possible prostitutes.[21] Yet, Degas's milliner works constitute a notable exception. His portraits do not include, for example, the covetous male gaze typically present in late-century images of dancers, actresses, and other women thought to be selling their bodies.[22] Also conspicuously absent in Degas's paintings are shop windows that suggest male visual consumption of female boutique workers, such as in Tissot's *La Demoiselle du magasin* (1883–1885), which depicts a male passerby peering into the female-staffed shop through a storefront display. Instead, in canvases such as four different compositions painted from 1879 to 1886 that were all entitled "At the Milliner's" (*Chez la modiste*), Degas represents enclosed, intimate spaces that seem protected from the prying, sexualizing gaze of male onlookers.[23] Moreover, he typically renders his female hatmakers active participants in their work rather than motionless objects of consumption. As Ruth Iskin writes of such compositions portraying hatmakers and their customers, "It is noteworthy that none of the women in these works are depicted as merely displaying fashion, or as passive. Rather, each is fully engaged in the activity typical to her class or profession."[24] That Degas's milliners are distanced from feminine figures of disrepute and are shown as dynamic, industrious, and absorbed in creating colourful works of beauty supports the thesis that he may have perceived some commonalities between the artistry of women who crafted fashion accessories and the work of the elite male painter.

This emphasis on the artistic side of hatmakers' work informs Degas's representation of their spatial environments. Some millinery paintings, such as several of the *Chez la modiste* compositions, spotlight women trying on completed headpieces, occasionally aided by a salesgirl or friend. Although the spaces are somewhat vaguely rendered,[25] they are clearly meant to be areas of fashion consumption, such as boutiques or department stores. In contrast, other images specifically emphasize the act of crafting hats. For instance, in *Les Modistes* (c. 1882, before 1905), the figure on the right works busily on making adjustments to an ornamented hat, while in the foreground bright pastel pieces of cloth – splashes of colour in an otherwise muted palate – allude to the future task of embellishing the accessory with decorative fabrics. (see figure 6.2)[26] Similarly, in the *Chez la modiste* from 1879/86 which is featured on the cover of this book, the young woman's absorption in her task, along with the appearance of a pin held in her lips, place focus on the process rather than the product of fashion construction.[27] Infrared reflectography and X-radiography of this canvas have revealed that Degas painted over an important detail of dress – a lace sleeve decoration – that would have more obviously rendered the woman a customer rather than a hatmaker, in so doing possibly changing the identity of the central figure from client to milliner.[28] Although many of Degas's images are still ambiguous in terms of whether they depict salesgirls, hatmakers, or bourgeois shoppers – especially in the case of the latter painting as Gloria Groom has convincingly shown[29] – for the reasons just outlined I understand them to indicate the artist's broader interest in milliners engaging in fashion creation. These paintings are thereby pertinent to this present discussion, since they highlight construction over sales and emphasize the setting not as a store but rather as the workshop of female garment labourers. In particular, *Les Modistes* provides an instructive example of how Degas's different representations of space fundamentally impact the meanings of his paintings.

Electromagnetic imaging, this time of *Les Modistes*, indicates that, here too, Degas painted over details that would have given the space the appearance of a hat boutique, altering it into a construction atelier by replacing a display of ornamented hats in the foreground with the tabletop workspace seen in the version on exhibit today.[30] The setting of the modified painting thus changes the focus of the composition, recasting the same figures as producers rather than shoppers. As with other hatmaker images, Degas includes multiple workers in *Les Modistes*, gesturing towards the idea of mass production both in the fashion industry and in other arenas related to large-scale commerce. Of these canvases, Allan observes, "We might see a single milliner

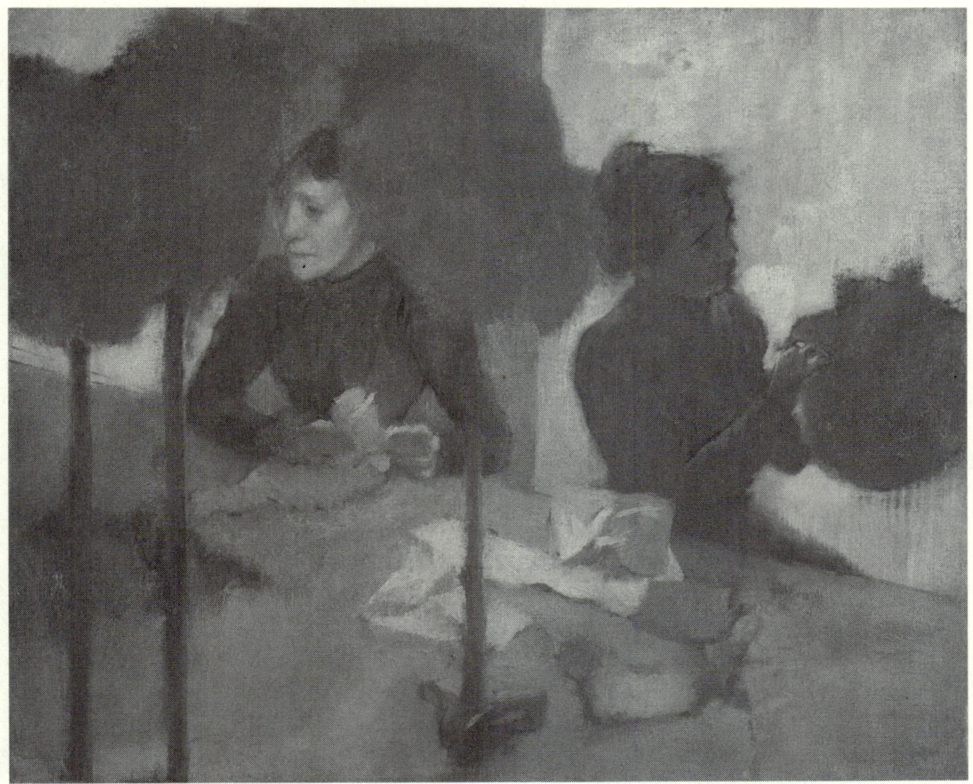

6.2 Edgar Degas, *Les modistes* (*The Milliners*), c. 1882 – before 1905. Oil on canvas. Unframed: 59.1 x 72.4 cm (23 1/4 x 28 1/2 in.). Framed: 77.8 x 91.1 x 6.4 cm (30 5/8 x 35 7/8 x 2 1/2 in.). Reproduced courtesy of the J. Paul Getty Museum, Los Angeles.

assessing her work, but more frequently we see pairs of women working. Degas thus draws attention to the serial nature of production."[31] The evolution of the melancholy scene in *Les Modistes*, reworked to emphasize garment fabrication and perhaps to suggest group labour, can be taken as Degas's critique of the mechanical, assembly-line practices arising during this era of increased industrialization. The colourless clothing, despondent expression, and static hands of the woman on the left express the drabness, immobility, and isolation that characterized, for some critics, the day-to-day experience of the urban working class.

In the revised painting, as Iskin suggests, "The secluded atelier appears desolate" and the modiste seems "alienated."[32] Furthermore, any potential intimacy with her companion seems compromised by the lack of interaction between them. Even the relationship of the central figure to the products of her labour is complicated by the way in which the hats in the foreground seem to crowd in, displacing her from view. This rather bleak interpretation of the painting has been used to posit fears that Degas may have harboured about the commodification of high art in the age of mass reproduction. In particular, the image might have signalled his distaste at being obliged to sell his paintings (due to his brother's loss of their family fortune), thereby reducing once purely artistic creations into saleable objects.[33]

However, the setting of *Les Modistes*, like its central characters, can likewise be viewed slightly differently if the broader trope of the hat-maker's atelier is re-examined in light of Degas's own aesthetic work. For, as scholars have suggested, Degas's renderings of hatmaking workshops, especially in late examples from the series, imply links between these rooms and the painter's studio. Unlike the majority of Impressionists, who painted sites outdoors and on location (*en plein air*), Degas preferred the sanctuary of his atelier where he sketched settings from memory. The painter's studio was thus a location with deep personal significance. While paintings of hatmakers pictured by some of his contemporaries include tools like scissors, cabinets of artificial flowers, and other objects underscoring the hat-constructing trade,[34] Degas's millinery settings are generally devoid of such identifying markers, forming indistinct rooms that could equally recall an artist's studio[35] or, in their relative bareness, perhaps evoke a blank canvas prepped to receive painterly inspiration. Analysing the image on this book's cover, *Chez la modiste* from 1879/86, Groom notes that the "ornately executed and only partially finished hats ... exist side by side," a detail that likens the setting to "representations of artist' studios, where finished paintings occupy the same space as unfinished canvases."[36] Instead of implements, Degas's works highlight the animated hands of *modistes* that have been understood to echo the expressive gestures of painters with their brushes.[37] Even the bleak attitude of *Les Modistes* supports the reading of hat ateliers as painters' studios, for it is logical to think that the process of artistic creation might, at times, have felt as dreary and isolating as this scene seems to project. On the other hand, isolation could also fuel productivity. Perhaps most tellingly, especially in his latest canvases, Degas depicts his milliners in solitary compositions, representing their work as, in Iskin's words, "a quiet ritual far removed from the metropolitan world of consumers' demands and the pressures of productivity."[38] Their workspaces, Iskin continues, here seem imbued with "the quiet privacy of an artisanal space of production."[39] In this way, the hatmakers at work mirrored Degas's own mature years, a period in which he entered into seclusion and became engrossed in abstract compositions, breaking from the realist depictions of society that had captured his attention earlier.

These resemblances notwithstanding, it would be a mistake to infer that the painter viewed hatmakers as his equals. A distinction must be made between Degas's perception of painting as an act requiring mastery and his likely attitude towards the more instinctive (and thus less difficult) handcrafting of the *modiste*. Allan evokes this, noting, "Ultimately, [Degas] could approach millinery as a serious male artist, rather than paint, unthinkingly, like a female craftswoman doing what came naturally to her."[40] Still, as Iskin puts it, the late-series lone milliners appear to be "engaged in the decoration of hats as work performed for its own sake."[41] Take, for example, the focused woman of *Chez la modiste* (see cover), who is surrounded by the multihued fruits of her labour: beautiful artlike objects that, reminiscent of paintings, seem to be displayed expressly for (our) viewing pleasure.[42] Intensely occupied with the manual creation of decorative aesthetic objects in atelier-like spaces, Degas's milliners appear to reflect his own *l'art-pour-l'art* concerns rather than the authentic conditions of women garment labourers. His treatment of the *modiste* space thus suggests interpreting the milliner series as not primarily about female hatmakers at all, but more fundamentally as the male painter's meditation on his own aesthetic concerns and artistic process.

"Petticoat Crises" in Huysmans's *En Ménage*

Degas's deployment of milliners at work to explore matters relating to himself as a high-art painter can be compared to Huysmans's equally self-referential treatment of female seamstresses. Like Degas, who reworked the figure of the *modiste* numerous times, Huysmans examined the workspaces of women garment makers in several of his writings, most notably in a short newspaper article published in *Le Gaulois* entitled "Robes et Manteaux" (1880) that he revised a year later and incorporated into his novel *En Ménage* (1881). This analysis takes both texts into consideration, focusing on important differences in their respective depictions of the seamstress's atelier. Appropriately enough for this study of the author of *A rebours*, I read the relationship between the two texts somewhat "against the grain," examining the novel for the ways in which it illuminates the short newspaper article rather than the other way around. This method is informed by my interpretation of the short piece as, paradoxically, the achievement of a text that is evoked but never actually realized in the novel.

En Ménage chronicles the parallel experiences of writer André Jayant and painter Cyprien Tibaille, friends dually afflicted with creative impotence that mirrors the stagnation and emptiness of their respective domestic arrangements and sexual encounters. André, the protagonist, opens the narrative by returning home and surprising his wife Berthe in bed with another man. Taking leave of Berthe, André sets up living quarters in an apartment, retaining his former maid Mélanie to attend to domestic chores while he attempts, unsuccessfully, to write. While he is living in his bachelor's abode André has several ultimately lacklustre affairs, first with the fashionable courtesan Blanche and then with Jeanne, a former mistress with whom he later reconnects. As befits this story of hollowness and futility, in the end André agrees to turn a blind eye to Berthe's indiscretion and the two resume their unfulfilling domestic partnership as though they had never separated. Cyprien, who is more bitingly pessimistic about matters of the heart than his complacent, phlegmatic friend, nonetheless enters into a stable living arrangement with the corpulent Mélie, a street prostitute-turned-nursemaid who tends to Cyprien's many physical ailments in a perverted version of marital bliss. The concluding page of the novel, wherein Cyprien notes that both men have been "emptied"[43] ["vidés"[44]], highlights the lack of productive vigour that characterizes them creatively, as Cyprien ends up painting not masterpieces but commercial wallpaper, while André, distracted by his affairs with women, spends more time reading others' texts than writing anything of his own.

For good reason, then, *En Ménage* has been called "a book about nothing,"[45] a novel featuring a banal plot that leads its characters anticlimactically back to where they began, thus mimicking the very inertia of its leading men. Yet, despite its relatively mundane subject matter, the work is not without interest. The few critics who have examined *En Ménage* point out its intriguing internal narrative tensions, which manifest in the text's inclination to undermine naturalism even as it describes it.[46] Moreover, Huysmans's tendency to vacillate between treating his protagonists either ironically as parodies of writer and painter,[47] or more genuinely (and sympathetically) as creative men afflicted with productive sterility,[48] subverts facile interpretations of his point of view of the experience of the modern urban artist. These two characteristics of the novel – its challenge to the literary genre it represents and its ambiguous commentary about how aesthetic work is produced – underpin the following analysis of Husymans's depiction of the female garment worker in her atelier and her role in supporting the concerns of the male writer.

Scholars have pointed out that the figure of Jeanne was likely inspired by Huysmans's long-time lover Anna Meunier, herself a seamstress (and later the proprietor of her own dressmaking business) who provided the author with first-person accounts of working in an atelier. Huysmans intended to incorporate Anna's reports into a novel about the Siege of Paris to be entitled *La Faim* that he began in the 1870s but ultimately abandoned.[49] In his classic biography of Huysmans, Robert Baldick notes the existence of a copy of *En Ménage* dedicated to "Jeanne – Anna Meunier,"[50] which seems to confirm the source of the seamstress prototype from the writer's own life. But, in fact, the centrality of the *couturière* in Huysmans's fiction transcends mere biographical resonance. Amy Reid calls attention to the recurring *ouvrière* in novels such as *Marthe* (1876) and *Les soeurs Vatard* (1879), works that join *En Ménage* in featuring working-class women. Reid submits that these female labourers serve Huysmans's larger project to distance himself from naturalism, and, she argues, "to redefine literary truth as something that he could both express and control."[51] It is this critical moment in Huysmans's development as a novelist that we will explore in its relation to his representation of fashion atelier dislocations in which female garment makers toil.

That Huysmans selected the seamstress as one of his protagonists in *En Ménage* is consistent with a larger leitmotif of fashion that is woven thematically and figuratively throughout *En Ménage*. Fashion and aesthetic creation (or lack thereof, in this case) intersect, for instance, in the symbolic "malady" that strikes André repeatedly after he leaves his wife. The "ailment," which causes André to think constantly about sex and transforms him from mild-mannered cuckold into an obsessive "skirt chaser," is named, tellingly, "les crises juponnières" or "petticoat crises," as Robert Ziegler has translated it.[52] Although clearly meant as a euphemism for André's debilitating and feverish carnal desires, the expression "crises juponnières" also privileges attire – *juponnières* or underskirts – over bodies, highlighting the erotic charge of women's undergarments and simultaneously downplaying the physical human forms that they clothe. Primal yearnings are thus filtered through the sartorial, as André's passions are displaced from flesh to women's lingerie. Indeed, André's lust not for the organic female body but for the seductive sweep of petticoats is clarified by the narrator, who declares, "He desired woman, not for the carnal embrace of her body, but for the rustling of her skirts" (translation modified)[53] ["Il désirait la femme, non pour l'étreinte charnelle de son corps, mais pour le frôlement de sa jupe"[54]]. This is further emphasized when, having found some relief through furtive sexual encounters with streetwalkers, André suddenly – if only temporarily – finds that "skirts did not trouble him anymore"[55] ["les jupes ne le tourmentaient plus"[56]]. These figurative expressions involving fashion that are evoked throughout the novel eventually manifest in spatial terms with the arrival in the plot of the dressmaker, Jeanne.

Jeanne, who works in a Parisian factory making ready-to-wear ladies' garments, is one of the "remedies" to André's recurring sartorialized pathology. In rekindling a romantic affair with his former mistress, André's petticoat crises are, for a time, quelled. The abatement of his lust endures until Jeanne tires both of André's deficient earning potential and of the dismissals that threaten her and her fellow seamstresses during the low season. Deciding to leave Paris for a more secure contract offered by a garment company in London, Jeanne takes leave of André and the narrative alike. Although Jeanne exits *En Ménage* before its completion, I would suggest that she is both a unique and a pivotal figure. One of her striking distinctions is that, of all the characters in the novel, Jeanne seems the only one to possess mainly estimable qualities.[57] Huysmans endows her with a "pretty figure"[58] ["jolie tournure"[59]] and "fine hands"[60] ["[de] fines mains"[61]], describing her as merry, energetic, and the very physical embodiment of an attractive *parisienne* (see chapter 2 for a discussion of this archetype). Comparing Jeanne to his wife Berthe, André deems his lover preferable, for she has "a more provocative body and mainly a softness of disposition, a fear of being in the way"[62] ["une tournure plus provocante, et surtout une douceur de caractère, une crainte de gêner"[63]], which are traits that he values over the "rough despotism"[64] ["rêche despotisme"[65]] of his overbearing wife. André's sincere affection for Jeanne prompts Baldick to rightly point out that Huysmans's treatment of their liaison is recounted "with unusual tenderness."[66] Huysmans also makes Jeanne admirably modest. She feels acutely ill at ease, for example, when waited upon by André's maid Mélanie, believing that she should not be treated as a superior by a working-class sister and particularly by Mélanie, who is married and thus "an honorable woman of the people"[67] ["une femme du peuple honnête"[68]], unlike Jeanne herself, who has compromised her honour by taking lovers. In friendship, and to repay Mélanie for her considerate service, Jeanne uses her skills as a seamstress to sew garments for the housemaid. The camaraderie that develops between Mélanie and Jeanne reflects Huysmans's positive impression of working-class women, who display compassion for one another, give of their labour freely, and, indeed, seem to achieve a more profound solidarity than the novel's romantically linked couples, whose connections end up to be merely tepid or indifferent.

During their liaison, André grows curious about the *maison* Larmange,[69] the garment factory where Jeanne works, and questions her about the daily activities taking place therein. The novel's portrait of the dressmaker's establishment are spatially informed in two ways: in terms of how the building fits into urban geography and in terms of Jeanne's description of the structure's interior. To turn first to the former case, as Huysmans specifies in both essay and novel, the maison Larmange is located on the rue du Quatre-Septembre. In the author's day, this street was in Paris's main fashion manufacturing district, an area where wholesale workshops (*maisons de gros*) and retail workshops (*maisons de détail*) were concentrated.[70] Adjacent to the Bourse, the nineteenth-century stock exchange, and a short distance from Worth and other haute couture shops on the rue de la Paix, its very placement halfway between the city's high fashion and high finance sites was emblematic of the rising impact of the ready-to-wear industry on the nation's economy. Moreover, the street lay southeast of the department store Le Printemps – a major location, like all nineteenth-century department stores, for buying and selling prêt-à-porter garments – as well as on the western edge of the Sentier district where textiles in the capital had been fabricated since the eighteenth century.[71] Cartographically speaking, then, Jeanne's atelier is positioned at the confluence of the city's spatial network of fashion production, consumption, and dissemination. Yet, the symbolism of the rue du Quatre-Septembre does not end there, for the street was also a commemoration of early Third Republic modernity itself. Formerly called the rue du Dix-Décembre in honour of the date that Louis-Napoléon Bonaparte was elected the first-ever president of the French Republic and became Napoléon III (10 December 1848), the street was renamed following his downfall to memorialize the day that the Second Empire ended and the new Third Republic was proclaimed (4 September 1870). By its very name, then, the rue du Quatre-Septembre signified "new" modernity, a fact that does not go unnoticed by Huysmans, who calls it in the article "Robes et Manteaux" a street "without history, brand new" ["sans histoire, toute neuve"].[72]

Huysmans's deliberate mentioning of the rue du Quatre-Septembre thereby underscores the atelier's literal and figurative placement in the larger metropole. Jeanne's description to André of the structure's interior also treats it in spatial terms. Dividing the building by floors, Jeanne starts at ground level, the domain of the live models (*filles-mannequins*) who don maison Larmange garments and parade them across shiny hardwood parquets. The relative luxury of their condition means the models are reviled by the seamstresses, the latter jealously treating the former as "harlots"[73] ["grues"[74]] and "good-for-nothings"[75] ["des rien-de-propre"[76]]. Separate from the showrooms on the first story, the upper floors of the factory are for the women who fabricate the garments, hunched over needlework for twelve-hour workdays. Unlike the models in their relatively luxurious showrooms, Jeanne and her colleagues are trapped in drafty dark rooms on the fifth floor. Huysmans notes that the seamstresses fall into three categories – skirtmakers, bodicemakers, and coatmakers ["les jupières, les corsagières et les confectionneuses de manteaux"][77] – but rather than focusing on their sewing tasks, he highlights other rituals, such as sniffing tobacco, by which they endeavour to find temporary relief from their gruelling work. Conditions on the upper floors are lamentable: in winter the space is frigid, and in summer the atelier becomes a sweatshop so swelteringly hot that most strip off their outer layers, stitching only in their undergarments.

Yet, despite their deplorable worksite, the communal aspect of the factory allows the women to foster a lively camaraderie that recalls the friendship between Jeanne and André's maid Mélanie. The garment makers spend their breaks chatting over baskets of packed lunch and discussing and interpreting each other's dreams; while on the clock they share the same reprimands from their snooty thread supplier and laugh together at childish pranks perpetrated on one another. Jeanne does not idealize the garment workers, for she admits that some take on airs and petty snobberies do arise. Hence, Huysmans upholds period reports of garment manufacturing ateliers in which "intimate conversations, gossip and rumors, and flaunting of the workshop rules and discipline were represented as the core of seamstresses' 'workculture.'"[78] However, he does so with a spin, presenting the dressmakers' gossiping and minor disobediences in a jovial and positive light. Rather than condemning their rough mannerisms, he seems even to celebrate the labouring women for their companionship, collective work ethic, and resiliency in the face of hardship.

That said, for the most part, the seamstresses are not portrayed as "respectable" women, and Jeanne's insider perspective allows Huysmans to indulge in the late-century stereotype generalizing *confectionneuses* as sexually promiscuous. Taking up Jeanne's point of view, he writes that "only very few good girls were among them"[79] ["il n'y avait, parmi elles, que très peu de bonnes filles"[80]], allowing for merely "*some* virgins scattered across the work-rooms" (translation modified)[81] ["les quelques vierges disséminées dans les ateliers"[82]]. In fact, the entire ready-to-wear operation in the rue du Quatre-Septembre, a street packed with petticoat, bustle, and false-hair boutiques, appears to involve *only* women of dubious repute, both as producers and consumers. Huysmans describes the urban thoroughfare, emblazoned with signs for women's clothing as far as the eye can see, as "a street, living from day to day, which was subordinated to the whims of a whole clientèle of actresses and prostitutes!"[83] ["une rue vivant au jour le jour, subordonnée aux engouements de toute une clientèle d'actrices et de filles!"[84]]. Adding his voice to those of Zola, Feydeau, and Rops, Huysmans thus reiterates period connections between illicit women (actresses and prostitutes) and fashion manufacturing.

By way of Jeanne's salty descriptions of these "loose" seamstresses, Huysmans is able to access the familiar street slang, grimy interiors, and candid references to sex associated with those from the working classes. Rather than finding such coarseness repellant, however, André is delighted by the crude piquancy of Jeanne's account of the dressmakers, who infuse the atelier's upper stories with not just erotic but more general transgressions of the senses. In addition to demanding details about the women's sexual practices, André eagerly inquires after the location and preparation of their pungent meals (on the sixth floor and warmed over shared gas stoves) and the scatological intimacies of their hygiene routines in the latrines.[85] Once aroused by this virtual entry into a feminine space of sensory overload, however, André smooths the harsh edges of Jeanne's narration into a sensual and appetizing fantasy that recalls Zola's seductive hypersexualization of Worms's haute couture salon in *La Curée* (see chapter 5). In particular, he lingers on the image of nearly nude female bodies, transforming Jeanne's blunt formulation of women who "[tug] their titties out of their bodice" (translation modified)[86] ["nainais [tirés] de son corsage"[87]] into his own lecherous fantasy consisting of a "perspective of busts showing in a row, in creased frames of linen, wide pears, with stalks the color of rust, chocolate, raspberry or mallow"[88] ["perspective de corsages laissant passer à la file, dans un cadre fripé de linge, de blanches poires aux queues couleur de rouille, de chocolat, de framboise ou de mauve"[89]]. Here the dressmaker's raw reportage is recast as a sexualized male daydream, as the sweaty breasts of tired garment workers become delectable fruits, ripe for André's picking.[90]

As this last example illustrates, there is a tension between the ways in which the same "facts" of the seamstresses' working conditions are interpreted. Tellingly, during the conversation about the dressmaking atelier, Huysmans's own tone is profoundly ambiguous. On the one hand, he presents André's perspective as that of an armchair voyeur who is titillated by the ability to penetrate second-hand into a feminocentric space otherwise barred from his view. Rather than endorsing André's attitude, though, Huysmans subverts it, framing it as the leering vision of an anti-heroic protagonist. Further supporting the reading that Huysmans condemns André's sexualized daydreaming is the fact that it is not the impotent writer but the productive seamstress who garners the author's sympathies through the friendships she cultivates with other working-class women and the generous gift of labour she bestows on Mélanie when she sews the maid a dress. Thus, when Jeanne confronts her distracted lover, her retort reads as Huysmans's authentic censure of André's covetous fantasies of the seamstresses' workshop:

– "Are you amused," Jeanne went on, rather melancholy, looking at André who smiled complacently in his armchair. – "Well! If you worked shut up in such rooms during the winter, full of drafts, heated by coke, lit, from two o'clock in the afternoon, by gaslamps, hanging so low that they burn you and make your hair fall, if you used to choke during the summer in the middle of a whole crowd who undressed to be comfortable, tug their titties out of their bodice, and weigh them to see who has them bigger and firmer, if you also had to withstand three or four months of slack season, you would see there was nothing to laugh at. – No, there is nothing to laugh at," she said again after a silence, in a convinced tone (translation modified).[91]

[– Ça t'amuse, reprit Jeanne, avec un peu de mélancolie, regardant André qui souriait, béatement, dans son fauteuil. Eh bien! si l'hiver, tu étais enfermé dans des pièces pareilles, pleines de courants d'air, chauffées au coke, éclairées dès deux heures de l'après-midi par des becs de gaz, pendus si bas qu'ils vous brûlent et vous font tomber les cheveux, si tu étouffais, l'été, au milieu de tout un monde qui se déshabille pour se mettre à l'aise, tire les nainais de son corsage et les soupèse afin de voir qui les a les plus gros et les plus fermes, si tu avais à supporter aussi trois ou quatre mois de morte saison, tu verrais qu'il n'y a vraiment pas de quoi rire. – Non, il n'y a pas de quoi rire, reprit-elle, d'un ton convaincu, après un silence.[92]]

In contrast with André's vision of ripe pears and soft lingerie, Jeanne offers a sobering list of miseries, including burned hair follicles, feelings of suffocation, and financial desolation during the dead season. Her repeated reproach, that there is "nothing to laugh at," gestures towards a more general social critique that criticizes those like the insensitive André who turn a blind eye to the very real sufferings of female garment workers. Reid, spotlighting the *ouvrières* in Huysmans's novels who "resist" the writer's attempts to control them by way of naturalist narration, persuasively argues, "In word and in deed working-class women challenge the artist's representation of them. They subvert his reading of their truth and highlight the blind spot of his subjective perspective."[93] Jeanne's comeback illuminates the true hardships of the garment sweatshop while shedding light on André's wilful ignorance about their lived realities and distasteful enjoyment of their plight.

On the other hand, following Jeanne's reprimand we read, "André apologised for his happy look, and he justified it by the picture (*spectacle*) she had drawn. – Never mind, I should like to see that, he said" ["André s'excusa de son air radieux et il le justifia par le spectacle qu'elle avait montré. – C'est égal, je voudrais voir ça, fit-il"].[94] Thus, as André is quick to counter, Jeanne can hardly blame him for being entertained by her revealing report, delivered, as it is, in such an engaging, tell-all style. Although readers might join Huysmans in condemning his protagonist for creating a pleasurable daydream of Jeanne's story of hardship, at the same time, Huysmans seems to suggest, André has a point. For, indeed, Jeanne's description of the ready-to-wear atelier is a compelling and vivid "spectacle" that entertains through its coarse liveliness, a characteristic typical of many naturalist narratives. In this way, the novel's passage about the garment atelier takes on larger literary implications, for the ensuing debate between Jeanne and André can be understood as an expression of the author's own uncertainty about how best to narrate experiences of life in the modern urban milieu. To Huysmans, creating idealized fantasies about the seamstresses in the atelier as André does seems unacceptable, an undesired consequence of the sexual pathology afflicting his feeble-minded protagonist. However, there is also a danger inherent to the language and imagery of Jeanne's graphically realist account. For, as her experience demonstrates, any critique of the rough conditions of sweatshops can be overshadowed by descriptions that transform the crudities of the atelier into a colourfully entertaining spectacle.

It has already been argued convincingly that *En Ménage* coincides with an important moment of transition in Huysmans's development as a writer, during a period when he was distancing himself from the methods of naturalist authors such as his former mentor Zola.[95] Turning away from the "scientific" techniques characteristic of Zola's work, Huysmans was in the process of cultivating a new voice that would flourish in such works as *A rebours* (1884) and establish him as a father of literary decadence.[96] Given this context, André's counterchallenge to Jeanne can be read as Huysmans's own doubts about naturalism, specifically its approach to realism based on gratuitous descriptions that could result, paradoxically, in an unrealistic type of "spectacle." In *En Ménage*, the discussion about the working-class fashion atelier is therefore crucial in that it allows Huysmans to express his ambivalence towards naturalism. However, his critique stops short of articulating an alternative solution for writing about the new subjects epitomizing early Third Republic modernity such as the ready-to-wear fashion workshop. Huysmans's hesitation about how to produce text about life in late-century Paris might be said to find its extreme in André, a writer who intends to pen a great novel about the modern cityscape but never actually does.

Part of André's problem is that he fails to realize that Jeanne's narrative is perfect fodder for chronicling urban modernity, a fact that Huysmans by contrast seems well to appreciate. Thus, although André is stifled and unable to write, the same cannot be said for Huysmans, who created not one but two separate texts (with plans for a third in the unpublished *La Faim*) from the rich inspiration he derived from the *maison de confection*. That is, the four chapters of *En ménage* that we have been discussing, which detail André's relationship with Jeanne and that contain her description of the *confectionneuses'* atelier, are clearly an extended version of his article "Robes et Manteaux," which appeared in print one year before *En Ménage*. That the short text was a direct precursor for the longer work implies the importance of the fashion-manufacturing locale to the novel more generally. Indeed, the novel reproduces most of the newspaper piece verbatim, albeit with a few notable changes. For instance, the novel particularizes the first section of the article, which originally portrays nameless men loitering outside the "Robes et Manteaux" atelier. In *En Ménage*, this section becomes instead a lengthy account of André as he lingers on the rue du Quatre-Septembre, impatient for Jeanne to descend after work. In the novel, the two passages concerning us here – André's delay in the street and Jeanne's description of the garment workers within – are separated by several chapters, while in contrast they form a single uninterrupted report in the newspaper piece. One result of these differences is that the scene in the newspaper report is generalized: there is no André or Jeanne but rather a generic "them" ["ils" and "elles"] describing the men below and the women toiling above. The article thus reads as more broadly applicable, as though the portrait might describe a universal experience of Parisian existence. In its brevity "Robes et Manteaux" is a concentrated slice of life, a crystallization of the dialogue and activities of the garment workers that is arguably more engaging and impactful than the drawn-out representation provided in the novel.

But what precisely is the nature of this impact? For another crucial disparity between the two versions is that the article is almost devoid of the social critique discernible in the novel. Jeanne's paragraph reproaching André that we examined above, for example, is absent from the shorter piece, in which a condensed reference to "the dressmakers' exhausting day" ["l'accablante journée des couturières"][97] is the only gesture in this direction. Instead of condemning André's lecherous gaze, then, the newspaper's portrait of the seamstress's workshop is merely invasive. Its opening phrase demonstrates its intrusive approach, focusing first on the seamstresses' male lovers pacing at street level: "Some men stride up and down the sidewalks of the rue du Quatre-Septembre" ["Des messieurs arpentent, de long en large, les trottoirs de la rue du Quatre-Septembre"].[98] The second sentence reiterates the men's perspective: "They verify the hour on the Bourse's clock dial, and at length cool their heels in front of a large door above which gleams in golden letters this inscription: 'Dresses and coats'; some looking indifferently aloft, others plunging their noses in a newspaper" ["Ils vérifient l'heure au cadran de la Bourse, et longuement ils font le pied de grue devant une grande porte au-dessus de laquelle flambe en lettres d'or cette inscription: "Robes et manteaux"; les uns regardent indifféremment en l'air, les autres se plongent le nez dans un journal"].[99] The items that the men examine – the Bourse clock, the golden letters of the sign, the sky, the newspaper – reinforce them as narrative focalizers and highlight the ocular quality of their point of view. As the essay proceeds to the interior space of the *confectionneuses'* atelier to describe the seamstresses above, it seems to trace what the men imagine seeing like a long cinematographic pan moving from street to upper floors, and back down again.

This technique is effective and compelling, leading the reader to the heart of the atelier to peek on the women as they snack, chat, and primp before bathroom mirrors. Without Jeanne to frame it, however, the depiction of space in "Robes et Manteaux" can only unfold one-sidedly, by way of the penetrating male gaze. This masculine perspective is emphasized in the essay's final phrase, which appears almost word for word in the corresponding sentence from the novel (see passage cited above): "it is a street living day to day, yielding to the passing fancies of the special clientele that it possesses, the clientele of a whole army of actresses and prostitutes" ["c'est la rue vivant au jour le jour, subordonnée aux engouements de la clientèle spéciale qu'elle possède, la clientèle de toute l'armée des actrices et de filles"].[100] In contrast to the novel, however, the short text amplifies the objectification and sexualization of women by suggesting that it is not only a select few involved with illicit sexuality but, in fact, "a whole army" of actresses and prostitutes. Absent the criticism of André that Jeanne provides later in *En Ménage*, this is the final image with which the reader is left.

I should clarify that this is not to suggest that *En Ménage* is an overall defence of mass-production labourers or more broadly concerned with their well-being. As the last example suggests, even if Huysmans celebrates the solidarity of female garment workers and indicates some sympathy for their difficulties in the second version that he wrote, ultimately he seems to see little difference between them and the alleged actresses and prostitutes who buy and wear the clothes that the seamstresses make. The reason that I am examining these variations between newspaper and novel is to point out that the two texts, although extremely similar, accomplish very different things, the former representing a slice of life in the urban capital, a typical moment of modernity

– the text, in short, that André never writes – and the latter serving as a platform for Huysmans's ruminations about narrative style. At the same time, what relates the two texts to one another is the dislocation that both feature: the female fashion atelier. What we have found, then, is that Huysmans, reminiscent of Degas, takes advantage of the feminine garment-making space to further his own artistic agenda. Bringing his planned story of the seamstress from the abandoned *La Faim* to textual fruition, first in *Le Gaulois* and then in an expanded work of fiction, Huysmans twice capitalizes on the seamstresses' atelier. Moreover, the dressmakers' space is pivotal to the discussion between André and Jeanne that enables Huysmans to articulate his own concerns about naturalism at a moment crucial to his development as an author. It provides the catalyst for Jeanne's retort, one that relates to the author's turn away from naturalist documentary techniques in the sense that, as Reid notes, "the woman's refusal to submit to the artist's authority calls into question the naturalist paradigm where observation produces truth."[101] The fashion dislocation is a space that helps Huysmans presage the new direction that his future literary production would take.

As we will see in the final section of this chapter, Rachilde's late-century fiction can be interpreted as an attempt to refashion some of the male-self-serving attitudes we have observed in works by Rops, Zola, Degas, and Huysmans by making women, not men, the primary beneficiaries of fashion creation. The jacket resewn for a female body described at the start of this chapter is a sartorial symbol of the process undertaken by Rachilde's heroines, put forth often in violent terms, to rip apart at the seams the conventions and ideologies constraining them because of their gender and attempt to refit them to their own specifications. Chapter 2 explored Rachilde's method of using fashion to trouble gender binaries on the dislocated staircase where women's experience of urban modernity is likened to that of the exceptional female performer. In this chapter, the focus will be on another spatial alignment that Rachilde established between the fictional protagonists that were ciphers for herself and the masculine-coded genius/artist symbolized by the male *grand couturier*. It will be argued that Rachilde's impetus to equate the creative productivity of her female characters with the talents of the artist-fashion designer was part of a broader call for woman's spatial appropriation of the metropole. To illuminate this spatial subtext of her novels, we will read Rachilde's technique to reimagine feminine access to the city through the lens of Michel de

Certeau's discussion of the strategies and tactics involved in navigating the urban environment.

Fashion and Power: The *Grand Couturier*

We have seen that Worth subverted long-standing tradition by fashioning himself into the first successful male *couturier* to the world's wealthiest female clientele.[102] Other high-profile entrepreneurs including Doucet and Poiret joined him in taking on roles of authority that seemed to concretize elite high fashion as the purview of men. Worth's role as a style authority was highly symbolic; writers such as the Goncourts, Feydeau, and Zola, along with the popular press, evoked him in their representations of the haute couture designer, helping to cement his position as fashion's reigning figurehead. At the same time, Worth enjoyed tangible effects that went far beyond the symbolic. These included the fortune that he amassed from his enormously successful clothing empire as well as his status in the business world as one of Paris's major employers. In 1871, for instance, Worth's staff numbered over a thousand, a massive figure especially given the recent political tumult of the Franco-Prussian War and the Commune.[103] Worth also exerted considerable sway on a national level through his involvement with France's important textile industries.[104] De Marly observes, for instance, that by forging direct relationships with producers of silk in Lyon, Worth "exert[ed] an influence over the placing of orders. He could tell the salesmen what patterns and materials he required, and explain what colours he wanted developed. Thus textile manufacturers began to respond to Worth's suggestions and to suit some of their products to his requirements."[105] Before Worth's time, she adds, "such a direct relationship did not exist between the woman dressmaker and the industry."[106] Troy concurs, noting, "For the first time, fashionable women's wear was the creation of a single designer who not only selected the fabrics and ornaments that made up any given outfit but who developed the design and produced the final product. Worth's success in consolidating these previously distinct operations enabled him to exercise extraordinary influence over the direction of France's luxury textiles industry and to gain control of all aspects of the dressmaking process."[107] Gilles Lipovetsky highlights the advantages of Worth's actions (and reputation) as the sovereign of style in terms of his increased social status, noting, "Worth's arrogance, the authority with which he addressed women of the highest society, must be understood in this context: more than a character trait, it must be seen as a rupture, as the assertion of a newly acquired right on the dressmaker's part to legislate freely in matters of elegance."[108] As Lipovetsky goes on to observe, the couturier's assertion of this right ultimately resulted in "unprecedented access to powers of initiative, leadership, and stylistic hegemony."[109] The terms "consolidating," "influence," "authority," "control," and "hegemony" in these scholars' arguments underscore how high fashion afforded Worth not merely symbolic, but concrete social and economic power as well.

It is important to mention that the haute couture industry in the second half of the nineteenth century was not, in fact, completely exclusive of women, for there *were* respected female designers of luxury garments who successfully helmed couture businesses, such as the Duluc sisters in the 1870s and 1880s and Jeanne Paquin in the 1890s. However, in sales and popular depictions, the male celebrity designer eclipsed all others such that to reign over high fashion, whether figuratively or financially, was apparently to be a man. As we saw earlier, starting in the Second Empire, the authority of the male dressmaker seems to have trumped even that of Empress Eugénie, despite her top rank in society and her own status as a style icon. Wilson observes that, although Worth initially needed Eugénie's sponsorship, "he, not she … remained the arbiter. The couturier alone could become the man above court factions and competing classes; he could, because he was an Artist and therefore was 'inspired,' create fashions that painters and later photographers then transformed into the symbol or signature of an epoch."[110] Wilson's analysis resonates with Troy's argument discussed in chapter 5, that part of the male designer's strategy was to promote himself as a master artist for whom gowns, rather than canvases, were chefs-d'œuvre. The image of the couturier as high artist is especially relevant to the following discussion of Rachilde, for the same metaphor recurs in her portraits of female protagonists who, like Worth and company, embody a nexus of creative mastery, fashion, and power. Reading Rachilde's heroines as archetypes of the high fashion designer provides a new optic through which to understand the complex subject of dress in her works.

Rachilde began contributing to the discourse of Parisian haute couture quite literally when, upon relocating to Paris from the provinces in the late 1870s, she secured a position in the capital city as a fashion reporter.[111] It was thus that she assumed the dual perspective of a woman in a male-dominated profession (writing) whose task it was to write about what had become a male-dominated industry (high fashion).[112] Rachilde's foray into commercial fashion writing did not last long; in 1880, she published her first novel *Monsieur de la nouveauté* (set, not co-incidentally, in a department store), marking the start of her career in literature. Still, fashion continued to play a crucial role in her writing during the years to follow, particularly in the novels written during the last two decades of the century – including *Monsieur Vénus* (1884), *Nono* (1885), *La Marquise de Sade* (1887), *L'Animale* (1893), and *La Jongleuse* (1900) – when Rachilde was "queen of the Decadents"[113] and created the heroine archetypes for which she is best-known. These works echo the perspective, popularized by Worth and other male designers, that fashion was a type of artistic endeavour involving expert skill and available only to a creative elite. Familiar with the clothing industry through her stint as a fashion reporter, Rachilde would have been well aware of the symbolic and material authority associated with the *grand couturier* as well as with the fact that the highest level of influence in the domain of high fashion had been secured by men. Against this contextual background, the collection of texts that she produced during these years evince an underlying impetus to wilfully (re)claim for women some of the status and privilege connected to the male high fashion designer.

The analysis in chapter 2 of Rachilde's texts concentrated on female protagonists as *wearers* of highly symbolic garments. Here we will focus instead on passages in which Rachilde's female characters *create* fashions, thereby assuming the authoritative role of male *grand couturier*. To examine the concept of creation in Rachilde's fiction is to call up the items that the author actually produced, which is to say, not clothes but literary texts prominently featuring them. This is a subject now well covered by scholars who have fruitfully analysed how Rachilde's use of fashion – from her own complicated forays into cross-dressing to the themes of disguising and costuming in her novels – was symbolic of nineteenth-century women's authorship itself.[114] And yet, this clear connection between the female writing experience and garment manipulation notwithstanding, the fact remains that none of the fictional heroines of Rachilde's major late-century novels are, in fact, writers.[115] Nor are they demonstrably productive as painters, drafters, or sculptors, despite their claims to high artistry.[116] On the other hand, all of them engage in some type of clothing design in the manner of male *grand couturiers*. In addition, they frequently exhibit the drive to occupy or exert influence over the spaces around them, often using fashion as a means to achieve spatial control. Significantly, this occurs in passages featuring dislocations that act as ad hoc fashion ateliers. These spontaneously generated garment studios appear across a body of Rachilde's texts, constituting a discursive theme in the novels that came to define her nineteenth-century voice.[117] What is of interest here is the way in which these works deploy dress to express a broader impetus to appropriate modern urban space.[118]

The "Essayage": Modelling in *La Jongleuse*

In chapter 2, we saw that Eliante Donalger's mansion in *La Jongleuse* is divided into two primary spaces, one devoted to the heroine's intimate decadent performance and the other to bourgeois sociability. I submit here that the structure can also be thought reminiscent of a *maison de couture*, for this is where Eliante generates the "costumes" that allow her to "juggle" the identities she adopts throughout the text. Yet, even though the majority of these garments are her designs, Eliante is never shown to be constructing them with her own hands. Her methods of garment production thereby align with those of the creative couturier rather than the seamstress. This is represented in a passage taking place in the garden side of the house (*côté jardin*), the "artistic" wing of the mansion where Eliante is at her most decadently creative. In this episode, the protagonist attempts to write a love letter to her husband while Ninaude, her Martiniquais servant, sits on the floor cross-legged in *"tailor-style"*[119] [*"en tailleur"* (original emphasis[120]]. This expression, which calls attention to itself through italicization, juxtaposes dress and status. As Schechner observes, "[Ninaude] is seated 'en tailleur,' and thus, obliquely evokes one of her roles which would have been to assist Eliante with her dressing as 'femme de chambre.'"[121] While the detail that Ninaude, a black maid, sits on the ground "en tailleur" does indeed reinforce the social (and implied racial) superiority of the wealthy white Eliante, who perches literally and figuratively above her, it suggests, too, that Eliante is not a lowly needleworker herself. As her creation of one-of-a-kind fashions throughout the novel demonstrates, Eliante is, instead, in a position to dictate her own designs, serving both as her own model and as her own (male) *grand couturier*.

The alignment of Eliante with the high fashion creator is evoked again in the "artistic" wing of the mansion in the prelude to the novel's climactic suicide scene. In this chapter, rife with theatrical metaphors, Eliante foregrounds her artistry by expertly dancing the flamenco before Léon, Missie, and a musician friend, Louise Fréhel. She then opens her personal cache of exotic garments to the two young women, declaring, "You must try on my robes"[122] ["Il faut essayer mes robes"[123]]. Thus arranging a type of *essayage*, a word used in the fashion industry to mean "clothes fitting," Eliante orchestrates an event that calls to mind a modelling session at the *grand couturier*'s:

> Behind the screens, one could hear the metal hooks clicking and the satins brushing against each other. An odor of fresh coquette mixed with the last sugary vapors of the meal … Soon Léon had around him, fluttering, whirling, stopping in front of mirrors or consulting his taste, all the beauties of a harem; the two girls changed costume four times.[124]

> [Derrière les paravents, on entendit cliqueter les agrafes de métal et se froisser les satins. Une odeur de fraîches femmes coquettes se mélangeait aux dernières vapeurs sucrées de la collation … Bientôt Léon eut autour de lui, papillonnant, tournoyant, s'arrêtant aux miroirs ou consultant son goût, toutes les beautés d'un harem; les deux jeunes filles changèrent quatre fois de costumes.[125]]

Although one of Rachilde's emphases in this passage is the exoticness of Eliante's sartorial collection – an orientalist phantasmagoria of Japanese, Turkish, and Malaysian clothing ornamented with bangles and bones – when these elements are removed, as is deliberately done by skipping over the middle of the passage in the citation above, the similarities with Worms's salon in *La Curée* or journalistic reports of the Maison Worth discussed in chapter 5 become more evident.[126] These similarities include groups of young women modelling outfits, multiple costume changes, the presence of delectable sweet treats, heady aromas of women's bodies, and the sounds and sights of luxury fabrics and garment fasteners. What is important to note is the role that Eliante plays in this passage, which is not that of a model but rather of the clothing collection's executor. Schechner observes that "Eliante actually displays the dresses on living mannequins (Missie and Mademoiselle Fréhel),"[127] adding that "in this scene, Eliante functions as a director, not a performer."[128] Reminiscent of Worth, reported to be the first designer to employ live models, Eliante compels the two elaborately clad female bodies to pose and parade before her.[129] Designing unique, hand-made outfits for these young women, she thus enacts the male style authority composing outfits for a fashionable female clientele.

The space in which this "fitting" takes place is itself suggestive of the male couturier's studio. Eliante's boudoir is a decadent haven outfitted with all the trappings of nineteenth-century Eastern-inflected exoticism. Upon first entering Léon is struck by the room's mysterious and opulent allure:

> This bedroom, vast and dark, looked like a temple … [the windows] let in no daylight, only sunshine … a sort of murky sunlight mixed with smoke from a fire … lions and panthers, brown bears and black, alternated, each one presenting its head in the center of a panel, quite dead heads with eyes shut, mouths closed, not losing their natural expression by showing the horrible artificial fangs of flashy adventurers' bedside rugs … ebony columns encircled with bronze, with silver, with marble bracelets, held strange idols … a pile of multicolored cushions and pale satins made up the bed.[130]

> [Cette chambre, vaste et sombre, avait un air de temple … [les fenêtres] ne donnaient point de jour, mais du soleil … une espèce de soleil trouble mêlé d'une fumée d'incendie … lions et panthères, ours bruns et ours noirs, alternaient, présentant chacun leur tête au centre du panneau, des têtes bien mortes, aux yeux clos, aux gueules fermées, ne perdant pas leur expression naturelle à montrer les horribles crocs artificiels des descentes de lit pour rastaquouères … des colonnes d'ébène cerclées de bronze, d'argent, de bracelets de marbre, portaient des idoles bizarres … un amas de coussins bariolés et des satins pâles formaient le lit.[131]]

The room, replete with animal heads, mysterious odours, and an abundance of ornamental objects plundered from France's colonies, is typical of the private chambers decorated by other rachildean heroines; similar bedrooms exist in all of her other novels studied here. Rachilde's decadent boudoirs are threatening yet attractive locations that spatially presage the danger posed by the exotic feminine Other who inhabits them. At the same time, these rooms also had an analogue in the world of Parisian high fashion: the highly decorated settings in haute couture establishments in which live models were routinely photographed.[132] Indeed, the boudoir described in *La Jongleuse* proves uncannily similar to the photography setting that the reporter Griffith happens upon during his visit to Worth's couture house in 1894. Observing this special room on the top floor, "where all the models are photographed,"[133] Griffith accompanies his article with a striking image of Mrs Brown-Potter – one of Worth's favourite clients – dressed in one of "the master's" creations and posing as Cleopatra (see figure 6.3).

Tellingly, a number of items in Eliante's boudoir are also to be found in Worth's staged interpretation of the Egyptian queen's chambers. These include temple-like columns, mysterious smoke, heads and pelts of giant savage felines and wild bears, a dangerous exotic woman, a luxurious bed. This is not to suggest that Rachilde sought to describe Worth's, or any specific haute couture photography studio per se. Nonetheless, the similarities between the image of Worth's photography room and *La Jongleuse* suggest an overlap between Eliante's boudoir and this space of constructed performance located in the haute couture *maison*.[134] Worth's common practice of taking in-house pictures of his finely dressed clients and models – Griffith notes that the photograph of Mrs Brown-Potter is but one example culled from many years' worth of albums[135] – is thus taken up narratively by Rachilde, who, through Eliante's kaleidoscopic array of attire, assumes the creative role of male grand couturier with a twist, creating garments not in image or material form but in her chosen artistic medium: text.[136]

As important as the metaphor of garments is to Rachilde's literary production, however, not all fashion creation in her novels is of equal merit. In *La Jongleuse*, Eliante disparages her niece's former job as a hat maker, recounting to Léon how she met Missie, "who had been made a milliner's apprentice," and declaring, "I said to this poorly brought-up young girl, *an errand girl* at heart: 'Instead of making hats, you will buy them to put on your head and you will try to forget your former wretchedness, with your workshop words by becoming educated'"[137] ["que l'on avait mise en apprentissage chez un modiste, et je dis à cette fille mal élevée, *trottin* dans l'âme, 'Au lieu de faire des chapeaux, vous les achèterez pour les mettre sur votre tête et vous tâcherez d'oublier l'ancienne misère, avec vos petits mots d'atelier en vous instruisant'"[138]]. Here Eliante displays the discriminatory attitude typical of Rachilde's heroines, belittling the labour of mass-produced fashion objects and scornfully associating such work with poor upbringing, coarse language, and ignorance. In this way, her depiction of the milliner's milieu recalls Huysmans's rendition of the working-class seamstress's atelier but includes none of the positive connotations of the collective spirit of labourers that he also incorporates. The elite artistry of the male

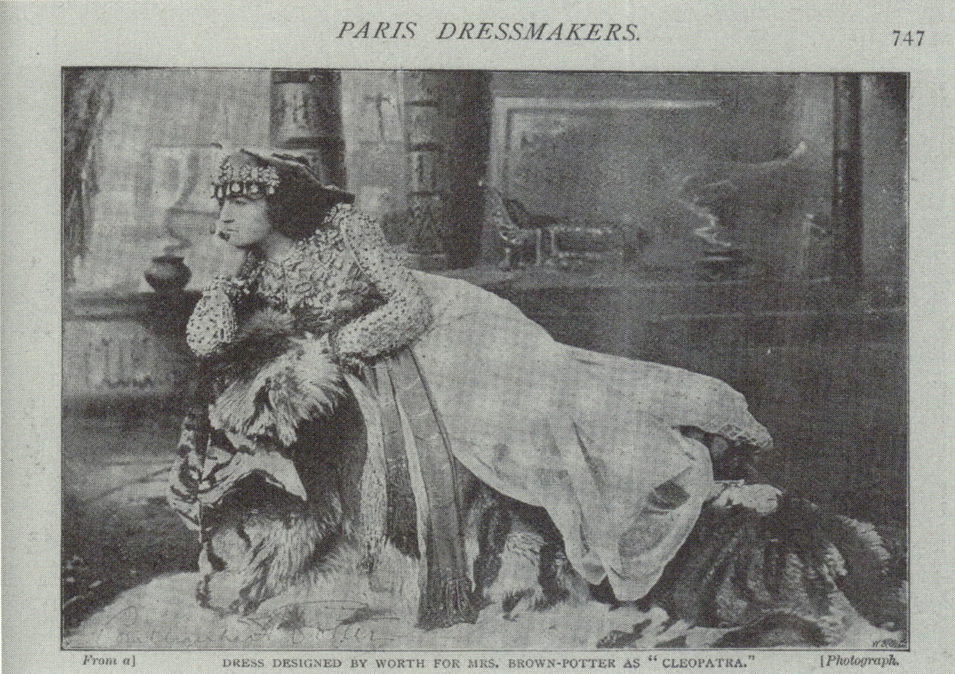

6.3 Anonymous, *Dress Designed by Worth for Mrs Brown-Potter as "Cleopatra,"* in *The Strand Magazine: An Illustrated Monthly,* ed. George Newnes (London: George Newnes Ltd, 1894), 747. Print from a photograph. Reproduced by permission of the General Research Division, the New York Public Library, Astor, Lenox, and Tilden Foundations.

designer *does* exist for Eliante, but it is found elsewhere, in figures such as Don Juan, whom she depicts in her own gender-bending retelling of the myth as a woman dressed in drag:

She had cut a doublet out of a chasuble of gold, put on violet slippers and took the lace from the altar of the Virgin, then also the strong sword decorated with precious stones of Saint Michael Archangel. She roamed the world in this disguise, turned Spain upside down, taking daughters from

their mothers and wives from their husbands, under the name of ...
Don Juan.[139]

[Elle avait taillé un pourpoint dans une chasuble d'or, mis des chausses
violettes et pris les dentelles de l'autel de la Vierge, puis aussi la forte épée
ornée de pierreries de saint Michel Archange. Elle courut le monde ainsi
déguisée, bouleversa l'Espagne enlevant les filles à leur mère et les femmes
à leurs maris, sous le nom de ... *Don Juan*.[140]]

In contrast with Missie, the lowly hatmaker, Eliante portrays Don Juan
as supremely powerful in the art of seduction, an androgyne endowed
with the shadow of a mustache who inventively restyles herself into a
man clothed in an outfit made especially subversive through its incor-
poration of profaned religious textiles.[141] It seems not a coincidence
that, rather than "sewing" her special disguise, Don Juan is said to
"cut" it (*tailler*), a subtle detail that aligns this male impersonator more
with the aggressive masculinity of slicing (echoed in Don Juan's phallic
sword) than the seamstress's apparently artless stitching using needle
and thread.

"An Electric Charge": The Photographic Flash

In the 15 November issue of *La Dernière Mode*, Mallarmé-as-Marguerite
de Ponty mentions having gleaned information for a fashion report
"from some great *couturière*s or their [male] rivals" (translation modified)[142] [près des grandes *couturière*s ou de leurs rivaux les couturiers[143]].
Although it is not altogether clear to whom Mallarmé refers in the
phrase "grandes couturières" – the feminine form of the masculine
grand couturier – the term "rivals" indicates an adversarial relationship
between the women and men of haute couture design. This gendered
hostility in high fashion is dramatized in Rachilde's *La Marquise de Sade*,
a text positing a basic antagonism between the sexes that plays out in
sartorial counterattacks perpetrated by a female self-fashioner. In the
novel, protagonist Mary Barbe evolves from a young girl dressed in the
couture of others to creative designer of her own troubling *toilettes*.
Emily Apter's examination of clothing in the novel analyses Mary as a
"weaponized woman" whose signature outfits, featuring armour-like
bodices, dagger-inspired necklines, thorn embellishments and piercing
hairpins, are expressions of the "war on the male sex" that she

symbolically wages.[144] As Apter notes, a key passage in the text with respect to fashion describes when twelve-year-old Mary plays the allegorical "spirit of war"[145] ["génie de la guerre"[146]] during a simulated army battle. For this high-profile event, which attracts spectators from across the region, the girl wears a flowing dress recalling the robes of ancient Amazon women warriors, "dressed," the text specifies, "with the help of a Parisian couturier who had created a masterpiece"[147] [s'habilla avec l'aide du couturier parisien qui avait créé un chef-d'œuvre"[148]]. Here Rachilde reinforces associations between male designer (the term is grammatically masculine) and artistry ("masterpiece"), as the Paris-based couturier is called upon as the one with the authority to make this special dress. An important detail, however, is that it is Mary, not the Parisian designer, who plays the role of "genius," a subtext suggested by the more common translation of the term "génie" cited above. Indeed, Mary does grow into her "genius," first in the masculine domain of science, where she becomes an adept anatomist and an expert poisoner thanks to her mastery of chemistry. But her innate sartorial "genius" further allows her to develop into her own clothing designer and to use dress ingeniously both as armour against the men who covet her and as a weapon to launch counterattacks. Her engagement gown is a case in point:

> Mary stood in the splendour of her eighteen years, dressed in singular attire, her engagement toilette. 'I want a dress the color of suffering' she had declared to her stunned dressmaker. The dress was the perfect embodiment of the cruel girl's idea! Over the eyecatching emerald green satin skirt a bodice was laced, an awkward fashion of the day, this velvet bodice spangled with bronze mesh whose purple and blue reflections were multiple. This bodice was high-cut yet it opened with an unexpected plunge between the breasts, whose rosiness struck one as heightened because of the intense velvet green. The bodice left her hips as if naked, and all down the folds of the very clinging skirt ran flowerless rose branches studded with thorns. Mary's perverse coquetry had exploded with a confidence bordering on naivety. Until that evening she had never taken much trouble over her clothes, and at one single attempt she had attained the sublime.[149]

> [Mary, debout, dans la splendeur de ses dix-huit ans, portait une singulière toilette, sa création des fiançailles. 'Je veux une robe couleur de

souffrance,' avait-elle déclaré à la *couturière* stupéfiée. Cette robe incarnait parfaitement l'idée qu'elle avait eue, la cruelle fille! Sur la jupe de satin vert émeraude, arrachant les yeux, se laçait une cuirasse, mode inconvenante de l'époque, une cuirasse en velours constellé d'un papillon mordoré à multiples reflets ou pourpres ou bleus. Ce corsage était montant et cependant s'ouvrait par une échancrure inattendue entre les deux seins, qu'on s'imaginait plus rose à cause de l'intensité de ce velours vert. La cuirasse laissait les hanches comme nues, et le long des plis de la jupe, très collante, couraient des branches de feuillage de rosier sans fleurs, criblées de leurs épines. La perverse coquetterie de Mary avait fait explosion avec une assurance frisant la naiveté. Jamais elle ne s'était souciée de ses chiffons avant ce soir-là, et d'un seul effort elle atteignait au sublime.[150]]

Vivid green, the gown's hue evokes absinthe, a drink known as the "green fairy" (*fée verte*) and thought to be fatally toxic, portending the "suffering" Mary inflicts on the men she will poison. But the dress is more than simply symbolic of her, for it is Mary's own "idea," a concept that she compels another person – the stunned female dressmaker – to sew for her. This hierarchical dynamic places Mary, like Worth, in the position of male designer holding power over the subordinate woman seamstress. The dress also demonstrates that Mary is born with masculine "genius," for she produces a "sublime" masterwork having no prior background in designing attire. Moreover, we find that "the discountenanced dressmaker had sworn that though it was original it was hardly the attire for a young engaged lady. Mary was fond of green ... she therefore paid no heed to the observations of the woman she paid to accomplish these extravagances"[151] ["La couturière contrariée avait avoué que si c'était original, ce n'était guère de mise pour une jeune fiancée. Mary aimait le vert ... elle n'écouta donc pas les réflexions de celle qu'elle payait pour accomplir des tours de force"[152]]. Recalling Eliante, who disdains women like Missie who fulfil the manual duties of garment production, Mary scorns her female dressmaker, a paid employee who merely "accomplishes" the "extravagant" and "singular" designs that Mary skillfully envisions.

The emerald dress connects Mary to a space in the novel that, like Eliante's bedroom, might be interpreted as another perversion of the fashion atelier's photography studio. This is the home laboratory of her uncle Célestin Barbe, a doctor whom Mary abhors because of his early abandonment of and later desire for her.[153] Described through Mary's eyes as she first discovers it, the laboratory is equipped, unsurprisingly, with an array of objects associated with scientific pursuits, such as stacks of leather-bound books, heating elements, vials, and surgical instruments. However, perhaps more surprisingly, the space is also reminiscent of Rachilde's opulent boudoirs and Worth's staged photography room. The lab is "hung in myrtle green draperies, with window and door curtains of Flemish greenery"[154] ["tendu de drap vert myrte, aux rideaux et aux portières en verdures flamandes"[155]] and features "velvet cases containing the most artistic jewels of steel, gleaming and mysterious"[156] ["des écrins en velours contenant les plus artistiques bijoux d'acier, luisants et mystérieux"[157]]. "Long animal hides"[158] ["longues peaux d'animaux"[159]] like those in Eliante's chamber and Worth's Cleopatra set make their appearance, and bones, recalling the embellishments on Eliante's oriental costumes, are present in the lab as a hanging skeleton. Finally, there is even a mannequin, "an anatomical Venus"[160] ["une Vénus anatomique"[161]] that "was stretched asleep in a corner … banished there like some discarded doll"[162] ["s'étendait endormie dans l'angle d'un mur … reléguée là comme une poupée devenue inutile"[163]]. The laboratory thus connects by way of the luxurious and exotic objects in it to the high fashion atelier. This link between the photography room of the haute couture *maison* and Mary's self-fashioning is strengthened later in the text when Célestin sees Mary in her brilliant green engagement dress and the effect is, tellingly, "electric": "For the poor tired eyes of Doctor Barbe all this green was like a charge of electricity"[164] ["Tout ce vert était, pour les pauvres yeux fatigues du docteur Barbe, comme une décharge électrique"[165]]. The "eyecatching"[166] (literally "eye-ripping") ["arrachant les yeux"[167]] green of Mary's dress which assaults Célestin's vision recalls the visual impact of flash powder, a compound of chemicals that, when mixed, produced a blinding flash that was commonly used by photographers during this period. The term "electrical" (*électrique*) itself connects Mary's garment to her uncle's place of work. For later one of Célestin's scientific instruments explodes in his laboratory, killing him and causing "a tremor of electricity"[168] ["un frisson électrique"[169]] throughout the mansion.[170] The explosion and electric blast in the extravagantly appointed laboratory echoes the ignition of flash powder used in the photography studio by the haute couturier to document his latest fashion creations.

If Mary is the couture-wearing woman of the novel, during the explosion she is not, however, the female body that is subject to the (camera's) flash. This job goes instead to the anatomical Venus, the cadaver replica that is found in the laboratory with Célestin's remains following the blast: "The anatomical Venus, detached from her pedestal, had leapt, still upright but decapitated, across its table on to a heap of shattered phials"[171] ["La Vénus anatomique, détachée de son piédestal, avait bondi, droite encore, mais décapitée, en travers de sa table, sur un amas de fioles brisées"[172]]. This decapitated female figure reinforces the juxtaposition of lab and fashion space by recalling the tailor's dummies that were used in the construction and display of garments in atelier workshops, boutiques, and department stores, and which were typically headless.[173] Beheaded and standing on shards of glass, the Venus symbolizes as well a female body painfully victimized, collateral damage in service of men's interests. This is the role that Mary rejects, refusing to be, like the Venus, a "discarded doll," a helpless mannequin that men dissect, whether through scientific probing or the objectifying photographic flash. Her refusal plays out in sartorial terms, for as we read in the description above of Mary's emerald dress, the garment is a manifestation of her "perverse coquetry" which "had exploded." Mary's clothes make her not the effaced woman of fashion like *La Curée*'s Renée, nor the passive model depicted in the photo, but the explosive flash itself. Her deployment of costume to deny female subjugation is reiterated in the novel's closing chapter, where Mary's preferred garment is "her dark velvet domino"[174] ["son domino loutre"[175]]. This long, hooded cloak fashioned of otter pelts, a counterpoint of darkness to the photographic flash, allows her to hide her body from penetrating male gazes and prey upon the ephebic cross-dressing men that she fantasizes about killing.

"Clothed with Transparent Rubber Skin": Fashioning Jacques Silvert

As the many references to art, the protagonist's masculinity, and the Pygmalion myth in *Monsieur Vénus* imply, Rachilde clearly sought to align her heroine Raoule with male artistry. My focus here will be Raoule's related skills as a fashion designer, which will then link to a larger commentary on women's spatial navigation of the city. As noted earlier, in spite of Raoule's self-declared artistic superiority, *Monsieur Vénus* does little to affirm her claim of being a great artist in the traditional sense, since her abilities as a fine painter or sculptor are never truly illustrated. Her talents for vestimentary design, on the other hand, are established throughout, notably in the novel's opening chapter, when Raoule goes in search of accessories and instead finds Jacques, whose body will become her ultimate "work of art." Explaining that she requires floral ornaments to affix to a water-nymph outfit for a costume gala, Raoule describes the plants she imagines wearing as Jacques produces sketches according to her stipulations. Although impressed with the young man's drafting abilities, Raoule suddenly intervenes, taking up her own pencil, we read, "to correct certain outlines"[176] ["pour rectifier certains contours"[177]] on his sketches. In one sense, the episode foreshadows Raoule's part in the refashioning of Jacques, for "correcting certain outlines" on his drawing is a euphemism for how she will recraft the young man into a version of himself that fully embraces his femininity. If, on the other hand, the encounter is understood through the lens of haute couture, what occurs is that Raoule dictates her imagined creation to Jacques and then makes adjustments to it, taking charge of the design process and claiming for herself the more powerful position of fashion creator to Jacques's inferior draftsman. The Silverts' decrepit attic apartment symbolically transforms, however temporarily, from an impoverished accessory sweatshop into an haute couture *maison*, with Rachilde's heroine at the helm.

Further highlighting the high fashion subtext is the detail that Raoule's water-nymph outfit is a "Grévin costume"[178] ["costume Grévin"[179]], a reference to the prominent caricature artist, Alfred Grévin (1827–1892) (see figure 2.1). Grévin is best known today for the Parisian wax museum that bears his name, but he also created garments for the theatre and high-society costume balls.[180] Readers would have instantly recognized Rachilde's reference, since *Monsieur Vénus* was published just two years after the highly publicized opening of Grévin's museum. To be sure, Rachilde was likely foreshadowing here Jacques's eventual transformation into a wax mannequin, fit for display among the other corpselike figures found in Grévin's exhibits. But the passage also confers sartorial authority onto the protagonist, since it specifies that Raoule, not the famous Grévin, creates the outfit's final touches. By inventing floral garnishes for the gown, Raoule makes changes to the made-to-order garment of a high-profile male designer, ultimately rendering his aesthetic opinion second to hers. In so doing, she undermines the gendered power dynamic associated with couturiers such as Worth, who, we have seen above, was known to be "despotic" with his female clientele. In masculinizing her role in the dress's creation, Raoule empowers herself and also relegates the biologically male Jacques to the position of female accessory maker, hiring him to accomplish the manual construction of the outfit's flowers from her own designs.

Ultimately, though, as readers of *Monsieur Vénus* well know, in spite of her alignment with the fashion designer Raoule *does* end up engaging in manual labour on a one-of-a-kind worn object. This occurs at the novel's infamous conclusion, when Raoule personally takes up a set of specialized tools to remove the nails, teeth, and hair from Jacques's corpse. Although the details are hazy, creation of the Jacques mannequin appears to involve some type of garment tailoring, for we read that the wax figure is "*clothed* with transparent rubber skin" (translation modified, emphasis added)[181] ["revêtu d'un épiderme de caoutchouc transparent"[182]], the verb "revêtir" meaning "to wear," "to don," or "to adorn" underscoring the vestimentary qualities of the rubber suit. Since it is specified that the rest of the mannequin is "made"[183] ["fabriqué"][184] by "a German"[185] ["un Allemand"[186]], one interpretation is that Raoule affixes the hair, nails, and teeth to the rubbery skin suit herself (indeed, it is difficult to imagine another person could be hired to do this gruesome job). The instruments that Raoule uses for this "very delicate task"[187] ["un travil très minutieux[188]] – *pince, marteau, ciseau*[189] or "pliers," "hammer" and "chisel" – call to mind implements of the skilled sculptor in accordance with the novel's Pygmalion theme.[190] One could suggest additionally that they evoke tools used in fabricating ornaments for clothing, such as buttons, beads, and hooks. The term "ciseau" is, moreover, the singular form of *ciseaux*, or a pair of scissors, an item having strong associations to garment making. To further follow the metaphor of tailoring, Raoule might be said to "accessorize" the rubber suit, adding to it the decorative embellishments she once found most eye-catching on Jacques's live body. Although certainly a ghastly analogy because of the human origins of such "ornaments," in a sense the notion of adorning the rubber skin with once-living materials echoes fashion's very real practice of garnishing clothing with the striking plumes, skin, fur, tusks, and shells of animals.[191] The point here is that it is Raoule, not a man, who puts the final artistic touches on the garment, thereby providing the last authoritative word of the *grand couturier*.

Fashioning Tactics: Women in the City

As we have seen above, the motif of women taking control of the process of garment creation manifested itself in a number of Rachilde's major late-century works. Another theme, established in *Monsieur*

Vénus and then taken up repeatedly in the following years, is a related meditation on woman's access to the urban milieu and fashion's role in facilitating this spatial appropriation. Often overshadowed by its deliberately scandalous challenge to gender normativity is the fact that *Monsieur Vénus* is a novel preoccupied with space. As Guri Ellen Barstad aptly puts it, the novel is formed of "numerous concrete and metaphoric spaces among which develop distinctive relationships and dynamics denoting a creative and vital quest" "[that] permit the protagonist, Raoule de Vénérande, to enlarge her own interior space" ["les nombreux espaces … concrets et métaphoriques qui développent entre eux des rapports particuliers et dynamiques dénotant une quête creative et vitale"] ["[qui] permett[ent] au personnage principal féminin, Raoule de Vénérande, d'élargir son espace intérieur"].[192] The point to which I have been building is that the identification between Rachilde's heroines and the specifically *male* fashion designer does not simply demonstrate a desire to appropriate the figure's privilege in symbolic terms, but also in spatial terms insofar as it allowed her to "enlarge" not just "interior" space, as Barstad evokes, but exterior as well. For Rachilde's writings form a discourse profoundly concerned with the possibility of women's uninhibited right of entry to the city, one that, Rachilde seems to perceive, was afforded only to men. Her attraction to the trope of the male *grand couturier* is therefore plausible, as he was the most powerful figure in fashion and was endowed with a man's privilege of urban access. To understand *Monsieur Vénus* and other novels by Rachilde in terms of gendered urban spatiality, a methodology that focuses on the nexus of city space and power is useful. It is thus that we turn to Michel de Certeau's formulation of the hierarchical dynamics at work in industrialized spaces as exemplified by the modern urban landscape.

Certeau's influential theories on how humans interact with city space are crystallized in his seminal set of essays translated into English in 1984 as *The Practice of Everyday Life*. For Certeau, the city is characterized by "strategies" that make it a "place" (*lieu*), "an instantaneous configuration of positions" that "implies an indication of stability."[193] This supposedly stable "place" of the city is constructed via a "strategic model"[194] which understands it as "a field of programmed and regulated operations."[195] However, against the "calculus of force-relationships"[196] that governs the city giving the (false) impression of its inherent stability, "tactics" arise in the form of what Certeau famously calls "everyday practices," examples of which include "talking, reading, moving about, shopping, cooking, etc."[197] Through such tactics, "the city is left prey to contradictory movements that counterbalance and combine themselves outside the reach of panoptic power … it is no longer a field of programmed and regulated operations."[198] "A tactic," he suggests, "insinuates itself into the other's place, fragmentarily, without taking it over in its entirety, without being able to keep it at a distance."[199] The city thus constitutes not a "place" administered by strategies of forced regulation but a "space": "a practiced place" "composed of intersections of mobile elements."[200]

The spatial navigation of Paris that Rachilde depicts can be understood as a narrative version of Certeau's "tactics," enacted by her female characters to challenge the regularizing, programming, surveilling, stabilizing, and ultimately male-serving ideologies of the "place" of the Haussmannian city. The effects of such limits on creative women's mobility in the late century are poignantly lamented in a journal entry written by the painter Marie Bashkirtseff (1858–1884), who was born close to the same year as Rachilde:

> What I long for is the freedom of going about alone, of coming and going, of sitting in the seats of the Tuileries, and especially in the Luxembourg, of stopping and looking at the artistic shops, of entering churches and museums, of walking about old streets at night; that's what I long for; and that's the freedom without which one cannot become a real artist.[201]

In their determination to overthrow restrictions placed on their movement in the city – crucial, Rachilde might have thought, to one's ability to "become a real artist" as Bashkirtseff suggests – Rachildean heroines are constantly "moving about," "insinuating" themselves, Certeau might say, into areas of the metropole that patriarchal social norms of the late-nineteenth-century seek to render off-limits to them. Mary Barbe, we read, "by night … roamed around"[202] ["rôdait la nuit"[203]], taking to the seedy streets to enact vengeance on men for their violence to women. Laure Lordès, protagonist of *L'Animale*, gambols across the city's skyline like a cat, this "rooftop vagabonding" ["vagabondages sur les toitures"][204] providing her only temporary escape from the cage-like immobility she suffers as a kept woman.[205] Renée Fayor of *Nono* sets herself in perpetual motion as an aggressive horse-riding *amazone*, enacting a subversive form of mobility in the countryside that she also deploys when she lives part-time in Paris. Raoule de Vénérande assumes the navigational practices of a male lover, installing Jacques in a series of enclosed locations and journeying to him rather than the reverse. Even Eliante Donalger, perhaps the most resigned and pessimistic of Rachilde's major nineteenth-century heroines, still travels continuously throughout the city, regularly entering and exiting her theatre-like mansion. Frequenting slums, leaping across rooftops, evading male supervision on horseback: Certeau might call these "contradictory movements," spatial negotiations that do not take the city over "in its entirety" all the while engaging with it "without being able to keep it at a distance." Rachilde's characters thus turn Certeau's "place" into "space," moving about in the metropole as it was not intended to be, particularly not by women.

Dress, which Certeau cites above as one of his "everyday practices," is part of their tactical approach to finding their way through the urban landscape.[206] Mary's fur domino, arm and armour in one, enables her to shadow her intended male victims through the dark recesses of the city. Raoule uses drag to circulate, clad in a suit in order to call upon Jacques on her own terms, "as a man." Laure dons a seductress's "red satin robe" ["peignoir de satin rouge"][207] and "velvet mules" ["mules de velours"][208] for her rooftop excursions, dismissing the garments' impracticality and favouring them because they enhance the sensual pleasure of her nocturnal roaming. Renée's mannish *amazone* outfits allow her a measure of spatial authority through solitary horse riding, this gesture towards symbolic social power reiterated by the regal connotations of her riding habit's impressive "royal appearance" ["un aspect tout royal"].[209] Eliante, a quick-change artist, dresses one moment as a bourgeois widow to visit Léon and at another attends society soirées clad in an impenetrable high-necked gown, her perpetual clothing transformations inside and outside the home constituting a technique to defy being defined and controlled by the men around her.

This insistence in Rachilde's fiction, that dress is crucial to women's spatial mobility in the city, is paralleled in the author's well-known request to cross-dress, which was submitted to the prefecture of Police in 1884. In her application letter, Rachilde notes that wearing men's clothing is necessary for her to make a living as a reporter, asking specifically, in her words, "that you allow me to wear, when traveling around Paris and the provinces, the most ungraceful clothing that exists in the world" ["que vous me permettrez de prendre, pour voyager dans Paris et en province, les vêtements les plus disgrâcieux qui soient au monde"[210]]. Rachilde's perhaps disingenuous characterization of men's clothing as "ungraceful" notwithstanding, the appeal highlights her association of male garb with the unfettered "traveling" around Paris necessary for her job as a reporter. An important point to recognize, though, is that the ability to be freely independent and integrated anonymously into the daily circulation of "respectable" public urban space – the very thing Rachilde's letter requests – is the one major spatial gift that Rachilde does not bequeath her heroines. For no matter what they wear, never are any of them shown navigating the socially sanctioned areas of Haussmann's modern city. They do not walk the boulevards, they do not take to newly built parks, they do not go to the Opéra, they do not shop at department stores, they do not visit museums. There are no strolling flâneuses among them, and only when starving and desperate does one, Laure Lordès, end up walking the streets to attempt prostitution ("Laure wandered the boulevard" ["Laure erra sur le boulevard"][211]). This omission of more normative ways to traverse the city seems deliberate: when Eliante belittles Missie's job in millinery, she calls her a "trottin," whose derivation, the verb "to trot" (*trotter*), implies the scampered movement of the delivery girl. Rachilde's protagonists do not scamper or "trot" through the city, eschewing such forms of movement that seem to them banal and undignified. A tension in her works, then, is that Rachilde's female protagonists do not seek to overcome spatial restrictions in ways that would allow them the same privileges inherent to male urban navigation and access of an everyday, quotidian, sort. For the painter Marie Bashkirtseff, who is cited above, the consequences of lacking such "freedom of going about alone, of coming and going" to the Tuileries, to the Luxembourg, to museums and so forth were severe, for this is part of what stood in the way of her becoming "a real artist."

These undeniable restrictions that Bashkirtseff and Rachilde faced notwithstanding, in the latter's case, the medium of fiction permitted her to compose textual worlds that recorded the realities that she and Bashkirtseff lived but in which the navigational challenges of women could be addressed on her own terms. In this way, her novels of Paris epitomize precisely what Janet Wolff calls on us to privilege, that is, "the perspective of women in the city," the study of which can "open up the possibility of seeing women's complex negotiations of city life, real obstacles and constraints, and ideological constructions which attempt to fix and constrain them."[212] Indeed, examining Rachilde's novels as we have just been doing – that is, with an eye to metropolitan movement – might be said to enact, as Wolff calls it, "a newly feminized urban theory,"[213] one that shifts the study of modernity to allow that "women become entirely visible in their own particular practices and experiences in the modern city."[214] Rachilde's literary works are surely to be included in Wolff's framework, for an important legacy of her heroines lies in their challenge to urban constraints facing women, a challenge that was spatially conceived and subverted through tactics lying at the intersection of artistry and modern dress.

Conclusion

It is not wholly surprising that Rachilde would choose the male *grand couturier* as a metaphor through which to envision more substantive power and mobility for the Third Republic woman. After all, high fashion was a world that she knew as a former fashion columnist, and as a woman, fashion was a domain accessible to her in ways that other spheres of power that interested her, such as the military, were not. Furthermore, the elitism and artistry associated with the male designer would have appealed to her, for she valued aesthetic superiority and sought to align herself with it. It is perhaps ironic that part of the couturier's allure for Rachilde would have been due to the fact that men had appropriated haute couture in the first place. As Troy observes of the couturier, "That he was male rather than female ... effectively raised the stature of the heretofore predominantly female dressmaking profession."[215] If Worth and his compatriots were essential to elevating the position of haute couture designer from lowly tailor to sartorial aristocrat, Rachilde's fiction can be interpreted as a textual attempt to reclaim some of the authority of the fashion milieu that men had, in fact, helped to establish.

Certeau's consideration of tactics and strategies of control in the city has been problematized for the way in which the model seems to accept the city's hegemonic "calculus of force-relationships" without seeking to overthrow its basic power inequities. Similarly, it has been posited that Rachilde's heroines, despite their disruptive and scandalous behaviours, do not imagine a regendered society and merely reassign masculine roles to select women while retaining the basic hierarchy between them. As Holmes puts it, her protagonists "seek [...] to usurp, not to transform, men's power"[216] for, indeed, "each heroine ends her story defeated, secluded in a fantasy world (Raoule, Mary Barbe) or dead (Renée, Laure, Eliante), while the society that has formed the context for the narrative apparently carries on much as before."[217] Rachilde's mitigated vision of social change, which ultimately preserves a system of patriarchal authority, can be understood in relation to the narrowness of her point of view of women in fashion more generally. Consistent with her attitude about her own role in literature and society, one that has been characterized as "a philosophy of extreme individualism,"[218] Rachilde's novels are concerned only with exceptional, self-fashioning, male-couturier-like women, who, though subversive, are not capable of (or interested in) profoundly disrupting the hierarchies of men's and women's roles themselves. One wonders how her vision might have shifted should she have tapped into the formidable force that the legions of women in the fashion milieu – seamstresses, milliners, flower makers, salesgirls, models, to name a few – could have represented in her texts if she had chosen to fictionalize them differently.

For some select women, gendered exclusion from the world of haute couture would resolve in their favour as the century turned. The early 1900s would usher in a new set of female *couturières* to join Jeanne Paquin – among them Madeleine Vionnet, Mme Grès, Coco Chanel and Elsa Schiaparelli – who would become prestigious designers in their own right, eventually outliving and eclipsing the name of Worth. For most working women, however, this would not be the case, as female sweatshops would only increase in numbers throughout the twentieth century and eventually become a world standard through the globalized exploitation of labour in former colonies and other marginalized regions.[219] Rachilde stands at a crossroads between these two trajectories. On the one hand, one can argue that she is no different from Degas and Huysmans in that all three turn to the figure of the woman in fashion to further their respective aesthetic projects. On the other hand, Rachilde's elitism was informed by the fact that she was herself subject to the sexist attitudes that plagued women, attitudes to which men like Huysmans and Degas were immune and against which she responded using her own set of authorial tactics.

To return to the regendered jacket with which we began this chapter, Rachilde's writing expresses tensions similar to those imbedded in this garment. The mismatched seams lining the *jaquette*'s front panels, for instance, bear witness to the difficulties inherent to refashioning a man's garment for a woman's body. Similarly, Rachilde's novels expose the challenges that women faced "fitting" into a society and literary world tailored not to them but to men. However, the coat has now been cut apart and restitched into something new, reappropriated for a female figure and never to be restored to an exclusively male silhouette. A wearable palimpsest, it bears the mark of its former owner but equally shows the markings – somewhat clumsily executed, perhaps – of the Third Republic woman who took ownership of it next. If there are problematic "imperfections" in Rachilde's unsympathetic attitude towards other women, they exist in tandem with the decadent breakthroughs that she pioneered and indelibly inscribed into the French literary landscape of the late nineteenth century, the literature of modernity.

Epilogue

To write a book with the word "modernity" in its title is to enter into a vast scholarly arena, one that has already produced countless volumes of rich inquiry and, if trends in academic publishing are to be believed, seems likely to find itself sustained into the future.[1] The wish, at least for this author, is to have contributed meaningfully to a corner of this wide-ranging discussion. At this juncture, then, one might ask, has *Fashioning Spaces* advanced our current conception of modernity and, if so, how? Will the reader arriving at these final pages have gleaned new insights about what it meant to be modern to those living in Paris in the late 1800s, and moreover, could these insights have broader implications beyond the relatively concentrated temporal and geographical focus that has concerned us here?

For answers – one hopes in the affirmative – we can return to the book's title and another term it brings into play, namely, *Mode*. Fashion, we have understood for some time, allured even as it troubled the chroniclers of late-century Parisian modernity who found their expression in the production of texts and images documenting the era. That garments *signify* in aesthetic representation is hardly a new idea; like any other detail that an author or artist includes in a work, clothing is a deliberate choice, meant to convey particular meanings about a subject's identity, mood, condition, character, and so on. Moreover, literary criticism in particular has long made use of sartorial metaphors in textual analysis: we speak of authors "weaving" together a narrative, of plot "threads," of our own "unveiling" of a work's underlying frictions or "unravelling" of its complexities. Writing of *La Curée* and describing the public health concerns addressed by Haussmann's architectural renewal, Alain Plessis, perhaps inspired by the fashion leitmotif in Zola's novel, notes, "If Paris transformed itself [under Haussmannization], it is that it was necessary to decontaminate the diseased, overpopulated city, assaulted more and more regularly by cholera, and also that the dynamism of this same city required that they alter and even retailor its fabric" ["Si Paris s'est transformé, c'est qu'il fallait bien assainir cette ville malade, surpeuplée, agressée de plus en plus régulièrement par le choléra, c'est aussi que le dynamisme de cette même ville exigeait que l'on retouche et même que l'on retaille son tissu"].[2] Plessis's use of terms that in French are strongly associated with sewing garments – "alter" (*retoucher*), "retailor" (*retaille*), "fabric" (*tissu*) – provides an example of this type of nod to fashion in the analysis of fiction.

If using the lexicon of dress as figures of speech in academic writing is a somewhat tenuous link between fashion and critical analysis, the practice gestures to a much more profound connection that *Fashioning Spaces* has sought to explore by introducing a third discourse on urban spatial theory. Thus, to call up a final term from this book's title – that is, *Spaces* – what this project has exposed is the repeated convergence in late-nineteenth-century literary, visual, and cultural creation of two themes working in tandem: the sartorial *and* the spatial. By way of an example, scholars have commented on the quality of "flatness" in some of Caillebotte's paintings,[3] one that articulates the city space as a series of surfaces. In Maupassant's *Bel-Ami*, the notion of "surfaces" is also put forth but in metaphorical terms to describe not physical space but social interactions. As we have understood by way of Foucault's treatment of the "virtual" in heterotopias, surface appearances in Maupassant's novel supplant interiority as the true marker of identity in the modern city. At the same time, as Varnedoe asserts, even very flat surfaces in Caillebotte's works can be offset by the sense of "a quite palpable space,"[4] belying a complexity to the painter's surface treatments of the city that in turn echo the deeply layered – ambivalent, beguiling, and contemptible – character that Maupassant creates of a "superficial" modern man like Duroy.

We could easily limit our thinking on Caillebotte to urban spatial considerations, but to turn as well to the sartorial motifs that recur with some frequency in his canvases reveals that fashion is itself a marker of the dimensionality that Varnedoe observes. For example, as Aileen Ribeiro contends in her reading of *Rue de Paris; Temps de pluie* [*Paris Street; Rainy Day*] (1877), perhaps Caillebotte's most iconic work, one way that the painter inserts a robust, third dimension into the painting is through the umbrellas that populate the composition and mitigate its flatness. She notes that the umbrella "creates a space around the person carrying it,"[5] this remark drawing the eye to the invisible yet perceptible sense of volume and depth surrounding the figures that the elegant accessories, repeated across the canvas, seem to delineate. Ribeiro, an art historian who specializes in the history of dress, calls attention to the fact that it is one of Caillebotte's favourite fashion objects that communicates this spatial tension in his art. When I connect Caillebotte to the literary example of Alphonse Daudet's *Sapho*, as I do in chapter 2, I depart from a strictly ocular reading to highlight the mutisensorial qualities of garments that the author projects. By foregrounding the haptic and sonoric features of dress in his novella, Daudet conveys the modern clothed body's presence in a manner that causes figures to fill space beyond the surfaces of their bodies. For in *Sapho*, as sounds made by costumes echo to all corners of rooms and pointed accessories dig ever deeper into the protagonist's flesh, the reader, like Caillebotte's viewer, perceives materiality, volume, and presence rather than the surface superficiality typically associated with fashion.

John Potvin, elaborating on Certeau's formulation of how agents tactically navigate cityscapes, affirms that "space allows … the embodied subject to *narrativize* fashion" (emphasis added).[6] Potvin's apt use of the term "narrativize" in the context of an urban-spatial discussion well invokes how location informs the uses of fashion in textual and visual narratives, the mechanisms of which *Fashioning Spaces* has been analysing. As we have seen, in literature and in its dialogues with art, it was in dislocations, those presumably insignificant and thereby often overlooked sites of the urban landscape, that the dynamics of modernity were catalysed through fashion's alternately rupturing and dazzling presence. Sustained attention paid to these locales, especially in fiction, indicates not merely how the French capital was itself a "fashion object" to be admired and consumed,[7] but also how narrative builders of the day contributed to this image of a pleasure-seeking, commodity-rich capital while simultaneously troubling perceptions of Paris's spectacular, phantasmagoric qualities. *Fashioning Spaces* focuses on three specific spatial arenas, but the model can be extended to encompass far more of what Potvin terms the "seemingly endless spaces and places which map out the city itself";[8] future analyses might focus on any number of these locales wherein the tensions, stagnations, and liberations of modernity occur.

What is being proposed in answer to the queries above, then, is that this approach conjoining dislocations and fashion impact not only how we conceive of modernity, but also how modernity might be studied if as-yet discrete theoretical and aesthetic discourses can be brought into conversation. Here I have drawn on spatial theory to examine fashion objects and on critical thinking on fashion to explore depictions of space. This method has brought to the forefront that the spatial and the sartorial meet in unexpected ways – architecture overlaps with bodies inhabiting built space; textiles from overseas colonies stand in for domestic politics of empire building, for instance – pointing to connections that have promising interdisciplinary and even transnational resonances.

To wit, the legacy of Haussmannization, true to its empire-building impetus, had repercussions far beyond the Hexagon's borders. The influence of urban planning under Napoléon III was a global phenomenon, and studies of other major urban centres – Buenos Aires, Tokyo, Tehran, Budapest, Mexico City, and (counterintuitively) London, to list only a few recent examples – repeatedly demonstrate this by naming Haussmann, specifically, in their analyses.[9] Whether directly related to analogous (neo)colonial instincts of those in power in other cities, symptomatic of a desire to associate with Paris's presumed status as a capital of high culture, or due to myriad other reasons, the archetype of Haussmannization clearly presents itself in many planning discourses of other cityscapes and in much scholarship that examines them. Fashion has proven an apt symbol of the modern in other national frameworks, as Regina Root has persuasively demonstrated in *Couture and Consensus: Fashion and Politics in Postcolonial Argentina*.[10] But even if dress is not always a fitting lens for the analysis of modernities outside of Paris, the concept of dislocations – or any other formulation called upon to describe non-sanctioned, problematic, or overlooked spaces that remain, nonetheless, linked to monumental spectacular analogues – might still be extrapolated to other locales. I hope that it is by now clear that I do not think Haussmannization *should* have been a model for other cities, or that I assume that my own conceptualizing about urban space would automatically be relevant to other global contexts. Rather, the thought of a potential extension of the notion of dislocations derives from a persistent pattern in academic studies, especially by critics working in historiography, which reiterates that Haussmannized Paris was, to varying degrees, referenced – politically, architecturally, socially, discursively – in other urban developments. That said, especially compelling to me in this body of research are cases when rising capitals rejected the Haussmann paradigm, eschewing efforts to become the next "Paris of the Middle East" or "Paris of the East" or "Paris of the Tropics," for instance,[11] to build their own modernities, for such examples might fruitfully be studied through the aesthetic works produced in reaction to these linked, yet distinctive, urban planning strategies.

For an example, we might draw on the novel *The Way to Paradise* [*El paraíso en la otra esquina*] (2003) by Peruvian-born writer Mario Vargas Llosa, the 2010 Nobel Laureate in literature and an author who has incorporated, played with, and refashioned 1800s Paris in a number of his texts.[12] In this biography-based work of fiction, Vargas Llosa charts a transnational cartography interspersing the Paris of socialist activist Flora Tristan in the early 1800s with memories of France's capital recalled by her wandering grandson, Paul Gauguin, during the last decades of that same century. Shifting narrative voices chapter by chapter, Vargas Llosa filters both depictions of Paris through his characters' travels to Peru, the French countryside, Tahiti, and the Marquesas Islands, creating a lyrical meshing of disparate times and places. I should clarify that my turn to how *The Way to Paradise* dislocates Parisian sites is not made with the presumption of impacting the scholarship of Latin American literature (which is not my area of expertise) but rather to suggest new avenues to considering the aesthetic production of modernity generated during the nineteenth century in France, that is, my own "home" discipline. For reading Vargas Llosa's vision of nineteenth-century Paris as he weaves the city through layered global spaces and physical sites inspires questions about his intertexts, Gauguin and Tristan. How might their respective paintings and writings be revisited with an eye to how both "dislocated" Parisian urbanism? Could attention to their nineteenth-century treatments of space imply what we think of today as a transnational consciousness, a twenty-first century concept that Vargas Llosa's novel evokes but that might likewise be traceable back to Tristan's and Gauguin's own representational works?

In closing, let us return to fashion in France's capital, and to the garment with which I opened chapter 6. The man's coat tailored into a *jaquette* for a woman, which is housed today, fittingly, in the Musée Galliera at the heart of Paris's fashion archives (see Figure 6.1), is a cogent symbol to invoke at the close of this study of fashion, space, and modernity in the post-Haussmannian city. Once a frock coat conferring the colourful glamour of the pre-Revolutionary *ancien régime*, the jaquette was then reimagined for a new bourgeois society, its crisp tailored lines and extreme bustle silhouette giving it the cut and look associated not with the past but with the new and modern. This type of reconfiguration, one documenting emerging social orders resulting from violent conflict, might call to mind Zola's textual appropriation of Garnier's classic Opéra *escalier* as a department-store staircase-cum-Commune barricade, all three spaces linked in their own way to the sartorial. In being completely transformed, the jaquette also recalls the mechanisms of the *robe à transformation*, a garment that resonates with "La Parure" and the total conversion of identity that, Maupassant suggests, a new dress represented to Mme Loisel, a protagonist who stands for a rising middle class superficial enough to fall victim to this alluring but false promise that fashion seems to offer. Yet, in the context of Rachilde's novels, the modified jacket reminds us that real changes, such as those related to gender expression and women's access to the metropole, were also projected in aesthetic works of the period. To give one last example, I will suggest that the jaquette is a sartorial cipher for the modern cityscape itself, an urban centre built with certain intentions under Haussmann that was then embraced but also questioned and contested by the writers and artists who inherited it. Their aesthetic work constitutes the textual and visual discourse existing alongside the official rhetoric of the period, the close examination of which, I hope, inspires us to think anew about how Third Republic urbanites may have experienced the metropolis and understood their roles in a city fashioned, not of locations, but of dislocations of the modern.

Notes

Introduction

1 The term "dislocation" has been used for a different purpose in Suzanne Nash, ed., *Home and Its Dislocations in Nineteenth-Century France* (Albany: State University of New York Press, 1993), a collection of essays in which "dislocations" refer to spaces related to homelessness. The word is used in broader terms in Daisy Connon, Gillian Jein, and Greg Kerr, eds., *Aesthetics of Dislocation in French and Francophone Literature and Art: Strategies of Representation* (Lampeter: Edwin Mellen Press, 2009), where it serves as an umbrella concept for a wide variety of dislocations, with an emphasis on those relating to notions of time and space.

2 T.J. Clark, *The Painting of Modern Life: Paris in the Art of Manet and His Followers*, rev. ed. (Princeton: Princeton University Press, 1999).

3 Rachel Bowlby, *Just Looking: Consumer Culture in Dreiser, Gissing, and Zola* (New York: Methuen, 1985); Michael B. Miller, *The Bon Marché: Bourgeois Culture and the Department Store, 1869–1920* (Princeton: Princeton University Press, 1981).

4 Christopher Prendergast, *Paris and the Nineteenth Century* (Cambridge: Blackwell, 1995), 4.

5 Joachim Schlor, *Nights in the Big City: Paris, Berlin, London 1840–1930*, translated by Pierre Gottfied Imhof and Dafydd Rees Roberts (London: Reaktion Books, 1998).

6 Walter Benjamin, *The Arcades Project*, translated by Howard Eiland and Kevin McLaughlin (Cambridge: Belknap Press, 1999); Susan Buck-Morss, *The Dialectics of Seeing: Walter Benjamin and the Arcades Project* (Cambridge, MA: MIT Press, 1989).

7 Vanessa Schwartz, *Spectacular Realities: Early Mass Culture in Fin-de-Siècle Paris* (Berkeley: University of California Press, 1998).

8 Sharon Marcus, *Apartment Stories: City and Home in Nineteenth-Century Paris and London* (Berkeley: University of California Press, 1999), 138.

9 A methodological inspiration has been Victoria Rosner's *Modernism and the Architecture of Private Life* (New York: Columbia University Press, 2005), which illuminates broader aesthetic and cultural concerns in modernist British literature as they were expressed through everyday lived spaces such as the home study and the drawing room.

10 Philippe Perrot, *Fashioning the Bourgeoisie: A History of Clothing in the Nineteenth Century*, translated by Richard Bienvenu (Princeton: Princeton University Press, 1994); Elizabeth Wilson, *Adorned in Dreams: Fashion and Modernity* (New Brunswick, NJ: Rutgers University Press, 2003); Gilles Lipovetsky, *The Empire of Fashion: Dressing Modern Democracy*, translated by Catherine Porter (Princeton: Princeton University Press, 1994); Valerie Steele, *Paris Fashion: A Cultural History* (Oxford: Berg, 1998); Ulrich Lehmann, *Tigersprung: Fashion in Modernity* (Cambridge, MA: MIT Press, 2000); Susan Hiner, *Accessories to Modernity: Fashion and the Feminine in Nineteenth-Century France* (Philadelphia: University of Pennsylvania Press, 2010). Although not expressly on fashion, Rae Beth Gordon's *Ornament, Fantasy and Desire in Nineteenth-Century French Literature* (Princeton: Princeton University Press, 1992) has also been important to my thinking on how literary criticism of decorative motifs and objects might be thoughtfully approached.

11 In this way, I take up where the chapter entitled "Costume" in Anne Green's *Changing France: Literature and Material Culture in the Second Empire* (London: Anthem, 2011) concludes.

12 This is a subject treated in the recent *Agrandir Paris, 1860–1970*, edited by Florence Bourillon and Annie Fourcaut (Paris: Publications de la Sorbonne, 2012), a collection of essays that studies Haussmannization not only in terms of the initial annexation of the Parisian suburbs starting in 1860 but also insofar as the mechanisms put into place at that time continued to develop throughout the Third Republic to impact the city and its surroundings.

13 Unless otherwise indicated, all translations are my own.

14 Charles Blanc, *L'Art dans la parure et dans le vêtement* (Paris: Librairie Renouard, 1875).

15 Ibid., 64.

16 Aileen Ribeiro, "Gustave Caillebotte: *Paris Street, Rainy Day*," in Gloria Groom, ed., *Impressionism, Fashion, and Modernity* (New Haven: Yale University Press, 2012), 194.

17 Clark, *Painting*, 46.

18 Ibid.

19 Although both materials derived from the same metallic element and were used industrially, steel was better suited for the crinoline cage (among other objects) as it was a stronger and more malleable alloy than wrought iron. For a comprehensive historical and cultural analysis of the crinoline, see Julie Wosk, *Women and the Machine: Representations from the Spinning Wheel to the Electronic Age* (Baltimore: Johns Hopkins University Press, 2001), 45–61.

20 Ibid., 45.

21 Leila Wittemore, "Theater of the Bazaar: Women and the Architecture of Fashion in 19th-Century Paris," *a/r/c architecture, research, criticism* 1, no. 5 (1994–95), 23.

22 Jean Sagne, "Marques de distinction" in Robert Delpire, ed., *Vanités: Photographies de mode des XIXe et XXe siècle* (Paris: Centre National de la Photographie, 1993), 11.

23 Diana de Marly, *The History of Haute Couture 1850–1950* (New York: Holmes and Meier, 1980), 7.

24 Green, *Changing*, 124.

25 Prendergast, *Paris*, 66.

26 Ibid.

27 Emile Zola, *Le Roman expérimental* (Paris: Charpentier, 1880), 1299–1302.

28 Benjamin, *Arcades*, 212.

29 Ibid., 421.

30 Ibid.

31 Ibid., 423.

32 Marcus, *Apartment Stories*, 2–3.

33 Schlor, *Nights in the Big City*, 16.

34 David Van Zanten, "Looking Through, Across, and Up: The Architectural Aesthetics of the Paris Street," in Groom, *Impressionism, Fashion, and Modernity*, 162.

35 Ruth E. Iskin, *Modern Women and Parisian Consumer Culture in Impressionist Painting* (Cambridge: Cambridge University Press, 2007), 89.

36 Kathryn Brown, *Women Readers in French Painting 1870–1890: A Space for the Imagination* (Farnham: Ashgate, 2012), 17.

37 Griselda Pollock, *Vision and Difference: Femininity, Feminism and the Histories of Art* (New York: Routledge Classics, 2003).

38 Indeed, I rely heavily on Pollock's formulation of the interstitial in "Interstitial Narratives: Rethinking Feminine Spaces of Modernity in Nineteenth-Century French Fashion Plates," *Nineteenth-Century Contexts* 36, no. 1 (2014), 1–33.

39 Reflecting nearly two decades later on her article "The Invisible *Flâneuse*: Women and the Literature of Modernity," a piece first published in 1985 that inspired many scholarly reactions, Janet Wolff put forth the challenge to "retire" the category of flânerie, in part because of analytical restrictions that she perceived stemming from the concept itself and the public/private binary to which it often gave rise ("Gender and the Haunting of Cities: Or, the Retirement of the Flâneur," in Aruna D'Souza and Tom McDonough, eds., *The Invisible* Flâneuse? *Gender, Public Space, and Visual Culture in Nineteenth-Century Paris* (Manchester: Manchester University Press, 2010), 28. It is my hope that *Fashioning Spaces* represents one way of answering Wolff's call to shift attention from the public/private dichotomy by analysing modernity through the intersection of urban theory and critical fashion studies.

40 Hollis Clayson, "Threshold Space: Parisian Modernism Betwixt and Between (1869 to 1890)," in Janet McLean, ed., *Impressionist Interiors* (Dublin: National Gallery of Ireland, 2008).

41 Ibid., 16.

42 John Potvin, introduction to John Potvin, ed., *The Places and Spaces of Fashion, 1800–2007* (New York: Routledge, 2009), 10–11.

43 Henri Lefebvre, *Rhythmanalysis*, translated by Stuart Elden (London: Continuum, 2004), 97.

44 Michel Foucault, "Other Spaces," in *Utopias*, edited by Richard Noble (Cambridge, MA: MIT Press, 2002).

45 Guy de Maupassant, *Romans*, edited by Louis Forestier (Paris: Gallimard, 1987), 218.

46 See Rosner, *Modernism*, chapter 4.

47 For more on the feminization of Madeleine's office, see Margot Irvine, "Spousal Collaborations in Naturalist Fiction and in Practice," *Nineteenth-Century French Studies* 37, nos. 1&2 (2008), 71, and Elisabeth-Christine Muelsch, "Belle Lectrices in *Bel-Ami* or How to Read the Female Reader," paper presented at the Twelfth International AIZEN Conference on Émile Zola and Naturalism, University of Texas at San Antonio, San Antonio, TX, 9–11 Oct. 2003.

48 Guy de Maupassant, *Bel-Ami*, translated by Douglas Parmée (London: Penguin, 1975), 67.

49 Maupasssant, *Romans*, 228.

50 Cited in Gloria Groom, "Spaces of Modernity," in Groom, *Impressionism, Fashion, and Modernity*, 172–3.

51 Jean-Pierre Leduc-Adine, "Architecture et écriture dans *La Curée*," in David Baguley, ed., *La* Curée *de Zola ou "la vie à outrance"*

(Paris: Société d'Etudes pour le Développement Economique et Social, 1987), 130.

52 Hiner, *Accessories*, 128.

53 Ibid., 13.

54 Rachilde, *Monsieur Vénus: A Materialist Novel*, translated by Melanie Hawthorne (New York: Modern Language Association of America, 2004), 118.

55 Rachilde, *Monsieur Vénus* (Paris: Flammarion, 1977), 132.

56 Hiner, *Accessories*, 210.

57 Ibid.

58 For example, the studies by Hiner, Lehmann, and Wilson, cited above. See also Barbara Vinken, "Eternity – A Frill on the Dress," *Fashion Theory* 1, no. 1 (1997), 59–68; and Peter Wollen, "The Concept of Fashion in *The Arcades Project*," *Boundary 2* 30, no. 1 (2003), 131–42. For Mallarmé's *La Dernière Mode*, see Damian Catani, *The Poet in Society: Art, Consumerism, and Politics in Mallarmé* (Bern: Peter Lang, 2003); P.N. Furbank and A.M. Cain, *Mallarmé on Fashion: A Translation of the Fashion Magazine* La Dernière Mode *with Commentary* (New York: Berg, 2004); chapter 2 in Rhonda K. Garelick, *Rising Star: Dandyism, Gender and Performance in the Fin de Siècle* (Princeton: Princeton University Press, 2009); Françoise Grauby, "Le Parfum de l'homme en noir: Mallarmé et *La Dernière Mode* (1874)," *Australian Journal of French Studies* 41, no. 1 (2004), 102–20; Jean-Pierre Lecercle, *Mallarmé et la mode* (Paris: Librairie Séguier, 1989); and Claire Lyu, "Stéphane Mallarmé as Miss Satin: The Texture of Fashion and Poetry," *L'Esprit Créateur* 40, no. 3 (2000), 61–71.

59 See works by Foucault and Lefebvre cited above. Also Henri Lefebvre, *La Proclamation de la Commune* (Paris: Gallimard, 1965); Jurgen Habermas, *The Structural Transformation of the Public Sphere: An Inquiry into a Category of Bourgeois Society*, translated by Thomas Burger (Cambridge, MA: MIT Press, 1991); Yi-Fu Tuan, *Space and Place: The Perspective of Experience* (Minneapolis: University of Minnesota Press, 2008); and Michel de Certeau, *The Practice of Everyday Life*, translated by Steven F. Rendall (Berkeley: University of California Press, 2011).

60 Certeau, *Practice*, 95.

61 Ibid., 117.

62 Tuan, *Space and Place*, 50.

63 Ibid., 102.

64 Lehmann, *Tigersprung*, xvii.

65 Furbank and Cain, *Mallarmé on Fashion*, 30.

66 Mallarmé, *Oeuvres complètes*, 496.

67 Furbank and Cain, *Mallarmé on Fashion*, 30.
68 Mallarmé, *Oeuvres complètes*, 496.

1   Fashioning the Commune Barricade

1 Albert de Lasalle, "Chronique Musicale: Le Nouvel Opéra," *Le Monde Illustré*, 5 Jan. 1875, 22.
2 Ibid., 23.
3 *Le Monde Illustré*, 16 Jan. 1875, 49.
4 Charles Nuitter, *Le nouvel Opéra* (Paris: Librairie Hachette, 1875), 81.
5 Ibid.
6 Ibid., 94.
7 Charles Garnier, *Le Nouvel Opéra de Paris* (Paris: Ducher, 1878), 1: 336.
8 Théophile Gautier, "Le Nouvel Opéra," *L'Artiste*, 1 Apr. 1866, 145. The spectacularity of fashionable audience members was not restricted to the *grand escalier*; Mary Cassatt's 1878 painting *At the Opera*, for example, demonstrates that artists of the period understood the visual play among spectators to continue from the staircase into the concert hall itself.
9 Lasalle, "Chronique Musicale," 22.
10 *Le Monde Illustré*, 9 Jan. 1875, 26.
11 The complexity of the relationship between the fashion industry and Garnier's building is demonstrated by the great number of players and strategies at work in the advertisement. For example, *Le Monde Illustré* was poised to benefit from the ad, which enabled it to court a variety of women subscribers. These included readers who wished to be "elegant" by following the sartorial trends of "certain figures of note" (presumably the upper-crust audience members of Garnier's Opéra) as well as frugal-minded shoppers who sought thrift without sacrificing style. Shop owner M. Lehoussel, the sole listed supplier of "le Nouvel-Opéra," was also set to profit from the spotlight of publicity trained on his boutique alone. The implication that this special fabric was carried by just one shop in Paris underscored the exclusivity and desirability of the silk, not simply to M. Lehoussel's clientele in the capital city but also to women subscribers living throughout France who wished to be as stylish as their Parisian sisters. As advertisements in provincial newspapers of the period suggest, Lehoussel actively sought customers located outside of Paris, offering to mail them swatches of the fabrics that he carried in his shop on the fashionable rue Auber (Anonymous, "La Mode, cette année," *Le Courrier des Alpes*, 5 May 1874, 4). The location of the boutique was itself significant, as the rue Auber runs along the southwest façade of Garnier's

Opéra, and the main entrance literally faced M. Lehoussel's establishment. Clients who ordered "Nouvel-Opéra" silk might have had the satisfaction of knowing that the fabric had once been but a stone's throw from the great edifice for which it was named. As the advertisement illustrates, the fashionability of Garnier's opera house helped stimulate a complex fashion economy that included fabric manufacturers, mass media, clothing boutiques, and customers within Paris as well as those far beyond the city's limits.

12 Before the inauguration of Garnier's new structure, the main opera house in Paris was located on the rue le Peletier. In addition to providing a space for performances of operatic works, the former opera house was well known for fashionable masked balls held there throughout the nineteenth century. The Opéra le Peletier's destruction by fire in 1873 intensified the need for its replacement, motivating Garnier to complete the new building ahead of schedule.

13 Garnier, *Nouvel Opéra*, 382.

14 Ibid. In 1863, Gautier posited that Garnier's staircase was being built expressly for a future event, which he called "une sortie d'Opéra" ("Nouvel Opéra," 145), seeming to refer to the mass departure of finely dressed audience members at the close of an act or evening. Like Garnier, Gautier described this spectacle-to-come in terms of the fine sartorial objects and clothed bodies that would one day parade down the *grand escalier*: "the cascade of diamonds, pearls, feathers, flowers, white shoulders, satin, velvet, moiré, tulle, lace, which … will bubble up on the white marble steps, in the twinkling of the brightest lights, encased in an enchanting architecture" ["cette cascade de diamants, de perles, de plumes, de fleurs, d'épaules blanches, de satin, de velours, de moires, de gazes, de dentelles, qui … écumera sur des degrés de marbre blanc, au scintillement des plus vives lumières, encaissé par une architecture féerique"] (145). In labelling the anticipated event a "marvel of modern civilization" ["cette merveille de la civilization moderne"] (145), Gautier highlighted the "modern" quality of this juxtaposition of architectural and sartorial display. In 1998, John Galliano, then head designer for Christian Dior, presented the house's autumn-winter collection on the steps of Garnier's Opéra, transforming the *grand escalier* into the runway show that the writings of Garnier and Gautier now seem to have predicted over a century earlier.

15 David Van Zanten has argued that part of what made Garnier's approach to architecture unique was the high importance he placed on the ways that humans interacted with their built surroundings, the notion that

"architecture is not a matter of principles but of experiences" (*Designing Paris: The Architecture of Duban, Labrouste, Duc, and Vaudoyer* (Cambridge, MA: MIT Press, 1987), 231). For more on Garnier's viewpoint, which distanced him from architectural trends of the previous decades, see Van Zanten, *Designing*, 230–3.

16 The *Trésor de la Langue Française* (*informatisé*) gives as a familiar definition of *attraper*: "to reproach, reprimand, scold" ["faire des reproches, réprimander, gronder"].

17 Bernadette Bonnier et al., *Félicien Rops: Rops suis, aultre ne veulx estre* (Brussels: Editions Complexe, 1998), 68–71.

18 François Mathey, ed., *Félicien Rops 1833–1898* (Brussels: Lebeer Hossmann, 1985), 113.

19 Ibid., 117.

20 Michel Draguet, *Le Cabinet des dessins Rops* (Paris: Flammarion, 1998), 36.

21 Bonnier, *Félicien Rops*, 57.

22 Draguet, *Cabinet*, 36.

23 I am grateful to one of the manuscript's anonymous readers for suggesting this military undercurrent linking Rops's and Zola's works.

24 Anne Zazzo, "Les Dessous du Second Empire," in Catherine Join-Diéterle et al., eds., *Sous l'Empire des crinolines* (Paris: Paris Musées, 2008), 65–6.

25 Benjamin, *Arcades*, 419.

26 One such example in the Musée Galliera's collection is an 1870s mother-of-pearl pocketbook engraved with a man and woman in eighteenth-century-style dress who are ascending the staircase of a house. The purse is pictured in Fabienne Falluel, "Les Accessoires sous le Second Empire: Une mode en contrepoint," in Join-Diéterle et al., *Sous l'Empire des crinolines*, 128.

27 Among the most common subjects depicted on new fans during the second half of the nineteenth century were, interestingly enough, historical ones: pastorals and romantic scenes inspired by the seventeenth and eighteenth centuries or based on well-known paintings from these periods (Falluel, "Accessoires," 132–9; Avril Hart and Emma Taylor, *Fans* (New York: Costume and Fashion Press, 1998, 92). This romanticizing of the past in the fans' thematics made them especially prized to nostalgic writers such as the journalist Octave Uzanne, who wrote an opulently decorated book in praise of the fan in 1882. One intriguing exception contradicting such historical settings in fans is a study that Gustave Caillebotte sketched for a fan depicting the clearly modern, newly erected buildings of the city upon which the man in his painting *L'Homme au balcon: Boulevard Haussmann* (1880) gazes. The fan study is pictured in

Kirk Varnedoe, *Gustave Caillebotte* (New Haven: Yale University Press, 1987), 144.

28 Furbank and Cain, *Mallarmé on Fashion*, 23.

29 Mallarmé, *Oeuvres complètes*, 493.

30 Furbank and Cain, *Mallarmé on Fashion*, 23.

31 Mallarmé, *Oeuvres complètes*, 493.

32 Hannah Thompson, *Naturalism Redressed: Identity and Clothing in the Novels of Emile Zola* (Oxford: Legenda, 2004).

33 Ibid., 156.

34 Habermas, *Structural Transformation*, 43.

35 Marcus, *Apartment Stories*, 186.

36 Emile Zola, *The Kill*, translated by Brian Nelson (Oxford: Oxford University Press, 2008), 50.

37 Emile Zola, *Les Rougon-Macquart*, edited by Henri Mitterand (Paris: Flammarion, 1960), 1: 368.

38 Zola, *Kill*, 50.

39 Zola, *Rougon-Macquart*, 1: 368.

40 See chapters 3 and 5 in Thompson's *Naturalism Redressed*.

41 Therese Dolan, "Guise and Dolls: Dis/covering Power, Re/covering Nana," *Nineteenth-Century French Studies* 26, nos. 2–3 (1989), 368–86.

42 Emile Zola, *Nana*, translated by George Holden (London: Penguin Classics, 1972), 241.

43 Zola, *Rougon-Macquart*, 2: 1286.

44 Ibid., 1287.

45 In addition to serving as a link between the courtesan and the Countess Sabine, the prostitute's hair functions as a narrative device. In the novel's second chapter, Nana's dishevelled chignon following a night of sexual pleasure and various efforts to recoiffe it provide the cadence that drives the chapter's plot.

46 Zola, *Nana*, 241.

47 Zola, *Rougon-Macquart*, 2: 1286.

48 Zola, *Kill*, 50.

49 Zola, *Rougon-Macquart*, 1: 369.

50 Ibid., 3: 1680.

51 Miller, *Bon Marché*, 5. Zola also visited two other Parisian department stores – Le Louvre and Le Printemps – but seemed to favour Le Bon Marché as his primary inspiration (*Carnets d'Enquêtes: Une Ethnographie inédite de la France*, edited by Henri Mitterand (Paris: Editions Plon, 1986), 147).

52 Emile Zola, *Au Bonheur des Dames (The Ladies's Delight)*, translated by Robin Buss (London: Penguin Classics, 2001), 116.

53 Zola, *Rougon-Macquart*, 3: 500.
54 Zola, *Ladies' Delight*, 414.
55 Zola, *Rougon-Macquart*, 3: 796.
56 Zola, *Ladies' Delight*, 97.
57 Zola, *Rougon-Macquart*, 3: 482.
58 Mieke Bal offers a compelling (counter)reading of Zola whereby his lengthy descriptions serve not to dominate narrative but rather as a motor for generating it ("Over-writing as Un-writing: Descriptions, World-Making, and Novelistic Time," in Ernesto Franco, ed., *The Novel*, vol. 2, *Forms and Themes* (Princeton: Princeton University Press, 2007), 571–610.
59 Zola, *Ladies' Delight*, 149.
60 Zola, *Rougon-Macquart*, 3: 533.
61 Zola, *Ladies' Delight*, 149.
62 Zola, *Rougon-Macquart*, 3: 533.
63 Zola, *Ladies' Delight*, 149.
64 Zola, *Rougon-Macquart*, 3: 533.
65 Zola, *Ladies' Delight*, 149.
66 Zola, *Rougon-Macquart*, 3: 533.
67 To read the Commune as an intertext for Zola's depictions of urban locations in *Au Bonheur des Dames* is consistent with Colette E. Wilson's argument that "the memory of Paris and the Commune lies at the very heart of Zola's carefully crafted descriptions of the city's topography" (*Paris and the Commune 1871–78: The Politics of Forgetting* (Manchester: Manchester University Press, 2007), 134) and extends this notion beyond the novels – *Le Ventre de Paris*, *L'Assommoir*, and *Une Page d'amour* – that Wilson studies. More recently still, Jann Matlock has read *La Curée* through the lenses of the Commune and Zola's participation in the mass-circulating press ("Everyday Ghosts: *La Curée* in the Shadow of the Commune," *Romanic Review* 102, nos. 3–4 (2011), 321–47.
68 Leslie Ann Minot, "Women and the Commune: Zola's Revisions," *Excavatio* 10 (1997), 60.
69 Peter Starr, *Commemorating Trauma: The Paris Commune and Its Cultural Aftermath* (New York: Fordham University Press, 2006), 149.
70 Vaheed Ramazani, "Gender, War, and the Department Store: Zola's *Au Bonheur des Dames*," *SubStance* 36, no. 2 (2007), 130.
71 Minot, "Women and the Commune," 57–8; Ramazani, "Gender, War," 131.
72 Scholars have done much to debunk the myth of the hysterically destructive *pétroleuse* and to point out the hypocrisy of misogynist discourses intent on explaining and reassigning blame for the event's horrors by way

of the demonization of women. See Gay L. Gullickson, *Unruly Women of Paris: Images of the Commune* (Ithaca: Cornell University Press, 1996); Carolyn J. Eichner, *Surmounting the Barricades: Women in the Paris Commune* (Bloomington: Indiana University Press, 2004); and Janet Beizer, *Ventriloquized Bodies: Narratives in Hysteria in Nineteenth-Century France* (Ithaca: Cornell University Press, 1994).

73 Gullickson, *Unruly Women*, 171–2.

74 Zola, *Ladies' Delight*, 249.

75 Zola, *Rougon-Macquart*, 3: 630–1.

76 A similar passage appears in Zola's sketched notes describing the staircase mannequins at the Louvre department store: "On the stairs, mannequins, jacket, dressing gown, headless, with the little wooden handle like the handle of a dagger, plunged into the soft red flannel, like the bloody severed stump of a decapitated body" ["Sur les marches, des mannequins, paletot, robe de chambre, sans tête, avec le petit manche de bois comme un manche de poignard, enfoncé dans le molleton rouge, qui fait comme la section saignante d'un décapité"] (Zola, *Carnets*, 186). That Zola later added the image of soldiers to the novel suggests he was deliberately highlighting a military theme in the final version.

77 Gullickson, *Unruly Women*, 17; Eichner, *Surmounting the Barricades*, 25.

78 Thomas S. Abler, *Hinterland Warriors and Military Dress: European Empires and Exotic Uniforms* (Oxford: Berg, 1999), 128; Odile Roynette, "L'Uniforme militaire au XIXe siècle: Une fabrique du masculin," *CLIO, Histoire, Femmes et Sociétés* 36 (2012), 115.

79 Gullickson, *Unruly Women*, 154; Eichner, *Surmounting the Barricades*, 188.

80 Gullickson, *Unruly Women*, 207.

81 Ramazani hypothesizes that the subject of war in this novel may have been overlooked by scholars precisely because it seems so uncomplicated ("Gender, War," 129–30). Janet Beizer addresses the notion of violence in Zola's works more generally through the lens of reader experience. For her, the tendency towards constant reiteration of mythic motifs is a narrative technique endemic to the Zolian oeuvre, one that has violent repercussions. For the reader, Beizer argues, revisiting these familiar narratives is akin to an act of forced aggression on the readerly process itself: "Like Denise ... readers are caught in the iron teeth of a machine, gripped by a legend, which is to say, by a *reading*, a master reading that arguably not only coerces ... but tyrannizes and even does violence to their own" (original emphasis, "*Au* (delà du) *Bonheur des Dames*: Notes on the Underground," *Australian Journal of French Studies* 8, no. 38 (2001), 399–400).

82 Raymond Trousson, "Emile Zola Chroniqueur de la Commune," *Travaux de littérature* 17 (2004), 454.

83 Ibid., 461.

84 Ibid.

85 Ibid., 463. One notes echoes of this scene in the aftermath of the Bonheur's first big sale, which Zola describes through the metaphor of carnage after a battle: "it was like a battlefield still hot from the massacre of materials ... ready-made clothes were heaped up like the greatcoats of wounded soldiers" (*Ladies' Delight*, 115) ["c'était comme un champ de bataille encore chaud du massacre des tissus ... les confections s'amoncelaient comme des capotes de soldats mis hors de combat"] (*Rougon-Macquart*, 3: 500). In the novel, the heaps of Communard bodies that Zola witnessed may have been echoed in the mounds of coats that, limp and empty, point implicitly to the lifeless bodies of the imagined soldiers that they once clothed.

86 Jeannene M. Przyblyski, "Revolution at a Standstill: Photography and the Paris Commune of 1871," *Yale French Studies* 101 (2001), 59.

87 Trousson, "Chroniqueur," 466–7.

88 Sylvie Aprile, *Le Siècle des exilés: Bannis et proscrits de 1789 à la Commune* (Paris: Centre National de la Recherche Scientifique Editions, 2010), 258.

89 Kristin Ross, *The Emergence of Social Space: Rimbaud and the Paris Commune* (Minneapolis: University of Minnesota Press, 1988), xix.

90 Ramazani, "Gender, War," 129. Zola was not the only author to steer clear of the Commune in his writings of the 1870s and 1880s. J.S. Wood notes that most novelists active during these decades who wrote about the events of 1870–71 similarly avoided the subject, opting instead to treat related yet separate topics such as the Franco-Prussian War, its provincial battles, and the subsequent loss of Alsace-Lorraine ("La Commune dans le roman," in James A Leith, ed., *Images of the Commune* (Montreal and Kingston: McGill-Queen's University Press, 1978), 70). Like Ramazani, Wood attributes the Commune's absence in fiction to the deep sense of trauma that Parisian writers continued to feel about the conflict, one that seemed to represent for them "a wound that was still bleeding" ["une plaie qui saignait encore"] (ibid.).

91 Zola, *Rougon-Macquart*, 3: 427.

92 Zola, *Ladies' Delight*, 41.

93 Zola, *Rougon-Macquart*, 3: 427.

94 Zola, *Ladies' Delight*, 41.

95 Zola, *Rougon-Macquart*, 3: 427.

96 Whittemore observes that such "theatrical and disorienting effects" ("Theatre," 21) that produced "a kind of erratic flow from department to department" (ibid.) were supposed to stimulate consumerism and were intentionally built into the structure of many nineteenth-century department stores by their architects.

97 Zola, *Rougon-Macquart*, 3: 491.

98 Ibid., 623.

99 Ibid., 789.

100 Gullickson, *Unruly Women*, 38.

101 Zola, *Ladies' Delight*, 172.

102 Zola, *Rougon-Macquart*, 3: 337.

103 Ibid., 556.

104 Zola, *Ladies' Delight*, 173.

105 Zola, *Rougon-Macquart*, 3: 557.

106 Simon Sadler, *The Situationist City* (Cambridge, MA: MIT Press, 1999), 122.

107 Nicholas White undertakes just such a reading, which posits Caroline Hédouin's pivotal importance in both novels ("The Lost Heroine of Zola's Octave Mouret Novels," *Romanic Review* 102, nos. 3–4 (2011), 369–90).

108 Zola, *Ladies' Delight*, 178.

109 Zola, *Rougon-Macquart*, 3: 561.

110 Marx references the 1848 barricades in *The Eighteenth Brumaire of Louis Bonaparte* and mentions them again in his defence of the Commune in 1871's *The Civil War in France*. The barricades are a recurrent theme in Engels's 1895 introduction to Marx's *The Class Struggles in France*. Hugo immortalized the barricades of 1832 in *Les Misérables* and, following the Commune, chose the 1871 barricades as the setting of his widely read poem, "Sur une barricade."

111 Zola, *Ladies' Delight*, 115.

112 Zola, *Rougon-Macquart*, 3: 500.

113 Mark Traugott, *The Insurgent Barricade* (Berkeley: University of California Press, 2010), 178–84.

114 In his 1868 *Instructions pour une prise d'armes* [*Instructions for taking up arms*], which included diagrams and directions on barricade building, famed insurrectionary Auguste Blanqui singled out stairs in his discussion of strategies for insurgents to make use of civilian houses during times of urban warfare: "When a house on the front lines of defense is particularly threatened, we demolish the first floor staircase and make openings in the floors of the various rooms on the second floor in order to fire on the soldiers who might invade the first floor to attach grenades

there. Boiling water could also play a useful role in this case. If the attack extends over a wide front, we cut off the stairs and pierce through the floors in all of the exposed houses. As a general rule, when time and other more urgent defensive work permits it, one should destroy the ground-floor staircase in all the houses of the sector except one, located on the least exposed backstreet."["Lorsque sur le front de défense, une maison est plus particulièrement menacée, on démolit l'escalier du rez-de-chaussée, et l'on pratique des ouvertures dans les planchers des diverses chambres du premier étage, afin de tirer sur les soldats qui envahiraient le rez-de-chaussée pour y attacher des pétards. L'eau bouillante jouerait aussi un rôle utile dans cette circonstance. Si l'attaque embrasse une grande étendue de front, on coupe les escaliers, et on perce les planchers dans toutes les maisons exposes. En règle générale, lorsque le temps et les autres travaux de défense plus urgents le permettent, il faut détruire l'escalier du rez-de-chaussée dans toutes les maisons de l'îlot, sauf une, à l'endroit de la rue derrière le moins exposé."] This correspondence between stairs in houses and barricades evokes the fluidity of spatial meanings in an urban environment beset by the strategies of popular uprising. As Kristin Ross rightly submits, Blanqui's manual transforms the interior home into a street battleground (*Emergence*, 38). Conversely, street barricades, serving as makeshift staircases, were public analogs to the demolished stairs in residences that Blanqui envisioned. The residential staircases destroyed by the Communards would have then been rebuilt by their own hands as staircase-barricades, turning the public boulevard into a space in which what had been razed in the home was reconstructed on the street.

115 Traugott, *Insurgent Barricade*, 185.

116 Przyblyski, "Revolution," 57.

117 Ibid.,64.

118 Lefebvre, *La Proclamation de la Commune*, 21.

119 Beizer, *Ventriloquized Bodies*, 216.

120 According to Gen Doy, "The Hôtel de Ville and the Vendôme column, destroyed by the Communards, were rebuilt afterwards in exactly the same way so as to efface memories of the Commune's existence as much as possible" ("The Camera against the Paris Commune," in Liz Heron and Val Williams, eds., *Illuminations: Women Writing on Photography from the 1850s to the Present* (London: I.B. Tauris, 1996), 26).

121 Georges Bell, *Paris Incendié: Histoire de la Commune de 1871* (Paris: E. Martinet, 1871).

122 Cited in Daryl Lee, "The Ambivalent Picturesque of the Paris Commune Ruins," *Nineteenth-Century Prose* 29, no. 2 (2002), 142. All translations of Bell are by Lee.

123 Lee, "Ambivalent," 146. See also chapter 5 of Colette Wilson's *Paris and the Commune* for a discussion of the period of tourism that followed the Commune in which photographs of ruins and shards of destroyed buildings were sold as souvenirs.

124 Furbank and Cain, *Mallarmé on Fashion*, 55.

125 Mallarmé, *Oeuvres complètes*, 523.

126 Furbank and Cain, *Mallarmé on Fashion*, 36.

127 Mallarmé, *Oeuvres complètes*, 501.

128 Furbank and Cain, *Mallarmé on Fashion*, 55.

129 Mallarmé, *Oeuvres complètes*, 523.

130 Furbank and Cain, *Mallarmé on Fashion*, 55.

131 Mallarmé, *Oeuvres complètes*, 523.

132 Furbank and Cain, *Mallarmé on Fashion*, 55.

133 Mallarmé, *Oeuvres complètes*, 523.

134 The *chapeau tyrolien* is favourably mentioned on three other occasions in *La Dernière Mode*, indicating that Mallarmé likely considered the hat highly fashionable. Yet, the accessory holds another possible allusion. In the 1870s the region of Tyrol was located, in part, in the southern territory of the German (formerly Prussian) Empire. One might also read Mallarmé's reference to the Tyrolean hat as the suggestion of a second (fashion) invasion of Paris by the Germanic forces that had controlled the city during the Siege of 1870–71.

135 Furbank and Cain, *Mallarmé on Fashion*, 55.

136 Mallarmé, *Oeuvres complètes*, 523.

137 Furbank and Cain, *Mallarmé on Fashion*, 55.

138 Mallarmé, *Oeuvres complètes*, 523.

139 Edmond de Goncourt, *Paris under Siege, 1870–1871: From the Goncourt Journal*, translated by George J. Becker (Ithaca: Cornell University Press, 1969), 310.

140 Cited in Janice Best, *Les Monuments de Paris sous la Troisième République: Contestation et Commémoration du passé* (Paris: L'Harmattan, 2010), 38.

141 Mallarmé, *Oeuvres complètes*, 492.

142 Cited in Lee, "Ambivalent," 153.

143 Ibid.

144 Simon Garfield, *Mauve: How One Man Invented a Color that Changed the World* (New York: W.W. Norton, 2002), 81.

145 For more on the fashionability of Renoir's *Parisienne*, see Iskin, *Modern Women*, 204–7.
146 Zola, *Ladies' Delight*, 39.
147 Zola, *Rougon-Macquart*, 3: 425.
148 Ibid.
149 Lee, "Ambivalent," 150.
150 The use of fashion to aestheticize the Commune may today be arriving at its most extreme – and commodified – expression by way of the contemporary French clothing company, La Commune de Paris 1871 (http://www.communedeparis.fr/accueil). The boutique fashion house, which debuted in 2010, sells garments, accessories, and home furnishings featuring violence-inspired graphic art including disembodied heads and pistols, T-shirts with political-sounding slogans such as "Couragé et Liberté," and a blue, white, and red colour scheme. In this way, it creates associations between its products and these evocations of the Commune that, despite their occasional historical inaccuracies, nonetheless resonate in popular culture today as fashionably "revolutionary." (Indeed, the "Couragé et Liberté" slogan derives from a misspelled banner which was fabricated during the French Revolution, not the Commune some eighty years later. The banner hangs today, coincidentally, in a starcase in Paris's Musée Carnavalet. I am grateful to Philippe de Carbonnières, conservator in the museum's Revolutionary and Imperial collection, for sharing with me his expertise about this object, and to Gérard Leyris for facilitating my research at the Musée Carnavalet.) Advertisements on the company's webpage include rifles and miniature canons as well as red ribbons streaming from shirts that are meant to simulate blood. In its efforts to capitalize on it the company simultaneously glorifies and tempers the violence of the historical event. Ironically, the clothing line, which makes light of the very brutality of the Commune that Zola found so disturbing, is today carried by Le Bon Marché, the original model for the novelist's fictional department store.
151 "Intime," *A History of Feminine Fashion* (London: Ed. J. Burrow and Co., 192?), 8.
152 Zola, *Ladies' Delight*, 260–1.
153 Zola, *Rougon-Macquart*, 3: 642.
154 Steven Wilson, "Nana, Prostitution and the Textual Foundations of Zola's *Au Bonheur des Dames*," *Nineteenth-Century French Studies* 41, nos. 1–2 (2012–13), 94.

155 This was not Zola's first depiction of clothing as animate. Describing the vibrant green and black garment in Claude Monet's 1866 painting *Camille*, Zola once asserted, "Notice the dress, how supple it is, how solid. It trails softly, it is alive, it declares loud and clear who this woman is" (cited in Gloria Groom, "Claude Monet: *Camille*," in Groom, *Impressionism, Fashion and Modernity*, 46).

156 Walter Benjamin, "Theses on the Philosophy of History," in Hannah Arendt, ed., *Illuminations*, translated by Harry Zohn (New York: Schocken, 1969), 257.

157 This intention is reflected in the subtitle of the *Rougon-Macquart*: "Natural and Social History of a Family under the Second Empire" ["Histoire naturelle et sociale d'une famille sous le Second Empire"].

158 Michael Mayerfeld Bell, "The Ghosts of Place," *Theory and Society* 26, no. 6 (1997), 813. See also Matlock, "Everyday Ghosts."

159 Bell, "Ghosts," 813.

2   Ups and Downs, Surface and Spectacle

1 Melanie Hawthorne examines Rachilde's short hair, questioning whether the rumours about it – the length of time she kept it clipped and what caused her to cut it – were truthful or rather an exaggeration spread largely by the author herself. See her *Rachilde and French Women's Authorship: From Decadence to Modernism* (Lincoln: University of Nebraska Press, 2001), esp. chapter 9, "The Photograph Never Lies."

2 George Sand (1804–1876), for instance, had already paved the way by wearing men's clothes in public earlier in the century. High-profile women celebrities from Rachilde's era, such as Colette (1873–1954) and Sarah Bernhardt (1844–1923), were also known to cross-dress. Rachilde can be situated within this group of women artists, whose reputations were built partly upon the public's knowledge (or perception) of their proclivities for wearing men's clothing.

3 See Hawthorne, *Rachilde*, and Diana Holmes, *Rachilde: Decadence, Gender and the Woman Writer* (Oxford: Berg, 2001).

4 Hawthorne, *Rachilde*, 145.

5 Those few who have studied Rachilde's works of theatre include Frazer Lively, "Rachilde, the Actor's Spectre, and Symbolist Dramaturgy: The Staging of *Madame La Mort*," *Nineteenth Century Theater* 23, nos. 1–2 (1995), 33–66; Melanie C. Hawthorne, introduction to *The Juggler*, translated by Melanie C. Hawthorne (New Brunswick, NJ: Rutgers University

Press, 1990); and Frantisek Deak, *Symbolist Theater* (Baltimore: Johns Hopkins University Press, 1993).

6 See Hawthorne, *Rachilde*; Holmes, *Rachilde*; Beizer, *Ventriloquized Bodies*; Dorothy Kelly, *Fictional Genders: Role and Representation in Nineteenth-Century French Narrative* (Lincoln: University of Nebraska Press, 1989); and Rita Felski, *The Gender of Modernity* (Cambridge, MA: Harvard University Press, 1995).

7 Rachilde, *Materialist*, 7.

8 Rachilde, *Monsieur Vénus*, 23. The opening pages of *La Jongleuse*, also set on a staircase, will be the subject of subsequent analysis.

9 Rachilde, *Materialist*, 97.

10 Rachilde, *Monsieur Vénus*, 110.

11 Rachilde, *Materialist*, 97.

12 Rachilde, *Monsieur Vénus*, 111.

13 The police ordinance forbidding women to wear men's clothing, a law established as a part of the Napoleonic Code of 1800 (although unenforced for many years), was finally repealed in 2013. Gretchen Van Slyke reproduces the 1800 ordinance which states, "Any woman, wishing to dress as a man, must present herself to the prefecture of police to obtain authorization" ["Toute femme, désirant s'habiller en homme, devra se présenter à la préfecture de police pour en obtenir l'autorisation"] ("Rebuilding the Bastille: Women's Dress-Code Legislation in the Nineteenth Century," in Carrol F. Coates, ed., *Repression and Expression: Literary and Social Coding in Nineteenth-Century France* (New York: Peter Lang, 1992), 217). Van Slyke notes that the French distinguished themselves from their English and German neighbours by stipulating that cross-dressing outside of carnival time was illegal for women but not necessarily for men. Rachilde was well aware of the laws against cross-dressing, as suggested by a letter that she sent to the Préfet of Police requesting official permission to wear men's clothing. See Hawthorne, *Rachilde*, 101–13, for a nuanced study of this letter and Rachilde's likely exaggerated reputation as a cross-dresser.

14 Rachilde, *Materialist*, 98.

15 Rachilde, *Monsieur Vénus*, 112.

16 Information on precisely how many women were actively cross-dressing and to what degree during this period is scant. However, Hawthorne provides persuasive evidence from contemporary newspapers to suggest that the practice was being adopted by far more than the ten women who had reportedly received official permission (*Rachilde*, 108).

17 Rachilde, *Materialist*, 99.

18 Rachilde, *Monsieur Vénus*, 112.
19 Rachilde, *Materialist*, 100.
20 Rachilde, *Monsieur Vénus*, 113.
21 Rachilde, *Materialist*, 100.
22 Rachilde, *Monsieur*, 113.
23 The philosopher Denis Diderot (1713–1784) originated the notion of "staircase wit" in *The Paradox of Acting* [*Paradoxe sur le comédien*], a text written in the 1770s but published posthumously in 1830. Diderot recalls an episode in which he was unable to think of a retort to another's comment until he found himself at the bottom of the stairs. This architectural detail would have suggested his departure from the premises by way of the ground floor exit, thus indicating that his reply had come too late: "This challenge disconcerts me and reduces me to silence, because a sensitive man, like myself, completely absorbed by objections against him, loses his head, and regains his wits only at the bottom of the staircase" ["Cette apostrophe me déconcerte et me réduit au silence, parce que l'homme sensible, comme moi, tout entier à ce qu'on lui objecte, perd la tête, et ne se retrouve qu'au bas de l'escalier"] (*Paradoxe sur le comédien* (Paris: A. Sautelet et Cie, 1830), 37). White fittingly cites Diderot's *esprit de l'escalier* in his analysis of a passage from *Pot-Bouille* in which Octave Mouret is left flustered and stuttering on a staircase ("Lost Heroine," 379).
24 Potvin, introduction, 9.
25 Hawthorne, introduction, xix.
26 Lively, "Rachilde," 48.
27 Rachilde, *The Juggler*, translated by Melanie C. Hawthorne (New Brunswick, NJ: Rutgers University Press, 1990), 205.
28 Rachilde, *La Jongleuse* (Paris: Des Femmes, 1982), 254.
29 *La Jongleuse* is composed of twelve chapters that alternate between extradiegetic narratives, which follow Léon's point of view, and epistolary exchanges between Léon and Eliante. This pattern, in which one narrated episode leads to one of letters, extends through the first ten chapters. In the final two chapters, Rachilde precipitously reverses this pattern, choosing to follow the tenth epistolary chapter with a brief telegrammed message from Eliante, comprising chapter 11. The omniscient narrator is thus in place to narrate the twelfth and final chapter, but in the electrifying dénouement, as Eliante literally performs her own death, Léon suddenly becomes the narrative focalizer.
30 In the program notes of the play's debut performance, Rachilde refers to *Madame La Mort* as a "drame cérébral" or "cerebral drama." Important to this discussion of spatiality in the novel is Rachilde's insistence that the

garden setting in Act II should not be understood literally and that the audience imagine it taking place in the mind rather than in an actual garden: "In saying: *cerebral drama*, I wanted to indicate that it concerns an action which, strictly speaking, has no locale … And if there is a setting called the *smoking room* or the *living room*, another called the *garden*, that is because it would be very difficult for everything to happen completely in the clouds. So I beg the spectators to let the setting count for almost nothing" (cited and translated by by Frazer Lively, introduction to *Madame La Mort and Other Plays*, translated and edited by Kiki Gounaridou and Frazer Lively (Baltimore: Johns Hopkins University Press, 1998), 21). Similarly, in *La Jongleuse*, the "cerebral" epistolary chapters do not take place in a designated physical space but rather in a sphere of pure textual discourse in which the characters can more freely express their emotions, uninhibited by the social expectations that spaces – like Eliante's mansion – place upon them in the intervening chapters.

31 See Hawthorne, introduction; Stephanie Schechner, "Dressing the Part: Fashion and Gender in Rachilde's *La Jongleuse*," *Excavatio* 20 (2005), 148–9; and Catherine McGann, "Juggling for Gender, Juggling for Love: Carnival in Rachilde's *La Jongleuse*," *La Revue Frontenac* 10–11 (1993–94), 177.

32 Hawthorne, introduction, xix.

33 Ibid., xx.

34 These include bringing herself to orgasm in the presence of Léon but without his participation (except insofar as he is a spectator) and presiding over exotic *tête-à-tête* meals with the young man.

35 I am grateful to one of the manuscript's anonymous readers for this observation. One major difference between play and novel is that in the former it is Paul who dies while in the latter Eliante, Madame La Mort herself, perishes from her self-inflicted injury.

36 Rachilde, *Juggler*, 6.

37 Rachilde, *Jongleuse*, 29.

38 Hawthorne, introduction, xx.

39 Rachilde, *Juggler*, 3.

40 Rachilde, *Jongleuse*, 25.

41 Rachilde, *Juggler*, 26. When Léon steps on her train ("her life"), he literally holds her back, symbolizing that he will permanently halt the progression of her life later when Eliante must kill herself to escape him as a dominating husband or lover. My thanks go to one of the manuscript's anonymous readers for suggesting this interpretation.

42 Rachilde, *Juggler*, 3.

43 Rachilde, *Jongleuse*, 26.

44 Rachilde, *Juggler*, 3.
45 Rachilde, *Jongleuse*, 26.
46 Schechner, "Dressing," 150.
47 Rachilde, *Juggler*, 6.
48 Rachilde, *Jongleuse*, 29.
49 Rachilde, *Juggler*, 4.
50 Rachilde, *Jongleuse*, 27.
51 Ibid.
52 Ibid.
53 Ibid.
54 Schechner provides an intriguing commentary on Rachilde's treatment of the body as a tool for both sensual gratification and power: "Bodies, for Rachilde, are not understood as biological entities, but rather as the conscious products of subjects who manipulate them at will for purposes of pleasure and social control" ("Dressing," 157).
55 Rachilde, *Juggler*, 106.
56 Rachilde, *Jongleuse*, 141. The fetishistic nature of Eliante's juggling costume is further evoked by the verb "sangler," which, as Schechner observes, evokes the word "blood" ["sang"] and can also mean to strike with a whip or strap ("Dressing," 156).
57 In 1901, one year after the appearance of *La Jongleuse*, sociologist Georg Simmel published the essay "Die Mode," a study of the dialectical tension in fashion to stimulate both conformity and distinction ("Die Mode," in Daniel Leonhard Purdy, ed., *The Fashion Reader* (Minneapolis: University of Minnesota Press, 2004), 289–309). For Simmel, the practice of constantly changing one's clothing is feminized and linked to the prostitute, whose "hatred against everything that has the sanction of law, of every permanent institution" is expressed in "the striving for ever new forms of appearance" (301). Simmel concludes that the prostitute's "continual striving for new, previously unheard-of fashions" constitutes "an aesthetic expression of the desire for destruction" (301). Among other things, Simmel's analysis lacks the impetus to view the prostitute as an expressive subject whose circumstances place her in the precarious position of needing to perform a multitude of selves through dress. Rachilde's novel provides a far more nuanced portrait of a woman's possible motivations to transform herself sartorially, pointing to this form of costuming as a method of identity expression while not denying its tolls on the wearer to reinvent herself incessantly. However, perhaps because Rachilde could empathize with Eliante's plight, *La Jongleuse* textually – and pessimistically – upholds Simmel's notion of the

performing woman's "desire for destruction" by condemning Eliante to take her own life. Even if her suicide is described as an expression of "supernatural joy," it is ultimately a destruction not of one but of the many identities Eliante has created.

58 Rachilde, *Juggler*, 4.

59 Rachilde, *Jongleuse*, 27.

60 Rachilde, *Juggler*, 18.

61 Rachilde, *Jongleuse*, 44.

62 For more on Fuller, see Rhonda K. Garelick, *Electric Salome: Loie Fuller's Performance of Modernism* (Princeton: Princeton University Press, 2009).

63 Quoted in Garelick, *Electric Salome*, 5.

64 Rachilde, *Juggler*, 5.

65 Rachilde, *Jongleuse*, 27–8.

66 Rachilde, *Juggler*, 5.

67 Rachilde, *Jongleuse*, 28.

68 We will return to the intersections of fashion and electrical flash photography in chapter 6.

69 McGann, "Juggling," 174.

70 Rachilde, *Juggler*, 109.

71 Rachilde, *Jongleuse*, 145.

72 McGann, "Juggling," 174.

73 James H. Johnson, "Paul Verlaine, Masks, and the French Fin-de-Siècle," *H-France Salon* 5, no. 1 (2013), YouTube video, 21:25, from the Panel "The Social Imaginary in Nineteenth-Century France," Society for French Historical Studies 59th Annual Meeting, Cambridge, MA, 5 Apr. 2013, posted by H-France2, 19 Apr. 2013, http://www.h-france.net/Salon/h-francesalon.html. I am grateful to Professor Johnson for his permission to cite this work.

74 Norma Broude, ed., *Gustave Caillebotte and the Fashioning of Identity in Impressionist Paris* (New Brunswick, NJ: Rutgers University Press, 2002), 1.

75 For an account of the rise in interest in Caillebotte's works since the 1970s, see Broude's introduction to *Gustave Caillebotte*.

76 Karin Sagner, "Gustave Caillebotte: An Impressionist and Photography," in Karin Sagner and Max Hollein, eds., *Gustave Caillebotte: An Impressionist and Photography* (Munich: Hirmer-Verlag, 2012), 21.

77 See Varnedoe's *Gustave Caillebotte* for more on the painter's perspectival manipulations.

78 These vertical views were one of the themes highlighted in several recent exhibitions featuring Caillebotte's paintings and period photographs. One exhibit focused on the painter's works alongside photographs by his

brother Martiel and was held first at Paris's Musée Jacquemart-André in 2011 and then at the Musée National des Beaux-Arts de Québec in 2012. Another exhibit, "Gustave Caillebotte: An Impressions and Photography," was held in Frankfurt in 2012–13. For the first see, Serge Lemoine et al., *De l'Intimité des frères Caillebotte: Peintre et photographe* (Paris: Skira Flammarion, 2011); for the last, see the catalogue edited by Sagner (cited above).

79 Van Zanten, "Looking," 154.

80 Michael Fried, "Caillebotte's Impressionism," in Broude, *Gustave Caillebotte*, 72.

81 One can contrast Caillebotte's views from windows and balconies on high with Manet's earlier *Le Balcon* (1868–69), which situates the spectator directly across from the subjects on the balcony and frames it in isolation from the rest of the building, thus de-emphasizing the notion of verticality.

82 There seems to be a trend correlating the work of visual artists and family histories in material fashion. Tissot, another painter whose works reflect a strong interest in clothing, had parents who worked in the textile and garment industries (Guy Cogéval and Stéphane Guégan, "James Tissot: *The Circle of the Rue Royale*," in Groom, *Impressionism, Fashion, and Modernity*, 146). Auguste Renoir's father and mother were a tailor and a dressmaker, respectively (Groom, "Social Network," 35), and may have influenced the artist's taste for painting scintillating gowns.

83 For an original reading of Caillebotte's treatment of masculine fashion as a sign of his ambivalence towards the privileges accorded to him by his class, see Tamar Garb, "Masculinity, Muscularity and Modernity in Caillebotte's Male Figures," in Broude, *Gustave Caillebotte*, 183–5.

84 Perhaps the most famous example is the chapter entitled "A Bird's-Eye View of Paris" ["Paris à vol d'oiseau"] in Victor Hugo's 1831 *Notre-Dame de Paris*. Gazing down upon the panorama of the city also occurs in texts by Balzac, Baudelaire, and Zola, which Prendergast explores in his chapter "The High View: Three Cityscapes" (in *Paris*). For a comparison of literary portraits of Paris and Algiers from the mid-1800s that view both cities from on high, see Seth Graebner, "The Bird's-Eye View: Looking at the City in Paris and Algiers," *Nineteenth-Century French Studies* 36, nos. 3&4 (2008), 221–39.

85 Attesting to his enduring popularity, many of Maupassant's writings have been adapted to film and television in numerous languages. Recent screen versions include a 2007 series of French telefilms based on a selection of short stories interpreted by New Wave director Claude

Chabrol, and the 2012 English-language movie *Bel-Ami* starring a high-profile Hollywood cast.

86 Bernard Urbani, "Espace et récit dans *Sapho* d'Alphonse Daudet," in Christian Chelebourg, ed., *Écritures XIX: Alphonse Daudet, pluriel et singulier* (Dives-sur-mer: Minard, 2003), 266.

87 Maupassant, *Romans*, 210.

88 Ibid.

89 Maupassant, *Bel-Ami*, 43–4.

90 Maupassant, *Romans*, 211.

91 One is reminded of the mirror on the staircase landing in Rachilde's *La Jongleuse*. However, in Rachilde's novel, Eliante does not contemplate her own reflection in the manner of Duroy, for all she can see is the image of Léon in pursuit of her. This contrast is highly gendered and might relate to thoughts that Rachilde may have been having later in her career about the modes of creative expression available to her, namely, performance and writing. As a woman in a publicly attended staircase, Eliante performs not for herself, like Duroy, but only for the invasive eyes of her male audience. In the odd-numbered "performance" chapters of *La Jongleuse*, she cannot attain what might be thought of as a subjective imaginary order, to borrow Lacanian terminology, which is accessible to the male Duroy, peering at his virtual self in the mirror. Instead, Eliante's subjective ability to tell her own story, to construct herself through self-narration, is limited to the even-numbered "cerebral" chapters of the novel, which are not composed of dazzling performances but, significantly, of intimate letters. By 1900, Rachilde's reputation as a scandalous cross-dressing authoress/performer had become a part of her past, yet she continued to produce texts at a prolific rate. Perhaps, like Eliante, she had found that writing, enacted privately, was a more viable arena for self-expression than the public world of self-fashioning that had been her stage during the previous decades.

92 Maupassant, *Bel-Ami*, 44.

93 Maupassant, *Romans*, 211.

94 Maupassant, *Bel-Ami*, 35.

95 Maupassant, *Romans*, 204.

96 Claudine Giacchetti, "La Conquête de l'espace dans *Bel-Ami*," *Revue Romane* 26, no. 2 (1991), 222.

97 Mary Louise Roberts, *Disruptive Acts: The New Woman in Fin-de-siecle France* (Chicago: University of Chicago Press, 2002), 230–1.

98 Foucault, "Other," 63.

99 Ibid., 66–7.

100 Stirling Haig, *The Madame Bovary Blues* (Baton Rouge: Louisiana State University Press, 1987), 161.
101 Ibid., 162.
102 The Forestiers' apartment where Duroy launches himself into high society is another heterotopia possessing the same conditions of entry as the staircase. The staircase is a conduit between two such spaces: the landing mirrors and the Forestiers' home.
103 Foucault, "Other," 63.
104 Maupassant volunteered for and served as an artillery soldier in the French army during the Franco-Prussian War of 1870–71 that ushered in the Commune. Interestingly, and not unlike Zola's works before the early 1890s, the Commune does not appear overtly in Maupassant's writings. Geoffrey Strickland, commenting on this lacuna, declares, "There is not a single allusion, incidentally, in the whole of Maupassant's fiction, as far as I have discovered, to the events of the Commune, despite the importance he gives in all his major writings to contemporary social history" ("Maupassant, Zola, Jules Vallès and the Paris Commune of 1871," *Journal of European Studies* 13 (1983), 294). The absence of direct references to the Commune in Maupassant's texts would seem further evidence of a generalized trauma among fiction writers following the horrific event, one that manifested itself in relative textual omission.
105 Foucault, "Other," 63.
106 Maupassant, *Bel-Ami*, 44
107 Maupassant, *Romans*, 211.
108 Maupassant, *Bel-Ami*, 44.
109 Maupassant, *Romans*, 211.
110 Foucault, "Other," 61.
111 Maupassant, *Bel-Ami*, 44.
112 Maupassant, *Romans*, 211.
113 Maupassant, *Bel-Ami*, 44.
114 Maupassant, *Romans*, 211.
115 Maupassant, *Bel-Ami*, 44.
116 Maupassant, *Romans*, 211.
117 Maupassant, *Bel-Ami*, 59.
118 Maupassant, *Romans*, 222.
119 Maupassant, *Bel-Ami*, 59.
120 Maupassant, *Romans*, 222.
121 As Giacchetti puts it, rather than emphasizing Duroy's ascent, "the gaze that transcends this space does not follow a trajectory of flight, because the opening leads us downward" ["le regard qui transcend cet espace ne

suit pas une trajectoire d'envol, car c'est vers le bas que nous entraîne l'ouverture"] ("La Conquête," 227).

122 Maupassant, *Bel-Ami*, 180.

123 Maupassant, *Romans*, 312.

124 Maupassant, *Bel-Ami*, 184.

125 Maupassant, *Romans*, 316.

126 Maupassant, *Bel-Ami*, 416.

127 Maupassant, *Romans*, 480.

128 Maupassant, *Bel-Ami*, 412.

129 Maupassant, *Romans*, 477.

130 Maupassant, *Bel-Ami*, 412.

131 Maupassant, *Romans*, 477.

132 Maupassant, *Bel-Ami*, 59.

133 Maupassant, *Romans*, 222.

134 Maupassant, *Bel-Ami*, 59.

135 Maupassant, *Romans*, 222.

136 Maupassant, *Bel-Ami*, 61.

137 Maupassant, *Romans*, 222.

138 The two figures are typically understood as Caillebotte and his brother Martial, who shared the flat on Boulevard Haussmann.

139 Urbani, "Espace," 259.

140 Alphonse Daudet, *Sapho* (Paris: Flammarion, 1995), 10.

141 Ibid., 9.

142 Translation of *Sapho*, 7–8.

143 Daudet, *Sapho*, 9.

144 Urbani, "Espace," 262.

145 Ibid.

146 Translation of *Sapho*, 11.

147 Daudet, *Sapho*, 12.

148 Translation of *Sapho*, 6.

149 Daudet, *Sapho*, 8.

150 Daudet's father had worked in the silk industry in the fabric's nineteenth-century capital, Lyon. As with painters of the era including Caillebotte, Tissot, and Renoir, Daudet's interest in this shimmering cloth may have been informed by his family's involvement in the textile trade.

151 Daudet, *Sapho*, 11.

152 Translation of *Sapho*, 13.

153 Daudet, *Sapho*, 13.

154 Translation of *Sapho*, 13.

155 Daudet, *Sapho*, 13.

156 Translation of *Sapho*, 13.
157 Daudet, *Sapho*, 13.
158 Translation of *Sapho*, 13.
159 Daudet, *Sapho*, 13.
160 Translation of *Sapho*, 13.
161 Daudet, *Sapho*, 13. The reference to Jean as a "piano mover" ["déména-geur de piano"] (ibid.) may be Daudet's tongue-in-cheek architectural reference to the *piano nobile* or "noble floor," an Italian phrase referring to the second storey that wealthy inhabitants of cities like Venice preferred over rooms on the ground floor that were musty and allowed in less light. The practice was common in France as well as in Italy. For more on the significance of the second floor in connection to the haute couture *maison*, see my discussion of Renée Saccard's *cabinet de toilette* in chapter 5.
162 Translation of *Sapho*, 9.
163 Daudet, *Sapho*, 13.
164 In nineteenth-century literature, the ascension of staircases when characters change lodgings often coincides with financial ruin, creating a rising-while-falling paradox. Balzac's Père Goriot, for example, moves to increasingly higher floors as his retirement money is squandered, and the Loisels in Maupassant's "La Parure" advance to lodgings up long flights of stairs after falling into massive debt. There is an architectural logic to this trope since, as Zola's *Pot-Bouille* illustrates, apartments on lower floors were often larger and more luxurious than higher flats, which lodged those of more modest means. Typically, apartments on the highest floors having the most arduous stair climbs were, not surprisingly, reserved for servants and poor students like Jean who could not afford to live on the more easily accessed storeys below. Caillebotte complicates this somewhat in his paintings by rendering the height of his building in the deluxe, newly contructed quarter behind the Opéra an emblem of optical power echoing the social prestige of wealthy fourth-floor inhabitants like himself.
165 Foucault ends his discussion of heterotopias with a lyrical description of the ship as "the heterotopia par excellence" ("Other," 68). For him, ships are symbols of imagination that thwart the regulatory operations of power that modern society has put into place: "In civilizations without boats," he writes, "dreams dry up, espionage takes the place of adventure, and the police take the place of pirates" (68).
166 Although the novel indicates that Arica is in Peru, the city was in fact lost to Chile as a result of the War of the Pacific involving Peru, Bolivia, and Chile (1879–84). Daudet likely would have been aware of this conflict,

which was highly publicized in the press. Given the simultaneity of *Sapho*'s serial publication in 1884, it may be the case that Daudet's naming of Peru as the location for Arica was a political commentary against the annexation.

167 I am grateful to Kate Baltais for this observation.

168 Traugott, *Insurgent Barricade*, 189.

3   Waiting for Change

1 For other treatments of these themes in nineteenth-century French literature, see, e.g., Larry Duffy, *Le Grand Transit Moderne: Mobility, Modernity and French Naturalist Fiction* (Amsterdam: Rodopi, 2005); and David F. Bell, *Real Time: Accelerating Narrative from Balzac to Zola* (Champaign: University of Illinois Press, 2004).

2 Clark, *Painting*, 257.

3 John Culbert, *Paralyses: Literature, Travel, and Ethnography in French Modernity* (Lincoln: University of Nebraska Press, 2011), 12.

4 Ibid., 7.

5 Iskin makes a similar case for fashion as the sole presence of movement in an otherwise immobile scenario in her analysis of Degas's *Les Modistes* (c. 1882 – before 1905). She points out that the multihued ribbons hanging from the hats in this painting are the only objects conveying motion against the milliner's inert expression and body: "The brightly colored ribbons stand out in the painting by their relatively large size and the yellow, pink, orange and green pastel contrast with the muted colors in the rest of the painting. These ribbons, as yet unformed materials to be used for ornamentation, are the only animated forms in the painting" (*Modern Women*, 110). See chapter 6 for my analysis of the space of the woman fashion worker in this same painting.

6 Clark examines a very similar hat in Manet's *Argenteuil, les canotiers* (1874). For Clark, the hat in Manet's work is imbued with a "flatness" that the painter used in many of his works as a metaphor for the expressionless ennui of modern life (*Painting*, 253). Somewhat in contrast, then, is the sense of vibrancy and fullness evoked in Clark's own description of the hat in Manet's work: "onto the surface is spread that wild twist of tulle, piped onto the oval like cream on a cake, smeared on like a great flourishing brushmark, blown up to impossible size" (164). Like the hat in Degas' painting, Clark's lively portrayal of this fashion object evokes animation and fullness, which offset the notion of splenetic flatness.

7 The first two definitions of the term *antichambre* listed in the *Trésor* are: "Entryway providing access to other rooms" ["Pièce d'entrée qui donne accès aux autres pieces"] and "Room that serves as a waiting room" ["Pièce qui sert de salle d'attente"](*Le Trésor de la Langue Française informatisé*).

8 Clayson, "Threshold Space," 15.

9 Rachilde, *Materialist*, 46.

10 Rachilde, *Monsieur Vénus*, 63.

11 Rachilde, *Materialist*, 46.

12 Rachilde, *Monsieur Vénus*, 63.

13 Rachilde, *Materialist*, 46.

14 Rachilde, *Monsieur Vénus*, 63.

15 *Le Trésor de la Langue Française informatisé*.

16 Ibid.

17 Ibid.

18 That the antagonism between two female characters is unleashed in a changing room in Madame Desforges's boudoir resonates with Jane Gallop's reading of divisions staged between women in the titular space of the Marquis de Sade's *La Philosophie dans le boudoir* ("The Liberated Woman," *Narrative* 13, no. 2 (2005), 95). For Gallop, the hostilities of women towards other women set in Sade's "very female" (94) boudoir allegorize troubling enmities existing in feminism of the twentieth century. I thank one of the manuscript's anonymous readers for pointing me to this reference.

19 The notion of Denise's servitude to Henriette is introduced two chapters earlier during the Bonheur's second sale, when Denise already senses Mme Desforges's "desire to treat her as a servant" (Zola, *Ladies' Delight*, 257) ["volonté de la traiter en servante"] (Zola, *Rougon-Macquart*, 3: 638).

20 Zola, *Ladies' Delight*, 305.

21 Zola, *Rougon-Macquart*, 3: 685.

22 Zola, *Ladies' Delight*, 304.

23 Zola, *Rougon-Macquart*, 3: 684.

24 Zola, *Ladies' Delight*, 303.

25 Zola, *Rougon-Macquart*, 3: 683. Madame Desforges's conflation of shop workers and domestic servants transcends gender, as suggested by an earlier passage describing a male employee who is similarly equated with a chambermaid. In this scene, Madame Desforges offers her hand to glove salesman Mignot "as calmly as she would give her foot to the chamber-maid who was buttoning her boots" (Zola, *Ladies' Delight*, 99) ["de l'air

tranquille dont elle elle donnait son pied à sa femme de chambre, pour que celle-ci boutonnnât ses bottines"] (Zola, *Rougon-Macquart* 3: 484). Mignot tries to use seduction to charm her into making a purchase but Madame Desforges is immune to his allure, prompting Zola's comment that "he was not a man" (Zola, *Ladies' Delight*, 99); "Il n'était pas un homme" (Zola, *Rougon-Macquart* 3: 484). Mignot's position at the Bonheur does more than link him to domestic servitude: it also emasculates and desexualizes him.

26 Zola, *Ladies' Delight*, 302–3.

27 Zola, *Rougon-Macquart*, 3: 682.

28 Zola, *Ladies' Delight*, 302.

29 Zola, *Rougon-Macquart*, 3: 682.

30 Zola, *Ladies' Delight*, 312.

31 Zola, *Rougon-Macquart*, 3: 692.

32 In haute couture fashion houses, which will be discussed at length in chapters 5 and 6, the pin girl was at the bottom of the hierarchy of seamstresses. De Marly observes that "the humblest member of staff in a couture house was the *arpette*, the apprentice, the girl who picked up the pins" (*History*, 99).

33 Mary Donaldson-Evans, "Pricking the Male Ego: Pins and Needles in Flaubert, Maupassant and Zola," *Nineteenth-Century French Studies* 30, nos. 3–4 (2002), 262.

34 Ibid.

35 Zola, *Ladies' Delight*, 314.

36 Zola, *Rougon-Macquart*, 3: 694.

37 As readers familiar with the novel will recognize, the two antechambers in this chapter are a microcosm for the troubling of formerly rigid social hierarchies occurring throughout *Au Bonheur des Dames* more generally. When describing the female staff of the department store, for example, Zola writes that "mixing daily with the customers, almost all the assistants took on airs and ended up in an indistinct social class, somewhere between the workers and the bourgeoisie" (*Ladies' Delight*, 152) ["Presque toutes les vendeuses, dans leur frottement quotidien avec la clientèle riche, prenaient des grâces, finissaient par être d'une classe vague, flottant entre l'ouvrière et la bourgeoisie"] (*Rougon-Macquart*, 3: 536). Neither fully working class nor respectably bourgeois, the salesclerks at the Bonheur exemplify a new, category-resistant class that, by its very indeterminateness, points to instabilities in social hierarchies. As in the antechamber, Zola uses fashion throughout the novel to illustrate the

class confusion inherent to the department store sales staff. Most memorable is his portrait of an impoverished Denise wearing a uniform made from the same luxury fabric that her affluent clients wear. This juxtaposition of sumptuous cloth and Denise's poverty makes her the class-defying paradox of "poverty in a silk dress" ["la misère en robe de soie"] (3: 507).

38 Starr, *Commemorating Trauma*, 157.

39 When Denise assists Madame Desforges at the second Bonheur sale, for instance, she is described as "patient and motionless" (Zola, *Ladies' Delight*, 255) ["immobile et patiente"] (Zola, *Rougon-Macquart* 3: 636). Earlier she helps Madame Desforges with a "patient serenity" (*Ladies' Delight*, 253) ["serenité dans la patience"] (*Rougon-Macquart*, 3: 634) that irritates her jealous rival.

40 Zola, *Ladies' Delight*, 305.

41 Zola, *Rougon-Macquart*, 3: 685.

42 Zola, *Ladies' Delight*, 359.

43 Zola, *Rougon-Macquart*, 3: 739.

44 Denise's improvements to working conditions echo those realized in the early 1870s by the Boucicauts, owners of the Bon Marché department store, which served as the main inspiration for Zola's fictional Bonheur. In the novel, these initiatives include retirement benefits for workers and the eradication of mass lay-offs, as well as enrichments such as a library, a games room, and classes on music, languages, and sports (*Rougon-Macquart*, 3: 728–9).

45 Zola, *Ladies' Delight*, 317.

46 Zola, *Rougon-Macquart*, 3: 697.

47 Zola, *Ladies' Delight*, 317.

48 Zola, *Rougon-Macquart*, 3: 697.

49 Brian Nelson's description of Aristide Saccard, Octave Mouret's precursor from the earlier *Rougon-Macquart* novel *La Curée*, could equally apply to Zola's attitude about the department store owner of *Au Bonheur*: "Zola's indictment of Second Empire society is unrelenting; but at the same time he cannot help admiring his protagonist for his phenomenal dynamism, which places him on the side of modernity and, for Zola, on the side of life and of the future" (introduction to *The Kill* by Emile Zola (Oxford: Oxford University Press, 2008), xxix).

50 I give the word "present" in quotation marks since the years of the Second Empire are the setting for his novels but Zola was, of course, writing after its fall.

51 Starr, *Commemorating Trauma*, 166.
52 Zola, *Ladies' Delight*, 321.
53 Zola, *Rougon-Macquart*, 3: 701.
54 Ibid., 2: 1664.
55 Emily Apter, "Celebrity Gifting: Mallarmé and the Poetics of Fame," in Edward Berenson and Eva Giloi, eds., *Constructing Charisma: Celebrity, Fame and Power in Nineteenth-Century Europe* (New York: Berghahn, 2010), 91.
56 Zola, *Rougon-Macquart*, 2: 1664.
57 Emile Zola, *Oeuvres complètes*, edited by Henri Mitterand (Paris: Cercle du livre précieux, 1962–69), 10: 1403–4.
58 See Janet Beizer, "Uncovering *Nana*: The Courtesan's New Clothes," *L'Esprit Créateur* 25, no. 2 (1985), 45–56; Peter Brooks, "Storied Bodies, or Nana at Last Unveil'd," *Critical Inquiry* 16, no. 1 (1989), 1–32; Dolan, "Guise and Dolls"; Thompson, *Naturalism Redressed*; and Heidi Brevik-Zender, "Tracking Fashions: Risking It All at the Hippodrome de Longchamp," in Potvin, *The Places and Spaces of Fashion*, 19–33.
59 Zola, *Nana*, 24.
60 Zola, *Rougon-Macquart*, 2: 1100.
61 Zola, *Nana*, 24.
62 Zola, *Rougon-Macquart*, 2: 1100.
63 Zola, *Nana*, 25–6.
64 Zola, *Rougon-Macquart*, 2: 1101.
65 Zola, *Nana*, 20.
66 Zola, *Rougon-Macquart*, 2: 1096.
67 Zola, *Nana*, 23.
68 Zola, *Rougon-Macquart*, 2: 1099.
69 Ibid., 1132.
70 Zola, *Nana*, 62.
71 Zola, *Rougon-Macquart*, 2: 1133.
72 Ibid.
73 Zola, *Nana*, 73.
74 Zola, *Rougon-Macquart*, 2: 1143.
75 Zola, *Nana*, 63.
76 Zola, *Rougon-Macquart*, 2: 1135.
77 Zola, *Nana*, 63.
78 Zola, *Rougon-Macquart*, 2: 1135.
79 Zola, *Nana*, 72.
80 Zola, *Rougon-Macquart*, 2: 1144.
81 Ibid., 2: 1347.

82 For more on the style of Haussmann's residential buildings, see Marcus, *Apartment Stories,* and Van Zanten, "Looking."

83 Zola, *Nana,* 312.

84 Zola, *Rougon-Macquart,* 2: 1347.

85 Emile Zola, *L'Invention des lieux,* edited by Olivier Lumbroso (Paris: Les Éditions Textuel, 2002), 404–5.

86 Zola, *Nana,* 144.

87 Zola, *Rougon-Macquart,* 2: 1203.

88 Zola, *Nana,* 144.

89 Zola, *Rougon-Macquart,* 2: 1203.

90 David Baguley, *Emile Zola, L'Assommoir* (Cambridge: Cambridge University Press, 1992), 40.

91 Zola, *Nana,* 21.

92 Zola, *Rougon-Macquart,* 2: 1097.

93 Zola, *Nana,* 144.

94 Zola, *Rougon-Macquart,* 2: 1203.

95 Zola, *Nana,* 145.

96 Zola, *Rougon-Macquart,* 2: 1204.

97 See Brevik-Zender, "Tracking Fashions" for more on the fashionability of the Bois de Boulogne horse races.

98 Zola, *Nana,* 352.

99 Zola, *Rougon-Macquart,* 2: 1382.

100 *Le Trésor de la Langue Française informatisé.*

101 Charles Baudelaire, *Oeuvres complètes,* edited by Claude Pichois, 2 vols. (Paris: Gallimard, 1975–76), 2: 468.

102 Ibid.

103 I am grateful to Kimberly Chrisman-Campbell for providing me explanations and resources about this accessory.

104 The Arrow collar is still worn today as part of a man's tuxedo ensemble.

105 Alan Flusser, *Dressing the Man: Mastering the Art of Permanent Fashion* (New York: HarperCollins, 2002), 122.

106 For the history and changing meanings of detachable collars in nineteenth- and twentieth-century America, see Carole Turbin, "Collars and Consumers: Changing Images of American Manliness and Business," *Enterprise and Society* 1, no. 3 (2002), 507–35.

107 John S. Farmer and W.E. Henley, eds., *Slang and Its Analogues Past and Present* (London: Harrison and Sons, 1891) 2: 252.

108 Turbin, "Collars," 512. For all of its pragmatic qualities, the turnover *col brisé* still does not seem to be a style that appealed to Zola personally, as

most photographs of the author wearing low, fully attached shirt collars would suggest.

109 Zola, *Rougon-Macquart*, 1: 560.

110 Zola, *Nana*, 35.

111 Zola, *Rougon-Macquart*, 2: 1110.

112 Zola, *Nana*, 436.

113 Zola, *Rougon-Macquart*, 2: 1456.

114 Zola, *Oeuvres complètes*, 10: 1173.

115 Ibid., 1194.

116 Ibid., 1193.

117 Ibid.

118 Ibid.

119 Ibid., 1200.

120 Zola, *Nana*, 311.

121 Zola, *Rougon-Macquart*, 2: 1346.

122 Zola, *Nana*, 345.

123 Zola, *Rougon-Macquart*, 2: 1376.

124 For more on the links between Nana's status as a high-class courtesan and a fashion trend-setter, see Dolan, "Guise and Dolls," and Brevik-Zender, "Tracking Fashions."

125 The theory of the "trickle-up" effect suggests that fashion originates not (only) in the privileged, wealthy classes but rather from the lower classes, whose styles "percolate up" into middle-class and haute couture garments. Dick Hebdige influentially examined the phenomenon in his classic study on punk fashion; see *Subculture: The Meaning of Style* (London: Methuen, 1979). Although the trend is thus associated most often with twentieth-century postmodernity, as Jennifer Craik submits, it can be traced much earlier (Jennifer Craik, *Fashion: The Key Concepts* (New York: Berg, 2009), 118).

126 Zola, *Nana*, 311.

127 Zola, *Rougon-Macquart*, 2: 1346.

128 Zola, *Nana*, 311.

129 Zola, *Rougon-Macquart*, 2: 1347. Citing similarities between the Empress Eugénie and the protagonist of Zola's novel, Dolan demonstrates that Nana is a (perverted) cipher for Napoléon III's stylish wife ("Guise and Dolls," 380). Through this overlapping of the noble woman and the prostitute, Zola uses Nana's fashionability to reiterate one of his favourite notions, that all women are equally perverted regardless of rank.

130 Zola, *Rougon-Macquart*, 2: 1659.

131 Ibid.

132 Ibid., 1666.
133 Ibid., 1677.
134 Ibid.
135 Zola, *Nana*, 221.
136 Zola, *Rougon-Macquart*, 2: 1269.
137 Ibid., 2: 1677.
138 Variants of the term "gai," including "gaieté," "gaillard," and "gaiement," appear numerous times throughout the Longchamp chapter of *Nana*. Interestingly, for this discussion on fashion, according to the *Oxford English Dictionary* one of the definitions of the term "gaiety" in English is "Bright appearance or ornamentation; showiness; showy dress" (*Oxford English Dictionary Online*). I have not been able to confirm a sartorial nuance in the French term, but as is often the case, the English word derives from Old and Middle French, thus it is possible that at one point the French word contained a connotation relating it to dress.
139 Zola, *Rougon-Macquart*, 2: 1692.
140 Ibid., 2: 1656.
141 For more on the bleak conditions in Paris during the Siege, see Part One of Alistair Horne, *The Fall of Paris: The Siege and the Paris Commune 1870–1871* (London: Macmillan, 1965). Lefebvre provides a contrasting narrative, wherein the Siege occasioned not immobility but rather fomented the revolutionary spirit that would explode during the subsequent Commune. For Lefebvre, Parisians during the Siege lived "an intense social life, in a spontaneous effervescence which quite naturally tends to become political" ["une vie sociale intense, dans une effervescence spontanée qui tend tout naturellement à devenir politique"] (*Proclamation*, 181). For him, the capital was a privileged locale of restless activity where "a mass in the making offered itself to our eyes, ready to take new forms, a sensitive, attentive, febrile mass, which had nothing in common with a passive milieu that might be troubled by exterior forces" ["une masse en fusion s'offre à nos yeux, prête à prendre des formes nouvelles, masse sensible, attentive, fébrile, mais qui n'a rien d'un milieu passif qu'agiteraient des forces extérieures"] (181).
142 John Milner, *Art, War and Revolution in France 1870–1871* (New Haven: Yale University Press, 2000), 125.

4 Maupassant, Transformation, and the Unexotic Exotic

1 Cited in Catherine Join-Diéterle, "Robes à transformation," in Join-Diéterle et al., *Sous l'Empire des crinolines*, 101.

2 Elizabeth Wilson elaborates on dress as a marker of "the compartmental-ized, obsessionally sub-divided life of the bourgeoisie" (*Adorned in Dreams*, 35). She notes, "There were morning gowns, tea gowns, dinner gowns, walking dress, travelling dress, dress for the country, dress (later) for different kinds of sport, deep mourning, second mourning, half mourning; costumes that no longer reflected a clear rank or status, but rather a socially defined time of day, or occasion, or an individual state of feeling" (35).

3 Steele, *Paris Fashion*, 123.

4 Catherine Join-Diéterle, "Revisiter le style Second Empire," in Join-Diéterle et al., *Sous l'Empire des crinolines*, 24.

5 Guy de Maupassant, "The Necklace," translated by David Coward, in *A Day in the Country and Other Stories* (Oxford: Oxford University Press, 1998), 175.

6 Guy de Maupassant, *Contes et nouvelles* (Paris: Gallimard, 1974), 1205.

7 Maupassant, "Necklace," 176.

8 Maupassant, *Contes*, 1205.

9 Maupassant, "Necklace," 168.

10 Maupassant, *Contes*, 1198.

11 Maupassant, "Necklace," 175.

12 Maupassant, *Contes*, 1205.

13 Mary Donaldson-Evans, "The Last Laugh: Maupassant's 'Les Bijoux' and 'La Parure,'" *French Forum* 10, no. 2 (1985), 167.

14 Wilson, *Adorned*, 246.

15 Maupassant, "Necklace," 169.

16 Maupassant, *Contes*, 1199.

17 Maupassant, "Necklace," 169.

18 Ibid.

19 Ibid.

20 Maupassant, *Contes*, 1199.

21 Floriane Place-Verghnes, "'La Parure': Pour une pragmatique de la défamiliarisation," *French Studies* 55, no. 1 (2003), 49.

22 Maupassant, "Necklace," 172.

23 Maupassant, *Contes*, 1202.

24 Maupassant, "Necklace," 172.

25 Maupassant, *Contes*, 1202.

26 Maupassant, "Necklace," 173.

27 Maupassant, *Contes*, 1203.

28 Donaldson-Evans, "Last Laugh," 169.

29 Maupassant, "Necklace," 168.

30 Maupassant, *Contes*, 1198–9.

31 Maupassant, "Necklace," 168.

32 Maupassant, *Contes*, 1198.

33 Maupassant, "Necklace," 176.

34 Maupassant, *Contes*, 1206.

35 Donaldson-Evans, "Last Laugh," 171.

36 Ibid., 170.

37 Maupassant, "Necklace," 176.

38 Maupassant, *Contes*, 1206.

39 Ibid.

40 Place-Verghnes, "Parure," 52.

41 Louis Forestier, notice to *Romans*, by Guy de Maupassant, edited by Louis Forestier (Paris: Gallimard, 1987), 1339.

42 Ibid.

43 For another (not incompatible) explanation, see Mary Louise Roberts's gloss of Madeleine's last name as it relates to the word "forest" (*forêt*), a location featured in a key passage involving this character. Roberts, *Disruptive Acts*, 236.

44 Maupassant, "Necklace," 175.

45 Maupassant, *Contes*, 1204.

46 Place-Verghnes, "Parure," 44.

47 Ross, *Emergence*, 4.

48 Hiner, *Accessories*, 77.

49 Ibid., 80.

50 Ibid., 83.

51 Ibid.

52 Heidi Brevik-Zender, "Fashion and Fractured Flânerie in Guy de Maupassant's *Bel-Ami*," *DIX-NEUF* 16, no. 2 (2012), 235.

53 Maupassant, *Bel-Ami*, 290.

54 Maupassant, *Romans*, 391.

55 Théophile Gautier, "Théâtres," *La Presse*, 6 Jan. 1845, 1.

56 Furbank and Cain, *Mallarmé on Fashion*, 107.

57 Mallarmé, *Oeuvres complètes*, 568.

58 Furbank and Cain, *Mallarmé on Fashion*, 154.

59 Mallarmé, *Oeuvres complètes*, 608.

60 Furbank and Cain, *Mallarmé on Fashion*, 198.

61 Mallarmé, *Oeuvres complètes*, 646.

62 Maupassant, *Bel-Ami*, 61.

63 Maupassant, *Romans*, 224.

64 Forestier, notice, 1362.

65 Maupassant, *Bel-Ami*, 61.
66 Maupassant, *Romans*, 224.
67 Maupassant, *Bel-Ami*, 290.
68 Maupassant, *Romans*, 391.
69 Iskin, *Modern Women*, 199, 204, 214. Degas's ballerinas, especially his famous sculpture of the *Petite danseuse de quatorze ans*, vividly capture the Parisienne's stylish up-turned nose.
70 Ibid., 218.
71 Ibid., 219.
72 Marni Reva Kessler, *Sheer Presence: The Veil in Manet's Paris* (Minneapolis: University of Minnesota Press, 2006), 100.
73 Ibid., 126.
74 Cited in Susan M. Barrow, "East/West: Appropriation of Aspects of the Orient in Maupassant's *Bel-Ami*," *Nineteenth-Century French Studies* 30, nos. 3&4 (2002), 316.
75 Ibid.
76 Maupassant, *Romans*, 199.
77 The veil's connections to eroticism are highlighted in another passage in which Clotilde and Madeleine Forestier both wear the accessory to a sensual dinner held in a private room of a restaurant. As the group becomes intoxicated with alcohol and fine food, Maupassant turns to clothing to express the party's increasingly relaxed inhibitions. Beginning with the image of lifting veils, he then connects these garments to the sexualized metaphor of lifting skirts: "They had reached the stage of witty suggestiveness, of words, veiled yet revealing, that are like a hand lifting up a skirt" (Maupassant, *Bel-Ami*, 108) ["Ce fut le moment des sous-entendus adroits, des voiles levés par des mots, comme on lève des jupes"] (Maupassant, *Romans*, 258).
78 Maupassant, *Bel-Ami*, 116.
79 Maupassant, *Romans*, 264.
80 Maupassant, *Bel-Ami*, 100.
81 Maupassant, *Romans*, 252.
82 Maupassant, *Bel-Ami*, 100.
83 Maupassant, *Romans*, 252.
84 Maupassant here seems to anticipate the twentieth-century writings of Gaston Bachelard bemoaning the lack of intimacy fostered by Parisian apartments. Bachelard, highly critical of modern urban dwellings, describes the way in which their tight consolidation of rooms actually discourages interpersonal closeness: "The different rooms that compose living quarters jammed into one floor all lack one of the fundamental

principles for distinguishing and classifying the values of intimacy"
(Gaston Bachelard, *The Poetics of Space*, translated by Maria Jolas
(Boston: Beacon Press, 1994), 27). Maupassant's narrative erasure of the
sexual encounter between Duroy and Clotilde might gesture towards a
similar sentiment, whereby the cramped space of Duroy's apartment
paradoxically seems to hinder intimacy between the two characters.

85 As Forestier remarks, Maupassant's references to colonial development in
Algeria and Morocco in *Bel-Ami* were actually thinly disguised allusions
to Tunisia, the country that Ferry had been targeting as the next candidate
for an increase in French expansionism. He writes, "Minister Ferry was
defeated on the question of Tunisia on 30 March 1885, several days before
the publication of *Bel-Ami* in serial form. Before this he had favoured a
French presence in Tonkin, in Madagascar, in sub-Saharan Africa and
in Tunisia. It is the history of the takeover of this last country that
Maupassant transposes under the guise of Moroccan affairs" ["le
ministère Ferry fut mis en minorité sur la question tunisienne le 30 mars
1885, quelquels jours avant la publication de *Bel-Ami* en feuilleton.
Auparavant, il avait favorisé la présence française au Tonkin, à
Madagascar, en Afrique noire et en Tunisie. C'est l'histoire de la mainmise
sur ce dernier pays que Maupassant transpose sous le couvert d'affaires
marocaines"] (notice, 1326).

86 Forestier, notice, 1326.

87 Kessler, *Sheer Presence*, 100.

88 Maupassant, *Bel-Ami*, 116.

89 Maupassant, *Romans*, 264.

90 Ibid., 266.

91 Nicholas White, *The Family in Crisis in Late Nineteenth-Century French
Fiction* (Cambridge: Cambridge University Press, 2004), 89.

92 Cited in Carla Calargé, "Une Fissure dans l'édifice colonial: Inquiétante
étrangeté ou agentivité féminine? Le cas de quatre nouvelles de
Maupassant," *Nineteenth-Century French Studies* 41, nos. 1–2 (2012–13), 108.

93 Culbert, *Paralyses*, 100.

94 Maupassant, *Bel-Ami*, 116.

95 Maupassant, *Romans*, 264.

96 Maupassant, *Bel-Ami*, 61.

97 Maupassant, *Romans*, 224.

98 Barrow, "East/West," 325.

99 Seth Graebner's examination of similarities between written depictions of
aerial views of Algiers and Paris after 1830 supports the notion that
authors were already thinking then of the relationship between

colonization abroad and the concurrent rise of urban development in France. Graebner argues that the relationship between accounts of Algiers and Paris in the nineteenth century can be called "symbiotic" due to likenesses in descriptions of the two metropoles "underlying the colony's contribution to the vision of modernity [in Paris]" ("Bird's-Eye View," 227). Graebner's study focuses on an earlier group of writers than those discussed here. For Maupassant, writing later in the century after many decades of French colonial imperialism, the relationship seems far less mutually beneficial than the term "symbiotic" optimistically implies.

100   Barrow, "East/West," 325.

101   Dorian Bell takes up this theme in the context of *Pierre et Jean*, a novel published four years after *Bel-Ami* and in which Bell studies tensions stemming from the "dueling imperatives toward the particular and the universal" ("Maupassant and the Limits of the Self," *Romanic Review* 101, no. 4 (2010), 781). I thank Edward Troy for calling my attention to Duroy's Everyman qualities.

102   For more on how fashion enables Duroy's anonymous penetration of the urban crowd, see Brevik-Zender, "Fashion and Fractured Flânerie," 226.

103   Maupassant, *Bel-Ami*, 99.

104   Maupassant, *Romans*, 251.

105   Maupassant, *Bel-Ami*, 103.

106   Maupassant, *Romans*, 254.

107   White, *Family in Crisis*, 88.

108   Culbert, *Paralyses*, 32.

109   Hiner, *Accessories*, 82.

110   Ross, *Emergence*, 76.

111   My analysis of *Bel-Ami* resonates with Kristin Ross's later study, *Fast Cars, Clean Bodies: Decolonization and the Reordering of French Culture* (Cambridge, MA: MIT Press, 1996). In this work, Ross explores decolonization a century later, examining the post–Second World War "conversion from exterior to interior colonialism" (*Fast Cars*, 8) that took place domestically in France through the rise of Americanization and consumer culture.

112   Maupassant, *Romans*, 480.

113   Maupassant, *Bel-Ami*, 416.

114   Maupassant, *Romans*, 480.

5   Places and Spaces of Haute Couture

1   *Le Trésor de la Langue Française informatisé.*

2   Ibid.

3 I am grateful to one of the manuscript's anonymous readers for this observation.

4 See Nancy L. Green, "Art and Industry: The Language of Modernization in the Production of Fashion," *French Historical Studies* 18, no. 3 (1994), 731. The feminization of the term "couturier" is actually much older; the *Trésor de la Langue Française* dates the definition "woman who sees to sewing" ["femme qui s'occupe de couture"] to around the year 1150 and the feminine form of the noun "cousturiere" appears around 1200.

5 See de Marly, *History*, 11; and Caroline Weber, *Queen of Fashion: What Marie Antoinette Wore to the Revolution* (New York: Picador, 2007), 103.

6 Alison Matthews David, "Cutting a Figure: Tailoring, Technology and Social Identity in Nineteenth-Century Paris" (Ph.D. diss., Stanford University, 2002), 8.

7 For more on the sometimes ambivalent relationship that these men had to their identities as couturiers, see chapter 1 of Nancy J. Troy, *Couture Culture: A Study in Modern Art and Fashion* (Cambridge, MA: MIT Press, 2003).

8 Alexandra Bosc, "Le Couturier et ses clientes dans la seconde moitié du XIXe siècle," in Olivier Saillard and Anne Zazzo, eds., *Paris Haute Couture* (Paris: Skira Flammarion, 2012), 22; Green, "Art," 729. The first union for dressmakers was established in 1868 (Françoise Tétart-Vittu and Gloria Groom, "Key Dates in Fashion and Commerce, 1851–89," in Groom, *Impressionism, Fashion and Modernity*, 274). The group's name, Chambre Syndicale des Confectionneurs et des Tailleurs pour Dames, bears witness to the profession's official recognition of the moniker "tailleur pour dames."

9 Troy notes the popularity of the couture house as a setting for plays and revues in the early twentieth century (*Couture*, 93–4). Feydeau's play, written when the notion of the couture house was still in its infancy and in the process of defining itself, may have paved the way for these later theatrical works. The setting of comedic plays in spaces of less glamorous (feminine) areas of clothing production dates at least back to the early decades of the nineteenth century, when vaudevilles were commonly set in places where seamstresses and hatmakers worked. I am grateful to Susan Hiner for bringing these works to my attention.

10 Henry Gidel, introduction to *Georges Feydeau: Théâtre complèt*, edited by Henry Gidel, vol. 1 (Paris: Garnier, 1988), 17.

11 Peter F. Parshall, "Feydeau's 'A Flea in Her Ear': The Art of Kinesthetic Structuring," *Theatre Journal* 33, no. 3 (1981), 356; and Gidel, introduction, 31.

12 Feydeau, *Théâtre complèt*, 250. There is a temptation to interpret these moments through the lens of Mikhail Bakhtin's notion of the

carnivalesque, whereby such sartorial inversions signal subversions of gender and class. However, for this reader, the overemphasis in farce on the rapid turnover of such moments of dressing-up – that they occur primarily to incite quick laughs rather than more lingering identity reversals – serves to dispel subversive potential rather than encourage it.

13 Norman R. Shapiro, "Suffering and Punishment in the Theater of Georges Feydeau," *Tulane Drama Review* 15, no. 1 (1960), 120.

14 Shapiro, "Suffering," 118.

15 Feydeau, *Théâtre complèt*, 265.

16 Parshall, "Feydeau's 'A Flea,'" 358.

17 Feydeau, *Théâtre complèt*, 277.

18 Ibid.

19 Leonard C. Pronko, *Georges Feydeau* (New York: Frederick Ungar, 1975), 55.

20 Feydeau, *Théâtre complèt*, 260–1.

21 Prohibitively expensive garments, then as now, were one sign of the haute couture fashion designer. A designer for Félix, a contemporary of Worth's, known for the exorbitant prices of its garments, reportedly once said to a client, "Ah madame, if you say the word there is absolutely no limit as to what your gown may cost" (Anonymous, "Many Women in Mourning," *Pittsburg Press*, 30 June 1901, 15).

22 Tuan, *Space and Place*, 50.

23 Ibid., 3.

24 Ibid.

25 Ibid., 102.

26 Ibid., 4.

27 Ibid., 3.

28 Feydeau, *Théâtre complèt*, 268.

29 Ibid.

30 Ibid,. 274.

31 Bassinet specifies that his apartment building is located at 70 rue de Milan (Feydeau, *Théâtre complèt*, 235). This street in the 9th arrondissement not far from Garnier's Opéra was adjacent to the renovated Gare Saint-Lazare train station; many artists and writers of the 1860s and 1870s used the area and its new structures as subjects to depict the industrialization and motion of urban modernity. Under Haussmannization, the area became a residential neighbourhood of bourgeois and upper-class homes. Feydeau likely intended for the address on the rue de Milan to exemplify the newly modernized city that these monuments and apartment buildings architecturally and cartographically represented.

32 Feydeau plays with the fact that the preposition "à" can mean "for" or "to." Thus, Moulineaux is flustered when he misunderstands and thinks Aubin is asking him what he is doing "to" his wife, whereas Aubin is simply inquiring about the garment that Moulineaux (the tailor) is fabricating "for" Suzanne.

33 Feydeau, *Théâtre complèt*, 262.

34 Ibid., 278.

35 Ibid., 260.

36 Ibid., 265.

37 Ibid., 305.

38 Pronko, *Feydeau*, 13.

39 Feydeau, *Théâtre complèt*, 259.

40 "Apprêter, parer quelqu'un avec beaucoup de soin et de coquetterie" (*Le Trésor de la Langue Française informatisé*).

41 Feydeau himself uses the diminutive "ette" for "loose" women in other plays, such as the actress Lucette from *Un fil à la patte* (1894) and the dancing girl La Môme Crevette from *La Dame de chez Maxim* (1899).

42 Habermas, *Structural Transformation*, 44.

43 Ibid.

44 Ibid., 45.

45 Shapiro, "Suffering," 117; Pronko, *Feydeau*, 196.

46 Gidel, introduction, 21.

47 Shapiro, "Suffering," 117.

48 Gidel, introduction, 71; Pronko, *Feydeau*, 19–20.

49 Gidel, introduction, 46–55; Shapiro, "Suffering," 126; Pronko, *Feydeau*, 50–1.

50 Feydeau, *Théâtre complèt*, 277.

51 Ibid., 275.

52 This link between Feydeau's farces and the notion of the "infernal machine" that pits chance in a losing battle against fate would later become strongly associated with surrealism, in part through the tellingly named 1934 play *La Machine infernale* by Jean Cocteau (Pronko, *Feydeau*, 74, 196–9; Shapiro, "Suffering," 124). The paths of Feydeau and Cocteau have crossed posthumously in a collection of monologues by the two playwrights that highlight their shared interest in this theme. See Jean Cocteau and Georges Feydeau, *Thirteen Monologues*, translated by Peter Meyer (London: Oberon, 1996).

53 Feydeau, *Théâtre complèt*, 259.

54 Ibid., 296.

55 Ibid., 297.

56 Ibid.
57 The concept of "homeopathy" was common knowledge to authors in the
   nineteenth century; Balzac, Baudelaire, and Huysmans, among others,
   cited the term in their writings.
58 Noëlle Benhamou, "*En Ménage, En rade*: Huysmans et la maladie
   du mariage," in Noëlle Benhamou, ed., *En ménage: En rade de
   Joris-Karl Huysmans, 1881* (Paris: Editions du Boucher, 2009),
   http://www.leboucher.com/pdf/huysmans/huysmans.pdf, 35.
59 Zola, *Kill*, 264.
60 Zola, *Rougon-Macquart*, 1: 599.
61 Ibid., 460–75.
62 Ibid., 474.
63 Zola, *Kill*, 140.
64 Zola, *Rougon-Macquart*, 1: 466.
65 Renée follows in the footsteps of her literary sister, Emma Bovary, who is
   likewise ruined, in part, by uncontrollable fashion purchases.
66 Martine Agathae Coste counts an impressive eighteen well-described
   outfits worn by Renée through the course of the novel ("Vêtir l'hypocrisie:
   La haute couture sous le Second Empire à travers *La Curée* d'Emile Zola,
   in Frédéric Monneyron, ed., *Vêtement et littérature* (Perpignan: Presses
   univéristaires de Perpignan, 2001), 216).
67 For Coste, Zola's treatment of fashion in *La Curée* is, in fact, "*necessary* to
   its plot" ["nécessaire à l'intrigue"] (emphasis added, "Vêtir," 216).
68 Nelson, introduction, xvii–xviii.
69 Like other detractors of Haussmanization, Zola criticized what he viewed
   as an overly rapid expansion of the city's infrastructure and the callous
   way in which such excessive growth exacerbated the plight of the urban
   poor. He further accused Napoléon III and Baron Haussmann of building
   a city principally for the entertainment, display, and pleasure of the
   wealthy at the expense of an increasingly displaced working class. For
   other critiques by Zola and his contemporaries of Haussmannization
   during the decade leading up to the drafting of *La Curée*, see the summary
   by Mitterand (Zola, *Rougon-Macquart*, 1: 1572–3). See the chapter, "The
   View from Notre Dame," in Clark's *The Painting of Modern Life* for critical
   responses by Manet and other visual artists.
70 Paul Rabinow, *French Modern: Norms and Forms of the Social Environment*
   (Cambridge, MA: MIT Press, 1989), 76.
71 Ibid., 77.
72 Alain Plessis, "*La Curée* et l'Haussmannisation de Paris," in Baguley, La
   Curée *de Zola*, 99.

73 Prendergast, *Paris*, 9.

74 Spatially distinct city spaces such as parks, monuments, and train stations were to be connected together through this logic of boulevards and bridges, a topography of conduits echoed underground in orderly sewers and man-made waterways that were intended to promote healthy living conditions. For the priorities and procedures of Second Empire urbanization from Haussmann's point of view, see his 1890 autobiography, *Mémoires du Baron Haussmann*. For a discussion of recent critical analyses that nuance what David Van Zanten has convincingly termed Haussmann's primarily "self-serving" account of urban development in these years, see his, "Paris Space: What Might Have Constituted Haussmannization," in Christian Hermansen Cordua, ed., *Manifestoes and Transformations in the Early Modernist City* (Farnham: Ashgate, 2010), 179–80.

75 Foucault, "Other," 61.

76 Larry Duffy makes the point that Zola returns to the notion of Haussmannian circulation in some later works of the *Rougon-Macquart*, most notably, in his text on the *grand magasin*. Duffy notes, "*Au Bonheur des Dames* is arguably the novel which most fully describes these new forms of exchange based on 'circulation' in a city in the final stages of its transformation, not least because the development of the department store was an inevitable corollary of Haussmannization" (*Le Grand Transit*, 128).

77 Coste, "Vêtir," 221.

78 Ibid.

79 Troy, *Couture*, 18–19; de Marly, *History*, 14–23; "Intime," *History of Feminine Fashion*, 3–6.

80 Troy, *Couture*, 28. Others disagreed that the *grand couturier* was a high artist. In response to the Salon of 1879, Joris-Karl Huysmans indirectly challenged the claims to artistry of men like Worth by using the figure of the haute couture designer to disparage contemporary painters that he disliked. Although he does not provide names, his critiques were likely levied at Alfred Stevens and Tissot, both of whom produced portraits of fashionable Parisians that Huysmans belittled. For Huysmans, who echoed critiques against "*peintre-couturiers*" levied by Zola during the previous decade, these artists created second-rate works that relied too heavily on dress as a prop to signify modernity. He described works produced by such fashion-focused artists as "canvasses that Worth might have painted if he had had a painter's disposition" ["tableaux que Worth eût peints s'il avait eu un tempérament de peintre"] (Joris-Karl

Huysmans, *Oeuvres complètes* (Paris: G. Crès et Cie, 1928), 6: 41), going on to note, "The painter of modernity is not simply an excellent 'couturier' as are, unfortunately, most of those who, under the pretext of modernity, envelope a model in various silks" ["Le peintre moderne n'est pas seulement un excellent 'couturier' comme le sont malheureusement la plupart de ceux qui, sous prétexte de modernité, enveloppent un mannequin de soies variées"] (43). By implying that lesser painters focused more on depicting modern garments than modern mores, Huysmans linked the work of haute couture fashion designers to the inferiority that he associated with substandard Salon artists.

81 Peter Wollen, *Addressing the Century: 100 Years of Art and Fashion* (Berkeley: University of California Press, 1999), 8. Wollen may be referring to the rising practice of artists opening their ateliers to customers, one that relates to changing spatial navigations in the Haussmannizing metropole. Manuel Charpy argues that, starting in the 1860s, it became fashionable for artists to receive clients in their studios in the manner of ad hoc weekly salons. By calling on "their painter," middle- and upper-class art buyers discovered entirely new areas of the city, including suburbs that were at this time being subsumed into Paris proper. Charpy writes, "The 'atelier visit' became a ritual and the atelier a worldly space, where the visitor could in a single visit discover fashionable artwork, clothing, trinkets, and neighborhoods" ["La 'visite à l'atelier' devient un rituel et l'atelier un espace mondain où le visiteur peut en une seule visite découvrir les oeuvres, les vêtements, les bibelots et les quartiers à la mode"] ("Quartiers à la mode et attraction des Marges: Législateurs du goût et conquêtes urbaines après 1860," in Flore Bourillon and Annie Fourcaut, eds., *Agrandir Paris: 1860–1970* (Paris: Publications de la Sorbonne, 2012), 188).

82 Susan North, "Redfern Limited: 1892 to 1940, *Costume* 43 (2009), 86.

83 Zola, *Kill*, 91–2.

84 Zola, *Rougon-Macquart*, 1: 413.

85 Zola, *Kill*, 92. Nelson explains that the Pythoness was "a woman believed to be possessed by a soothsaying spirit, like the priestess of Apollo at Delphi" (introduction, 272n92).

86 Zola, *Rougon-Macquart*, 1: 413.

87 Zola, *Kill*, 92.

88 Zola, *Rougon-Macquart*, 1: 413.

89 Priscilla Parkhurst Ferguson, *Paris as Revolution: Writing the Nineteenth-Century City* (Berkeley: University of California Press, 1997), 147.

90 "Intime," "A Parisian Prince of Dress," *The Lady's Realm*, vol. 9 (London: Hutchinson, 1901), 25.

91 Hippolyte Taine, *Notes sur Paris*, 18th ed. (Paris: Hachette, 1913), 145.

92 Ibid. The detail of the velvet blouse supports the notion that Taine was caricaturizing Worth, whose penchant for wearing smocklike garments of rich fabrics was well known (M. Griffith, "Paris Dressmakers," in *The Strand Magazine: An Illustrated Monthly*, edited by George Newnes (London: George Newnes Ltd, 1894), 745). Elizabeth Wilson, for example, notes, "Toward the end of his life Worth took to dressing like Rembrandt, with a velvet beret, rich cloak and the flowing tie that was the symbol of the artist amongst the romantics and bohemians" (*Adorned*, 32). However, the eccentricities of Worth's creative process and alleged despotism may have been more the stuff of self-perpetuating legend, since many period accounts derive from the memoires of Worth's clients who could have exaggerated such elements for dramatic effect (see, e.g., de Marly, *History*, 209nn9, 10, 13, and 14; and Perrot, *Fashioning*, 248n34). Not all depictions of Worth were unflattering. M. Griffith's report of meeting Worth in 1894 describes him in kinder terms as a "dear picturesque old veteran" (Griffith, "Dressmakers," 745) and praises the "care and forethought of the master for those who work for him" (747). It is worth pointing out the role of scholarship in reproducing some of the stereotypes surrounding the figure of the *grand couturier* in this period. For example, de Marly's classic study *The History of Haute Couture* begins with a chapter tellingly entitled "Worth, the First Fashion Dictator." Philippe Perrot's influential *Fashioning the Bourgeoisie* cites accounts by several of Worth's contemporaries, including Taine and the historian Vicomte d'Avenel, which seem to colour his own description of the elite couturier as a haughty and self-centred fashion dictator: "'The autocrat of taste … and spiritual director in matters of fit,' noted for his arrogance, as much as for his professional qualities, treated even the wealthiest women with incredible condescension. He received them only if they were properly introduced and presented, made them wait for hours, then admitted them, a cigar in his mouth, into his boudoirs, where, indolent and majestic, surrounded by piles of fabrics carelessly thrown on the furniture, he would look them over in silence until the judgment fell and an order was given" (Perrot, *Fashioning*, 185).

93 Zola, *Kill*, 90.

94 Zola, *Rougon-Macquart*, 1: 412.

95 Another similarity is the term *avorton*, meaning a "monstrous runt" or, more crudely, "aborted fetus," which Zola uses to refer to Maxime in the

paragraph before his description of Worms's waiting room salon (*Rougon-Macquart*, 1: 411). The repetition of this jarring term in *La Curée* supports the argument that Zola was inspired by Taine's earlier text.

96 For analysis of another metaphor, that of the couturier as a stand-in for the naturalist novelist, see Thompson, *Naturalism Redressed*, 38–9. The caricaturing of high fashion couturiers seems to have morphed later in the century from hyperbolic portraits like those cited here to images of businessmen with the rational sense necessary to head large enterprises. Social economist Léon de Seilhac's 1897 assertion that men were better suited than women to lead large fashion companies is notable for its overt sexism towards the latter who, for him, could be either artistic or business-minded but not both: "In a large industry, women are ill-equipped to direct business affairs. Either they may be organized and confuse that organization with economy, afraid to throw themselves in, lacking the nerve to risk enormous expenses that they are not sure of recuperating. Or women running a business may have good taste and be artistic but, as a result, too often lack order. Men alone can direct so considerable an 'industry.'" ["Dans une grande industrie, une femme est peu apte à diriger les affaires. Ou bien elle aura de l'ordre et confondra cet ordre avec l'économie, aura peur de se lancer, n'osera se risquer dans des frais énormes, qu'elle n'est pas assurée de récupérer. Ou bien la femme, à la tête d'une affaire, aura du goût, sera artiste, et par suite trop souvent désordonnée. L'homme seul peut diriger une 'industrie' aussi considérable"] (Léon de Seilhac, *L'Industrie de la couture et de la confection à Paris* (Paris: Didot, 1897), 13). Seilhac's paternalism was easily challenged by the example of women such as Jeanne Paquin, who by 1897 had turned her *maison de couture* into one of the most successful businesses in the industry.

97 Zola, *Kill*, 90–1.

98 Zola, *Rougon-Macquart*, 1: 412.

99 See Thompson, *Naturalism Redressed*, 78, for more on Zola's startling use of the term *lesbiennes* in this passage. Thompson aptly points out that the specificity of the fashion location – that the word is used in the context of the couturier's atelier – contributes to Zola's implicit link of "the erotic import of costume to the female desiring economy" (78). This connection resurfaces in later novels through Zola's juxtaposition of high fashion and lesbian desire in *Nana* and *Au Bonheur*.

100 Griffith, "Dressmakers," 745.

101 Ibid., 748.

102 Compared with the House of Worth, little interest has been paid to Maison
Félix, which was, nonetheless, one of the major Parisian couture houses of
the late nineteenth century. In 1901 one newspaper reporter noted, "Even
in the palmiest days of Worth, often styled the greatest man dressmaker of
the world, the house of Mr Felix could boast a proud supremacy"
(Anonymous, "Many Women," 15). Félix was a fashion house jointly
owned by brothers Auguste (1831–1910) and Emile (1841–1930)
Poussineau, the former a one-time hairdresser to Empress Eugénie. Their
maison was the clothier to many well-known actresses, including Sarah
Bernhardt, one of the most recognizable celebrities of the day. In 1882,
when the Musée Grévin enjoyed its highly anticipated and well-publicized
debut, it was Félix's gowns that were used to clothe the wax figures of
Bernhardt and other famous personalities in the museum's life-sized wax
dioramas (Arnold Mortier, "Le Musée Grévin," *Le Figaro*, 23 Mar. 1882), 1).
The enterprise's popularity in the last decades of the century is suggested
by the 1897 launch of its own monthly fashion periodical entitled *Félix-
Mode*, a small-format luxury gazette which included in every issue a report
signed by "Félix," at least one full-colour fashion plate, descriptions and
patterns of Félix gowns, and special offers for made-to-order dresses
offered only to subscribers to the periodical. The Maison Félix's role as
a figurehead of high fashion was cemented when it was tapped to help
organize the Pavillon de la Mode fashion exhibit at the 1900 Universal
Exposition that featured thirty tableaux of mannequins dressed by only
the most elite couture houses of the fin-de-siècle (T. Bentzon, "Woman at
the Paris Exhibition," *Outlook*, 29 Sept. 1900, 260; Iskin, *Modern Women*,
217). The 1901 article by "Intime" in the *Lady's Realm*, entitled "A Parisian
Prince of Dress," went so far as to refer to Félix as "the recognised leading
costumier[sic] of Paris" ("Intime," "Parisian Prince," 22). When Félix
abruptly closed its doors that same year, the Pittsburg Press reported that
the designer had been the "World's Greatest Modist," declaring, "Many
Women in Mourning: Closing of Mr Felix's Dress-Making Establishment
the Cause" (Anonymous, "Many Women," 15).
103 Griffith, "Dressmakers," 748.
104 The name appeared both with and without the French *accent aigu*.
105 Ibid., 748–50. In contrast, the images of the Maison Worth in Griffith's
article focused not on space but on people, highlighting Worth's two sons
and a society woman dressed in a Worth-designed costume, making
their only concession to location a relatively small photograph of the
building's exterior.

106 Griffith, "Dressmakers," 747.
107 Zola, *Rougon-Macquart*, 1: 404.
108 Zola, *Kill*, 84.
109 Zola, *Rougon-Macquart*, 1: 404.
110 Zola, *Kill*, 93.
111 Zola, *Rougon-Macquart*, 1: 414.
112 Zola, *Kill*, 93.
113 Zola, *Rougon-Macquart*, 1: 414.
114 Renée's attire is also a surprising amalgamation of a masculinized army uniform and a feminized ruffled skirt, one that suggests the threatening destabilization of gender roles that she later enacts while playing masculine aggressor as well as feminine prey to Maxime's androgyne. The outfit's military theme marks Renée as both dangerous and sullied due to popular perceptions about the impropriety of women dressing in uniform. As Roynette notes, "until 1914, the idea of a feminine uniform remained transgressive and … representations of women in military dress reflected a profoundly debased image of them" ["jusqu'en 1914, l'idée d'un uniforme féminin reste transgressive et … les représentations de la femme en habit militaire renvoient une image profondément dévalorisante de celle-ci"] ("L'Uniforme militaire," 122).
115 Zola, *Kill*, 154.
116 Zola, *Rougon-Macquart*, 1: 481–2.
117 Ibid., 411.
118 Zola, *Kill*, 90.
119 Zola, *Rougon-Macquart*, 1: 411.
120 As others have pointed out, this dress is a rendering of Renée's own position as "prey" to her predatory husband and her allegorizing of the Second Empire more generally. Ferguson's astute reading summarizes it well: "Worms's outfits make up the archives of the Second Empire. Renée's deer hunt gown plays on the double sense of *la curée*, since it figures her own situation as quarry and also the larger hunt that designates the regime as a whole" (Ferguson, *Revolution*, 147).
121 Ibid.
122 Zola, *Rougon-Macquart*, 1: 439.
123 Zola, *Kill*, 93.
124 Zola, *Rougon-Macquart*, 1: 415.
125 Zola, *Kill*, 93.
126 Zola, *Rougon-Macquart*, 1: 414.
127 Larry Duffy points out that another of Zola's fashion spaces, the Au Bonheur *grand magasin*, similarly replicates the constant circulation of

busy urban boulevards, representing a smaller version of both the larger metropolis and its financial networks: "The department store, then, precisely because of the movement which it generates and of which it is a part, while being an integral element of the city, can ... be considered a microcosmic working model for Paris, and for the economic system determining its transformation (*Le Grand Transit*, 132).

128 Griffith, "Dressmakers," 745.

129 "Intime," "Parisian Prince," 25.

130 Cited in Perrot, *Fashioning*, 185.

131 Zola, *Rougon-Macquart*, 1: 414.

132 Zola, *Kill*, 93.

133 Zola, *Rougon-Macquart*, 1: 414.

134 Troy observes a later type of conflation of domestic space and the *maison de couture* in her study of the early-twentieth-century designer Paul Poiret, who staged elaborate costumed soirées at his Parisian mansion that were also ways for him to display his latest clothing lines. She notes, "Poiret's *hôtel* was a business setting that doubled as a domestic space in which his wife circulated like a mannequin and his friends tried out his latest styles at extravagant costume parties" (Troy, *Couture*, 192).

135 Griffith's report on the *maison de couture* of Morin and Blossier, one of Worth's contemporaries, summarizes the typical layout of fashion establishments: "The business premises are five stories high; the first and second floors are used for show and fitting rooms, and the other three floors for office and work-rooms" (Griffith, "Dressmakers," 750).

136 For its location on the second floor and the various types of rooms found within it, Renée's *appartement* corresponds to Françoise Tétart-Vittu's description of period haute couture establishments: "Large, specialized fashion houses (the future purveyors of haute couture) ... remained above street level. Located on the 'noble' floor of a new building or a former private mansion, and reached by a graceful staircase, these *maisons* consisted of a series of comfortably furnished rooms: the waiting room, its walls hung with the portraits of famous clients or medals won at international trade shows, where customers could sit and look over the styles offered by the house or illustrated in fashion magazines; the show room; a fitting room; and rooms devoted to various individual accessories, such as lingerie or hats" ("Shops versus Department Stores," in Groom, *Impressionism, Fashion, and Modernity*, 211–12).

137 Zola, *Kill*, 115.

138 Zola, *Rougon-Macquart*, 1: 439.

139 Zola, *Kill*, 150.

140 Zola, *Rougon-Macquart*, 1: 476–7.
141 Zola, *Kill*, 150.
142 Zola, *Rougon-Macquart*, 1: 477.
143 Zola, *Kill*, 150.
144 Zola, *Rougon-Macquart*, 1: 477.
145 Zola, *Kill*, 150.
146 Zola, *Rougon-Macquart*, 1: 477.
147 Zola, *Kill*, 150.
148 Zola, *Rougon-Macquart*, 1: 477.
149 Zola, *Kill*, 150.
150 Zola, *Rougon-Macquart*, 1: 477.
151 Zola, *Kill*, 150.
152 Zola, *Rougon-Macquart*, 1: 477.
153 Zola, *Kill*, 151.
154 Zola, *Rougon-Macquart*, 1: 478.
155 Zola, *Kill*, 150.
156 Zola, *Rougon-Macquart*, 1: 477.
157 Zola, *Kill*, 150.
158 Zola, *Rougon-Macquart*, 1: 477.
159 Zola, *Kill*, 150.
160 Zola, *Rougon-Macquart*, 1: 477.
161 Thompson, *Naturalism Redressed*, 64.
162 The *maillot* illustrates Coste's observation of Zola's "incessant slippery play in descriptions of Renée's outfits between fabric and skin, between *flesh and silk*" ["jeu de glissement incessant dans la description de toilettes de Renée entre tissu et peau, entre *chair et soie*"] (original emphasis, "Vêtir," 219).
163 Zola, *Kill*, 239.
164 Zola, *Rougon-Macquart*, 1: 572.
165 Zola, *Kill*, 243.
166 Zola, *Rougon-Macquart*, 1: 576.
167 Zola, *Kill*, 224.
168 Zola, *Rougon-Macquart*, 1: 556.
169 Zola, *Kill*, 239.
170 Zola, *Rougon-Macquart*, 1: 572.
171 Wilson, *Adorned*, 3.
172 Zola, *Kill*, 242.
173 Zola, *Rougon-Macquart*, 1: 576.
174 Zola, *Kill*, 242.
175 Zola, *Rougon-Macquart*, 1: 576.

176 Ibid., 479.
177 Jean Borie, "Préface" in *La Curée* by Emile Zola (Paris: Gallimard, 1981), 29.
178 Zola, *Kill*, 238.
179 Zola, *Rougon-Macquart*, 1: 571.
180 Ibid., 571.
181 Nelson, introduction, xxvii.
182 Anne Anlin Cheng, *Second Skin: Josephine Baker and the Modern Surface* (New York: Oxford University Press, 2011), 138.
183 Borie, "Préface," 34.
184 For more on the metaphor of the department store as machine, see chapter 3 in Duffy's *Le Grand Transit*.
185 Cited in Ferguson, *Revolution*, 246.

6 A Woman's Work(space)

1 Olivier Saillard ed., *Le XVIIe au goût du jour: Couturiers et créateurs de mode au Grand Trianon* (Versailles: Editions Artlys, 2011), 26.
2 Ibid.
3 I am grateful to Alexandra Bosc, Conservatrice du Patrimoine and Curator of the Nineteenth-Century Department, for sharing her expertise about these items as well as images and documentation of the museum's impressive holdings.
4 One early twentieth-century costume historian noted that, as of 1884, garments characteristically had "gentlemanly little collars and *revers* on walking dresses, and quasi-military froggings of velvet," expressly referring to these tailored details as "'mannish' touches" ("Intime," *History*, 33).
5 Guy Tomel, "Nos Petites *couturières*," *Le Monde Illustré*, 31 July 1897, 84.
6 David, "Cutting a Figure," 187.
7 Alexandra Bosc, "Le Costume Tailleur: Histoire d'un succès," in Saillard and Zazzo, *Paris Haute Couture*, 32.
8 Green, "Art," 730.
9 Ibid.
10 Lorraine Coons, "'Neglected Sisters' of the Women's Movement: The Perception and Experience of Working Mothers in the Parisian Garment Industry, 1860–1915," *Journal of Women's History* 5, no. 2 (1993), 52–3; David, "Cutting a Figure," 186–7.
11 De Marly, *History*, 106.
12 As Coons indicates, the "sweating system" also included the vast numbers of women who sewed or did finishing work on garments and

accessories from home ("Neglected," 55). For the ways in which these women were represented in socialist and other political discourses, see Judith DeGroat, "Virtue, Vice, and Revolution: Representations of Parisian Needlewomen in the Mid-Nineteenth Century," in Beth Harris, ed., *Famine and Fashion: Needlewomen in the Nineteenth Century* (Aldershot: Ashgate, 2005), 201–14. For a sympathetic, yet ultimately paternalistic attitude towards women factory seamstresses from a period source, see Seilhac, *Industrie*, 34–78.

13 Nancy L. Green, *Ready-to-Wear and Ready-to-Work: A Century of Industry and Immigrants in Paris and New York* (Durham, NC: Duke University Press, 1997), 157.

14 De Marly, *History*, 106.

15 Iskin, *Modern Women*, 68.

16 Green, *Ready-to-Wear*, 140.

17 Iskin, *Modern Women*, 60; Gloria Groom, "Edgar Degas: *The Millinery Shop*," in Groom, *Impressionism, Fashion, and Modernity*, 318–19n4.

18 Scott Allan, "Degas's *Milliners* and the Craft of Painting" (unpublished lecture, Curator's Spotlight Series, Getty Center, Los Angeles, CA, 20 Nov. 2011), 14. I am grateful to Allan, Assistant Curator of Paintings at the J. Paul Getty Museum, which owns *Les Modistes*, for sharing his unpublished lecture and insights with me.

19 Iskin, *Modern Women*, 71.

20 Allan, "Milliners," 15–16.

21 Judith G. Coffin observes that sexual promiscuity was a common theme in representations of women garment manufacturers: "Engravings of women workers in the clothing trades were often a pretext for pornographic or erotic fantasies and merged the commerce in fabrics and clothing with a traffic in women. Eighteenth- and early nineteenth-century engravings of *lingères*, for instance, showed women flirting with their male clients and provided voyeuristic peeks at groups of women together behind closed doors … Unlike representations of male labor, which focused on the worker and the work process, those of female labor centered instead on commerce and sales and on women as vendors or beautiful objects" ("Credit, Consumption, and Images of Women's Desires: Selling the Sewing Machine in Late Nineteenth-Century France," *French Historical Studies* 18, no. 3 (1994), 758).

22 Iskin, *Modern Women*, 68–9.

23 The *Chez la modiste* from 1879–86 is held at the Art Institute of Chicago; two, from 1881 and 1882, respectively, are at the Metropolitan Museum of Art in New York; and a fourth, from 1882, is at the Musée d'Orsay in Paris.

24 Ibid., 68.

25 Iskin points out that Degas's paintings of hats being bought and sold are spatially unclear, for it is not certain whether his ladies are shopping in small family boutiques, large-scale department stores, or haute couture salons (*Modern Women*, 88–92). Tétart-Vittu concurs, noting, "Despite the notable characteristics of various types of fashion establishments, in his numerous depictions of millinery shops, Edgar Degas did not fully describe the space of the store" ("Shops vs Department Stores," 212).

26 Groom, "Edgar Degas," 223.

27 Ibid., 222.

28 Ibid.

29 Ibid.

30 Iskin, *Modern Women*, 108–9. In her intriguing reading of this shift, Iskin describes Degas's decision to transform what may have been a customer into a hatmaker in terms of an ongoing dialogue with Manet, which involved Degas's desire to depict a working-class woman in homage to the former's "Un Bar aux Folies-Bergère" (98).

31 Allan, "Milliners," 4.

32 Iskin, *Modern Women*, 110.

33 Allan, "Milliners," 19.

34 See Iskin's analysis of milliners painted by Paul Signac (*Modern Women*, 77) and Eva Gonzales (96).

35 Allan, "Milliners," 3.

36 Groom, "Edgar Degas," 223.

37 Allan, "Milliners," 4. Although it was not likely his intention, Degas's milliner paintings resonated with a rising discourse, crystallizing around fashion, as the garment industry recognized that profits were to be made in elevating ready-to-wear objects to the status of art more readily associated with haute couture. Green describes the efforts of some clothing companies to associate prêt-à-porter with artistry "by reappropriating a language of art, even within the context of mass production" ("Art," 723). "Manufacturers in particular," she notes, "sought to legitimate the more standardized product by maintaining that it still contained an inherent artistic component" (732).

38 Iskin, *Modern Women*, 107.

39 Ibid., 106.

40 Allan, "Milliners," 21.

41 Iskin, *Modern Women*, 107.

42 Groom observes that period depictions of artists' studios often showed works on easels ("Edgar Degas," 223); in *Chez la modiste* (1879–86), the

hats are propped up on wooden stands that recall these pieces of
equipment associated with painters.

43 Joris-Karl Huysmans, *Living Together (En Ménage)*, translated by
J.W.G. Gandiford-Pellé (London: Fortune Press, 1969), 204.

44 Joris-Karl Huysmans, *En Ménage* (Geneva: Droz, 2005), 324.

45 Robert E. Ziegler, "Huysmans's *En Ménage* and the Unwritable Naturalist
Text," *Forum for Modern Language Studies* 29, no. 1 (1993), 18.

46 Donaldson-Evans argues, for example, that Huysmans's treatment of
medical pathology in the novel reveals his intent to subvert the scientific
biases of Zolian naturalism ("Huysmans's *roman-abattoir*: *En ménage*,"
Stanford French Review 13, nos. 2–3 (1989), 195), while Ziegler describes it
as "a self-autopsying book auguring the death of the literary movement it
exemplifies" ("Huysmans's *En Ménage*," 29). For Amy Reid, *En Ménage*
exemplifies "an on-going power struggle between the author and his
documentary sources" that heralds Huysmans's ultimate break with
naturalism ("Resisting Documents: Huysmans's Struggle to Represent
Working-Class Women," *French Literature Studies* 28 (2001), 81).

47 Donaldson-Evans, "Huysmans's *roman-abattoir*," 199; Benhamou,
"Maladie," 7.

48 Ziegler, "Huysmans's *En Ménage*," 20.

49 Gilles Bonnet, introduction to *En Ménage*, by Joris-Karl Huysmans
(Geneva: Droz, 2005), 13; Reid, "Resisting," 80–1.

50 Robert Baldick, *The Life of J.-K. Huysmans* (Cambs: Dedalus, 2006), 94.

51 Reid, "Resisting," 86.

52 Ziegler, "Huysmans's *En Ménage*," 21.

53 Huysmans, *Living Together*, 89.

54 Huysmans, *En Ménage*, 145.

55 Huysmans, *Living Together*, 93.

56 Huysmans, *En Ménage*, 150.

57 Green has shown that, as part of a larger movement to promote the
superiority of French clothing manufacturing, the late nineteenth century
saw an idealization of the female garment worker. She writes, "French
fashion critics as well as industrialists wrote veritable love poems to the
Parisian seamstress … Her nimble fingers were lauded, her supposedly
innate skill admired. Women's 'goût naturel,' their 'instinct d'élégance'
were also almost ritualized explanations for the large number of women
in a now-feminized trade" ("Art," 734). Huysmans's relatively affirming
portrait of Jeanne, in addition to paying homage to Anne Meunier, may
be a literary echo of this trend.

58 Huysmans, *Living Together*, 127

59 Huysmans, *En Ménage*, 204.

60 Huysmans, *Living Together*, 127.

61 Huysmans, *En Ménage*, 204.

62 Huysmans, *Living Together* 152.

63 Huysmans, *En Ménage*, 243.

64 Huysmans, *Living Together*, 152.

65 Huysmans, *En Ménage*, 243.

66 Baldick, *Life*, 95.

67 Huysmans, *Living Together*, 143.

68 Huysmans, *En Ménage*, 229.

69 I have found no evidence of a *maison* Larmange. However, Baldick observes that Anna Meunier, the presumed model for Jeanne, worked for a dressmaker located on the rue du Quatre-September called "Hentenaar's" (Baldick, *Life*, 94), a name that shares in reverse order the "ar" and "en" sounds with the (seemingly fictitious) "Larmange."

70 Green, *Ready-to-Wear*, 79.

71 Ibid.

72 Joris-Karl Huysmans, "Robes et Manteaux," *Le Gaulois*, 6 June 1880, 1.

73 Huysmans, *Living Together*, 147.

74 Huysmans, *En Ménage*, 234.

75 Huysmans, *Living Together*, 147.

76 Huysmans, *En Ménage*, 235.

77 Ibid.

78 Coffin, "Credit," 758.

79 Huysmans, *Living Together*, 147.

80 Huysmans, *En Ménage*, 235.

81 Huysmans, *Living Together*, 147.

82 Huysmans, *En Ménage*, 235.

83 Huysmans, *Living Together*, 126.

84 Huysmans, *En Ménage*, 203.

85 Ibid., 237–8.

86 Huysmans, *Living Together*, 148.

87 Huysmans, *En Ménage*, 236.

88 Huysmans, *Living Together*, 148.

89 Huysmans, *En Ménage*, 236.

90 Earlier we examined how underskirts, not flesh, incite André's petticoat crises; here women's body parts are once again mediated through the sartorial by way of the rumpled undergarments against which the women's "pears" nestle.

91 Huysmans, *Living Together*, 148.

92 Huysmans, *En Ménage*, 236.
93 Reid, "Resisting," 87.
94 Huysmans, *En Ménage*, 236.
95 Ziegler notes, "Despite a warm, deferential relationship with Zola, who qualified [*En Ménage*] as 'banal yet poignant,' Huysmans had already begun to show signs of distancing himself philosophically from the master" ("Huysmans's *En Ménage*," 18).
96 To be sure, narrative categories such as naturalism and decadence are notoriously slippery, and critics have done much to expose that these two allegedly antithetical approaches actually have much overlap. The point here is that a formal break between Huysmans and the naturalists was posited and perceived, regardless of the extent to which such a divide registered itself in literary works.
97 Huysmans, "Robes," 1.
98 Ibid.
99 Ibid.
100 Ibid.
101 Reid, "Resisting," 87.
102 This transition, whereby men replaced women as the top clothing makers for the world's elite, was, at times, a rocky one. The Princess Metternich, who eventually became a strong supporter and launched Worth into high society, initially found it implausible that a man would approach her to make a gown. Reportedly, when first asked, she refused to meet the Englishman since, before Worth's time, "a dressmaker was by definition a woman" (de Marly, *History*, 19). Some critics of the day took the couturier's interest in ladies' dress as a sign of his questionable virility (Perrot, *Fashioning*, 328). Others had opposite fears, worrying that it was improper for men to gain familiar access to the bodies of aristocrats above their station, or to be within dangerous touching distance of "respectable" wives, mothers, and daughters of the bourgeoisie. De Marly's is a vivid description of period anxieties over potential impropriety between the male couturier and his female clients: "What a shock it was to the mid-nineteenth century that a man should be making dresses on women, seeing them in a state of undress, touching their bodies, and ordering them to parade before him. Moralists were appalled. They declared that Maison Worth et Bobergh must be a house of orgies" (*History*, 21–2). See the above analysis of *Le Muscle du grand couturier* (and Figure 5.1) for Rops's take on the male designer's problematic sexuality. For more on the perceived "promiscuity of fitting sessions" ["promiscuité des séances d'essayage"] in the haute couture maison, see Bosc, "Le Couturier," 22.

103 As de Marly notes, "The fact that Worth still had 1,200 employees in 1871, the year of the lull between the fall of the Second Empire and the establishment of the Third Republic, suggests that he may well have had more before then" (*History*, 106).

104 If Griffith's interview with Worth is to be taken at face value, Worth himself was acutely aware of how his opinion dictated the production of textiles. His alleged response to Griffith's simple yet profound query, "What is really the origin of fashion, M. Worth?" ("Dressmakers," 746) is telling, first for its suggestion of fabric as inspiration for design, and second for its frank awareness of the snowball effect to industry resulting from his personal preference for a given cloth: "It is difficult to enter into all the details which influence changes of style; but briefly I may say that, when a manufacturer invents any special fabric or design, he sends me a pattern, asking if I can make use of it. That fabric may require a severe style of dress, or if light and soft, is adapted for draperies, puffings, etc. If the material pleases me, I order a large quantity, to be specially made for me, and design my dresses accordingly. A purchase by a large firm of a great quantity of material influences other firms, and that material, and the style it is best suited to, becomes the fashion" (ibid.).

105 De Marly, *History*, 18. An early twentieth-century reporter detailed Worth's formidable impact on various fabric industries as follows: "When Worth first entered the business of dressmaking, the only materials of the richer sort used for woman's dress were velvet, faille, and watered silk. Satin, for example, was never used. M. Worth desired to use satin very extensively in the gowns he designed, but he was not satisfied with what could be had at the time; he wanted something very much richer than was produced by the mills at Lyons. That his requirements entailed the reconstruction of mills mattered little – the mills were reconstructed under his directions, and the Lyons looms turned out a richer satin than ever, and the manufacturers prospered accordingly. On parallel lines, he stimulated also the manufacture of embroidery and *passementerie*. It was he who first started the manufacture of laces copied from the designs of the real old laces. He was the first dressmaker to use fur in the trimming of light materials – but he employed only the richer furs, such as sable and ermine, and had no use whatever for the inferior varieties of skins" ("Intime," *History*, 6–7).

106 De Marly, *History*, 18.

107 Troy, *Couture*, 19.

108 Lipovetsky, *Empire*, 75.

109 Ibid., 87.

110 Wilson, *Adorned*, 32.

111 This profession was a logical one for her to pursue since, before moving to Paris, Rachilde had written fashion columns for regional newspapers in the southwestern commune of Périgueux where she then lived (Emily Apter, "Weaponizing the *Femme Fatale*: Rachilde's Lethal Amazon, *La Marquise de Sade*," *Fashion Theory* 8, no. 3 (2004), 257).

112 Rachilde chronicled her beginnings as a fledging fashion journalist years later in an article entitled "Young Reporter" ["Jeune Reporter"] where she recounts being sent to report on the gowns worn by "a fashionable actress" ["une actrice en vogue"], likely a reference to Sarah Bernhardt ("Jeune Reporter," [*Comedia*?] [30 June 1921?]).

113 Holmes, *Rachilde*, 113.

114 See Hawthorne, *Rachilde*, and Holmes, *Rachilde*, for the most developed studies on this subject.

115 Eliante of *La Jongleuse* perhaps comes closest, for she writes long letters that constitute much of the novel's epistolary chapters. Also, Hawthorne makes the case that the cross-dressing heroine of *Madame Adonis* (1888), who passes well enough to masquerade as her own brother, is not technically a writer but can be understood to symbolize the woman author who must adopt a male pseudonym and identity in order to achieve success in a masculine world of letters (*Rachilde*, 76).

116 The oft-cited example is Raoule de Vénérande's declaration "I'm a boy … an artist whom my aunt calls her nephew"(Rachilde, *Materialist*, 37) ["Je suis un garçon, moi … un artiste que ma tante appelle son neveu"] (Rachilde, *Monsieur Vénus*, 53), which suggests that Raoule's artistry is dependent on her masculinity.

117 The intersection of location and fashion creation in isolated novels by Rachilde has been taken up in Guri Ellen Barstad, "Espaces et construction de soi dans *Monsieur Vénus* de Rachilde," *Excavatio* 23, nos. 1–2 (2008); McGann, "Juggling"; Schechner, "Dressing"; Heidi Brevik-Zender, "Decadent Décors and Torturous Textiles: Fatal Fashions and Interior Design in the Fin-de-Siècle Novels of Rachilde," in Alla Myzelev and John Potvin, eds., *Fashion, Interior Design and the Contours of Modern Identity* (Farnham: Ashgate, 2010), 105–23; and Heidi Brevik-Zender, "Fashion and Fin-de-Siècle Feminisms in Rachilde's *La Jongleuse*," *French Review* 87, no. 3 (2014), 131–44. However, none of these studies seeks to examine connections between the two themes more generally across her late-century works.

118 The spatial appropriation suggested in Rachilde's texts can be thought of as a way to enlarge the city for women through increased access. It is

perhaps not a coincidence that the theme of spatial amplification in her works developed simultaneously with ideologies of expansionism broadly at work in France during this period, both in terms of the peripheral limits of Paris and the nation's continued imperialist strategies in overseas colonies. See the introduction to this book for discussions of the former and chapter 2's analysis of Maupassant's *Bel-Ami* for the latter.

119 Rachilde, *Juggler*, 133.

120 Rachilde, *Jongleuse*, 174. See above discussion of the traditional seated position of the tailor and Rops's *Le Muscle du grand couturier* (see Figure 5.1).

121 Schechner, "Dressing," 155.

122 Rachilde, *Juggler*, 189.

123 Rachilde, *Jongleuse*, 234.

124 Rachilde, *Juggler*, 189.

125 Rachilde, *Jongleuse*, 234–5.

126 As Holmes observes, the objects in Eliante's boudoir are also meant to conjure up her transgressive and dangerous sexuality: "these signifiers of violence and eroticism indicate her refusal to abide by the codes that govern female behaviour and heterosexual relations" (*Rachilde*, 138).

127 Schechner, "Dressing," 155.

128 Ibid.

129 Despite assurances such as those by an early twentieth-century publication declaring that "the House of Worth was the first to adopt the custom of showing its creations on living mannequins" ("Intime," *History*, 7), this claim has been contested (see, e.g., de Marly, *History*, 100). The point here is not whether Worth really was the first to use live models but rather that women parading as mannequins was a typical practice in haute couture *maisons* of the period, which is confirmed by multiple sources (see chapter 5).

130 Rachilde, *Juggler*, 74.

131 Rachilde, *Jongleuse*, 104–5.

132 It is reasonable to assume that Worth established his in-house photography studio to catalogue the garments created in his atelier over the years. Beyond this pragmatic indexing relationship between photography and fashion, however, is Sagne's compelling observation that "it is not improbable … that photography, in allowing the rapid execution of portraits and facilitating their dissemination, could have accelerated the erosion of fashion, contributing to its frenzy of renewal and exciting capacities for creation and innovation" ["il n'est pas improbable … que la photographie, en autorisant la réalisation rapide de portraits, en facilitant

leur diffusion ait pu accélérer une usure de la mode et participer à cette frénésie de renouvellement, exciter la capacité de création et d'innovation"] ("Marques," 12). Hence, as Sagne suggests, photographic images may have had functions beyond inciting consumerism, for they could fuel genuine creativity and innovation in fashion design. Moreover, as Elizabeth Anne McCauley submits, there is no indication that Worth used these images for commercial purposes ("Photography, Fashion, and the Cult of Appearances," in Groom, *Impressionism, Fashion, and Modernity*, 199). Nonetheless, photographs such as those taken at Worth's establishment were related by medium to a larger phenomenon taking hold in this period whereby mass photographic images of well-dressed subjects were widely circulated, many with the intent to encourage sales. Worth's impetus to photograph his gowns may have helped to speed up the public's desire for new garments by, paradoxically, fixing outfits in a static image of a (past) historical moment. This visual permanency would implicitly render the fashions depicted not fresh and new but instantly outmoded, creating a "need" to purchase the next latest look. Roland Barthes, among others, has theorized on this process whereby fashion photography stimulates consumption by generating a perception of need. See Roland Barthes, *The Fashion System*, translated by Matthew Ward and Richard Howard (Berkeley: University of California Press, 1990).

133 Griffith, "Dressmakers," 748.

134 If the haute couture photography studio was set up to support the *sartorial* innovations of Worth and fellow designers, this did not, however, render it a space of *photographic* innovation. As Sagne points out, rather than seeking to create modern new compositions to serve as backdrops for their models, early fashion photographers relied instead on traditional settings gleaned from classical portraiture: "Photography strove to plagiarize the most academic of paintings, those of Carolus-Duran and Bonnat, Helleu, Henner, Gervex and Lévy-Dhurmer. Charming tableaus, reconstructed exterior scenes with a backdrop of mountains, or else easily fashioned out of cardboard, evocations of greenhouses and superb romantic landscapes appropriated all the accessories of the portrait studio, the most tired clichés, to serve fashion" ["La photographie s'ingéniait à plagier la peinture la plus académique, celle de Carolus-Duran et Bonnat, celles de Helleu, Henner, Gervex et Lévy-Dhurmer. Des tableaux charmants, des reconstitutions d'extérieur avec fonds de montagnes, ou practicables en carton-pâte, des évocations de serres et de superbes paysages romantiques récupéraient tous les accessoires du studio de portrait, poncifs les plus éculés, pour servir la mode"]

("Marques," 15). Figure 6.3, in which the "exotic" temple of Cleopatra seems upon close inspection nothing more than a painted backdrop, might exemplify this "clichéd" practice. It was not until the end of the century, when technology evolved such that fashion photographers could take their models outdoors, that they began to distance themselves from, in Sagne's words, "the power of heavy-handed references to painting and the smothering design contraints of specialized reviews" ["le prégnance des références lourdes à la peinture, du carcan étouffant du dessin des revues spécialisées"] (18). This possible echo in fin-de-siècle fashion photography of the *plein air* innovations of painters such as the Impressionists is a subject worth future examination.

135 Griffith, "Dressmakers," 748,

136 Rachilde explains her task to depict garments through the written word in the article "Jeune Reporter," which describes her first job as a fashion columnist. Responding to a "famous" actress's suggestion that the young woman journalist simply draw her dresses rather than describing them in words, Rachilde recalls saying, "I will try to paint … by my pen" ["Je tâcherai de peindre … à la plume"]. This article, which is undated but likely written in the 1920s, summarizes Rachilde's lifelong efforts to project her writing project as an art ("to paint") and her habit of framing this notion through the lens of fashion.

137 Rachilde, *Juggler*, 127.

138 Rachilde, *Jongleuse*, 165–6.

139 Rachilde, *Juggler*, 200.

140 Rachilde, *Jongleuse*, 248–9.

141 This motif occurs also in Rachilde's *L'Animale*, in which protagonist Laure Lordès makes a stylish travelling suit out of holy objects from a church. See Brevik-Zender, "Decadent Décors," 149–54.

142 Furbank and Cain, *Mallarmé on Fashion*, 143.

143 Mallarmé, *Oeuvres complètes*, 599.

144 Apter, "Weaponizing," 252, 254.

145 Rachilde, *The Marquise de Sade*, translated by Liz Heron (Cambs, UK: Dedalus, 1994), 154.

146 Rachilde, *La Marquise de Sade* (Paris: Gallimard, 1996), 163.

147 Rachilde, *The Marquise*, 155.

148 Rachilde, *La Marquise*, 164.

149 Rachilde, *The Marquise*, 155.

150 Rachilde, *La Marquise*, 196.

151 Rachilde, *The Marquise*, 185.

152 Rachilde, *La Marquise*, 196.

153 Rachilde's heroines are highly distrustful of men of science and medicine. See Hawthorne, *Rachilde*, 190, for an analysis of the recurring figure of the malevolent doctor in her works.

154 Rachilde, *The Marquise*, 170.

155 Rachilde, *La Marquise*, 180.

156 Rachilde, *The Marquise*, 170.

157 Rachilde, *La Marquise*, 180.

158 Rachilde, *The Marquise*, 171.

159 Rachilde, *La Marquise*, 180.

160 Rachilde, *The Marquise*, 171.

161 Rachilde, *La Marquise*, 180.

162 Rachilde, *The Marquise*, 171.

163 Rachilde, *La Marquise*, 180. Hawthorne's explanation of the "anatomical Venus" in her translation of *Monsieur Vénus* highlights the recurring presence of the female mannequin in Rachilde's fiction. Anatomical Venuses, Hawthorne informs, were "the wax models of female figures used to teach anatomy ... these models, with detachable abdomens that revealed the inner workings of the female reproductive system but also with seductive poses and winsome facial features, were used as teaching aids in the medical profession" (Rachilde, *Materialist*, 209).

164 Rachilde, *The Marquise*, 185.

165 Rachilde, *La Marquise*, 197.

166 Rachilde, *The Marquise*, 184.

167 Rachilde, *La Marquise*, 196.

168 Rachilde, *The Marquise*, 242.

169 Rachilde, *La Marquise*, 257.

170 It is suggested that Célestin, driven by Mary to commit suicide, sets off the explosion himself.

171 Rachilde, *The Marquise*, 243.

172 Rachilde, *La Marquise*, 258.

173 The image of headless mannequins famously appears in Zola's opening to *Au Bonheur des Dames* (see chapter 1) but is also featured in Rachilde's own department-store novel, *Monsieur de la nouveauté*, which was published two years before Zola's text. For a visual example of a headless shop mannequin see Tissot's 1883 painting *La demoiselle du magasin* [*The Shop Girl*].

174 Rachilde, *The Marquise*, 273.

175 Rachilde, *La Marquise*, 291.

176 Rachilde, *Materialist*, 13.

177 Rachilde, *Monsieur Vénus*, 28.

178 Rachilde, *Materialist*, 12.

179 Rachilde, *Monsieur Vénus*, 27.

180 For more on Grévin's wax museum, see Michelle E. Bloom, *Waxworks: A Cultural Obsession* (Minneapolis: University of Minnesota Press, 2003); and Schwartz, *Spectacular Realities*.

181 Rachilde, *Materialist*, 208.

182 Rachilde, *Monsieur Vénus*, 227.

183 Rachilde, *Materialist*, 210.

184 Rachilde, *Monsieur Vénus*, 227.

185 Rachilde, *Materialist*, 210.

186 Rachilde, *Monsieur Vénus*, 228.

187 Rachilde, *Materialist*, 208.

188 Rachilde, *Monsieur Vénus*, 225.

189 Ibid., 224–5.

190 Representing another possible reading, Hawthorne translates Rachilde's word *ciseau* as "scalpel" (Rachilde, *Monsieur Vénus*, 208), rightly calling to mind a surgeon and underscoring the dark malevolence that Rachilde ascribes to Raoule through her association with the typically evil men of medicine in her novels.

191 Rachilde had a strong affection for animals; as a child, she may have found more solace in their companionship than in that of humans, and, as an adult, she repeatedly identified herself with the figure of the werewolf (Hawthorne, *Rachilde*, 231–3, 21–7). As Hawthorne submits, though, "while she loved animals, she was accustomed to seeing them suffer and often accepted that she could do nothing about it" (231). To read the Jacques mannequin as an object dressed in grisly yet fashionable trim may suggest Rachilde's underlying critique of the late-century garment industry's rampant destruction of birds, small mammals and other creatures to embellish the stylish dress of humans.

192 Barstad, "Espaces," 294.

193 Certeau, *Practice*, 117.

194 Ibid., xix.

195 Ibid., 95.

196 Ibid., xix.

197 Ibid.

198 Ibid., 95.

199 Ibid., xix.

200 Ibid., 117.

201 Cited in Pollock, *Vision*, 98.

202 Rachilde, *The Marquise*, 271.

203 Rachilde, *La Marquise*, 288.
204 Rachilde, *L'Animale* (Paris: Mercure de France, 1993), 195.
205 That Rachilde seems to allude in this novel to the imagery of the
     celebrated Baudelaire – that other lover of cats, Parisian rooftops, and
     decadence – supports the notion of her desire to align her writing project
     with male genius.
206 For more on fashion as an expression of Certeau's "everyday" (*quotidien*),
     see Michael Sheringham, "Fashion, Theory, and the Everyday:
     Barthes, Baudrillard, Lipovetsky, Maffesoli," *Dalhousie French Studies* 53
     (2000), 145).
207 Rachilde, *Animale*, 175.
208 Ibid.
209 Rachilde, *Nono* (Paris: Mercure de France, 1994), 117.
210 Cited in Hawthorne, *Rachilde*, 105.
211 Rachilde, *Animale*, 243.
212 Wolff, "Gender," 24.
213 Ibid.
214 Ibid., 28.
215 Troy, *Couture*, 19.
216 Holmes, *Rachilde*, 131.
217 Ibid., 115.
218 Ibid., 76.
219 See Ellen Israel Rosen's study of globalized labour in the twenty-first-
     century fashion industry (*Making Sweatshops: The Globalization of the U.S.
     Apparel Industry* (Berkeley: University of California Press, 2002), 4).

Epilogue

1 A search on the Modern Language Association International Bibliography
   for the term "modernity" in publication titles of peer-reviewed studies
   from the past five years – 2008 to 2013 – listed 194 works, an increase
   from the 168 works listed for the previous five-year stretch.
2 Plessis, "Curée," 104.
3 The term "flatness" is used throughout Varnedoe's influential *Gustave
   Caillebotte*, for example.
4 Varnedoe, *Gustave Caillebotte*, 150.
5 Ribeiro, "Gustave Caillebotte," 189.
6 Potvin, introduction, 2.
7 Ibid., 3.
8 Ibid.

9 See J.P. Daughton, "When Argentina Was 'French': Rethinking Cultural
  Politics and European Imperialism in Belle-Époque Buenos Aires," *Journal
  of Modernity History* 80, no. 4 (2008), 839–42, 852; Shun-ichi J. Watanabe,
  "Tokyo: Forged by Market Forces and Not the Power of Planning," in
  David L.A. Gordon, ed., *Planning Twentieth-Century Capital Cities* (New
  York: Routledge, 2006), 103; Asef Bayat, "Tehran: Paradox City," *New Left
  Review* 66 (2010), 101; Alexander Vari, "From 'Paris of the East' to 'Queen
  of the Danube': International Models in the Promotion of Budapest
  Tourism, 1885–1940," in Eric G.E. Zuelow, ed., *Touring beyond the Nation:
  A Transnational Approach to European Tourism History* (Farnham: Ashgate,
  2011), 105; Mauricio Tenorio Trillo, "1910 Mexico City: Space and Nation
  in the City of the *Centenario*," in William H. Beezley and David E. Lorey,
  eds., *¡Viva México! ¡Viva la independencia! Celebrations of September 16*
  (Wilmington: Scholarly Resources, 2001), 173; and Dennis Hardy,
  "London: The Contradictory Capital," in Gordon, *Planning Twentieth-
  Century Capital Cities*, 97. Haussmannization is referenced throughout
  Arturo Almandoz, ed., *Planning Latin America's Capital Cities, 1850–1950*
  (London: Routledge, 2002) in essays treating Santiago, Rio de Janeiro,
  Mexico City, Caracas, and Lima. I am grateful to Brian Bockelman and
  Alexander Vari for directing me to some of these studies.
10 Regina A. Root, *Couture and Consensus: Fashion and Politics in Postcolonial
  Argentina* (Minneapolis: University of Minnesota Press, 2010), see esp.
  chapter 5.
11 Beirut has been dubbed the "Paris of the Middle East" due in part to its
  development as a modern cosmopolitan capital when under mandated
  French control during the first half of the twentieth century. For a study of
  the Budapest tourism industry's rejection of the name "Paris of the East"
  in favour of the nationalistic Hungarian moniker "Queen of the Danube,"
  see Vari, "From 'Paris of the East.'" For more on Francisco Pereira Passos,
  whose early twentieth-century remodelling of Rio de Janeiro garnered
  him the nickname "Tropical Haussmann," see Jeffrey D. Needell, *A
  Tropical* Belle Époque: *Elite Culture and Society in Turn-of-the-Century Rio de
  Janeiro* (Cambridge: Cambridge University Press, 1987). Mike Davis uses a
  similar phrase evoking the Baron in "Haussmann in the Tropics," the title
  of one chapter in *Planet of Slums* (New York: Verso, 2006); Davis's sharp
  critique of the widespread areas of urban poverty that have resulted from
  Haussmann-inspired urban planning projects across the globe.
12 I am grateful to Leslie Raymond Williams for introducing me to Vargas
  Llosa's works and to the broader concept of Paris as a symbol in
  twentieth-century Latin American fiction.

Bibliography

Abler, Thomas S. *Hinterland Warriors and Military Dress: European Empires and Exotic Uniforms*. Oxford: Berg, 1999.

Allan, Scott. "Degas's *Milliners* and the Craft of Painting." Unpublished lecture, Curator's Spotlight Series, Getty Center, Los Angeles, CA, 20 Nov. 2011.

Almandoz, Arturo, ed. *Planning Latin America's Capital Cities, 1850–1950*. London: Routledge, 2002.

Anonymous. "La Mode, cette année." *Le Courrier des Alpes* (5 May 1874): 4.

Anonymous. "M. Lehoussel, propriétaire de l'*Union des Indes*." *Journal de la Savoie* (27 Mar. 1874): 4.

Anonymous. "Many Women in Mourning." *Pittsburg Press* (30 June 1901): 15.

Aprile, Sylvie. *Le Siècle des exilés: Bannis et proscrits de 1789 à la Commune*. Paris: CNRS Editions, 2010.

Apter, Emily. "Weaponizing the *Femme Fatale*: Rachilde's Lethal Amazon, *La Marquise de Sade*." *Fashion Theory* 8, no. 3 (2004): 251–66.

– "Celebrity Gifting: Mallarmé and the Poetics of Fame." In *Constructing Charisma*, ed. Edward Berenson and Eva Giloi, 86–102. New York: Berghahn, 2010.

Bachelard, Gaston. *The Poetics of Space*. Translated by Maria Jolas. Boston: Beacon Press, 1994.

Baguley, David. *Emile Zola, L'Assommoir*. Cambridge: Cambridge University Press, 1992.

Bal, Mieke. "Over-writing as Un-writing: Descriptions, World-Making, and Novelistic Time." In *The Novel*, vol. 2, *Forms and Themes*, ed. Ernesto Franco, 571–610. Princeton: Princeton University Press, 2007.

Baldick, Robert. *The Life of J.-K. Huysmans*. Cambs: Dedalus, 2006.

Barrow, Susan M. "East/West: Appropriation of Aspects of the Orient in Maupassant's *Bel-Ami*." *Nineteenth-Century French Studies* 30, nos. 3–4 (2002): 315–28.

Barstad, Guri Ellen. "Espaces et construction de soi dans *Monsieur Vénus* de Rachilde." *Excavatio* 23, nos. 1–2 (2008): 294–302.

Barthes, Roland. *The Fashion System*. Translated by Matthew Ward and Richard Howard. Berkeley: University of California Press, 1990.

Baudelaire, Charles. *Oeuvres complètes*. Edited by Claude Pichois. 2 vols. Paris: Gallimard, 1975–76.

Bayat, Asef. "Tehran: Paradox City." *New Left Review* 66 (2010): 99–122.

Beizer, Janet. "Uncovering *Nana*: The Courtesan's New Clothes." *L'Esprit Créateur* 25, no. 2 (1985): 45–56.

– *Ventriloquized Bodies: Narratives in Hysteria in Nineteenth-Century France*. Ithaca: Cornell University Press, 1994.

– "*Au* (delà du) *Bonheur des Dames*: Notes on the underground." *Australian Journal of French Studies* 8, no. 38 (2001): 393–406.

Bell, David F. *Real Time: Accelerating Narrative from Balzac to Zola*. Champaign: University of Illinois Press, 2004.

Bell, Dorian. "Maupassant and the Limits of the Self." *Romanic Review* 101, no. 4 (2010): 781–801.

Bell, Georges. *Paris Incendié: Histoire de la Commune de 1871*. Paris: E. Martinet, 1871.

Bell, Michael Mayerfeld. "The Ghosts of Place." *Theory and Society* 26, no. 6 (1997): 813–36.

Benhamou, Noëlle. "*En ménage, En rade*: Huysmans et la maladie du mariage." In *En ménage: En rade de Joris-Karl Huysmans, 1881*, edited by Noëlle Benhamou. Paris: Editions du Boucher, 2009. http://www.leboucher.com/pdf/huysmans/huysmans.pdf.

Benjamin, Walter. "Theses on the Philosophy of History." In *Illuminations*, translated by Harry Zohn, edited by Hannah Arendt New York: Schocken, 1969.

– *The Arcades Project*. Translated by Howard Eiland and Kevin McLaughlin. Cambridge: Belknap Press, 1999.

Bentzon, T. "Woman at the Paris Exhibition." *Outlook* (29 Sept. 1900): 259–64.

Bernard, Claude. *An Introduction to the Study of Experimental Medicine*. Translated by Henry Copley Greene. New York: Dover, 1957.

Best, Janice. *Les Monuments de Paris sous la Troisième République: Contestation et commémoration du passé*. Paris: L'Harmattan, 2010.

Blanc, Charles. *L'Art dans la parure et dans le vêtement*. Paris: Librairie Renouard, 1875.

Bloom, Michelle E. *Waxworks: A Cultural Obsession*. Minneapolis: University of
   Minnesota Press, 2003.
Bonnet, Gilles. Introduction to *En Ménage*, by Joris-Karl Huysmans, 7–25.
   Genève: Droz, 2005.
Bonnier, Bernadette, Véronique Leblanc, Didier Prioul, and Hélène Védrine,
   eds. *Félicien Rops: Rops suis, aultre ne veulx estre*. Brussels: Editions
   Complexe, 1998.
Borie, Jean. Préface to *La Curée*, by Emile Zola, 7–35. Edited by Jean Borie.
   Paris: Gallimard, 1981.
Bosc, Alexandra. "Le Couturier et ses clientes dans la seconde moitié du
   XIXe siècle." In *Paris Haute Couture*, ed. Olivier Saillard and Anne Zazzo,
   22–5. Paris: Skira Flammarion, 2012.
– "Le Costume Tailleur: Histoire d'un succès." In *Paris Haute Couture*, ed.
   Olivier Saillard and Anne Zazzo, 32. Paris: Skira Flammarion, 2012.
Bourillon, Florence, and Annie Fourcaut. *Agrandir Paris, 1860–1970*. Paris:
   Publications de la Sorbonne, 2012.
Bowlby, Rachel. *Just Looking: Consumer Culture in Dreiser, Gissing, and Zola*.
   New York: Methuen, 1985.
Brevik-Zender, Heidi. "Tracking Fashions: Risking It All at the Hippodrome
   de Longchamp." In *The Places and Spaces of Fashion, 1800–2007*, ed. John
   Potvin, 19–33. New York: Routledge, 2009.
– "Decadent Décors and Torturous Textiles: Fatal Fashions and Interior
   Design in the *Fin-de-Siècle* Novels of Rachilde." In *Fashion, Interior Design
   and the Contours of Modern Identity*, ed. Alla Myzelev and John Potvin,
   105–23. Farnham: Ashgate, 2010.
– "Fashion and Fin-de-Siècle Feminisms in Rachilde's *La Jongleuse*." *French
   Review* 87, no. 3 (2014): 131–44.
– "Fashion and Fractured Flânerie in Guy de Maupassant's *Bel-Ami*."
   DIX-NEUF 16, no. 2 (2012): 224–42.
– "Interstitial Narratives: Rethinking Feminine Spaces of Modernity in
   Nineteenth-Century French Fashion Plates." *Nineteenth-Century Contexts*,
   (2014): 1–33.
Brooks, Peter. "Storied Bodies, or Nana at Last Unveil'd." *Critical Inquiry* 16,
   no. 1 (1989): 1–32.
Broude, Norma, ed. *Gustave Caillebotte and the Fashioning of Identity in
   Impressionist Paris*. New Brunswick, NJ: Rutgers University Press, 2002.
Brown, Kathryn. *Women Readers in French Painting 1870–1890: A Space for the
   Imagination*. Farnham: Ashgate, 2012.
Buck-Morss, Susan. *The Dialectics of Seeing: Walter Benjamin and the Arcades
   Project*. Cambridge, MA: MIT Press, 1989.

Calargé, Carla. "Une Fissure dans l'édifice colonial: Inquiétante étrangeté ou agentivité féminine? Le cas de quatre nouvelles de Maupassant." *Nineteenth-Century French Studies* 41, nos. 1–2 (2012–13): 105–21.

Catani, Damian. *The Poet in Society: Art, Consumerism, and Politics in Mallarmé.* Bern: Peter Lang, 2003.

Certeau, Michel de. *The Practice of Everyday Life.* Translated by Steven F. Rendall. Berkeley: University of California Press, 2011.

Charpy, Manuel. "Quartiers à la mode et attraction des marges: Législateurs du goût et conquêtes urbaines après 1860." In *Agrandir Paris: 1860–1970,* ed. Flore Bourillon and Annie Fourcaut, 185–202. Paris: Publications de la Sorbonne, 2012.

Cheng, Anne Anlin. *Second Skin: Josephine Baker and the Modern Surface.* New York: Oxford University Press, 2011.

Clark, T.J. *The Painting of Modern Life: Paris in the Art of Manet and His Followers.* Rev. ed. Princeton: Princeton University Press, 1999.

Clayson, Hollis. "Threshold Space: Parisian Modernism Betwixt and Between (1869 to 1890)." In *Impressionist Interiors,* ed. Janet McLean, 30–51. Dublin: National Gallery of Ireland, 2008.

Cocteau, Jean, and Georges Feydeau. *Thirteen Monologues.* Translated Peter Meyer. London: Oberon Books, 1996.

Coffin, Judith G. "Credit, Consumption, and Images of Women's Desires: Selling the Sewing Machine in Late Nineteenth-Century France." *French Historical Studies* 18, no. 3 (1994): 749–83.

Cogéval, Guy, and Stéphane Guégan. "James Tissot: *The Circle of the Rue Royale.*" In *Impressionism, Fashion, and Modernity,* ed. Gloria Groom, 146–51. New Haven: Yale University Press, 2012.

Connon, Daisy, Gillian Jein, and Greg Kerr, eds. *Aesthetics of Dislocation in French and Francophone Literature and Art: Strategies of Representation.* Lampeter: Edwin Mellen Press, 2009.

Coons, Lorraine. "'Neglected Sisters' of the Women's Movement: The Perception and Experience of Working Mothers in the Parisian Garment Industry, 1860–1915." *Journal of Women's History* 5, no. 2 (1993): 50–74.

Coste, Martine Agathe. "Vêtir l'hypocrisie: La haute couture sous le Second Empire à travers *La Curée* d'Émile Zola." In *Vêtement et littérature,* ed. Frédéric Monneyron, 215–23. Perpignan: Presses univérsitaires de Perpignan, 2001.

Craik, Jennifer. *Fashion: The Key Concepts.* New York: Berg, 2009.

Culbert, John. *Paralyses: Literature, Travel, and Ethnography in French Modernity.* Lincoln: University of Nebraska Press, 2011.

Daudet, Alphonse. *Sapho*. Translated by Anonymous. New York: Modern
  Library, 1950[?].
– *Sapho*. Paris: Flammarion, 1995.
Daughton, J.P. "When Argentina Was 'French': Rethinking Cultural Politics
  and European Imperialism in Belle-Époque Buenos Aires." *Journal of
  Modernity History* 80, no. 4 (2008): 831–64.
David, Alison Matthews. "Cutting a Figure: Tailoring, Technology and Social
  Identity in Nineteenth-Century Paris." Ph.D. diss., Stanford University, 2002.
Davis, Mike. *Planet of Slums*. New York: Verso, 2006.
DeGroat, Judith. "Virtue, Vice, and Revolution: Representations of Parisian
  Needlewomen in the Mid-Nineteenth Century." In *Famine and Fashion:
  Needlewomen in the Nineteenth Century*, ed. Beth Harris, 201–14. Aldershot:
  Ashgate, 2005.
de Marly, Diana. *The History of Haute Couture 1850–1950*. New York: Holmes
  and Meier, 1980.
Deak, Frantisek. *Symbolist Theater: The Formation of an Avant-Garde*. Baltimore:
  Johns Hopkins University Press, 1993.
Diderot, Denis. *Paradoxe sur le comédien*. Paris: A. Sautelet et Cie, 1830.
Dolan, Therese. "Guise and Dolls: Dis/covering Power, Re/covering Nana."
  Nineteenth-Century French Studies 26, nos. 3–4 (1998): 368–86.
Donaldson-Evans, Mary. "The Last Laugh: Maupassant's 'Les Bijoux' and
  'La Parure.'" *French Forum* 10, no. 2 (1985): 163–74.
– "Huysmans's *roman-abattoir*: *En ménage*." *Stanford French Review* 13, nos. 2–3
  (1989): 193–210.
– "Pricking the Male Ego: Pins and Needles in Flaubert, Maupassant and
  Zola." *Nineteenth-Century French Studies* 30, nos. 3–4 (2002): 255–66.
Doy, Gen. "The Camera against the Paris Commune." In *Illuminations: Women
  Writing on Photography from the 1850s to the Present*, ed. Liz Heron and
  Val Williams, 21–31. London: I.B. Tauris, 1996.
Draguet, Michel. *Le cabinet des dessins Rops*. Paris: Flammarion, 1998.
Duffy, Larry. *Le Grand Transit Moderne: Mobility, Modernity, and French
  Naturalist Fiction*. Amsterdam: Rodopi, 2005.
Eichner, Carolyn J. *Surmounting the Barricades: Women in the Paris Commune*.
  Bloomington: Indiana University Press, 2004.
Falluel, Fabienne. "Les Accessoires sous le Second Empire: Une mode en
  contrepoint." In *Sous l'Empire des crinolines*, ed. Catherine Join-Diéterle et al.,
  120–39. Paris: Paris Musées, 2008.
Farmer, John S., and W.E. Henley, eds. *Slang and Its Analogues Past and Present*,
  vol. 2. London: Harrison and Sons, 1891.

Felski, Rita. *The Gender of Modernity*. Cambridge, MA: Harvard University Press, 1995.

Ferguson, Priscilla Parkhurst. *Paris as Revolution: Writing the Nineteenth-Century City*. Berkeley: University of California Press, 1997.

Feydeau, Georges. *Théâtre complet*, vol. 1. Edited by Henry Gidel. Paris: Garnier, 1988.

Flusser, Alan. *Dressing the Man: Mastering the Art of Permanent Fashion*. New York: HarperCollins, 2002.

Forestier, Louis. Notice to *Romans*, by Guy de Maupassant, 1324–1341. Edited by Louis Forestier. Paris: Gallimard, 1987.

Foucault, Michel. "Other Spaces." In *Utopias*. Edited by Richard Noble, 60–8. Cambridge, MA: MIT Press, 2009.

Fried, Michael. "Caillebotte's Impressionism." In *Gustave Caillebotte and the Fashioning of Identity in Impressionist Paris*, ed. Norma Broude, 66–116. New Brunswick, NJ: Rutgers University Press, 2002.

Furbank, P.N., and A.M. Cain. *Mallarmé on Fashion: A Translation of the Fashion Magazine* La Dernière Mode *with Commentary*. New York: Berg, 2004.

Gallop, Jane. "The Liberated Woman." *Narrative* 13, no. 2 (2005): 89–104.

Garb, Tamar. "Masculinity, Muscularity, and Modernity in Caillebotte's Male Figures." In *Gustave Caillebotte and the Fashioning of Identity in Impressionist Paris*, ed. Norma Broude, 175–96. New Brunswick, NJ: Rutgers University Press, 2002.

Garelick, Rhonda K. *Rising Star: Dandyism, Gender, and Performance in the Fin de Siècle*. Princeton: Princeton University Press, 1998.

– *Electric Salome: Loie Fuller's Performance of Modernism*. Princeton: Princeton University Press, 2009.

Garfield, Simon. *Mauve: How One Man Invented a Color that Changed the World*. New York: W.W. Norton, 2002.

Garnier, Charles. *Le Nouvel Opéra de Paris*, vol. 1. Paris: Ducher, 1878.

Gautier, Théophile. "Théatres." *La Presse* (6 Jan. 1845): 1–3.

– "Le Nouvel Opéra." *L'Artiste* (1 Apr. 1866): 19–20.

Giacchetti, Claudine. "La Conquête de l'espace dans *Bel-Ami*." *Revue Romane* 26, no. 2 (1991): 219–29.

Gidel, Henry. Introduction to *Théâtre complet* by Georges Feydeau, 9–108. Edited by Henry Gidel. Paris: Garnier, 1988.

Goncourt, Edmond de. *Paris under Siege, 1870–1871: From the Goncourt* Journal. Translated by George J. Becker. Ithaca: Cornell University Press, 1969.

Gordon, Rae Beth. *Ornament, Fantasy, and Desire in Nineteenth-Century French Literature*. Princeton: Princeton University Press, 1992.

Graebner, Seth. "The Bird's-Eye View: Looking at the City in Paris and Algiers." *Nineteenth-Century French Studies* 36, nos. 3–4 (2008): 221–39.

Grauby, Françoise. "Le Parfum de l'homme en noir: Mallarmé et *La Dernière Mode* (1874)." *Australian Journal of French Studies* 41, no. 1 (2004): 102–20.

Green, Anne. *Changing France: Literature and Material Culture in the Second Empire.* London: Anthem, 2011.

Green, Nancy L. "Art and Industry: The Language of Modernization in the Production of Fashion." *French Historical Studies* 18, no. 3 (1994): 722–48.

– *Ready-to-Wear and Ready-to-Work: A Century of Industry and Immigrants in Paris and New York.* Durham, NC: Duke University Press, 1997.

Griffith, M. "Paris Dressmakers." In *The Strand Magazine: An Illustrated Monthly.* Ed. George Newnes. 745–51. London: George Newnes Ltd, 1894.

Groom, Gloria. "The Social Network of Fashion." In *Impressionism, Fashion, and Modernity*, ed. Gloria Groom, 33–43. New Haven: Yale University Press, 2012.

– "Claude Monet: *Camille.*" In *Impressionism, Fashion, and Modernity*, ed. Gloria Groom, 44–51. New Haven: Yale University Press, 2012.

– "Spaces of Modernity." In *Impressionism, Fashion, and Modernity*, ed. Gloria Groom, 165–85. New Haven: Yale University Press, 2012.

– "Edgar Degas: *The Millinery Shop.*" In *Impressionism, Fashion, and Modernity*, ed. Gloria Groom, 218–31. New Haven: Yale University Press, 2012.

Gullickson, Gay L. *Unruly Women of Paris: Images of the Commune.* Ithaca: Cornell University Press, 1996.

Habermas, Jurgen. *The Structural Transformation of the Public Sphere: An Inquiry into a Category of Bourgeois Society.* Translated by Thomas Burger. Cambridge, MA: MIT Press, 1991.

Haig, Stirling. *The Madame Bovary Blues.* Baton Rouge: Louisiana State University Press, 1987.

Hardy, Dennis. "London: The Contradictory Capital." In *Planning Twentieth-Century Capital Cities*, ed. David L.A. Gordon, 87–100. New York: Routledge, 2006.

Hart, Avril, and Emma Taylor. *Fans.* New York: Costume and Fashion Press, 1998.

Haussmann, Georges. *Mémoires du Baron Haussmann.* vol. 2. Paris: Victor-Havard, 1890.

Hawthorne, Melanie C. Introduction to *The Juggler*, by Rachilde, xi–xxxiv. Translated by Melanie C. Hawthorne. New Brunswick, NJ: Rutgers University Press, 1990.

– *Rachilde and French Women's Authorship: From Decadence to Modernism.* Lincoln: University of Nebraska Press, 2001.

Hebdige, Dick. *Subculture: The Meaning of Style.* London: Methuen, 1979.

Hiner, Susan. *Accessories to Modernity: Fashion and the Feminine in Nineteenth-Century France*. Philadelphia: University of Pennsylvania Press, 2010.

Holmes, Diana. *Rachilde: Decadence, Gender and the Woman Writer*. Oxford: Berg, 2001.

Horne, Alistair. *The Fall of Paris: The Siege and the Paris Commune 1870–1871*. London: Macmillan, 1965.

Huysmans, Joris-Karl. "Robes et Manteaux." *Le Gaulois* (6 June 1880): 1.

– *Oeuvres complètes*, vol. 6. Paris: G. Crès et Cie, 1928.

– *Living Together* (*En Ménage*). Translated by J.W.G. Sandiford-Pellé. London: Fortune Press, 1969.

– *En Ménage*. Geneva: Droz, 2005.

"Intime." "A Parisian Prince of Dress." *The Lady's Realm*, vol. 9. London: Hutchinson, 1901.

"Intime." *A History of Feminine Fashion*. London: Ed. J. Burrow and Co., 192?.

Irvine, Margot. "Spousal Collaborations in Naturalist Fiction and in Practice." *Nineteenth-Century French Studies* 37, nos. 1–2 (2008): 67–80.

Iskin, Ruth E. *Modern Women and Parisian Consumer Culture in Impressionist Painting*. Cambridge: Cambridge University Press, 2007.

Join-Diéterle, Catherine. "Revisiter le style Second Empire." In *Sous l'Empire des crinolines*, ed. Catherine Join-Diéterle et al., 18–28. Paris: Paris Musées, 2008.

– "Robes à transformation." In *Sous l'Empire des crinolines*, ed. Catherine Join-Diéterle et al., 101–3. Paris: Paris Musées, 2008.

Join-Diéterle, Catherine, et al., eds. *Sous l'Empire des crinolines*. Paris: Paris Musées, 2008.

Kelly, Dorothy. *Fictional Genders: Role and Representation in Nineteenth-Century French Narrative*. Lincoln: University of Nebraska Press, 1989.

Kessler, Marni Reva. *Sheer Presence: The Veil in Manet's Paris*. Minneapolis: University of Minnesota Press, 2006.

Lasalle, Albert de. "Chronique Musicale: Le Nouvel Opéra." *Le Monde Illustré* (9 Jan. 1875): 22–3.

Lecercle, Jean-Pierre. *Mallarmé et la mode*. Paris: Librairie Séguier, 1989.

Leduc-Adine, Jean-Pierre. "Architecture et écriture dans *La Curée*." In La Curée *de Zola ou "la vie à outrance,"* ed. David Baguley, 129–39. Paris: Société d'Etudes pour le Développement Economique et Social, 1987.

Lee, Daryl. "The Ambivalent Picturesque of the Paris Commune Ruins." *Nineteenth-Century Prose* 29, no. 2 (2002): 138–61.

Lefebvre, Henri. *La proclamation de la Commune*. Paris: Gallimard, 1965.

– *Rhythmanalysis*. Translated by Stuart Elden. London: Continuum, 2004.

Lehmann, Ulrich. *Tigersprung: Fashion in Modernity*. Cambridge, MA: MIT Press, 2000.

Lemoine, Serge, Anne de Mondenard, Eric Darragon, and Julien Faure-Cornoton. *De l'Intimité des frères Caillebotte: Peintre et photographe*. Paris: Skira Flammarion, 2011.

Lipovetsky, Gilles. *The Empire of Fashion: Dressing Modern Democracy*. Translated by Catherine Porter. Princeton: Princeton University Press, 1994.

Lively, Frazer. "Rachilde, the Actor's Spectre, and Symbolist Dramaturgy: The Staging of *Madame la Mort*." *Nineteenth-Century Theatre* 23, nos. 1–2 (1995): 33–66.

– Introduction to *Madame la Mort and Other Plays*, by Rachilde, 3–53. Edited and translated by Kiki Gounaridou and Frazer Lively. Baltimore: Johns Hopkins University Press, 1998.

Lyu, Claire. "Stéphane Mallarmé as Miss Satin: The Texture of Fashion and Poetry." *L'Esprit Créateur* 40, no. 3 (2000): 61–71.

Mallarmé, Stéphane. *Oeuvres complètes*, vol. 2. Paris: Gallimard, 1998.

Marcus, Sharon. *Apartment Stories: City and Home in Nineteenth-Century Paris and London*. Berkeley: University of California Press, 1999.

Mathey, François, ed. *Félicien Rops 1833–1898*. Brussels: Editions Lebeer Hossmann, 1985.

Matlock, Jann. "Everyday Ghosts: *La Curée* in the Shadow of the Commune." *Romanic Review* 102, nos. 3–4 (2011): 321–47.

Maupassant, Guy de. *Contes et nouvelles*. Paris: Gallimard, 1974.

– *Bel-Ami*. Translated by Douglas Parmée. London: Penguin, 1975.

– *Romans*. Edited by Louis Forestier. Paris: Gallimard, 1987.

– "The Necklace." Translated by David Coward. In *A Day in the Country and Other Stories*, 168–76. Oxford: Oxford University Press, 1998.

McCauley, Elizabeth Anne. "Photography, Fashion, and the Cult of Appearances." In *Impressionism, Fashion, and Modernity*, ed. Gloria Groom, 197–207. New Haven: Yale University Press, 2012.

McGann, Catherine. "Juggling for Gender, Juggling for Love: Carnival in Rachilde's *La Jongleuse*." *La Revue Frontenac* 10–11 (1993–94): 171–92.

Miller, Michael B. *The Bon Marché: Bourgeois Culture and the Department Store, 1869–1920*. Princeton: Princeton University Press, 1981.

Milner, John. *Art, War and Revolution in France 1870–1871*. New Haven: Yale University Press, 2000.

Minot, Leslie Ann. "Women and the Commune: Zola's Revisions." *Excavatio* 10 (1997): 57–65.

Montel, Nathalie. "L'Agrandissement de Paris en 1860: Un projet controversé." In *Agrandir Paris, 1860–1970*, ed. Florence Bourillon and Annie Fourcaut, 99–111. Paris: Publications de la Sorbonne, 2012.

Mortier, Arnold. "Le Musée Grévin." *Le Figaro* (23 Mar. 1882): 1.

Muelsch, Elisabeth-Christine. "Belles Lectrices in *Bel-Ami* or How to Read the Female Reader." Paper presented at the Twelfth International AIZEN Conference on Émile Zola and Naturalism, University of Texas at San Antonio, San Antonio, TX, 9–11 Oct. 2003.

Nash, Suzanne, ed. *Home and Its Dislocations in Nineteenth-Century France.* Albany: State University of New York Press, 1993.

Needell, Jeffrey D. *A Tropical* Belle Époque: *Elite Culture and Society in Turn-of-the-Century Rio de Janeiro.* Cambridge: Cambridge University Press, 1987.

Nelson, Brian. Introduction to *The Kill,* by Emile Zola, vii–xxix. Oxford: Oxford University Press, 2008.

North, Susan. "Redfern Limited: 1892 to 1940." *Costume* 43 (2009): 85–108.

Nuitter, Charles. *Le nouvel Opéra.* Paris: Librairie Hachette et Cie, 1875.

Parshall, Peter F. "Feydeau's 'A Flea in Her Ear': The Art of Kinesthetic Structuring." *Theatre Journal* 33, no. 3 (1981): 355–64.

Perrot, Philippe. *Fashioning the Bourgeoisie: A History of Clothing in the Nineteenth Century.* Translated by Richard Bienvenu. Princeton: Princeton University Press, 1994.

Place-Verghnes, Floriane. "'La Parure': Pour une pragmatique de la défamiliarisation." *French Studies* 55, no. 1 (2003): 39–53.

Plessis, Alain. "*La Curée* et l'Haussmannisation de Paris." In La Curée *de Zola ou "la vie à outrance,"* ed. David Baguley, 97–105. Paris: Société d'Etudes pour le Développement Economique et Social, 1987.

Pollock, Griselda. *Vision and Difference: Femininity, Feminism and the Histories of Art.* New York: Routledge Classics, 2003.

Potvin, John. Introduction to *The Places and Spaces of Fashion, 1800–2007,* ed. John Potvin, 1–18. New York: Routledge, 2009.

Prendergast, Christopher. *Paris and the Nineteenth Century.* Cambridge: Blackwell, 1995.

Pronko, Leonard C. *Georges Feydeau.* New York: Frederick Ungar, 1975.

Przyblyski, Jeannene M. "Revolution at a Standstill: Photography and the Paris Commune of 1871." *Yale French Studies* 101 (2001): 54–78.

Rabinow, Paul. *French Modern: Norms and Forms of the Social Environment.* Cambridge, MA: MIT Press, 1989.

Rachilde. "Jeune Reporter." *Comedia* [?] (30 June 1921?).

– *Monsieur Vénus.* Paris: Flammarion, 1977.

– *La Jongleuse.* Paris: Des Femmes, 1982.

– *The Juggler.* Translated by Melanie C. Hawthorne. New Brunswick, NJ: Rutgers University Press, 1990.

– *L'Animale.* Paris: Mercure de France, 1993.

– *The Marquise de Sade*. Translated by Liz Heron. Cambs, UK: Dedalus, 1994.
– *Nono*. Paris: Mercure de France, 1994.
– *La Marquise de Sade*. Paris: Gallimard, 1996.
– *Monsieur Vénus: A Materialist Novel*. Translated by Melanie Hawthorne. New York: Modern Language Association of America, 2004.
Ramazani, Vaheed. "Gender, War, and the Department Store: Zola's *Au Bonheur des Dames*." *SubStance* 36, no. 2 (2007): 126–46.
Reid, Amy. "Resisting Documents: Huysmans's Struggle to Represent Working-Class Women." *French Literature Studies* 28 (2001): 79–95.
Ribeiro, Aileen. "Gustave Caillebotte: *Paris Street, Rainy Day*." In *Impressionism, Fashion, and Modernity*, ed. Gloria Groom, 186–96. New Haven: Yale University Press, 2012.
Roberts, Mary Louise. *Disruptive Acts: The New Woman in Fin-de-siecle France*. Chicago: University of Chicago Press, 2002.
Root, Regina A. *Couture and Consensus: Fashion and Politics in Postcolonial Argentina*. Minneapolis: University of Minnesota Press, 2010.
Rosen, Ellen Israel. *Making Sweatshops: The Globalization of the U.S. Apparel Industry*. Berkeley: University of California Press, 2002.
Rosner, Victoria. *Modernism and the Architecture of Private Life*. New York: Columbia University Press, 2005.
Ross, Kristin. *Fast Cars, Clean Bodies: Decolonization and the Reordering of French Culture*. Cambridge, MA: MIT Press, 1996.
– *The Emergence of Social Space: Rimbaud and the Paris Commune*. Minneapolis: University of Minnesota Press, 1988.
Roynette, Odile. "L'Uniforme militaire au XIXe siècle: Une fabrique du masculin." *CLIO, Histoire, Femmes et Sociétés* 36 (2012): 109–28.
Sadler, Simon. *The Situationist City*. Cambridge, MA: MIT Press, 1999.
Sagne, Jean. "Marques de distinction." In *Vanités: Photographies de mode des XIXe et XXe siècles*, ed. Robert Delpire, 10–21. Paris: Centre National de la Photographie, 1993.
Sagner, Karin. "Gustave Caillebotte: An Impressionist and Photography." In *Gustave Caillebotte: An Impressionist and Photography*, ed. Karin Sagner and Max Hollein with Ulruch Pohlmann, 16–33. Munich: Hirmer-Verlag, 2012.
Saillard, Olivier, ed. *Le XVIIIe au goût du jour: Couturiers et créateurs de mode au Grand Trianon*. Versailles: Editions Artlys, 2011.
Schechner, Stephanie. "Dressing the Part: Fashion and Gender in Rachilde's *La Jongleuse*. *Excavatio* 20 (2005): 146–62.
Schlor, Joachim. *Nights in the Big City: Paris, Berlin, London 1840–1930*. Translated by Pierre Gottfried Imhof and Dafydd Rees Roberts. London: Reaktion Books, 1998.

Schwartz, Vanessa. *Spectacular Realities: Early Mass Culture in Fin-de-Siècle Paris*. Berkeley: University of California Press, 1998.

Seilhac, Léon de. *L'Industrie de la couture et de la confection à Paris*. Paris: Didot, 1897.

Sennett, Richard. *The Fall of Public Man*. New York: W.W. Norton, 1992.

Shapiro, Norman R. "Suffering and Punishment in the Theater of Georges Feydeau." *Tulane Drama Review* 15, no. 1 (1960): 117–26.

Sheringham, Michael. "Fashion, Theory, and the Everyday: Barthes, Baudrillard, Lipovetsy, Maffesoli." *Dalhousie French Studies* 53 (2000): 144–54.

Simmel, Georg. "Die Mode." In *The Fashion Reader*, ed. Daniel Leonhard Purdy, 289–309. Minneapolis: University of Minnesota Press, 2004.

Starr, Peter. *Commemorating Trauma: The Paris Commune and Its Cultural Aftermath*. New York: Fordham University Press, 2006.

Steele, Valerie. *Paris Fashion: A Cultural History*. Oxford: Berg, 1998.

Strickland, Geoffrey. "Maupassant, Zola, Jules Vallès and the Paris Commune of 1871." *Journal of European Studies* 13 (1983): 298–307.

Taine, Hippolyte. *Notes sur Paris*. 18th ed. Paris: Hachette, 1913.

Tétart-Vittu, Françoise. "Shops versus Department Stores." In *Impressionism, Fashion, and Modernity*, ed. Gloria Groom, 209–17. New Haven: Yale University Press, 2012.

Tétart-Vittu, Françoise, and Gloria Groom. "Key Dates in Fashion and Commerce, 1851–89." In *Impressionism, Fashion, and Modernity*, ed. Gloria Groom, 270–9. New Haven: Yale University Press, 2012.

Thompson, Hannah. *Naturalism Redressed: Identity and Clothing in the Novels of Emile Zola*. Oxford: Legenda, 2004.

Tomel, Guy. "Nos Petites *couturières*." *Le Monde Illustré* (31 July 1897): 84–5.

Traugott, Mark. *The Insurgent Barricade*. Berkeley: University of California Press, 2010.

Trillo, Mauricio Tenorio. "1910 Mexico City: Space and Nation in the City of the *Centenario*." In *¡Viva México! ¡Viva la independencia! Celebrations of September 16*, ed. William H. Beezley and David E. Lorey, 167–98. Wilmington: Scholarly Resources, 2001.

Trousson, Raymond. "Emile Zola chroniqueur de la Commune." *Travaux de littérature* 17 (2004): 449–68.

Troy, Nancy J. *Couture Culture: A Study in Modern Art and Fashion*. Cambridge, MA: MIT Press, 2003.

Tuan, Yi-Fu. *Space and Place: The Perspective of Experience*. 6th ed. Minneapolis: University of Minnesota Press, 2008.

Turbin, Carole. "Collars and Consumers: Changing Images of American Manliness and Business." *Enterprise and Society* 1, no. 3 (2000): 507–35.

Urbani, Bernard. "Espace et récit dans *Sapho* d'Alphonse Daudet." In *Écritures XIX: Alphonse Daudet, pluriel et singulier*, ed. Christian Chelebourg, 259–73. Dives-sur-mer: Minard, 2003.

Van Slyke, Gretchen. "Rebuilding the Bastille: Women's Dress-Code Legislation in the Nineteenth Century." In *Repression and Expression: Literary and Social Coding in Nineteenth-Century France*, ed. Carrol F. Coates, 209–19. New York: Peter Lang, 1992.

Van Zanten, David. *Designing Paris: The Architecture of Duban, Labrouste, Duc, and Vaudoyer*. Cambridge, MA: MIT Press, 1987.

– "Looking Through, Across, and Up: The Architectural Aesthetics of the Paris Street." In *Impressionism, Fashion, and Modernity*, ed. Gloria Groom, 153–63. New Haven: Yale University Press, 2012.

– "Paris Space: What Might Have Constituted Haussmannization." In *Manifestoes and Transformations in the Early Modernist City*, ed. Christian Hermansen Cordua, 179–210. Farnham: Ashgate, 2010.

Vari, Alexander. "From 'Paris of the East' to 'Queen of the Danube': International Models in the Promotion of Budapest Tourism, 1885–1940." In *Touring beyond the Nation: A Transnational Approach to European Tourism History*, ed. Eric G.E. Zuelow, 103–27. Farnham: Ashgate, 2011.

Varnedoe, Kirk. *Gustave Caillebotte*. New Haven: Yale University Press, 1987.

Vinken, Barbara. "Eternity – A Frill on the Dress." *Fashion Theory* 1, no. 1 (1997): 59–68.

Watanabe, Shun-ichi J. "Tokyo: Forged by Market Forces and Not the Power of Planning." In *Planning Twentieth-Century Capital Cities*, ed. David L.A. Gordon, 101–14. New York: Routledge, 2006.

Weber, Caroline. *Queen of Fashion: What Marie Antoinette Wore to the Revolution*. New York: Picador, 2007.

White, Nicholas. *The Family in Crisis in Late Nineteenth-Century French Fiction*. Cambridge: Cambridge University Press, 2004.

– "The Lost Heroine of Zola's Octave Mouret Novels." *Romanic Review* 102, nos. 3–4 (2011): 369–90.

Whittemore, Leila. "Theatre of the Bazaar: Women and the Architecture of Fashion in 19th-Century Paris." *a/r/c architecture, research, criticism* 1, no. 5 (1994–95): 14–25.

Wilson, Colette E. *Paris and the Commune 1871–78: The Politics of Forgetting*. Manchester: Manchester University Press, 2007.

Wilson, Elizabeth. *Adorned in Dreams: Fashion and Modernity*. Rev. ed. New Brunswick, NJ: Rutgers University Press, 2003.

Wilson, Steven. "Nana, Prostitution and the Textual Foundations of Zola's *Au Bonheur des Dames*." *Nineteenth-Century French Studies* 41, nos. 1–2 (2012–13): 91–104.

Wolff, Janet. "Gender and the Haunting of Cities: Or, the Retirement of the Flâneur." In *The Invisible* Flâneuse? *Gender, Public Space, and Visual Culture in Nineteenth-Century Paris*, ed. Aruna D'Souza and Tom McDonough, 18–31. Manchester: Manchester University Press, 2010.

Wollen, Peter. *Addressing the Century: 100 Years of Art and Fashion*. Berkeley: University of California Press, 1999.

– "The Concept of Fashion in *The Arcades Project*." *Boundary 2* 30, no. 1 (2003): 131–42.

Wood, J.S. "La Commune dans le roman." In *Images of the Commune*, ed. James A. Leith, 69–82. Montreal and Kingston: McGill-Queen's University Press, 1978.

Wosk, Julie. *Women and the Machine: Representations from the Spinning Wheel to the Electronic Age*. Baltimore: Johns Hopkins University Press, 2001.

Zazzo, Anne. "Les Dessous du Second Empire." In *Sous l'Empire des crinolines*, ed. Catherine Join-Diéterle et al., 60–9. Paris: Paris Musées, 2008.

Ziegler, Robert E. "Huysmans's *En Ménage* and the Unwritable Naturalist Text." *Forum for Modern Language Studies* 29, no. 1 (1993): 18–30.

Zola, Emile. *Au Bonheur des Dames* (*The Ladies' Delight*). Translated by Robin Buss. London: Penguin Classics, 2001.

– *Carnets d'Enquêtes: Une ethnographie inédite de la France*. Edited by Henri Mitterand. Paris: Editions Plon, 1986.

– *L'Invention des lieux*. Edited by Olivier Lumbroso. Paris: Les Éditions Textuel, 2002.

– *The Kill*. Translated by Brian Nelson. Oxford: Oxford University Press, 2008.

– *Nana*. Translated by George Holden. London: Penguin Classics, 1972.

– *Oeuvres complètes*. Edited by Henri Mitterand. 15 vols. Paris: Cercle du livre précieux, 1962–69.

– *Le Roman Expérimental*. Paris: Charpentier, 1880.

– *Les Rougon-Macquart*. Edited by Henri Mitterand. 5 vols. Paris: Flammarion, 1960.

Index